Lester **Beall**

Michael **Bierut**

Ed **Benguiat**

Morris Fuller **Benton**

David **Berlow**

Aaron **Burns**

Will **Burtin**

Tom **Carnase**

David **Carson**

Matthew **Carter**

Firmin **Didot**

Lou **Dorfsman**

W.A. **Dwiggins**

Robert **Estienne**

Davis **Farey**

Clause **Garamond**

Eric **Gill**

MIlton **Glaser**

Frederic W. **Goudy**

April **Greiman**

Gerard **Huerta**

Takenobu **Igarashi**

Nicholas **Kis**

Olaf **Leu**

Zuzana **Licko**

Listening to Type

	Greek source	Meaning
Photography	"phos" = light	light drawing *coined in 1834 by Hercules Florence shortly after its invention in the 1820s*
Topography	"topos" = place	place drawing *coined in ancient Greece*
Stenography	"stenos" = narrow	constricted writing *coined c1595 in England*
Iconography	"ikon" = likeness	pictorial representation *coined c1680 as a concentration in the growing area of art history*
Biography	"bios" = life	life writing *coined c1690*
Lithography	"lithos" = stone	stone drawing *coined c1805 shortly after its invention in 1797 by Alois Senefelder*

THEREFORE

	Greek source	Meaning
Typography	"typos" = form	(letter)form drawing *coined c1620*

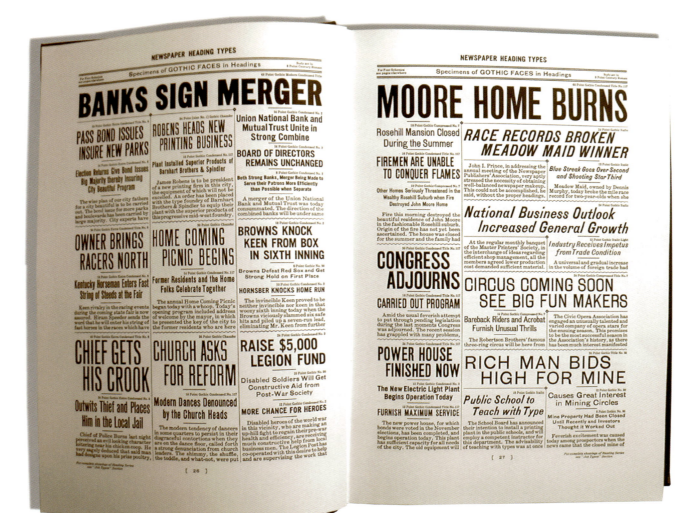

Listening to Type

Making Language Visible

Alex W. White

A spread from an early 20th-century type book. For some, this is a fascinating display and gets the blood circulating as powerfully as looking at the selection in the cases in an ice cream shop.

ALLWORTH PRESS
NEW YORK

"Language is not an abstract construction of the learned... but is something arising out of the work, needs, joys, affections, and tastes of long generations of humanity. Its base is broad and low, close to the ground." Walt Whitman, *Slang in America*

16 15 14 13 12 11 10 9 8 7 6 5 4 3 2 1

Published by Allworth Press
An imprint of Skyhorse Publishing, Inc.
307 West 36th Street, 11th Floor, New York, NY 10018
Book design, composition, and typography by
Alexander W. White, New York, NY

Library of Congress Cataloging-in-Publication Data
White, Alex W.
Listening to Type: The Practical Philosophy of Typography / Alex W. White – 2nd Edition
       p.   cm.
Includes bibliographical references and index.
ISBN 978-1-62153-535-5
Ebook ISBN 978-1-62153-538-6
1. Type and type-founding
2. Graphic design (Typography)
2. Type and type-founding History 20th century.
3. Graphic design (Typography) History 20th century.
I. Title.
    z250.w565 2005
    686.2'21dc22
    2004026955

Listening to Type

The Art of Making Language Visible

Contents

"If you think you are capable of living without writing, do not write." Rainer Maria Rilke To which I add, *"The same goes for designing."*

"Quantum potes tantum aude" or *"Whatever your talents, use them to their fullest."* Beatrice Warde's headstone, Surrey, England.

* Dwiggins (1880–1956) designed 280 books for Alfred A. Knopf, illustrated some, wrote extensively on design, and developed typefaces, seventeen of which were released by Linotype. Dwiggins said, *"I like to design type. Like to jiggle type around and see what comes out. Like to design ornaments. Like paper. Like ink on paper. Like bright colors. Handicapped by clock."*

Preface

We have seen the evolution of type from being professionally prepared and proofread to just another responsibility among many of the modern design professional. From 1450 through the early years of the 19th century, the printer was the typesetter and, quite often, the type designer as well. From the early 1800s to the early 1900s, the printer bought type from a foundry, a specialist who frequently developed his own technology for setting the characters. He thereby cornered the market on his particular typefaces, so if a printer wanted an additional size or weight or posture of type in a family, there was only the one place to get it.

As the 20th century progressed, offset lithography was improved to allow a printing plate to be made from a photographic negative. Because this didn't require pieces of wood and metal to be organized on a wooden chase, offset printing enabled a great deal more flexibility in the placement of design elements. Some printers found they enjoyed and were skilled at the organization of materials in readiness for this new kind of reproduction. They evolved into "graphic designers," a term that was invented in 1922 by William Addison Dwiggins.* These new graphic designers began expanding the possibilities of printing and technology. Letterforms and their spacing became much more plastic: letterforms and type became flexible and permutable.

In the mid-1980s, the computer became a companion in designers' offices. Throughout the 1990s, the definition of designer expanded to add the responsibilities of typesetter, proofreader, and photo retoucher. The computer has not yet proved to be *our* labor-saving device. But it also profoundly affected designers' ability to make their own letterforms, typefaces, and fonts, which in a way takes us full circle back to the first few hundred years of printing.

The greatest recent technical changes in type have taken place in the online sphere. These changes happen so quickly it is unwise to put them in a book because the information becomes out of date almost immediately.

Typography cannot be faked. It is either clear, interpretive of the content, and appropriate to its message, or it is a random treatment that only superficially looks daring and current. I am certain there is no Photoshop filter for instant typographic excellence. Typography can only be mastered one hard lesson at a time. It is not for every designer because it requires a love for language and a gift for details. But there are a double handful of common sense guidelines that will immediately improve everyone's use of type. I have tried to put them all in this book.

Thanks to Jenson, Griffo, Arrighi, Garamond, Caslon, Baskerville, Goudy, Tschichold, Dwiggins, Preissig, and Menhart, whose work has inspired me to see beauty and define type's workability for myself. ⊡ Carol Wahler and my fellow board members of The Type Directors Club, for the opportunity to deepen my appreciation of type and typography by their association, and for access to their extraordinary type library. ⊡ Tad Crawford, for encouraging this book's existence. ⊡ Rocky, for making the office a much nicer place each day. ⊡ And *Eponymous*.

This book is dedicated in loving memory of Honzíček (1928–2014).

Alex W. White

Greenwich CT

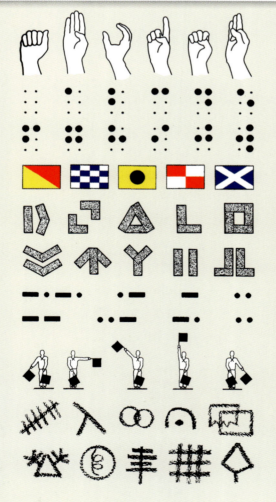

Taxonomy of Alphabets and Scripts

Alphabets	Scripts	Genera of Scripts	Families of Scripts
Czech			
Dinka			
English			
German			
Hawaiian			
Icelandic			
Irish			
Kazakh	Neoroman		
Latin			
Malay		Romanoid	
Navajo			
Serbo-Croatian			
Spanish			
Swedish			
Turkish			
Latin	Paleoroman		Hellenic
German	Fraktur		
Irish	Gaelic		
Buryat			
Chuvash			
Kazakh			
Russian			
Serbo-Croatian	Neocyrillic		
Udmurt		Cyrilloid	
Ukrainian			
Yakut			
Old Church Slavic	Paleo-cyrillic		
Modern Greek	Neohellenic	Hellenoid	
Coptic	Coptic		
Hindi-Urdu			
Marathi			
Nepali	Devanagari		
Panjabi			
Assamese		Devanagaroid	
Bengali	Bengali		
Gujarati	Kaithi		
Oriya	Oriya		
Panjabi	Gurmukhi		
Tibetan	Tibetan		
Kannada	Kannada		
Telugu	Telugu	Telugoid	Brahmic
Tamil	Tamil	Tamiloid	
Malayalam	Malayalam	Keraloid	
Burmese			
Mon	Burmese	Burmoid	
Shan			
Lao	Siamese	Saimoid	
Thai			
Armenian	Armenian	Armenoid	
Georgian	Khutsuri	Paleokart-veloid	Mesropic
Georgian	Mkhedruli	Neokart-veloid	
Amharic	Ethiopic		
Ge'ez			
Cherokee	Sequoyah		
Korean	Hangul		
Cree	Evans		
Eskimo			
Hebrew			
Karaim	Hebrew		
Yiddish			
Arabic			
Hindi-Urdu			
Kazakh			
Panjabi	Naskhi	Araboid	
Pashto			
Persian			
Turkish			

ALPHABET	CHARACTERS
Arabic	**28**
Etruscan	**17**
Greek, Early	**21**
Greek, Classical	**20**
Hebrew, Old	**19**
Latin, Early	**20**
Phoenician	**19**
Roman	**26**

Verbal Communication

Writing

Visual Communication

A selection of alphabets show how cultures determine how many sounds require symbols. Galileo (1564-1642) said, *"What loftiness of mind was that of man who thought of a way to communicate, though separated by the longest of intervals of space and time, to speak with those as yet unborn. All through various groupings of simple letters on paper."*

Writing is where spoken language and visual language meet, and should look like spoken language frozen in time and place. This may be all the guide you need as a typographer.

Reading directions have included back and forth (*boustrophedon* by the early Greeks, *above*), spiraled, vertical, right to left, and our familiar left to right.

Speaking vastly preceded writing. Today, "Negotiated speaking" is a cornerstone of political life.

Writing is visible speech. There are several ways of communicating in addition to speaking and writing: American Sign Language shows A–F; Braille shows A–J; Semaphore shows A–G; Morse Code spells COMMUNICATION; Nautical flags show ONIUM; the first symbol of the Ground–Air Emergency Code shows AIRCRAFT BADLY DAMAGED; and the first hobo symbol (each of which can stand for entire sentences) says YOU'LL BE CURSED AT HERE.

There are multiple alphabets for the world's languages. Letterforms are shared among *related* languages.

Introduction

> *"The duty of typography is to be the agent and general interpreter of wisdom and truth. In short, it portrays the human spirit."* Pierre Simon Fournier (le Jeune), 1764

Humans have been on earth for about 500,000 years. Before writing, people kept all information in their heads. The first written language dates from around 3,500BC and the alphabet from about 1,500BC. Writing evolved in many places more or less at once, each civilization taking and expanding on what they learned through trading and travel. Writing makes it possible to pass information across space and time: I wrote this in Greenwich, Connecticut in 2015. You are reading it in another place time.

Language existed first only as spoken systems. They were gradually given graphic representations. The earliest written systems were unrelated to spoken language, so people had to learn two languages. The Phœnicians were the geniuses who figured out that a correlation between spoken sounds and written symbols would require learning only one language. Their invention is the *alphabet*.

قوم من الرواة ينحلون الشعر تأبط شرا ويذكرون انه كان يتبع اماه من
وكان لها ابن من هذيل وكان يدخل عليها رحلا فلما قارب الغلام الح
قال لها من هذا الرجل الداخل عليك قالت صاحب كان لأبيك قال و

没 上 許 話 點 回 一 情 幾 那 你 先 九
來 帝 多 ○ 兒 來、四 也 個 一 的 生 七

βμην τῶν Λακεδαιμονίων, μὴ ἐπεὶ τὰ μακρὰ τείχη τὰ
το, ἔλθοιεν ἐπὶ σφᾶς, ἡγήσαντο κράτιστον εἶναι ἀνατειχίσ

עשה בְחֶפְצוֹ כֹל · אֲזַי מֶלֶךְ שְׁמוֹ נִקְרָא : וְאַחֲרֵי וְאֵין שֵׁנִי · לְהַמְשִׁיל לו
כְלוֹת הַכֹּל · לְבַדּוֹ יִמְלוֹךְ נוֹרָא : וְהוּא הָיָה בְּלִי תַּכְלִית · וְלוֹ הָעֹז וְ

知 〱 に 劇 て 躍 弘 仗 と 實 紅 其 前 友 とち れ 小 ら 紅
る て 想 と も 動 るず 有 の 葉 實 に 社 小 々 仗 說 弘 葉

дежзіийклмнопрстуфхцщчшщъыьѣэюяѳѵаб
вгдежзиийклмнопрстуфхцщчшщъы

حقّی ایدوب مایهٔ طپش زاهد ساقز شرابنی پنهان چکوب د
مسون بو صودن کم ساقزلی در تاریخی سلطان احمدڭ جاری ز

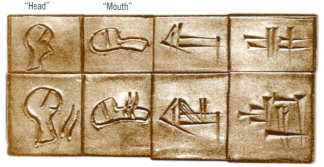

3100BC "Head" 2800BC "Mouth" 2500BC 700BC

Gutenberg propelled Western knowledge and culture by inventing *movable, reusable* type. This is a detail of his c1454 *Gotische Schrift* ("Gothic Script") shown at actual size.

Simple *pictographs* represented objects but they couldn't represent ideas, so they were combined into *ideograms*: "mouth" plus "water" means "drink." These hybrid symbols were

associated with sounds, so the symbols could be combined into abstract representations of sounds, cuneiform, wedge marks in clay, an early precursor of our alphabet.

A letter is a sound *and* an object: *An eagle and an elephant have two. A tiger, a moose, a bear, a turtle, and a snake have one. Humans don't have any. What are we talking about?*

Some of the world's most used — or previously used — alphabet systems: Arabic, Chinese, Egyptian hieroglyphics, Egyptian hieratic script, Greek, Hebrew with vowels (indicated by dots), Japanese, Javanese, Russian, and Turkish.

The variety and beauty of letterforms can be appreciated separate of their linguistic meaning, for their own sake. But the essential, inescapable function of writing is to transmit information. Any letter by itself is a mark taken out of its context. Letters must be seen in groups of words and sentences, as members of their families. We read by recognizing word shapes.

Type history and rules

Writing systems evolved from symbol systems. When humans needed to record complex abstract ideas, symbols were no longer adequate. Languages that combined symbols into new meanings began to emerge. Eventually, written symbols carried no meaning of their own at all. Our Roman alphabet, for example, is a collection of abstract symbols that represent sounds, and work only in combination.

Movable type was invented in China in 1041AD. Gutenberg figured out to make metal letters that could be used on a printing press in about 1450AD.

Display type was invented around 1500, when the quantity of printed material began to accumulate and identifying content became essential (type's evolution is a history of developments that solved technical, economic, cultural, and aesthetic problems). With improvements in speed, metal type was in use until the 1960s.

"Whenever social historians attempt to suggest the few most significant intellectual achievements of man, nearly always the one mentioned first is 'writing' — or (a) reference to man's initial development of a visible language." From the editorial statement in the first issue of *Visible Language* magazine, 1971.

"Type is the first impression of what you are about to read. Each typeface, like a human face, has a subtle character all its own… Since you must have type in order to have words, why not make sure those words are presented in the most elegant, or the most powerful, or softest way possible?" Roger Black

Section One
Type & Design

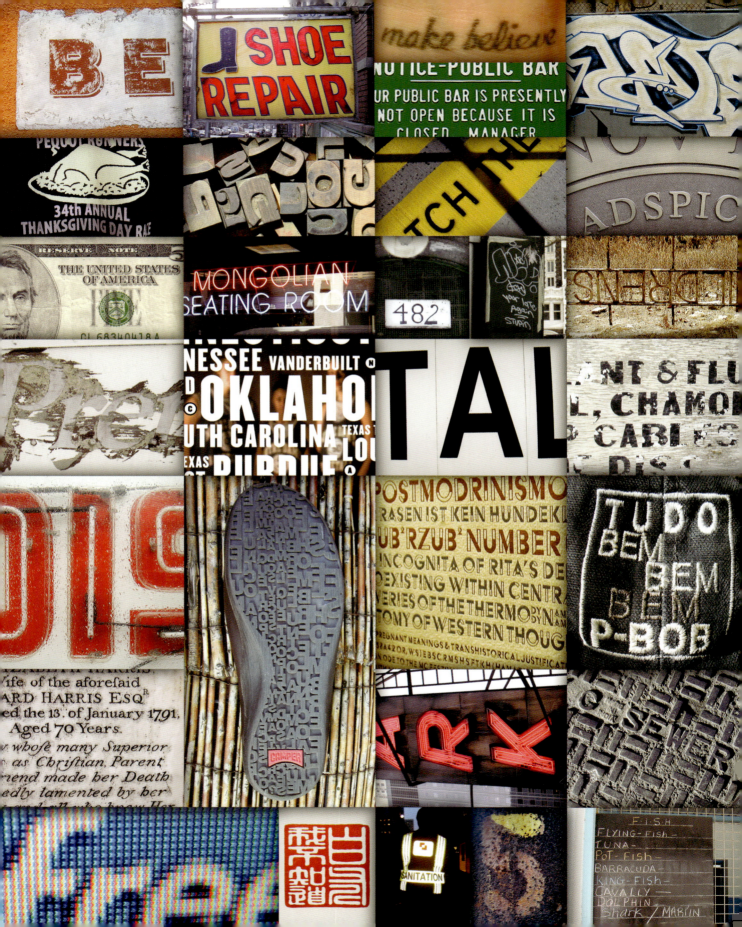

Glyphs (marks that represent sounds) have several alternatives that may not look alike, yet each represents the same sound. Each version must be learned.

a	n	t	e	b	s	r	i
d	l	th	œ	z	ɔ	m	c
v	p	æ	ɛ	f	w	u	ω
ɤ	ie	h	k	aʊ	ŋ	ʃh	⍵
g	y	oʊ	tʃh	a	j	th	wh
ue	ɔi	ʒ	z				

There are 44 sounds in English but our alphabet has only 26 characters, forcing letter combinations to describe the "missing" 18 sounds. This "phonetic alphabet" has exactly 44 glyphs.

ẒE PIPLZ UILL EÇÏV
THE PEOPLES WILL ACHIEV

ÇERIŞT ΓOUL OF S
CHERISHED GOAL OF S

ẒEÏ PÜL ẒEÏR EFFO
THEY POOL THEIR EFFORTS

REZOLUTLI END EI
RESOLUTELY AND A

END FRENDŞIP EN
AND FRIENDSHIP AMO

S.B. Telingater's 1968 alphabet of *glyphs*, marks with a direct relationship to their sounds, with additional pronunciation guides.

A	∧	F	⌐	L	∿	R	⌒
B	3	G	<	M	∼	S	⌣
C	C	H	ᔑ	N	ζ	T	⊤
D	∂	I	I	O	⊃	V	∪
E	ϭ	K	k	P	∠	X	⌣
		Q	⌐	Z	≠		

An early shorthand, the Tironian alphabet, was invented to record speeches in the Roman Senate, c63BC. The J, U, W, and Y weren't added to the Latin alphabet for another 1,200 years.

We see type everywhere. It is so pervasive that we are often not even aware of seeing it. Because we are given so many visual messages every day — counted in the thousands — we have trained ourselves to block type out. As typographers, we have to figure out ways of getting through our audience's barriers, which is becoming harder all the time. Which of the samples here seem most visible? Why do you suppose that is? If you can begin to determine what makes *you* look, you can apply those insights to your work on messages you are paid to prepare for *others* to notice. Informed typography begins with a keen interest in what makes visual messaging work and a dedication to self-reflection as your first and probably best model of efficacy.

What is type and where is it found?

f in finding a solution the typographer can produce a piece of work that has a quality of absolute correctness... an aesthetic appeal which will induce the reader to read and arouse a sense of covetousness in the sophisticate, it may be called a piece of inspired typography." Alan Dodson

For a design to work effectively, the type must be an integral part of the composition. If the type is altered or removed, the piece should fall apart. It doesn't matter if it's a poster, an advertisement, or corporate identity. Type strategy includes crafting a size and weight sequence for headlines, subheads, captions, and text so all work as one to make a distinctive and explanatory design.

Typography is, according to the dictionary, "the art or process of printing with type." The root words that make up *typography* are *typo* (type) and *graphy* (drawing), so it literally means *drawing with type*. My definition is: *Applying type with eloquence to reveal the content clearly and memorably with the least resistance from the reader.*

A B C

abcde

abcdfe

abcdefg

Quousque ta ndem abute-

Quousque tanden
tilina, patientia n
diu nos etiam fu
ludet? quem ad
frenata jactabit a
ABCDEFGH

Quousque tandem a
patientia noftra? qua

det? quem ad finem fefe
dacia? nihilne te nocturnu
nihil urbis vigiliæ, nihil
confenfus bonorum omni
tiffimus habendi fenatus lc
ra vultufque moverunt? pa
ABCDEFGHIJKL

Quousque tandem abutere, Ca
quamdiu nos etiam furor ifte
quem fefe effrenata inftabit a

Italic

Spabefgomty *Spabefgomty* Spabefgomty **Spabefgomty**

Spabefgomty SPABEFGOMTY Spabefgomty *Spabefgomty*

Spabefgomty Spabefgomty **Spabefgomty** Spabefgomty

Spabefgomty Spabefgomty *Spabefgomty* *Spabefgomty*

Spabefgomty Spabefgomty SPABEFGOMTY Spabefgomty

Lettering (and type) is flexible, showing its plasticity in this Saul Steinberg example in which visual embellishment of a two-letter word suggests thoughts unsaid.

Letterforms can be abstracted to become more than mere representations of sounds: they can be manipulated to represent *ideas*. Traced studies use JJ (consulting), O (oil), DP (cable), G (printing), X (fencing), D (security), and the British pound sign (farming). Some messages don't require any letters or words at all: a bright red triangle indicating "danger" and a realistic rendering of a polar bear are all that's needed in a northern Norway road sign.

c1500BC Cuneiform writing in clay, shown actual size. Behind it is a type sample sheet printed in Glasgow in 1783. Unlike those long-ago days of metal type, in which making a new font (at the time a "font" was one typeface in a single size) took up to a full year to craft, designers can today choose from the greatest variety of letterforms in the history of written language. That many of these types are so quirky as to be illegible is a mathematical certainty. That many are inappropriate for a given message is also numerically obvious. It is among the designer's responsibilities to be aware of the types available and to choose those that communicate clearly and with the correct tone for every message.

Type and sound

Type is one part of a learned language system that works through both hearing and sight: *Phonemes* are sounds we join together. English has about 40 phonemes, but we have only 26 letters. There are some sounds that are not represented, so letter combinations like EE, CH, SH, TH, NG, and OI, are necessary. *Glyphs* are written symbols that represent sounds. We have two styles of glyphs for every letter: majuscules and minuscules, or capitals and lowercase. There are, in addition, a variety of shapes for each letter within these two categories. And most phonemes can be written in multiple ways. For example, IE, Y, UY, IGH, EYE, I, and UI all represent the same phoneme in LIE, CRY, BUY, HIGH, EYE, SLIDE, and GUIDE.

Correlating spoken and written language was the great legacy of the Phœnicians, an ancient trading civilization in the Middle East. In the few thousands of years since the Phœnicians developed their characters, many evolutionary steps have produced the letters we now take for granted: word spaces and punctuation helped clarify meaning; lowercase letters grew out of medieval scribes needing faster writing processes; and sans serif types developed in response to social and intellectual changes in the 19th century.

The very essence of typography is translating the equivalencies of spoken language into printable form.

"A glyph space is formed by attaching the counterspace, letterspace, and line space to a letter. The idea of attaching white space to a letter is a typographic concept. It's the starting point for the divergence of type design and calligraphy." Cyrus Highsmith, *Inside Paragraphs: Typographic Fundamentals*

1 11

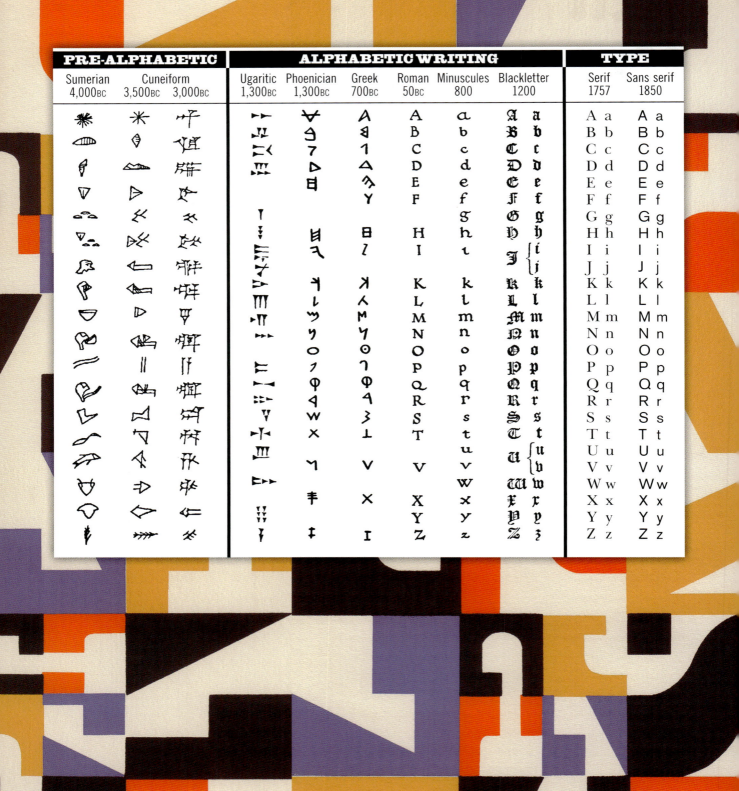

PRE-ALPHABETIC			ALPHABETIC WRITING						TYPE		
Sumerian 4,000BC	Cuneiform 3,500BC	3,000BC	Ugaritic 1,300BC	Phoenician 1,300BC	Greek 700BC	Roman 50BC	Minuscules 800	Blackletter 1200	Serif 1757	Sans serif 1850

...den in all en dag de

ist der mane nume-

graden der fische... Ge

Good typography addresses both the letterforms and the "not-letterforms," the space between characters, words, lines, and between blocks and columns of type. Poor typography results from concentrating only on the letters themselves. It is the contrast of the letter form to its surrounding space that makes type either less or more legible.

The lines above show the edges of the metal pieces that hold the raised letters for printing Johannes Gutenberg's 1448 *Astronomical Calendar*. The metal forced minimum letterspacing on typeset characters: the letters couldn't be any closer than the farthest left and farthest right edges of the metal pieces on which they were molded.

The earliest marks were pictographs, or representational drawings of objects. These evolved into abstract drawings, which in turn bore the *alphabet*: symbols representing spoken sounds.

In the background is a detail of a letterform-based artwork. Notice that the ground — the light areas — are as visually interesting as the figures, regardless of their color. That's because the letters have been cropped so tightly that they cannot be easily recognized. This illustrates that abstraction increases visual intrigue but hampers legibility.

Verbal emphasis should become an equivalent visual emphasis. This typographic process of giving appropriate form to language is called *frozen sound*: sounds are frozen into letters; groups of sounds are frozen into words; and groups of words are frozen into sentences.

Interpreting verbal language allows the reader to "listen to type." What do we mean by "listening to type"? Imagine listening to a recorded book. The reader's voice changes with the story, helping the listener hear various characters and emotions. A story told on paper should do the same thing.

Type as form

The letters we use are the product of 10,000 years of written evolution. At about the time of the first human communities — and the time of the first farming — the people living in what is now Iraq and Syria began to make marks that recorded their herds and harvests. At first, the marks were very representational. The mark for a cow looked like a cow. As speed and need imposed themselves, the marks became more and more abstract, until they couldn't be understood without having learned their meanings. A separation between spoken and written languages continued until the Phœnician's developed a system that used far fewer symbols, each symbol representing a specific sound. In their trading on the

"The intelligence of the typographic designer as communicator shines through. He or she is not playing around with abstraction, but instead manipulates letterforms and words clearly intended to be read, recognized, and understood." Edward A. Hamilton, Art Director, Time-Life Books

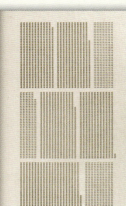

SPECIAL CENTENNIAL OFFER

COMPLETE

DO-IT-YOURSELF

DECLARATION OF INDEPENDENCE KIT

Everything You Need to Write
The Entire Declaration of Independence

RIGHT IN YOUR OWN HOME

Rise
to the Greatness
of the Founding Fathers
as You Write Sentences Like:

"When, in the course of human events...."

"In every stage of these oppressions, we
have petitioned for redress...."

"They, too, have been deaf to the voice
of justice and consanguinity."

And that Perennial Favorite,
"We hold these truths to be self-evident
...."

And Many, Many More!

HERE'S WHAT YOU GET:

(TURN PAGE)

JOIN THE CELEBRATION
ORDER YOUR KIT TODAY

Excerpted with kind permission from *Rutabaga in Eight Languages* by
Stephen G. Perrin, 35 School Street, Andover, MA 01810. A previous
collection of Stephen Perrin's typewriter pieces, *Earth Heart*, was
published by The Addison Gallery of American Art, Andover, MA 01810.

256   *Visible Language* : X 3 Summer 1976

Aoccdrnig to rscheearch at an Elingsh uinervtisy, it deosn't mttaer in waht oerdr the lteters in a wrod are. The olny iprmoatnt tihng is taht frist and lsat ltteres are in the rghit pacle. The rset can be a mses and you can siltl raed it wouthit a pobrelm. Tihs is bcuseae we dno't raed ervey lteetr individually, but as parts of familiar wrod shapes.

The order of letters affects meaning, as in this 1997 logo. Predictably, clothing bearing the French Connection United Kingdom logo is among f.c.u.k.'s best sellers.

An internet pass-along illustrates that letter order may not be as important as thought. It also shows that type has rhythm. A speaker who drones at a single speed is causing listeners extra work to dig out the content, presuming they care enough to make the effort. By comparison, a speaker who alters her rhythm of delivery, by pausing before beginning a new idea, for example, makes the content clearer by grouping information into sensible clusters.

Typographic order is manipulated in Stephen G. Perrin's 1976 *"Complete Do-It-Yourself Declaration of Independence Kit,"* which includes the correct characters and punctuation to produce your own document.

Comic books are particularly good at translating sounds into words. That the words being shown are *Ka-Boom, Kkshh-kkkkk, Smash,* and so forth can be a model of all expressive typography, though it is more difficult to do this with words that have more complex meanings. Children's books sometimes enlarge type to represent a shout, and make it smaller to represent a whisper. This rates as relatively lively typography.

Mediterranean, the Phœnicians passed their system on to the Greeks, who made changes as their spoken language required. The Greeks passed it on to the Romans, who made further changes, and we use the Roman (or "Latin") system with only a couple of minor changes.

Writing developed around 3,000BC. *Alphabetic writing*, where each sound is represented by a symbol, developed around 1,600BC — and is the greater development because it simplified language and made it accessible.

Typographers use elements and traditions inherited through generations of writing, printing, and reading. Many typographic rules were adopted from handwriting as printable type forms were developed in the 1400s and 1500s. Historically, typography was handled by the printer who cut his own typefaces, designed the page, and reproduced the design on paper. In the 20th century, typography and printing separated. Around 1950, typographers and typesetters became vendors who set type to the specifications of the designer or art director, itself having evolved into a new responsibility. Computers, forcing a new working methodology, have nearly obliterated the typography specialist since all type decisions are made on screen. Designers today are widely expected to be masters of an art form that takes years to learn.

It is important to understand the distinction between type and script. Script, or handwriting, was

"Between the two extremes of unrelieved monotony and typographical pyrotechnics there is an area where the typographic designer can contribute to the pleasure of reading and the understanding of what is being read."
Carl Dair

MP·CAESARI·DIV

TRAIANO·AVG·G

MAXIMO·TRIB·PO

AD·DECLARANDVM

MON·SET·LOC·VSTAN

13A

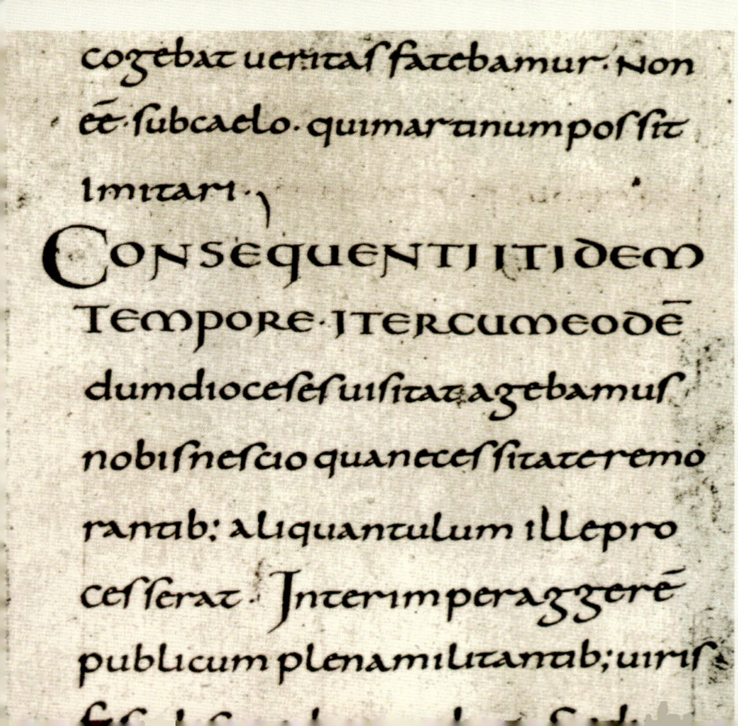

cogebat ueritaf fatebamur· Non
ēē ſubcaelo. quimartinumpoſſit
imitari·)
Consequenti itidem
Tempore·itercumeodē
dumdioceſeſuiſitatagebamuſ
nobiſneſcio quaneceſſitateremo
rantab: aliquantulum illepro
ceſſerat·Interimperaggerē
publicum plenamilitantab;uiriſ

QUOUSQUE tandem abutere
amdiu nos etiam furor iste tuus eluc
ta jactabit audacia? Nihilne te n
urbis vigiliae, nihil timor populi,

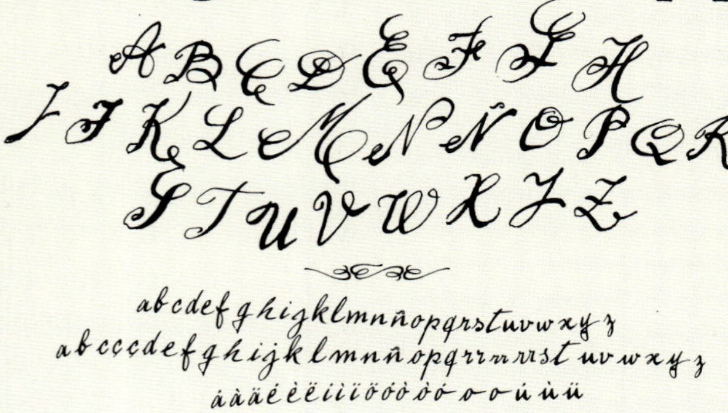

A B C D E F G H
I F K L M N N O P Q R
S T U V W X Y Z

abcdefghiklmnãopqrstuvwxyz
abcccdefghiklmnãopqrrnrust uvwxyz
àáâãéèeîíïöõóõô o o ũü

The term "type" refers only to movable letters used for reproduction. Script handwriting evolved from about 3,000BC.

The birth of type happened in 1450, when Gutenberg perfected movable, reusable metal type.

This sample, Gutenberg's second type (shown actual size) is a "round gothic" from the *Catholicon*, which he crafted in Mainz in 1460. It was made to look like the local handwriting of the time.

Perfectly proportioned capital letters were inscribed on Trajan's Column in c114AD.

Minuscule letters were developed in the process of copying books more quickly. These Carolingian minuscules on the *Sulpicius Severus* date from c810AD.

Script type looks more like handwriting than do italics, which share design characteristics with their roman siblings. The roman and italics are from a showing of Monotype's 1929 interpretation of Garamond, originally designed c1535. Script types often come with alternate characters to enhance to their handwritten quality. This script example is a typeface made by Pepe Gimeno from Andy Warhol's mother's writing.

the only "type" that existed until Johannes Gutenberg perfected the technique of casting identical letters out of metal in 1450. Script was developed by several civilizations simultaneously in what is now the Middle East and Far East. Writing has changed as the materials used have evolved from sticks in clay to reed pens to sticks on wax tablets to quill pens to steel pens to ballpoint pens to porous-tip pens to fingers on touch-sensitive screens. Handwriting has always been affected by its use: a casual, hurried hand for personal notes or an elegant, carefully modulated hand for official documents. In Latin script, the one the Western world uses, script capital letterforms reached their point of perfection with the Roman inscription on Trajan's Column in c114AD. Lowercase, or minuscule, letters didn't fully evolve until about the 9th century AD, as a result of speedier writing and improvements in both writing surface material and pens.

Today, we have two styles of type that emulate handwriting: italics and scripts. Italics are distinct from script types in that they are designed to complement a roman, or upright, typeface with which it shares design characteristics. Scripts are stand-alone types that look like handwriting. Italic types evolved in Venice in 1500, when the region's angled handwriting style was used as inspiration. Script types were introduced shortly after, but fell out of use until Robert Granjon's *Civilité* in 1557.

"Art is simply a right method of doing things." Thomas Aquinas, *Summa Theologiae*, c1265

LETTERFORM CHARACTERISTICS

SOUND (LETTER A)

ay
aah
ah uh
aw
silent

NAME (LETTER A)

"Aye"

Aleph

"Ox" in Semitic and Hebrew

Alpha

Greek

SHAPES (LETTER A)

PLACE IN ALPHABET

A = 1ST IN ALPHABET

B = 2ND IN ALPHABET

C = 3RD IN ALPHABET

D = 4TH IN ALPHABET

E = 5TH IN ALPHABET

F = 6TH IN ALPHABET

G = 7TH IN ALPHABET

H = 8TH IN ALPHABET

I = 9TH IN ALPHABET

RULES FOR USE

1 | Change in sound when combined with certain other letters

2 | Capitalization at the beginning of sentences and names

3 | Cannot be combined in odd pairings and doubled in others

TYPE CHARACTERISTICS

FAMILY

A type family is a series of RELATED FONTS THAT SHARE stylistic attributes. Some fa milies have only two (the mi nimum) or three versions, WHILE SOME FAMILIES HAV e dozens of members. Sof tware makes creating varia tions relatively effortless. FROM THE 1450S UNTIL T he 1950s, a font would t ake up to a year to comp lete, making each und ERTAKING A SIGNIFICAN t financial risk and co mmitment. A type fam

Fairfield LH

STRESS

aA
Roman

aA
Oblique

aA
Italic

WEIGHT

aA
Light

aA
Book/Regular

aA
Medium

aA
Bold

aA
Black

CASE

a b c d e f
g h i j k l m
n o p q r s t
u v w x y z

Minuscules

A B C D E F
G H I J K L M
N O P Q R S T
U V W X Y Z

Majuscules

SIZE

4point Type is measured in points, which is one seventy-seco

6pt Type is measured in points, which is

8pt Type is measured in points,

10pt Type is measured in p

12pt Type is measured i

14pt Type is measure

18pt Type is meas

24pt Type is me

30pt

48pt

60pt

72pt

90pt

POSITION

Above

Left —— Right

Below

COLOR (VALUE)

Areas of type create "color," by which we actually mean the darkness or "value" of the type. This assumes all comparative types are of equivalent size. **Areas of type create "color," by which we actual-ly mean the darkness or "value" of the type. This assumes all com-parative types are of equivalent size.** Areas of type create "color," by which we actually mean the darkness or "value" of the type. This assumes all comparative types are of equivalent size. Areas of type create "color," by which we actually mean the darkness or "value" of the type. This assumes all comparative types are of equivalent size. Areas of type create "color," by which we actually mean the darkness or "value" of the type. This assumes all comparative types are of equivalent size. Areas of type create "color," by which we actually mean the darkness or "value" of the type. This assumes all compara-tive types are of equivalent size. **Areas of type create "color," by which we actually mean the darkness or "value" of the type. This assumes**

TREATMENT

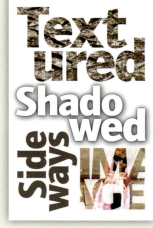

Text ured

Shado wed

Side ways

IMA GE

Hermann Zapf drew a variety of forms of each letter in 1944 studies for a calligraphic type.

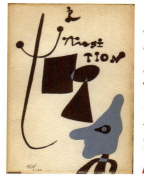

Type can be abstracted to its essentials and still be readable. Spanish artist Joan Míro (1893–1983) used lettering in many of his paintings. This is a 1936

cover for *Transition* magazine. Richard Kegler and Michael Want digitized Míro's characters into a highly decorative typeface in 1993.

A student exercise in merging two glyphs into a new letter-form requires identifying a sound and the critical characteristics of both letters, then preserving the two in balance.

This chart shows the characteristics of letters and type. Any one of them can be manipulated to create emphasis and, in combination, can be used to create distinctive, expressive type that serves the message-sender's need for visibility and the reader's need for a focal point and clarity.

To the five *letter* characteristics we may add that *type* glyphs have additional characteristics:

1 | **It is a member of a family**
2 | **It has a dominant stress**
3 | **It has weight**
4 | **It has a case**
5 | **It has size**
6 | **It has a position**
7 | **It has a color** ("typographic color" is considered its *value* — its lightness or darkness — not its *hue* — its redness or blueness)
8 | **It has a treatment** or a lack of a treatment

The characteristics of type

An alphabet — there are many, of which Latin is the most familiar to us — is made of *glyphs*. According to linguist Earl M. Herrick, each written letter has five characteristics: It has a name. ⊡ It has a specific spoken pronunciation. ⊡ It has a place in the alphabetical order. ⊡ It is subject to rules for its use. In Polish, for example, the sequence of letters *szcz* is permissible. In English, that sequence is not, unless used in a word of Polish assimilation. ⊡ It has a certain basic shape or, often, a few basic shapes. The letter A, for example, may be shown as A, *A*, a, or *a*. The letter's shape is an abstraction that Eric Gill was describing when he said, "A capital A does not cease to be a capital A because it is sloped backwards or forwards, because it is made thicker or thinner, or because serifs are added or omitted."

Utility in type is closely related to its generic styling. There is beauty and opportunity in taking generic style and exaggerating it to create something new. For example, Helvetica, the most popular and generic sans serif face, is nostalgic and evokes a time — the 1950s and 1960s — when there was less clutter and noise of competing messages. Helvetica doesn't avoid complexity, but ensures complexity doesn't exist for its own sake. Because of readers' familiarity with it, Helvetica needs a design treatment *in display settings* to become visible.

"Basically, a graphic designer's job is to be a translator, to put information into a visual form that gives people a better understanding of the content… Not to make it prettier, but to make it more understandable."
Wendy Richmond

Lettering has been used in art throughout the centuries, as in Fra Angelico's *The Death of Saint Dominic*. The saint's words are upside down, indicating death is already here.

But lettering itself became the focal point in art in the 20th century. Shown are samples by René Magritte *Table-Ocean-Fruit*, 1927 (the labels do not correspond with the objects

with which they are paired); Paul Klee *Halme* (*Blades*), 1938 (Klee used pictographs and letterforms in his work throughout the 1930s); and Maurice LeMâitre *Dionysian Hymn for

Beatrice, 1968. LeMâitre was a *letterist*, a French movement begun in 1946 which uses largely non-readable lettering in addition to figurative and abstract elements.

American painter Jasper Johns is known for his works using layered and manipulated numbers. In this 1961 work, *0 through 9*, Johns uses the spaces inside and around each of the figures to determine the forms and counterforms of the painting. The result is an abstract study that reveals its own development.

Elegant typography

What is elegance in typography? It is presenting all necessary information with no unnecessary complexity. It is the distillation of content to its essence. It is, in other words, *expressive clarity*.

Designers want to challenge the reader, to provoke them and to entertain them. We also want to design on the edge — or at least to tip our hats at the edge and acknowledge the design era in which we practice. We want to serve the profession and the art of typography. But how? The way to create expressive typography is to predigest the copy, understand the message, and show off its meaning and its importance to the reader. Contrast type style, size, weight, position, color, or treatment to show hierarchy and give enough information for the reader to decide whether to become involved with the text.

Complexity will not get a message across because, though it may be interesting to look at, the message won't be legible. Simplicity will not get a message across because, though it may be easy to read, the item's importance won't be recognized. Only *expressiveness* combined with *lack of complexity* will make the message both interesting and legible.

Choosing a typeface that enhances the content is important: words are symbols of emotions and ideas that manipulate the reader.

"Pretentious [letterforms] oppose the utilitarian task of typography. The more uninteresting a letter is in itself the more useful it is in typography." Piet Zwart (1885–1977) Choosing the right typeface is not as important as using a neutral typeface well. By using fancy letters, the danger is that typography will begin and end with choosing the typeface. That is not typography, but fashion. The most forward-looking design is generally the first to look dated. On the other hand, traditional, conservative design looks timeless, but it is highly derivative. How can these two ends be balanced?

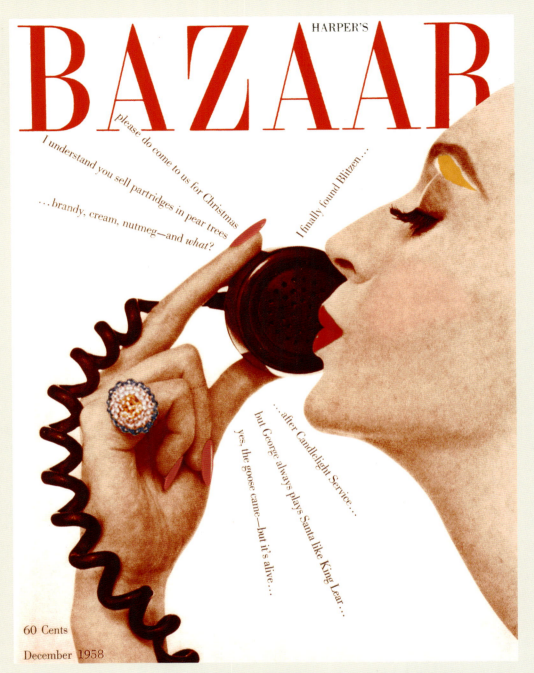

HARPER'S BAZAAR

please do come to us for Christmas

I understand you sell partridges in pear trees

...brandy, cream, nutmeg—and what?

I finally found Blitzen...

...after Candlelight Service...

but George always plays Santa like King Lear...

yes, the goose came—but it's alive...

60 Cents

December 1958

This 24-point headline is set as if it was just large text. Default settings have been left intact.

This improved 24-point headline is set as if every interspace was meaningful. It is darker and more visible.

Text and display may work together to convey a single idea, as in Don Egensteiner's 1960 ad by and for Y&R Advertising that appeared in Fortune magazine.

An idea may be expressed many ways depending on how the primary type is handled. Display type is most successful when it provides two or three opportunities for a browser to decide whether the story is worth their time and attention. Headline, subhead, and captions are the three areas that are the persuaders. The primary type sets the tone and typographic attitude. The secondary type supports and explains the primary type.

"BAZAAR" is clearly display type: it is big and it is meant to be seen first on this 1958 cover by Henry Wolf. The radiating type, though text size, is also display type since it is meant to attract attention. Size alone is not a determinant for text or display type: intention is.

Spacing is more visible in display type. Look carefully at these two examples. The only difference between them is *the organization of space*. The one on the right is a considerably better arrangement. Think of display type not as typesetting, but as *shape management* in which each character and each space is a discrete shape. Digital font spacing is generally optimized for text sizes, so default settings have to be massaged for larger type.

Text and display

Text is generally thought of as the small, gray type that contains the bulk of a message. Display is the big type that is supposed to stop the browser rushing to get the big ideas. Once upon a time in the history of printing, there was so little printed matter in existence, display type was unnecessary. Those who could read would read whatever they got their eyes on. Labelling was relatively insignificant. As more books became available, naming their contents — from book covers to headings — became a benefit. The earliest display type was simply bigger text. The 1800s industrial revolution brought an avalanche of display faces to make advertising messages more visible. In today's hyperactive information and media environment, readers require us to state immediately and convincingly what our message is, or to be ignored entirely.

Display type has traditionally been defined as type over 18 points in size. Typographic treatments in recent years have changed the definition to *any type whose purpose is to be seen first*. Display type is therefore properly called *primary type*, regardless of size.

The purpose of primary display type is to lure the reader to secondary type and then into the text, so keep primary type short and provocative. Once in the text, nothing should be done to repel the hard-won reader.

"Type, like the spoken voice, can be powerfully bold or elegantly understated. It can shout or gracefully inform. It can be stuffy or informal, universal or parochial, traditional or state of the art, highly complex or primitive."
Anonymous

But unless the reader grasps something of value, his conversion from a looker to a reader will not occur. Put interesting information where it can be found. Break the type into palatable chunks and recognize that *captions* are the first type many readers cover.

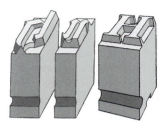

Type has been made of metal since about 1450. These characters, when printed, would read **Hnh**

Lettering has color and texture, as this dark, rough woodcut example by J.V. Videní shows. Or lettering may be even-toned and gritty as in this c1930

quilt by Lena Moore. The letters are cut and sewn individually onto the background fabric. Or lettering may be light and organic, as this 2003

illustration by Lauren Redniss shows. Ignoring traditional baselines, the letters serve as the illustration's shading.

A typographer adds value to the content by interpreting it for maximum absorption. This magazine cover prints parts of letters in red on pages of a 1040 US income tax filing report, then the pages are tiled into a composite message and photographed. The appropriateness of the treatment is critical: this solution wouldn't work for a different problem.

The language of type

> "Type is a medium of philosophical enjoyment. It is interesting to discover typographic rules containing inconsistencies in logic, which are in use only because of tradition. It is also interesting to ponder the origin of these errors, the practical reasons for their perpetuation, and to suggest remedies." Bradbury Thompson

The rightness of a type is determined by what it is *used for.* Advertising must be visually competitive, so it needs typefaces that are slightly "different." Text, having been reached as a result of persuasive display type, has already won its readers, so using a "different" typeface would only impede absorption. Low-resolution type, on-screen display for example, benefits from certain type characteristics: relatively uniform stroke weight, open letterspacing, and short, thick serifs. Some types have been designed specifically for such use.

Type attracts readers. Type arouses emotions. Like color, some types are cool and some are warm. Each type has a feel created by the relationship of the thick and

V ı fuperum fæuæ memorem ıunonıſo

M ulta quoque'& bello paſſus dum cond

I nferret'q, deoſ latıo : genuſ unde' lat

A lbanıq, patreſ, atque' altæ' moema ı

Script handwriting of Antonio Sinibaldi, Florence 1480

alıos : infta alios . Ego teram aut Platonen

alter deum fecit fine corpore : alter fine an

tandem inquit : Veriora uidentur Tıtı T

fumma : Cloatinam Tıtus Tatius dedicaı

Roman type of the de Spira brothers, Venice 1469

hāno piu graue boce che lefemine . Del fanc

e tutto fuori . Non parla fenon dopo lannc

di fei mefi : elquale prodigio fignifico laruı

mincıono a parlare prefto penono piu a a

Roman type of Nicolas Jenson, Venice 1470

lttera eft pars mínima uo cís indíuídua .   Su

ræ uigíntiq̃tuor · alpha . uíta . gamma . delta . ep

thíta . íota . cappa . gní . xí . omícron . pi . ro . fıgm

chí . pfí . omega . Harum uocales quidem fep

First type of Aldus Manutius, Venice 1495

dulo Angèle ; quod meminiſſe te certo

ſcio ; ut fructus ſtudiorum noſtrorum͚,

quos ferebat illa aetas nō tam maturos , q̃

uberes , femper tibi aliquos promeremus :

Second type of Aldus Manutius, Venice 1495

Quare multarum quoq; ge
ipſo benedicédas oés gente
aperte prædıctum eft : cuius
fed fide cōfecutus eft : qui p
filium : quem primum omı
cæteris qui ab eo nafcerétu
eorum futuræ fignum : uel
tinétes maiores fuos imitar

Quare multarum quoq; ge
ipso benedicédas oés gente
aperte prædictum est : cuiu
sed side cósecutus est : qui p
filium : quem primum omn
cæteris qui ab eo nasceréti
eorum futuræ signum : uel
tinétes maiores suos imitaı

POETRY IS WHAT MILTON SAW WHEN DON MAR-QUIS

RELATE HEADLINE to text by repeating the design treatment on the initial caps. Good craftsmanship calls for alignment of the initial's baseline with the one of the text baselines. It is usual to have it agree with the third or fourth text base-

Type's color can be used to guide the reader from primary to tertiary information. Dark to light is most logical and functional.

Unify a type design by applying a special headline treatment to other display type, like an initial cap. This fading headline illustrates the onset of blindness and is adapted to

the initials in the story. Add meaning to the type: there are an infinite number of ways of doing this. The appropriateness of your solution distinguishes you as a typographer.

Glowing words are placed seemingly at random on a stairway at Lincoln Center for the Performing Arts in New York City, an intentional, tasteful, and amusing treatment.

Roman type development shown over fifteen years: the first example shows the local handwriting style of the time. Type was made to emulate handwriting, so each printer crafted letterforms that echoed his region's writing style.

Nicolas Jenson's 1470 roman (*far left*) and a recent digital interpretation show many small æsthetic judgments that must be made in a typeface revival.

thin strokes, the proportion of width to height, the way corners meet, and a myriad of other stylistic traits. But regardless of tone, type must be legible and, at least in text settings, must add clarity.

Type treatments have an attribute of rightness or wrongness, determined by the message, the medium, and the audience. What works splendidly for one situation may not work at all for another. Putting the reader's needs first is always a right decision. Erik Spiekermann says: "Design for the user. If you want to get something from somebody, why not make it easy for them to give it to you? Design top left to bottom right. Put the most important (information) first. Things that belong together get placed together."

Type has "color"; that is, it is relatively light or dark gray. Darker type generally attracts attention and so is used at larger sizes. Readers are most comfortable with "medium," "normal," or "book" weights, so these are best for text settings. Lightweight type is somewhat more legible than bold type at text sizes, but is less legible as it gets smaller.

Where did type come from? It evolved from handwriting. Today type comes from four sources: fonts that are found on or are added to your computer; letters and alphabets you design yourself in specialized programs like Font Lab; letters you find and scan in; and letters you

"Perfect typography must be unorthodox typography. It may mean using wrong fonts, cutting hyphens in half, using smaller punctuation marks, in fact, doing anything that is needed to improve the appearance of typography. There should be no rule except to make type pleasing to the eye." Aaron Burns

SCONSIDERATO

per Angela diCampo
Modi di dire a azioni uno fine

Ne ho fin sopra i capelli di questo brutto tempo

|In questo lavoro imprevedibile può andare benis simo o malissimo

Nella grande raccolta do annotazioni e disegni contenuti nelle carte superstiti di multe sono le idee, molti e progetti incompiuti. La construzione di modelli che realizza no i progetti vinciani e che sono esposti in questo e in altri musei del mondo ha in primo luogo una funzione didattica sparsi in molti manoscritti e specialmente nel codice Atlantico sono i progetti di macchine per volare, navigare e perfino per camminare sopra l'acqua o lavorare sotto la sua superficie.

Fra tanti accurati disegni o schizzi sommari, fra tante ingegnose e geniali intuizione non mancano i sogni impossibili e prevale l'incompiuto.

Nessuna meraviglia che anche in questo campo si siano ripetuti i tentativi di dare un corpo materiale a idee che in qualche caso erano ancora fantasmi della mente, appena tradotti in pochi segni tracchiati sulle carte. Non che egli si limitasse a un

La construzione di modelli che realizzano progetti vinciani e che sono esposti in questo e in altri musei del mondo ha in primo luogo una funzione didattica.

che realizza no i progetti vinciani e che sono esposti in questo e in altri musei.

Del mondo ha in primo luogo una didattica sparsi in molti manoscritti e specialmente nel codice Atlantico sono i progetti di macchine per volare, navigare e perfino per camminare sopra l'acqua o lavorare sotto la sua superficie. Fra tanti accurati disegni o schizzi sommari, fra tante ingegnose e geniali intuizione non mancano i sogni impossibili e prevale l'incompiuto meraviglia che anche in questo campo si siano.

Ripetuti i tentativi superstiti di multe sono le idee, molti e progetti incompiuti. La construzione di mo delli accurati e di dare un corpo materiale a idee che in qualche caso erano ancora fantasmi della mente, appena tradotti in pochi segni tracchiati sulle carte. Non che egli si limitasse a un ella grande raccolta do annotazioni e disegni contenuti nelle carte.

Nel codice Atlantico sono i progetti di macchine per volare, navigare e perfino per camminare sopra l'acqua o lavorare sotto la sua superficie.

Tanti accurati disegni o schizzi sommari, fra tante ingegnose e geniali intuizione non mancano i sogni impossibili e prevale l'incompiuto meraviglia che anche in questo discorso mentale parla di oggetti e

che realizza no i progetti vinciani e che progetti di macchine per volare, navigare e perfino per camminare sopra l'acqua o lavorare sotto la sua superficie. Fra tanti accurati disegni o schizzi sommari.

Ingegnose e geniali intuizione non mancano i sogni impossibili e prevale l'incompiuto meraviglia che anche in questo si siano. Ripetuti i tentativi superstiti di multe sono le idee, molti e progetti incompiuti.

Ne abbiamo avuto abbastanza della violenza!

e perfino per camminar sopra l'acqua o lavorare sotto la sua superficie. Fra tanti egni contenuti nelle carte. Nel codice sono i progetti di macchine per volare, navigare e perfino per camminare sopra l'acqua o lavorare sotto la sua superficie.

Disegni o schizzi sommari, fra tante ingegnose e geniali intuizione non mancano i sogni impossibili e prevale meraviglia che anche in questo discorso mentale parla di oggetti e sono esposti in questo e in altri musei. Del mondo ha in primo luogo una didattica sparsi in molti manoscritti e specialmente nel codicequarantesima che sviluppa una velocità di rotazione presso

54
D'ACCORDO

55
D'ACCORDO

President's Day Sale

45% to 70% off every President in stock.
Nothing held back.
Republicans and Democrats.
One or two independents, too.
When they're gone,
they're gone until November.

Pennsyltucky
Where deals are made edging on insanity.

Reductions off original prices. No adjustments to prior purchases. Cannot be combined with any other offer. Presidents labelled to show state of origin. Sale ends when all Presidents are gone.

Abraham Lincoln
16 not be-sixteenth President. Our time campaigns to Vote Obama-Defeated

Medium **_Black Italic_**   MEDIUM SMALL CAPITALS   **Black** _Italic_ **Bold** Roman

A type family can have many members, some that look more related than others.

Some font variations can look like near twins, while others seem to share fewer common traits. Type family members

may share or have contrasting angle, serifs, texture, weight, and width.

A _typeface_ is a set of related characters. A _font_ is a digital vehicle for those characters. Sketches for _Palatino Regular_, Hermann Zapf's first typeface shows corrections, c1950.

Design can be split into two broad categories: editorial (information for its own sake) and advertising (information that persuades an action). There are ten applications of editorial type, eight of which are shown in the example: ❶ headline, ❷ subheads, ❸ captions, ❹ breakouts, ❺ text, ❻ department headings, ❼ bylines and bios, and ❽ folios and footlines. The remaining two, coverlines and contents, do not appear on typical interior pages so are not included in this illustration. Because advertising is simpler in message and presentation, fewer type applications are needed: ① headlines, ② subheads, ③ captions, ④ text, and ⑤ logos and taglines.

draw or write yourself then scan in and place as images.

Let's pause for a moment and talk about where type goes. Design can be split into two broad categories: _editorial_ and _advertising_. There are ten type applications of editorial type, eight of which are indicated in the example at left. Because advertising is by necessity simpler in message and presentation, there are fewer type applications needed: five are all that are needed.

What is a typeface? What is a font?

A typeface is a collection of characters that share design attributes (see page 30). A typeface is the _design_ of the letters. A font is, today, the software file that describes related scalable characters. Until the advent of phototype in the 1960s, a font was a collection of related metal letters in a single size. The _scalability_ of phototype made a font a collection of related characters without regard to typeset size. Today's _font_ is a single weight that can be set at any size.

Will Burtin wrote in 1963, "Each typeface is a piece of history, like a chip in a mosaic that depicts the development of human communication. Each typeface is also a visual record of the person who created it — his skill as a designer, his philosophy as an artist, his feeling for the details of each letter and the resulting impressions of an alphabet or a text line."

"People who love ideas must have a love of words. They will take a vivid interest in the clothes that words wear."
Beatrice Warde

Ag
AGaramondPro-
Regular.otf

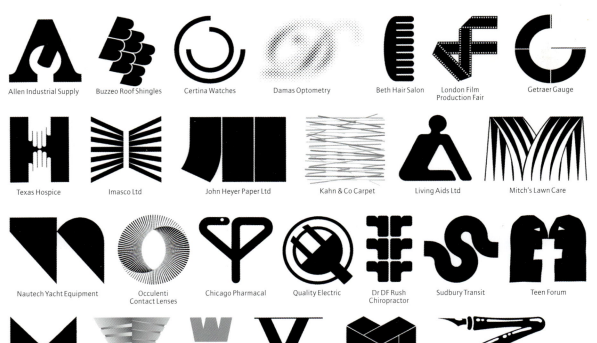

Allen Industrial Supply

Buzzeo Roof Shingles

Certina Watches

Damas Optometry

Beth Hair Salon

London Film Production Fair

Getraer Gauge

Texas Hospice

Imasco Ltd

John Heyer Paper Ltd

Kahn & Co Carpet

Living Aids Ltd

Mitch's Lawn Care

Nautech Yacht Equipment

Occulenti Contact Lenses

Chicago Pharmacal

Quality Electric

Dr DF Rush Chiropractor

Sudbury Transit

Teen Forum

Ursula Flower Shop

Vail Blinds

Willis Painting

Xpedx Freight

York Centre

Zemkie Copywriting

ABCDEFGHIJKL
MNOPQRSTUVW
XYZ&123456789
0abcdefghijklmn
opqrstuvwxyz?!;:

FF Bodoni Classic

ABCDEFGHIJK
LMNOPQRSTU
VWXY&Z12345
abcdefghijklm
nopqrstuvwxyz

ITC Bodoni Seventy-Two Book

ABCDEFGHIJK
LMNOPQRSTU
VWXY&Z12345
abcdefghijklm
nopqrstuvwxyz

Lanston Bodoni

ABCDEFGHIJK
LMNOPQRSTU
VWXY&Z12345
abcdefghijklm
nopqrstuvwxyz

Monotype Bodoni

ABCDEFGHIJK
LMNOPQRSTU
VWXY&Z12345
abcdefghijklm
nopqrstuvwxyz

Bauer Bodoni

ABCDEFGHIJK
LMNOPQRSTU
VWXY&Z12345
abcdefghijklm
nopqrstuvwxyz

Berthold Bodoni Old Face

ABCDEFGHIJK
LMNOPQRSTU
VWXY&Z12345
abcdefghijklm
nopqrstuvwxyz

Berthold Bodoni Antiqua

ABCDEFGHIJK
LMNOPQRSTU
VWXY&Z12345
abcdefghijklm
nopqrstuvwxyz

WTC Our Bodoni

ABCDEFGHIJK
LMNOPQRSTU
VWXY&Z12345
abcdefghijklm
nopqrstuvwxyz

Giambattista Bodoni's original metal types from 1818.

A scalable outline description is used to print a letter. A cruder bitmap description shows the letter on screen, and the printed letter is the result. The design of letters themselves is not copyright protected in the US, but the outline description is. Making changes to an outline description file (a font) requires permission from the type designer who made it. You may, however, print characters, scan, and outline them, and make alterations to these new "character descriptions." Respect type designers' work: don't steal their fonts.

An *alphabet* is a group of characters that represent sounds. A *typeface* is an alphabet that has consistent design attributes. This is not a typeface but merely an A–Z collection of letterform logotypes. They do show how letters can be abstracted to convey additional meaning.

Eight interpretations of the same source design, Bodoni's type of 1800. Sensitivity to details will reveal differences in specific character shapes and overall typographic color.

Looking at type

More than ever before in human history, we take type for granted. The computer has made type and its arrangement a daily practice for nearly everyone. The mystery of type well used is diluted by day-to-day familiarity. But when type was a new invention nothing about type was taken for granted. Even Latin typeforms were invented (opposite) by copying the handwriting in northern Italy. Each printer had to make his own type — there were no type foundries yet — so each had his own style. By seeing one another's work, printers developed type designs rapidly, though each font required months of non-paying work to complete.

Ideally, typographers transform an author's copy into palatable, easy-to-read text. In reality, we see quite a bit of type that does nothing to make the content easier to read. Why? What are the rules of legibility that are being broken or, worse still, ignored?

Typography isn't *typesetting*. Typesetting, traditionally a craft by specialists, has, in the digital evolution, often come to mean allowing the computer's default settings to dictate final outcomes. Typography, on the other hand, is in part knowing how to set defaults for optimal spacing and legibility while recognizing the moments when breaking the defaults is exactly the right decision.

It may well be true that rules are made to be broken,

"Why worship typographic tradition? We pay our debt to the past when we preserve craft laws and principles that the old typographers handed down. But progress demands that we add some achievement of our own to the heritage."
Unknown, c.1932

Modern Latin	A B C D E F H I K L M N O P Q
Early Latin	A B ᴄ D E F H ꙅ K L M N O Γ Q
Early Greek	Λ Δ ᴄ Δ ᴈ Ⅎ B ꙅ K Γ ꟼ L ʔ O Π
Phoenician	ᵏ Ϥ ᴧ Δ ᴈ ᴪ Ｉ ☲ ꙅ ㇵ ㇵ ㄥ ㇷ ʔ O Ꝑ
Early Aramaic	ᴋ ᵞ ʌ ᵞ Ʒ ﹅ ﹅ ᴗ ᴗ ᴗ ʕ ᴗ ʕ O ﹅
Early Arabic	ㄴ ㄴ ㄴ ㄅ ᴑ ᴑ ᵹ ᴗ ᴗ ᴗ ㄴ ㄴ ㄴ ᴗ ㄴ

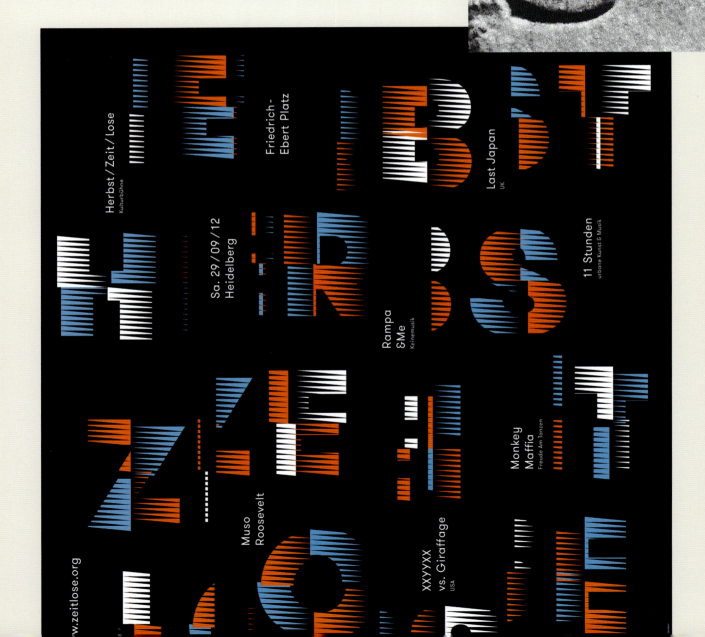

moukamouka

Type is both the shape of the letters themselves and the spaces around and within the letters (top).

Emil Ruder made a study of negative space within characters using a variety of typefaces.

Ninety percent of typography is about *manipulating the emptiness* that surrounds type. The first four lines of this example are set without wordspacing. The middle four lines are set

with normal wordspacing and the last four lines are set with 200% wordspacing. Reading becomes more difficult when wordspacing is out of proportion to letter spacing.

Our modern Latin letters — as well as modern Arabic — evolved in different directions from the Phœnician alphabet, as shown in the chart compiled by linguist Thomas Milo. Our alphabet — only capital letters, minuscules weren't developed until about 750AD — passed through the Greeks and Romans and had characters added or deleted to meet the needs of its changing users. The Romans perfected the alphabet's forms on the Trajan Column in 114AD (actual size). Letters were drawn with a broad reed pen or painted with a square-ended brush on stone, then chiseled, slightly accentuating the ends.

Legibility is injured but readability is enhanced by letterform manipulation in this poster detail by Götz Gramlich. The lettering reads: HERBST ZEIT LOSE.

but you shouldn't break typographic rules until you know what they are. Originality comes from knowing what has come before: an understanding of both type history and current practice leads to variety and innovation. Using type well requires an understanding of the following:

Legibility A measure of a type's ability to be read under normal reading conditions. It is a result of assessing the inherent legibility of a typeface and applying optimal spacing attributes.

Readability A measure of the type's ability to attract and hold a reader's interest. Increasing readability often causes a reduction in legibility, so care must be taken, particularly in text settings, where legibility is more important than in display type.

Shapes of letters Latin letters can be grouped into four categories based on their shapes: vertical (il, EFHILT); curved (acegos, COQS); a combination of vertical and curved (bdfhjmnpqrtu, BDGJPRU); and diagonal, or oblique (kvwxyz, AKMNWXYZ). Letters within each group are more likely to be mistaken for each other.

Shapes of words & All-caps/lowercase We do not read by looking at individual letters. We read by recognizing word shapes, which is a combination of the external shape and internal structure of the empty areas. Familiar letterforms create familiar word shapes, speeding the reading process.

"Choose a typeface that works with the sound you want to make." Anonymous

	XXX Condensed	XX Condensed	X Condensed	Condensed	Regular	Extended
Roman	R	R	R	R	R	R
Antique	R	R	R	R	R	R
Gothic	R	R	R	R	R	R

Type cases were placed above each other. The upper case held capitals, or majuscules, and the lower case held numerals and non-capital letters, or minuscules. The California Job Case (right) became the standard storage system because it fit all characters in a more efficient single tray.

There are three letter shapes in our alphabet: vertical, round, and diagonal. These shapes often do not fit together evenly, causing spacing problems that must be fixed.

AИTIQUEЯIA TЯIBECA

The shapes of letters includes their direction. Right reading-ness is manipulated in this logo for a shop in New York.

Tops of letters are more identifiable than bottoms, and right sides are more identifiable than left sides.

Type was cut in a *series* beginning in the 1830s and by the 1880s, a *series* usually included at least the six variations, as shown in the three families here: Roman (serifed), Antique (slab serifed), and Gothic (sans serif).

Adrian Frutiger's studies for *Univers* included pasted together repeatable parts for consistent curves. A typeface requires consistency of form applied to the alphabet's wide variety of letterforms. The original *Univers* had 45,000 glyphs spanning twenty-seven weights and postures.

ALL-CAPS WORD SHAPES ARE MORE ALIKE, WHICH SERIOUSLY SLOWS READERS. *LIKE ITALICS, ALL CAPS SHOULD BE USED IN TEXT SPARINGLY, ONLY TO CREATE EMPHASIS.* **IN DISPLAY TYPE, ALL CAPS INCREASES VISIBILITY AND WORKS WELL IN SHORT HEADLINES.** ALL CAPS TAKES UP TO 35 PERCENT MORE SPACE THAN LOWERCASE OF THE SAME SIZE. USE LINING FIGURES, WHICH LOOK LIKE CAPITAL LETTERS (1234567890) IN ALL-CAPS SETTINGS SO NUMBERS DON'T DRAW UNNECESSARY ATTENTION TO THEMSELVES.

Type size is measured in points in the United States (72 to the inch) and measured in millimeters in the rest of the world. Text sizes range from 8 to 12 points, depending on x-height. Type size is closely related to line length: reading is affected by having more than about 50 to 60 characters per line. A design should be adjusted to balance type size and line length to achieve that number of characters per line. If there are more than 60 characters per line, linespacing must be added. ▣ Use size contrast to make the most important words most visible. Ordinarily, this means making display type larger than text. More creatively, small display type can whisper with significance if all the other type is uniformly large. ▣ If text is too small, it can't — and almost certainly won't — be read. Large

"In 1951, when I was a typesetter's apprentice, I held letters — or rather, type — in my hand for the first time. It was made of lead. I carefully placed them in order, starting at the left and ending on the right so that they became a line. I have never forgotten this lesson of order." Olaf Leu

This is Wilke Roman set so there are an average of seventy characters per line, including word spaces. This setting, which is 10-point type, forces the reader to traverse a column that is too wide. The easiest way to determine optimal type size for a given column width is to try setting a specific type and counting characters. If setting more than the optimal number of characters per line cannot be avoided, add a few points of linespacing. This will give readers a comfortable return path to the beginning of the next line.

This is Wilke Roman set so there are an average of fifty characters per line, including word spaces. This is an ideal setting for reading comfort. The column width necessary for this ideal setting calls for 14-point type.

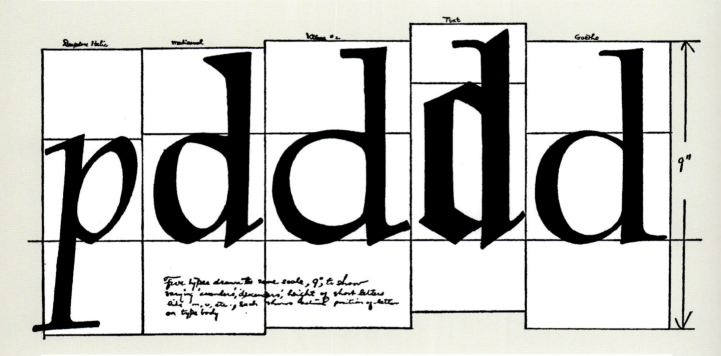

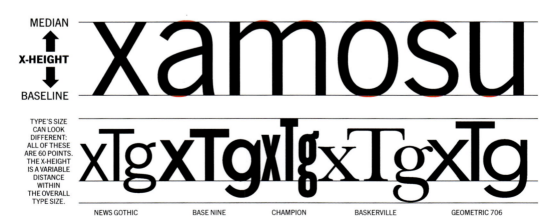

MEDIAN

X-HEIGHT

BASELINE

TYPE'S SIZE CAN LOOK DIFFERENT: ALL OF THESE ARE 60 POINTS. THE X-HEIGHT IS A VARIABLE DISTANCE WITHIN THE OVERALL TYPE SIZE.

NEWS GOTHIC BASE NINE CHAMPION BASKERVILLE GEOMETRIC 706

defgh

defgh

dunhill

A lack of descenders allows lines of lowercase type to be set tighter on the Daily Telegraph's 1865 "news bill."

Ascenders are exaggerated in this logo for a British purveyor of men's quality goods.

Capitalization is one way to emphasize beginnings. Bradbury Thompson suggested alternatives in 1945, basing his ideas on the simplicity of the idealistic *monalphabet*, using

only lowercase letters: ● use a bullet before each sentence; underline the initial letter; **s**et the first character in bold; **e**nlarged lowercase letters can substitute for capitals.

Relative x-height is shown in this 1940 study by Frederic Goudy. Letters from five of his typefaces are drawn to the same scale. The overall heights are equivalent and indicate the type's "body," or the size of the metal block on which it was cast.

text looks like yelling and forces the reader to read lines in sections rather than as a whole. ⊡ When setting small type, use medium weight and a face with a large x-height. Use a slightly condensed face — saving width — and increase the point size to make copy fit and maximize legibility. Or do your readers a real favor and cut some copy to make the remaining text larger, more openly spaced, and much more legible.

x-height The *perceived* size of type is determined by its x-height, the distance from the baseline to the top of the lowercase letters' median (*opposite*). It is called the x-height because an ordinary lowercase *x* has neither ascender nor descender. Other lowercase letters that lack ascenders and descenders, like *a*, *m*, *o*, *s*, and *u*, have rounded tops and bottoms of the letters that slightly exceed the baseline or median. ⊡ X-height is not a unit of measurement, but a distance within the overall size of the type, which is measured from the tops of the ascenders to bottoms of the descenders. All 60-point types, for example, are equivalent in overall size, but their appearance can very greatly because the x-height occupies different proportions of that distance. ⊡ A large x-height makes type look larger, because more of the overall area is occupied by lowercase letterform. A large x-height imposes proportionally short ascenders and descenders. Types

"Even with all the beauty and ingenuity of a well-designed typeface, a single letterform is still the lowest common denominator. When we experience disappointment with letters, let's not be afraid to do what comes naturally: let's draw." Gerard Huerta

Safengomby
Optima

Safengomby
Dead History

Safengomby
Poppl-Laudatio

Safengomby
Rotis SemiSerif

Safengomby
Syndor

Safengomby
Rotis SansSerif 55

Safengomby
Rotis SemiSans 55

Safengomby
Rotis SemiSerif 55

Safengomby
Rotis Serif 55

Semi-serif faces fill a gap between serif and sans serif faces. Sometimes a semisans can be mistaken for a serif face whose serifs have been chopped off (far left). *Rotis*, among a few others, has a semisans by virtue of it being midway in a family that extends from a sans serif to a serif version, giving the designer a set of four typographic voices that inherently relate to each other.

Type weight is shown in this 1971 chart for the development of *Typos*, a large family of Japanese typefaces. The versions are arranged in increasing horizontal stroke widths from top to bottom and in increasing vertical stroke widths from left to right in 100ths of the square unit in which each is shown. Equivalent weight flexibility can now be achieved through a single Multiple Master font.

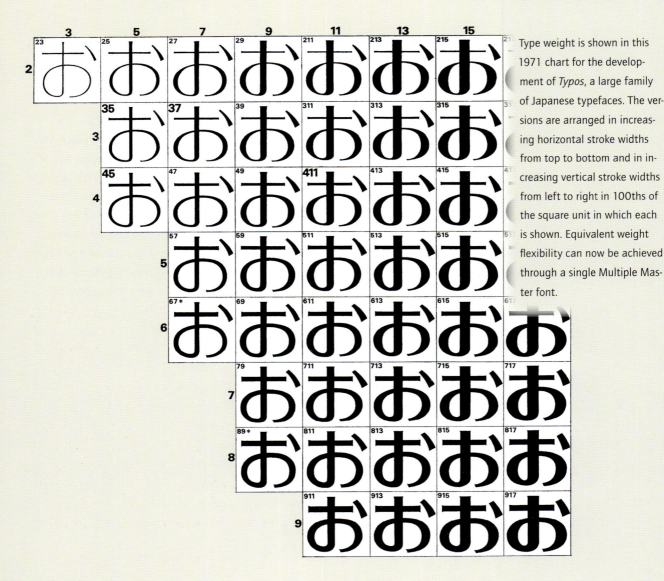

Serifs are exaggerated to their fullest in this extremely dark 1895 display face. The maximum darkness provided visibility for advertising headlines.

Cactus Roman might be called a "super-serif" because its spikes are essentially serifs placed rhythmically over the entire body of each letter.

Two lettermarks that don't just *have* serifs, they *use* them. The *H* uses 6 different serifs attached to a simple, bold armature. The *E* is made entirely of serifs.

Linotype's *Univers Next* has a total of 63 weights and, overlapping only 9 weights, show a notable proportional progression of both stroke weight and length.

with large x-heights require additional line-spacing to compensate for their lack of built-in negative space.

Serif/sans serif Types that have small lines at the ends of major strokes have serifs, types without are sans serif. Serifs aid reading across lines but they force too much space between letters in display type. That is why serifs are often preferred for text and sans serif types are preferred for display. ⊡ Serifs help direct eyes horizontally. Because they poke out beyond the edges of characters, they force a certain amount of space between characters. Sans serif can be just as readable as serif faces if you open the letterspacing a bit and add extra linespacing to compensate for the lack of horizontal direction. ⊡ Were serifs an aesthetic refinement by Roman carvers, or were they only products of the tools in use at the time? There are no Roman writing manuals in existence, so we must guess. In the time of Christ, letterers used reed pens and brushes for smaller works and chisels for monumental works. They painted letters on stone before chiseling them out. So serifs were both a result of the tools in use *and* an aesthetic decision.

Weight Type's weight is described as hairline, book, medium, bold, and black and is determined by the ratio of each character's negative space to its strokes: larger counter spaces are found on light faces, and small counter spaces are found on bold faces. ⊡ Medium weight is most readable: type that is too light doesn't stand out from the paper; type that is too bold has counters that fill in and are indistinguishable. ⊡ Type with extreme contrast between its thinnest and thickest strokes makes poor reading because of "dazzle." ⊡ Regardless of typeface used, reversing type out of a background makes it look smaller and thinner. Compensate by making it a little bigger and bolder, until the optical discrepancy becomes invisible.

Italics are used to emphasize or differentiate short passages, like quotes, titles, and foreign terms, from roman text settings. They are most effective when used sparingly. If used too much they make text looks frenetic and their meaning as *special information* becomes unclear. Italics, which are not as easy to read as roman, slow readers to the point of abandonment. Italics are also lighter than their roman equivalents, so are a bit harder to discern from their background. ⊡ Some designers believe that italics, with their diagonal stress, suggest *action* and *speed* and have dynamic qualities. That is more an aesthetic perception than a factual one, but the idea that italic type is *fast* or *racy* is almost always used as a graphic crutch. Italics were invented as a way to emulate regional handwriting in 1501 and to fit more type in the same space. In

ribus bris annotandas uoces studium necessa
rium · quod partim pro uoluntate cuiusq. fit
partim usu proprio : et obseruatione communis

160 years of italic type development: Cursive script, Italian c1500

se, suaq; confirmet: nec ulli alteri sapere concedit; ne se
desipere fateatur. sed sicut alias tollit ; sic ipsa quoq; ab
alijs tollitur omnibus . Nihilo minus enim philosophi
sunt , qui eam stultitiæ acusant . Quancunq; lauda-

First italic type by Aldus Manutius, Venice 1501

N ulla uia est. tamen ire iuuat, quo me rapit ardor,

I nuiaque audaci propero tentare iuuenta.

V os per inaccessas rupes, et inhospita euntem

Ludovico degli Arrighi's second italic type, Rome 1527

Fert Fatum parteis in-re quacunque gerenda ,
    Fato Romani post tot discrimina , post tot
Prælia, debellatum Orbem rexere monarchæ :
Roma caputq; fuit Mundi, priùs exiguus grex

First italic type with oblique capital letters, Basel 1525

Christianiß. Regis primus elecmosynarius, vir
tum editis suis in sacras literas hypomnematis,
tum euulgandis virorum doctorum ac piorum
monumētis de Republica literaria optime me-

Claude Garamont's italic type, Paris 1545

Æadem, is admonenti Gubernatrici ut
Amstelodamo, non modo non a paruerit, sed
Missuma Gubernatrice Turrium a secret
urbe Protinus abscendere, non Exaudito R

Christopher van Dyck's italic type, Amsterdam 1660

Roman	Italic	Reverse Italic
Manifest	***MENTA***	***Adams***
Wells 1828	Wells 1828	Wells 1828
Sound 18	***Thunder***	**Chesters**
Page 1859	Wells & Webb 1840	Cooley 1859

STOP FOR **SUPER SHELL** *AND* **GO**

Italics — and reverse italics — are used to illustrate speed in Zero's (Hans Schleger) 1950 British modernist poster for a gasoline company.

Wood samples illustrate the three basic type styles: roman, italic, and reverse italic, sometimes called backslope or contra-italic. The last has never been a common style because,

even in brief display settings, it is difficult to read. Wood type can be found at flea markets, like these from an open-air market in Manhattan.

Use genuine small caps and old style figures to ensure even type color, the surest mark of careful typography. Merely reducing the point size produces characters that are too light.

the modern era, motion can be indicated in a more creative and convincing way. ⊡ Most readers want to be unaware of letters. They find a lot of italics "fancy" and disturbing.

Capitalization has evolved into a systemic way of signalling kinds of content. Until the late 1700s, capitalization was a free-form way of indicating emphasis. Elisha Coles, an English printer, wrote in 1674, *"Whatsoever words the Author laies any kind of stress of force upon, these he either writes in a different character, or else prefixes a Capital before them, or both."* Today, capitalizing the first letter of a word indicates a proper name or the beginning of a sentence.

Initial capitals are used to indicate the starting point of text or to break text into manageable chunks. They must be base-aligned with one baseline of text, usually the third or fourth. The first line of text must be spaced closely to the initial, especially important with initial letters that are open on the top right corner like *A* and *L*. The first few words of text may be set in all caps as a transition.

Small caps and **old style figures** are used in lowercase text so typographic color is maintained. Small caps are a bit bigger than the x-height and visually weighted with lowercase characters. Regular capital letters would be too dark and assertive. Using genuine small

caps is much better than simply reducing the size of regular caps, which look too light (above). Old style figures (1234567890) are sometimes called "lowercase numbers." Use old style figures in text and use lining figures (1234567890) with all-caps and in tables and charts.

Alternate characters Typefaces may include second versions of some letters, like **A** and **A** or **T** and **T**. Some types include "biform" alternate characters, which may be large lowercase letters that replace caps, or small caps that replace lowercase letters. Some faces have complete sets of alternate characters that feature longer or shorter ascenders and descenders.

Ligatures A *ligature* is a pair of letters joined into a single glyph. At bottom left is a detail of a specimen sheet showing 292 ligatures designed by Ludovico Vicentino degli Arrighi and printed in Venice in 1529. Gutenberg's c1450 printing emulated local manuscript writing, which had carefully justified lines. He crafted 290 letters, abbreviations, and ligatures to make even lines. Printers found that many characters impractical when they made their own fonts and rapidly reduced their total characters until today's ligatures include only fi, fl, and sometimes ff, ffi, and ffl, st, and ck. Using joined letters resolves intercharacter spacing problems and adds distinction

Typography is the art of visual communication. No argument can absolve typography from its duty to transmit ideas in writing. A printed work that cannot be read is a product without purpose. - Emil Ruder

an	land	em	empty
ar	yard	en	men
as	ask	er	ever
be	label	ff	effort
de	side	is	his
ec	piece	it	item
ed	edge	ns	tonsil

Gutenberg's 290 letters, abbreviations, and ligatures were impractical to use, so printers reduced their numbers. But technology has made additional characters much easier to use. These ligatures in Century Schoolbook are excerpted from a larger set by Joseph S. Scorsone.

		Greeks	c600BC	written
˘	subscript	Greeks	c600BC	written
ᵕ	subscript	Romans	c200BC	written
_	subscript	Carolingian minuscule	c800	written
⁄	character	Carolingian minuscule	c900	written
-	character A	Anglo-Saxon	c1100	written
=	character	Gothic	c1300	written
⩘	character B	Gothic	c1450	type
⁄	character C	Latin	c1470	type
-	character D	Latin	c1495	type
-	character E	European standard	c1549	type

Hyphens evolved from the Greeks who put a bowl-shaped character under the last letter of a compound word that continued on the next line. The hyphen went through several changes over the next 20 centuries, until the 1600s, when standardization became necessary as printing expanded. Even then, it didn't represent syllabic breaks for another 100 years.

Chart by F.M. O'Hara, Jr.

A – *B* – Gutenberg – *C* – Jenson – *D* – Manutius – *E* – Estienne

PUNC: Punctuation Graphs of Sentences

ANDREAE
ALTHAMERI
BRENZII
Annotationes in Epistolam
beati I·A·COBI
iamprimum editae.
Cum Indice.
Argentorati apud Ioannem
Schottum. 1527.

Change.
For a dollar.
The NY Lottery

left to right Punctuation indicates the structure of thought in this 1983 study of thought abstraction by G. Perlman and T.D. Erickson; commas used purely as decorative elements in 1527; add a period. Imply significance.

Hyphens center on the x-height. Adjust them for all caps by moving them up to the optical center of the caps.

HYPHENS CENTER ON THE X-HEIGHT. ADJUST THEM FOR ALL CAPS BY MOVING THEM UP TO THE OPTICAL CENTER OF THE CAPS.

Hyphens center on the x-height (the midpoint of lowercase letters). When setting all caps, the hyphen should be moved up to look centered on the cap height.

x-height. Ad-

X-HEIGHT. AD-

CAP LINE
MEDIAN
BASELINE

Hyphenate
Hyphen-
ate

Fnagle®
Comive™
Fnagle®
Comive™

An ellipsis is a character made of three spaced dots. It can indicate an edited segment or, as above, a pause in thinking.	The hyphen has two jobs: to mark joined or compound words, and to indicate word continuation at the end of a line. New meanings emerge when these two tasks coincide.	*Avant Garde* magazine's logo grew into an expanded set of joined characters for headlines. Avant Garde and Lubalin Graph (A.G. with serifs) were drawn by Tony DiSpigna in 1970.	Register® and Trademark™ symbols should be sized to blend into the color of type. Set them smaller than the text's point size (*bottom examples*). Small sans serif symbols read better.

to a design. *Logotypes* are preset words like *AND*, *For*, *of*, and *The*.

Fractions Pre-made combinations most used: ¼, ½, ¾. Other fractions can be made from superior and inferior characters. ▣ *Superior* and *inferior figures* are used to make fractions. In *Define styles*, set *Super/subscript size* at 60 percent and the *Superscript position* at 28 percent and the *Subscript position* at 0 percent.

Titling capitals Designed with altered proportions — usually lighter weight — and refined serifs, titling caps are to be used at display sizes.

Swash characters Characters with ornamental flourishes. There are three categories: swash letters that begin or end words; "demonstrative" swash letters that relate well to neighboring characters; and fancy caps that are ornamental alternate characters. Swash caps should never be used in all-caps settings for two reasons: they are based on calligraphic lettering (which would never use them this way), and they are meant to be appreciated only a few at a time.

Superior letters A selection of 12 characters used in French and Spanish to abbreviate words: abdeilmnorst.

Hyphenation is the practical necessity of breaking words into syllables at the end of lines of type. It should only be used in text settings, never in display (with the lone exception when the idea of "breaking" is the

point of the headline itself). There are two kinds of hyphenation: "hard rag," a rougher edge caused by a large hyphenation zone setting that more liberally allows words to be pulled to the next line without hyphenation, and "soft rag," a smoother, more pleasing edge, caused by a small hyphenation zone setting that breaks words more frequently. An ideal ragged edge should look like a torn sheet of paper. Best of all is the "saw-tooth" edge, which has alternating long and short lines. ▣ A *hyphen* is the shortest horizontal bar. It indicates a broken word at the end of a line of text. The next longer bar is an *en-dash*, which is the width of half the point size of the type. It is a separator between numbers and compound words. The longest bar is an *em-dash*, which is the width of the point size of the type. It is used for breaks in dialogue. Depending on the font, some en- and em—dashes are too long and create noticeably light spots on the page. Substitute the hyphen to preserve even type color, which takes precedence over using the "correct" mark.

Punctuation There are two kinds of punctuation: *elocutionary*, the earliest marks that indicate pauses for reading aloud; and *syntactic*, much more recent marks that indicate thought groupings. ▣ Among the first to use a punctuation system was Aristophanes of Byzantium in 260BC, who used marks to indicate

I II 66 99 9 6 9

"That will be fine." English, U.S.

'That will be fine.' English, U.K.

« Je pars demain. » French

„Danke gleitfalls." German

«Quería desayuno.» Spanish

Paula Scher's comma made of smaller commas shows the power in even our smallest glyph. The comma flipped is an apostrophe — or a British quote mark — as in this telecom's wordmark.

"Ambidextrous" quote marks were invented for typewriters to reduce the number of keys (*top left*). Proper English quote marks are in the shapes of 6s and 9s.

1		8		100	
2		9		200	
3		10		300	
4		11		400	
5		12		600	
6		20		800	
7		40		1000	

0 1 2 3 4 5 6 7 8 9

Cuneiform numerals are very early marks in clay. Machines that could read numerals were developed in the late 1950s. Anton Stankowski developed abstracted numerals

c250BC India *Nana ghat*

900AD India *Devanagari*

950 Eastern Arabic

976 Spain *Ghobar*

1400 Italy

1545 Paris *Garamont*

1794 Berlin *Unger Fraktur*

1908 New York *News Gothic*

for machine reading (*bottom left*) c1960. He left only the necessary vertical lines of each figure. Numerals develop quickly after the zero is invented in India in about 700AD.

three different lengths of spoken pauses. Greek and Roman authors each used his own variety of dots and virgules — a slash (/), from *virgula*, "rod" — and his own placements to indicate word separations, pauses, and ends of sentences. In general though, a·dot·separated·words.a·dot·at·the·baseline· indicated·a·pause·like·a·modern·comma.a·raised·dot· at·the·cap·height ·indicated·a·stop·like·a·modern· period˙ Standards for punctuation began only with the development of printing. ⊡ Shakespeare's punctuation is meant to guide spoken delivery: his system uses a comma for a short pause, a semicolon for a longer pause, a colon for an even longer pause, and a period for a full stop — which Shakespeare would sometimes put in the middle of a sentence. ⊡ Hyphens, parentheses, and brackets center on the lowercase x-height. When used with all caps, they must have their baselines adjusted to center on the cap height.

Quote marks There is a difference between inch (") and foot (') marks, which are a leftover from the typewriter, and real quote marks. Quote marks should look like 6s and 9s: "xxx" and 'xxx.' Quote marks have evolved since their first use in Paris as sideways *V*s in 1557. English printers replaced them with inverted commas before a quote and apostrophes, which had been invented in the early 1600s, at the end of a quote.

Numerals Numbers came before written language. The numbers 1, 2, 3, 4, 5, 6, 7, 8, and 9 were developed in India c250BC. They added the 0 in about 400AD. The name for numbers, *arabic numerals*, was attached when Arabs brought the Hindu system to Europe through trading. In addition to the numbers themselves, Hindus also invented the placement of ones in the far right column, tens in the next column, hundreds in the third column, and so on. ⊡ Roman numerals evolved around 30BC from the Etruscans and Greeks, and used letters to represent numbers: *I* for one, *V* for five, *X* for ten, *L* for fifty, *C* for hundred, and *M* for thousand. Though elegant to look at, the Roman system is not as easy to use in mathematical figuring as the Hindu system. That is why we see Roman numerals used on buildings and watch faces but not on spreadsheets. ⊡ Our capital letters evolved from the Romans while our numerals evolved from Indian characters. These are two separate sources of character shapes: numerals don't look like they belong in the same style. To avoid dark spots in text settings, use old style figures ("lowercase numbers") with lowercase type, which have ascenders and descenders. Use lining figures ("capital numerals") with all caps. Old style figures are available in "expert fonts." Lining figures developed only in the 1800s, with the increase in all caps advertising headlines.

ABCDEFGabcdefghi

Serif *Old Style* Adobe Garamond

ABCDEFGabcdefghijk

Serif *Old Style* Garamond 3

ABCDEFGabcdefgh

Serif *Old Style* Sabon

ABCDEFGabcdefgh

Serif *Transitional* Baskerville

ABCDEFGabcdefghi

Serif *Transitional* Bell

ABCDEFGabcdefgh

Serif *Transitional* New Caledonia

ABCDEFGabcdefghij

Serif *Modern* Bodoni

ABCDEFGabcdefg

Serif *Modern* Didot

ABCDEFGabcdefghi

Serif *Modern* Modern No.20

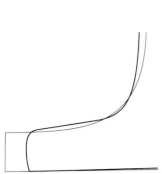

Sabon is Jan Tschichold's 1964 interpretation of Claude Garamont's c1560 type. This shows the change in serif shape in the original *Sabon* (thin line) and the updated *Sabon Next*.

The Romans painted serifs at the end of strokes. All serif types today are evolved from this process. These are the constituent strokes to make a dozen painted letters.

Elaborate serifs evolved in the mid- to late-1800s to make advertising display type more noticeable. There are four categories: Antique, Clarendon, Latin, and Tuscan.

The flamboyant serifs on Eric Gill's *Golden Cockerel Initials* are enhanced by adding antique steel-engraved details on this monochromatic magazine cover by Rodrigo Sánchez.

eight categories, two broken into subcategories that are very useful to know. Remember, however, that type design is an art and, like all art, some typefaces fit in more than one category at a time. Even something as simple as serif/sans serif can't be definitively determined on many faces where that very distinction is meant to be blurred. So category names describe type characteristics, not precise historical dating.

1. **Serif** Type with cross-lines at the ends of strokes. There are four categories of serif types: Old Style (1450s–1600s), Transitional (1700s), Modern (late 1700s), and Slab Serif (1800s).

Serif Old Style The first types designed were based on Roman capitals for majuscules and humanist bookhand for minuscules. They are designed and used best for text setting. *Garamond* is the basis of nearly 1,000 fonts, including third-generation digital interpretations of phototype interpretations of metal type interpretations. Robert Slimbach's 1989 *Adobe Garamond* is perhaps the most accurate representation of Claude Garamond's original early 1600s design, though *Garamond 3* (1936, from Morris Fuller Benton's 1917 American Type Founders designs), and Jan Tschichold's *Sabon* (1967) are also fine examples. *Garamond* has relatively bold serifs because of coarse paper, which had to be dampened

before printing to accept an impression, and the wooden press, which could not be adjusted to lighten the impression. **Venetian Old Style** Based on the handwriting of Italian scribes, it first appeared in about 1470. It is characterized by axes angled to the left, bracketed serifs, an angled cross stroke on the lowercase ℮, and low stroke contrast (thins aren't very thin because printing at the time wasn't able to handle such delicacy). **Aldine Old Style** are types designed in the style of Aldus Manutius's 1490 characters. They have greater stroke contrast and the cross stroke on the lowercase ℮ is horizontal. **Dutch Old Style** or **Geralde** evolved from a blending of German blackletter and Aldine Old Style, so they have darker color, larger x-height, and greater stroke weight contrast.

Transitional serif Types that show the evolution from Dutch Old Style to Modern in the mid-1700s, and show characteristics of both: more accentuation between thick and thin strokes, flat serifs, and very slightly inclined axes on curves. Designed and used best for text setting. No longer based solely on handwritten examples, these were the first type refinements of letters as shapes in their own right. John Baskerville (1706–1775) was an English master calligrapher who became one of the most influential type designers in history. His types were lighter than Old Style, and the

ABCDEFGabcdefg

Serif *Slab* Clarendon

ABCDEFGabcdefc

Serif *Slab* Rockwell

ABCDEFGabcdefghi

Serif *Slab* Thesis Serif

ABCDEFGabcdefgl

Sans serif *Grotesque/New Grotesque* Univers

ABCDEFGabcdefgl

Sans serif *Geometric* Futura

ABCDEFGabcdefghij

Sans serif *Humanist* Syntax

ABCDEF*Gabcdefghijklmnop*

Script *Italian minuscule* Poetica

ABCDEFGabcdefghijklmno

Script *Brush* Pelican

ABCDEFGabcdefghijklmnc

Script *Monoline* Alpha Crunch

Aside from his famous **Univers** family, Adrian **Frutiger** has created many other

Frutiger schuf neben seiner berühmten Univers viele weitere bekannte Schriften wie z. B. die Linotype Centennial oder auch

well known typefaces such as Linotype **Centennial** and **Meridien**,

Meridien, die vielseitige Vectora oder auch die Versailles, sowie viele weitere Schriften, die bei der Linotype Library erhältlich sind.

the versatile **Vectora**™ or even **Versailles**™ as well as many other

son fameux Univers, Frutiger a créé des caractères typographiques de renommée mondiale tel le Linotype Centennial, le Meridien,

typefaces which are also available from Linotype Library.

utre le très puissant Vectora, le Versailles, et de nombreux autres caractères également disponibles chez Linotype Library.

Slab serifs are highlighted with matching underlines in this logotype by Domenic Lippa and Lucy Groom of Pentagram Design in London. Note the skillful negative space control.

Type designer Adrian Frutiger says *"Every reader has a matrix of letterforms stored in their subconscious. When reading, the perceived characters are compared with those in this matrix and are either readily accepted or rejected as being too foreign… Gradually the matrix is expanded and the characters develop flexible contours. The limits of this range of readability have been defined by the similar design elements of all roman type. Any new sans serif type which strives for optimal legibility will fall into the same patterns."*

---

curved emphasis was more vertical. Baskerville also reinvented the way paper was made, using heated plates to smooth the surface (equivalent to today's *wove* surface), and he developed a darker quality ink. Nevertheless, his type refinements were not universally well received: Benjamin Franklin wrote Baskerville that a friend of his reported "Baskerville eyepain" caused by the "thin and narrow strokes of your letters."

Modern serif First faces designed based not on a handwritten model but on the idealized shape of letters themselves. They first appeared in the late 1700s. Firmin Didot and Giambattista Bodoni were the primary evolutionists. Modern faces are the result of several technical advancements of the period. Copperplate engraving allowed much greater detail and paper quality continued to improve in smoothness. Modern types have a more mechanical appearance — constructed rather than drawn — and they have extremely high stroke contrast, vertical axes, and horizontal, unbracketed serifs. They are particularly well-suited for display and can be difficult to read in continuous text. **Didones** were created during the 18th century. **Twentieth-Century Moderns** are more stylized and have more pronounced stroke contrast.

Slab serif The Industrial Revolution in the mid-1800s introduced mass production and advertising. Posters encouraged very bold, highly visible types. First called "Egyptians" after the popularity of archaeological discoveries taking place at the time, slab serifs are extremely effective for display use. All slab serif types are distinguished by relatively consistent stroke weight and serifs that are as thick — or thicker — as the vertical strokes. The search for even bolder, more visible faces in the late 1800s lead to types without serifs so letters can be more tightly packed together. These came to be known as *grotesques* or *sans serifs*. **Clarendons** have bracketed serifs, or curves where the serif meets the character's strokes. **Unbracketeds** have serifs that meet the strokes without curves. **Neo Clarendons** Twentieth-century refinements of earlier slab serifs with increased usefulness for text settings.

2. Sans serif Sans means *without* in French. Sans serif types, therefore, are types that have no serifs. The earliest sans serif letterforms were written 2,000 years ago, but in 1816 William Caslon IV tried to market the first sans serif type. Vincent Figgins, calling the type "Sans surryph," and William Thorowgood, calling it "Grotesque," tried their versions in England in 1832. The term "Gothic" was applied to these new types in America. Jan Tschichold and the Bauhaus and de Stijl movements spread the use of sans serif types in the 1920s. There are three categories of sans serifs:

ABCDEFGHIJKLMN

Glyphic Lithos

ABCDEFGHIJKLM

Glyphic Trajan

ABCDEFGhijklmnopqr

Blackletter Dampfplatz (Steam Room)

ABCDEFGhijklmnop

Blackletter Deutsche Zierschrift (German Decorative Writing)

ABCDEFGhijklmn

Monospaced OCR-B

ABCDEFGabcde

Decorative/Display Lietz Alexander Nero

Decorative/Display Propinquity

Symbol Sutnar 1941

Capitals
ABCDEFGHIJKLMNOPQRSTUVWX

Lowercase
abcdefghijklmnopqrstuvwxyz

Lining figures
0123456789

Old style figures
0123456789

Small caps
ABCDEFGHIJKLMNOPQRSTUVWXYZ

Superscript and Subscript figures
$0123456789X_{0123456789}$

Punctuation
.,:;-¿?¡!/".."|•'[{()}]

Fractions
¼ ½ ⅛ ¾ ⅝ ⅔

Accented characters
åçéîñöü ÅÇÉÎ

Ligatures & Diphthongs
ff fi fl ffl æ Æ Œ

Reference & Miscellaneous marks
©®™ &$¢£†‡§¶

A font contains more than the standard 26 capitals and lowercase letters. The minimum is usually about 150 characters. Typefaces intended for text settings require many more characters than display types. This expansion of glyph interactions requires a more experienced eye, so many type designers begin by designing sets of display characters.

These characters are sans serif grotesque — exactly as the Pennsylvania Department of Transportation designed it. A group of type fans paid for custom plates, each of which carries a small portion of this invitation's message. Such complex exploitation of word breaks is an example of creativity that is bound to be seen, read, and remembered.

Grotesque/New Grotesque, Geometric, and Humanist. All have relatively little stroke contrast and are highly legible as display and, with added spacing, successful as text.

Sans serif Grotesques/New Grotesques First released sans serifs. New Grotesques are more recent — generally Swiss — designs that are refinements of earlier grotesques. Erik Spiekermann says of one: "Univers, the classic European face, is the first family with mathematical weights: 21 weights from very light to very heavy and legible under nearly every condition."

Sans serif Geometrics Bauhaus-inspired simplicity, mono-weight strokes, and near-geometric perfection make these harder to read than grotesques.

Sans serif Humanists are based on Roman proportions, look somewhat hand drawn, and blend features of both serif and sans serif. They have the greatest stroke contrast of the sans serifs.

3. Script Script faces, more so than italics, resemble handwriting. Scripts can be arranged by chronology, style (from formal to casual), or by intended use. The best may be a system based on similarity to actual handwriting: Italian miniscule (*Poetica*), English interpretations of Italian letters, Brush scripts (*Pelican*), Broad pen scripts, Monoline scripts (*Alpha Crunch*), and the catchall category of Combination scripts.

4. Glyphic Based on stone carving rather than pen drawing. Characters have low stroke contrast and are best used as all-caps, which is the way source carvings were rendered.

5. Blackletter Northern European scripts at the time of Gutenberg's movable type. Also called *Gothic* and *Old English* and used from about 1150 through the 1600s. There are three main varieties of blackletter: Textura, Schwabacher, and Fraktur.

6. Monospaced Types in which all letters and numerals occupy the same width, making a vertical and horizontal grid, useful for tabular and columnar arrangements.

7. Decorative All the types that don't fit in the other categories. Because their letterforms are either elaborate or abstract, decorative types are rarely useful for text settings. Many decorative faces lack lowercase characters and full punctuation.

8. Symbol, **ornament**, and **dingbats** Illustrations and symbols whose complexity is limited only by the number of bezier points in their outline descriptions. The first ornament typeface was created in 1478. *Sutnar 1941* (*bottom left*) has two "characters" for each illustration: one line drawing (printed here in black) and one solid shape (printed here in white). The font's kerning is carefully adjusted so they perfectly overlap when keystroked in the correct order.

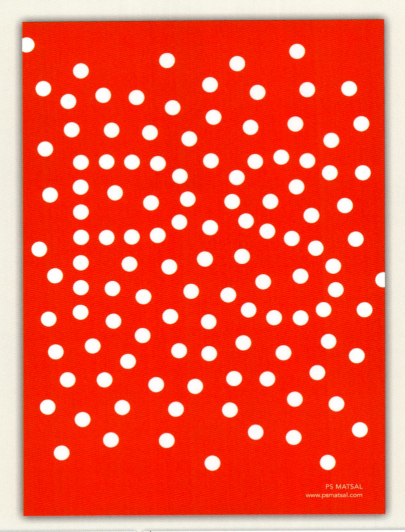

PS MATSAL
www.psmatsal.com

The three elements designers use, type, image, and space, overlap where they may be mistaken for one another. Those three overlaps are where good design takes place.

Ground can exist behind (*top left*) or in front of a figure (*bottom left*). Ground is sometimes ambiguous and exists in both places simultaneously (*top and bottom right*).

Equal letter, word, and line-spacing turns reading into deciphering, as in *The Puzzle Gravestone*, Samuel Bean's 1865 commemoration

of his wife. Reading direction can be vertical, horizontal, or diagonal, and from left to right, right to left, downward or upward.

The dots are all identical in this poster by John Bark. What makes the message visible is the adjustment in *spacing* between them so the P and S become subtly visible. *"In typography, meaning is a condition of the position of an event in space. Position — order in space — matters. When concern for position is relaxed, visible language becomes loose in the joints."* Peter Burnhill

Lack of space results in a stuffed message. This can be used to advantage, when the message itself is stifling (*far left*, by Charles S. Anderson), or to disadvantage, by making reading all but impossible.

3 Space and type

By every measure as significant as the words to be printed, the empty spaces on the page are active shapes that contribute to the expression of the whole. We refer to this as unity — in all creative fields, the essential quality of design.*" Karl-August Hanke

The best space is invisible: it supports the message with subtlety and grace. In every instance when we notice space, there is either too much or too little of it. Either way, our attention has been drawn away from the message to the form in which the message is being delivered. That's bad for communication.

In typography, as in all design, space is there to make the foreground — the type, the design elements, the message — look good. Without attending to space, the filled-in areas will look misaligned, be packed too tightly, and, sometimes, be flying apart for lack of proximity.

Typography is 10 percent letter management and 90 percent space management. The designer's responsibility is to manage the space all around letterforms.

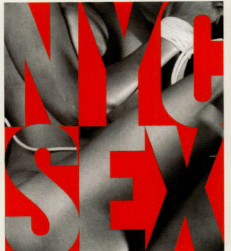

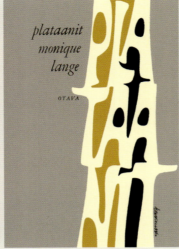

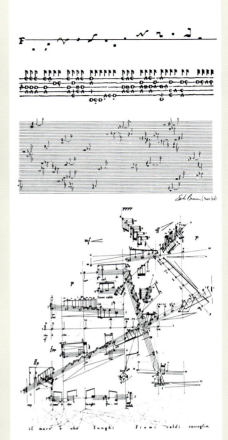

"The graphic signs called letters are so completely blended with the stream of written thought that their presence is as unperceived as the ticking of a clock in the measurement

"The graphic signs called letters are so completely blended with the stream of written thought that their presence is as unperceived as the ticking of a clock in the measurement

"The graphic signs called letters are so completely blended with the stream of written thought that their presence is as unperceived as the ticking of a clock in the measurement

"The graphic signs called letters are so completely blended with the stream of written thought that their presence is as unperceived as the ticking of a clock in the measurement

"The graphic signs called letters are so completely blended with the stream of written thought that their presence is as unperceived as the ticking of a clock in the measurement

"The graphic signs called letters are so completely blended with the stream of written thought that their presence is as unperceived as the ticking of a clock in the measurement

"The graphic signs called letters are so completely blended with the stream of written thought that their presence is as unperceived as the ticking of a clock in the measurement

"The graphic signs called letters are so completely blended with the stream of written thought that their presence is as unper-

"The graphic signs called letters are so completely blended with the stream of written thought that their presence is as unper-

Excellent type craftsmanship controls space between the lines and sections of type so the *flat planar shapes* of the three figures is emphasized, making this a noticeable design.

M SE MS.
CHOR S.
VIS AL ARTS.
M SICALS.
C LT RE.

Only one thing's missing.

Word spaces can be mistaken for missing characters. Gaps are the focal point — and the message — in this headline detail from a corporate ad.

Letterspaced caps are used to emphasize column width in Thomas Jefferson's *Summary View*, a 1773 document encouraging separation from England.

DISC DISC
TELE TELE
PEP PEP
AQU AQU
LES LES
CAR CAR

The edges of letterforms should be optically aligned at display sizes. Letters with little stroke at the alignment edge (T and A) must be moved farther than other letters (C).

"Not letterforms" appear in the foreground of these book covers by abstracting the negative shapes of abutting letters and bleeding to trim.

Space is a vital aspect of musical notation since pauses are as important as notes played. The history of music shows a variety of approaches: *neume notation* c900 with its arcs indicating pitch rises and falls in pitch; *tablature* c1500; a 50-line *staff* from 1952; and *partitioning*, in which the page is divided into sections that use space flexibly.

These three studies manipulate details of a single letterform and space into an abstract and unified whole that expresses a design idea: rhythm, texture/mass contrast, and organic/geometric contrast.

Not letterforms

The spaces surrounding and within letters are as significant as the letters themselves. In fact, the shapes around the letters *define* the letters. Managing the spaces between and around letters makes type more or less legible and more or less engaging for the reader.

Even color is achieved by managing spacing attributes (*opposite*). Excepting the top row in which the weights alone have been changed, none of the *letterforms* have been altered in these studies. The only changes are to the *spaces* between and around them.

Change the type weight The top row is set 12½-point solid Avenir Light, Roman, and Heavy.

Change the letterspacing The three paragraphs in the middle row are set 12½-point solid (no extra linespacing). The attributes have been adjusted in the left paragraph to tight letterspacing and open word spacing; the middle paragraph attributes are normal; and the right paragraph has open letterspacing and tight word spacing.

Change the linespacing The three paragraphs in the bottom row are set 12½ point. The left paragraph is set solid, that is, with no additional linespacing; the middle paragraph is set on 14 points of linespacing, that is, with 1½ points of additional linespacing; and the right paragraph is set on 16½ points of linespacing, that is, with 4½ points of additional linespacing.

"[Type] is a figure-ground synthesis in which the letterforms are the figure — the salient element — and the counterforms are the ground, the unnoticed element... The question (to) ask appears simple, 'What is good letterspacing?'" Charles A. Bigelow In answer, each letter should appear to be exactly in the optical center between its neighbors, and the overall typesetting should have even color.

Letterspacing is seen in proportion to word spacing. This paragraph is set with too much letterspacing, given its amount of word spacing. This causes the words to merge into line groupings and slows reading

Letterspacing is seen in proportion to word spacing. This paragraph is set with too little letterspacing given the amount of word spacing. This causes the lines of type to break into individual word groupings. Letterspacing is seen in propor-

This last paragraph is set with the right letterspacing, given the word spacing used. Each word retains its integrity as a discreet entity, yet the line's integrity is also maintained, making reading effortless. This

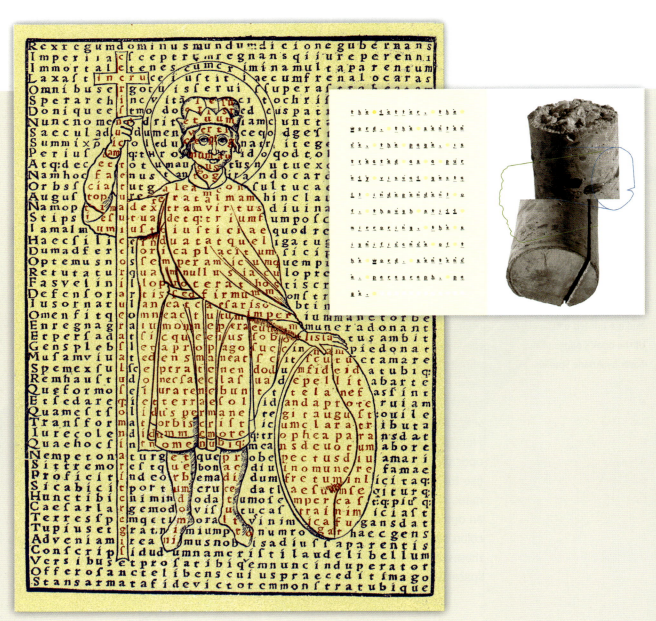

Tracking is macro spacing
−50% tracking
Tracking is macro spacing
−25% tracking
Tracking is macro spacing
Default tracking
Tracking is macro spacing
+25% tracking
Tracking is macro spacing
+50% tracking

Tracking is paragraph-wide spacing and affects all characters equally. Character spacing and word spacing are perceived as one: note how word spaces get smaller automati-cally as tracking is tightened and word spaces get larger automatically as tracking is widened. These defaults can be overridden in the Paragraph/ Justification control panel.

Kerning used to require cutting and filing the metal block on which the type was molded. Metal type discouraged even letterspacing for a physical reason: the metal blocks that held the letters had to abut. Characters that needed to be closer together would be labo-riously cut and filed to allow the metal bodies to be placed closer together.

Letterspacing is perceived as tight or loose in relation to word spacing. Letters make up words, so letters must be near enough that the word shape is visible. Similarly, words make up lines, so the words should be near enough that the line shape — which enhances left-to-right reading — is visible.

Experimental letterspacing appeared as early as 1503 by Thomas Anshelm in his *De laudibus sanctae crucis* in which type was set with equal letter and linespacing. Printed in black and red on bright yellow, this was at the time a difficult piece to prepare. A modern equivalent is by Bob Aufuldish that makes use of a horizontal and vertical grid. Both samples are meant to *be seen* rather than *read effortlessly.*

Letterspacing

The essence of letterspacing is to make the letters appear equidistant from one another. Readers should never be aware of type's spacing unless the purposeful tightening or loosening of spacing, which indicates an increase or decrease of reading speed, is an illustration of itself. Both text and display are affected by spacing. It is more important for display type to be properly spaced, however, because bad spacing is more noticeable at large type sizes.

Good letterspacing can be defined very simply as *invisible spacing*. Neither too tight nor too open, it should not draw attention to itself. Good letterspacing creates even type color: there should be enough space to separate letterforms without weakening the word units.

Letterspacing is perceived as tight or loose in rela-tion to word spacing. It should be tighter at display sizes than at text sizes so the letters create a darker, more vis-ible word shape. Condensed types should be more tightly letterspaced than either normal or expanded types. Small type should be more openly letterspaced so individual characters are more easily identifiable.

There are two ways to adjust letterspacing: *tracking* and *kerning. Tracking* refers to adjusting the spacing of all type in a word or paragraph. Default tracking charac-teristics can be customized in the Preferences panel of all

"Writing is not a series of strokes, but space, divided into characteristic shapes by strokes." Gerrit Noordzij

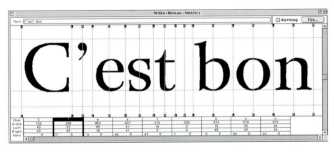

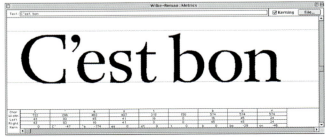

Tuńczyk

Tuńczyk

Avelãs

Avelãs

Vasárnap

Vasárnap

C'est bon French for *That's good.* Tuńczyk Polish for *Tuna fish.* Avelãs Portuguese for *Hazelnuts.* Vasárnap Hungarian for *Sunday.*

A"	ay	Fa	Ku	OX	RO	TA	U.	WA	xa	y.	'
A'	by	Fe	Ky	OY	RT	TC	U,	WC	xc	y,	,1
AC	CO	Fo	ka	oc	RV	TG	VA	WO	xe	'A	1.
AG	CT	Fr	ke	oo	RY	TO	VO	W.	xo	'.	1,
AO	CY	Fu	ko	ov	r'	TS	VY	W,	YA	',	10
AQ	Co	f'	L"	ow	r.	TV	V.	Wa	YG	.'	11
AT	Ce	fa	L'	ox	r,	TW	V,	We	YG	,'	14
AV	DA	fe	LA	oy	ra	TY	V:	Wi	YS	'A	16
AW	DV	ff	LC	PA	rc	T.	V;	Wo	Y.	'd	17
AY	DW	fi	LG	PO	rd	T,	Va	Wr	Y,	'o	31
Ac	DY	fl	LO	P.	re	T:	Ve	Wu	Y:	'r	41
Ad	e'	fo	LS	P,	ro	T;	Vi	Wy	Y;	's	51
Ae	ev	fs	LT	Pa	rw	Ta	Vo	wa	Ya	't	61
Aq	ew	ft	LV	Pe	rx	Tc	Vr	wc	Ye	'v	74
Au	ex	ij	LW	Po	ry	Ti	Vu	we	Yo	'w	76
Av	ey	KC	LY	Pr	SA	To	Vy	wo	Yu	'y	7.
Aw	FA	KG	Ly	py	ST	Tr	v.	w.	ya	"A	7,
Ay	FG	KO	OA	Qu	SY	Ts	v,	w,	yc	."	7:
a'	FO	Ka	OT	RA	s'	Tu	va	XC	ye	.'	81
av	F.	Ke	OV	RC	st	Tw	ve	XO	yo	.1	91
aw	F,	Ko	OW	RG	sy	Ty	vo	Xy	ys	,"	01

Avelãs
Avelãs

Check for equal spacing by flipping a headline upside-down so its shapes become noticeable, or by imagining equal amounts of water poured between characters.

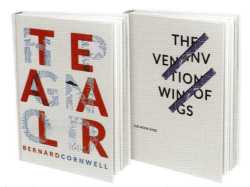

Precise spacing and active negative space are critical in logos, where only a few elements must create a carefully crafted, memorable impression.

The best way to sensitize yourself to perfect letterspacing is to pretend there are only two choices: either letterspacing is too open or it is too tight. *Perfect spacing is not*

an available choice. Your eyes will eventually be attuned to achieving perfect spacing. This student project is the result of nearly twenty developmental iterations.

Digital type's spacing is based on the rectangle surrounding the letterform (*far left*). Assigning kerning is a matter of adjusting character pairs, as in the *'e* pairing, which was reduced by 174 units. Additional kerning samples are shown near left, with the "befores" in gray and improved "afters" in black.

This chart shows the most significant kerning pairs. The most frequently used are in bold sans. Notice which characters are the most difficult "repeat offenders" so you can be particularly sensitive to adjusting their spacing when needed.

page makeup programs: one change that is often useful is reducing global word spacing in relation to character spacing. Tracking is *macro* space adjustment. *Kerning* refers to adjusting the space between a specific pair of letterforms. Kerning is *micro* space adjustment.

The closeness of a pair of characters should resemble that of their neighbors. Consistency and context are the keys to kerning. If the surrounding type is relatively open, kerning should make ill-fitting pairs more open. If the surrounding type is relatively tight, kerning should match the neighbor's tightness.

Before movable type was invented, scribes wrote and spaced characters by eye as they went. Gutenberg's first fonts included dozens of paired characters to emulate the written hand.

Programs automatically kern awkward letter pairs, a process that is more reliable at text sizes — where minor inconsistencies are acceptable — than at larger display settings, where inconsistent letterspacing is a telltale of mediocre design. It remains the designer's responsibility to create perfectly spaced display characters.

Fonts that are advertised as having hundreds or thousands of kerning pairs are inelegantly prepared. A well-designed font, one in which the spacing attributes have been thoughtfully perfected, should not need more than about one hundred kerning pairs.

"Bad spacing is bad spacing in any era." Aaron Burns (1922–1991)

conform to their monumental archetype. They are themselves set in different type. Beginning and ending as remnants, they do not support any over-arching structure, philosophical, literary-critical or other, but only resonate with each other. They offer no sanctuary as in a temple; they do not cling to any root. They are the visible image of the "decapitations" by which Derrida characterizes, or rather caricaturizes, earlier deconstructions in *Positions*. ("Dissemination," "The Double Session," "The White Mythology are practical re-stagings of all the false starts, beginnings, incipits, exergues, titles, fictive pretexts, etc.: decapitations)" (p. 62).

The micro-marginal insertions which punctuate the columns irregularly do not merely complement or add to the text. They supplement its activity in a thoroughly ambiguous way. They gnaw at the rectilinear stability of the columns, at the plenitude of their form. In the antistructural language of *Positions* they constitute a "creux" as well as a "relief": "the hollow is a relief but the lack and the surplus can never stabilize themselves in the plenitude of a form or of an equation, in the fixed correspondence of a symmetry or of a homology" (p. 63). In the holes or niches carved out of the phallic columns of India, Glas finds the anarchitectural model of its own anarchitextual activity:

"One cannot then lodge there. Whatever it be, dead or alive. It is neither a house, nor a sepulture. Who contemplates such a structure, who can, one wonders. And how an altar, (one wonders,) a habitat or a funerary monument, an urban system or a mausoleum, the family and the state can find their origins there" (p. 9).

In Glas, movable type exceeds its potential towards movable text, bringing the career of the bible to its term, or at least giving it a new twist, as this antepenultimate fragment suggests: "Time to perfect the resemblance between Dionysus and Christ" (p. 291). In fact, the antecedents of Glas—or more literally, its prototypes—are Biblical,

properly and benevolent in dispensation of energy. Eradication of a central, individuating being by means of its production of letters in terms of ever-errant discourse where . "Every author-remover (oteur) must jump-remove itself (s'oter) into its host-guest-other-author (hotre)" so that a named - limited, cited, positioned, univocal, and unilateral - son (nonfils) turns into a more 'incestuous' no-child of dubious familial origin"

Obviously the consequence of the sexual politics depends on a confusion of phonic and visual dimensions of writing. The duplicitous reading of words in paragrammer and anagram restores the veracity of the fantasm which transpires to the reader as a gift. The text before the eyes — between imaginary and real status - between a manifest and latent expression of the author — is an emergent, half-born form from which, as lure of the desire of writing, must force the reader to desire to write. We can hypothesize that since Partie Hélène Cixous has written texts which are half-orginary scenes. They body forth as a series of musical movements amplifying a fragment of life lived into a far more significant ensemble of given desires extended and repressed through the physical shape of words. Texts such as Angst and Préparatifs exact an entirely different process of reading, for the book has not only a therapeutic function — the writer writing 'out' of an exiguous or painful scene in the real in order to reduce mediation with an over-obstinate presence of practical familiar, or phallocentric thinking programming the mother, but also an instructively pleasurable configuration which releases the body from the seeming transparency of the mind pre-empting desire.

As such texts unwind and spiral away from half-events or truisms and weave in their motion traces of majestic psychic orchestrations, whether of accession to an undecidable status between male and female (Neutre), the loss of one's name (Prénoms de personne), the reach for a North African origin (Figure 7) in writing autobiography (Portrait du soleil), the anguish of paradoxical rapture toward another body in what a

substance Ponge's "cruche" assumes the characteristics of a person "cruche" can also mean which Roche creates finds its application in rather stupid person for the poet texts with encyclopedic ambitions speaks of "cruche" without article and reminds the What I propose to show reader that it knows how to sing however is that the language is incessantly passes from emptiness to fullness not based on a semantics but on which corresponds to a change in being semantics—is other words that The poet reveals the analogy between the jug does not set up a series of and the language Because of its shapes differentially- defined elements but contexts rather the jug resembles the letter "U" in the manipulation of a vowel unconnected at its center of of elements whose meaning is contextually defined word The jug that sings is thus The necessity for postulating such a endowed with a double sonority As the theory will hope become poetic discourse builds itself not on one or clear once the texts have been described several letters printed on the page the physical appearance of relation between the signified and signifier appears no the text which is foregrounded in Roche's longer altogether arbitrary At the end the records The first of the series poet mentions with his usual irony that his Compact (1966) presents itself as a commentaries concerning the jug could just as well typographical display eight or more apply to words thus rendering the analogy different types are used from beginning to established at the beginning even more complex and The different typefaces read He never does come to grips with the separately form more or less cohesive jug but engages in a series of reports narratives or descriptions verbal exercises What he says about the But since each type is in jug is also relevant to language a different person or tense read

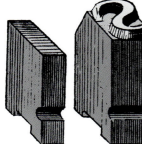

FRESH MADESUSHI

Justifying type requires forcing space between words. Narrow columns have too few word spaces, so this becomes visible.

Flush left type has even word spacing. Narrow columns will have leftover space at the right edge, where it is harmless.

J. B. Lenoir
B. B. King
J. A. T. P. Blues

J.B. Lenoir
B.B. King
J.A.T.P. Blues

This is six-point The Sans Semi Light Plain set justified across a measure of six picas. The word spacing is greater than the linespacing, so vertical "rivers" of white appear. This is one telltale sign of poor typography and

must be recognized and repaired. Otherwise, readers' eyes have a tendency to drift downward rather than across the lines of type in effortless reading. This is six-

Using the space bar to align columns is a poor solution: spacing increments are limited to the type size in use. So true alignment is unlikely.

Set tabs to create a true vertical alignment. You will have a sharp left edge and you will have fewer adjustments if the type size is changed later.

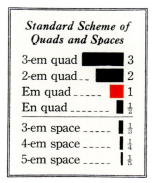

Standard Scheme of Quads and Spaces

3-em quad	▬	3
2-em quad	▪ ▬	2
Em quad	▬	1
En quad	▬	½
3-em space	▮	⅓
4-em space	▮	¼
5-em space	▮	⅕

Wordspacing in metal type is determined by metal pieces of fixed widths. The basic unit is an *em*, a square of the type size being used, as shown in this 1928 chart.

Man Ray's expression of reading relies on word spaces and non-existent letterspacing to help form word shapes as minimalist signals of set type.

Wordspacing – and linespacing – are effaced in Jan Tschichold's 1923 lettering, which reads:
The idea and the enduring are the guiding principles, not some person or some period.

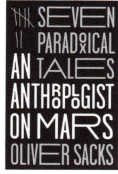

Wordspacing is critical when all letterforms are the same. But they can be narrowed when letterform contrasts are used to indicate words, as in this book cover by Cardon Webb.

Four experimental text settings from a 1978 issue of *Visible Language* magazine emphasize (*l–r*) the line, the word space, the column, and the word.

The surface of the metal spacers is below the printing surface of the letters to ensure they do not print. Original artwork adapted from *l'Encyclopédie*, 1765.

Too little word space confuses meaning, as shown by this sign in a Japanese luncheonette.

Justified type can cause uneven word spacing across a too-narrow column: flush left ensures consistent word spacing. Add a word space only after the last period in a string of initials. Rivers appear when word spacing is bigger than line spacing. Set tabs for accurate alignment.

Wordspacing

Typographer's work is judged by the spaces between words as well as between letters and lines. Using defaults does not always provide quality text type, and rarely provides quality display type. Ideal wordspacing, like ideal letterspacing, should be invisible. It should be just enough to separate word thoughts. Too much word spacing breaks a line of type into individual words.

Wordspacing didn't come into use until the 4th to 8th centuries. SCRIBESWEREREQUIREDTOUSEWORDSPACING WHILECONVERTINGALLCAPSWRITINGLIKETHIS into the then-new minuscule letters with majuscule initials. In medieval Europe, scribes made facing pages symmetrical. The ultimate expression of this was to write every line so it would perfectly fill the width of the column. The only way to do this was to abbreviate words, which came to be called *contractions*. With the development of movable type in the latter 1400s, such *justified* type was achieved by adjusting the spaces, rather than the words.

Wordspacing and letterspacing are seen relative to each other: open goes with open, tight with tight. ⊡ Grossly uneven word spacing occurs in justified type across a narrow measure. Set as flush left type. ⊡ Reduce wordspacing after small punctuation like periods and commas. Adding a full space simply makes a hole. This is especially important in display type.

"Two thoughts: one, word spacing and letterspacing are seen relative to each other. Open goes with open and tight goes with tight. Two, many types have too much word spacing as their default. Setting the word spacing at seventy to eighty percent of 'normal' is often ideal. Try it."
Anonymous

This is ten-point Barmeno Regular set to a measure of twenty-nine picas, the space that is available. Two points of additional linespacing have been added, equivalent to the "auto" linespacing default. When the character-per-line number exceeds sixty, reading becomes measurably more difficult. Counteract this unpleasantness by enlarging the type size or narrowing the column to get fifty to sixty characters per line, or, if the type size you are using is required, as in this example, by adding two to four points of linespacing.

50 chars per line | 60 chars per line

This is ten-point Mrs Eaves set with no additional linespacing. Because it has a small x-height, it requires less linespacing than the Barmeno example to the right.

This is ten-point Barmeno Regular set with no additional linespacing. Because it has a large x-height, it requires more linespacing than the Mrs Eaves example to the left.

Talk to the Hoof
Post Office Box 4
Stamford, Lincs
PE9 1NA, U.K.
44 0 1780 65587
talktothehoof.com

Talk to the Hoof
Post Office Box 4
Stamford, Lincs
PE9 1NA, U.K.
44 0 1780 65587
talktothehoof.com

GENESIS

IN THE BEGINNING, God created the heavens and the earth. The earth was without form and void, and darkness was over the face of the deep. And the Spirit of God was hovering over the face of the waters.

And God said, "Let there be light," and there was light. And God saw that the light was good. And God separated the light from the darkness. God called the light Day, and the darkness he called Night. And there was evening and there was morning, the first day.

And God said, "Let there be an expanse in the midst of the waters, and let it separate the waters from the waters." And God made the expanse and separated the waters that were under the expanse from the waters that were above the expanse. And it was so. And God called the expanse Heaven. And there was evening and there was morning, the second day.

And God said, "Let the waters under the heavens be gathered together into one place, and let the dry land appear." And it was so. God called the dry land Earth, and the waters that were gathered together he called Seas. And God saw that it was good.

heavens." So God cr
creature that moves,
kinds, and every win
it was good. And Go
and fill the waters in
there was evening an

And God said, "Le
to their kinds—lives
according to their ki
the earth according t
kinds, and everythin
And God saw that it

Then God said, "I
And let them have de
of the heavens and e
every creeping thing

So God creat
in the ima
male and f

And God blessed
multiply and fill the

Space between words is like mortar between bricks. A bricklayer's work is not judged by the quality of the bricks, but by the quality of the mortaring. Similarly, a typographer's work is judged not by the quality of the letters, but by the quality and consistency of the spacing. No rule in typography is more important than this one: if it *looks* right, it is right. Good typography requires consideration of every mark as well as every space. In a sense, typography is about sculpting the emptiness with letterforms.

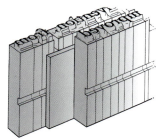

Except for very young children, we do not read single words at a time: we read in *saccadic jumps*, grouping a few words together in clusters. This paragraph is set in such saccadic groups. *Saccades* are quick, simultaneous movements of both eyes in the same direction. French ophthalmologist Émile Javal coined the word in the 1880s when he observed eye movement in silent reading and found that it involves a succession of individual movements.

Linespacing in metal type was increased by inserting bars of lead between slugs, or lines of type, hence the term *leading* (pronounced *ledding*). It is now properly called *linespacing*.

Fifty to 60 characters per line is the optimal number for ease of reading. Shorter lines are perceived as choppy and longer lines need additional linespacing. X-height determines the need for additional linespacing.

Linespacing looks inconsistent (*center left*) when lining figures are set amid a U/lc setting, as is typical in an address. Add space above such lines for optical equivalence.

The ESV (*English Standard Version*) *Reader's Bible* was created in 2014 for those who want to read the Bible as it was originally written — as an unbroken narrative. The wayfinding numbers and footnotes have been eliminated and the text is set in 9 point serif with an average of 64 characters per line.

Optimal line length

We read text in "saccadic jumps," in groups of three or four words (*see above*). Lines that are too short interrupt these saccadic jumps. *Minimum line length* must be at least one such group, that is, three or four words long. But beyond four groups – twelve to sixteen words — reading becomes effortful. *Maximum line length* should therefore not be more than about twelve words, or 50 to 60 characters. Otherwise, additional linespacing must be added. The text column you are reading in this book contain 52 to 58 characters per line.

Justified vs. flush left Justified type is set so each line is exactly the same length: leftover space at the end of each line is distributed between letters and words. In justified type across narrow columns, it is common for word spaces to vary from one line to the next, creating uneven color and revealing poor craftsmanship. Extremely uneven word spacing causes rivers — wiggly vertical columns. On the scale of typographic righteousness, this is bad. Flush left type, on the other hand, inserts even word spacing throughout a column and leaves emptiness at the end of each line. ☒ By working with hyphenation preferences, the ragged right edge can be adjusted. A smaller hyphenation zone yields more hyphens, but gives a smoother ragged edge. This is known as a *soft rag*. A *hard rag*, made when hyphens are disallowed or allowed

"This report, by its very length, defends itself against the risk of being read."
Winston Churchill
(The amount of verbiage and line length used affects the reader's interest in persevering through it. Therefore, write short and set type at the optimal number of characters per line.)

In addition to the five schemes diagramed above, paragraphs may be indicated in all sorts of creative ways. This treatment contrasts a single normal space after each period with exaggerated space after the period that completes a paragraph.   This technique is simple and elegant: it uses space in a fresh way by offering a new solution to an old problem. The only catch is that paragraphs cannot end at the coincidental end of a line of type.   No paragraphs should ever end at the top of a column. The last unfilled line of text looks carelessly abandoned in a highly visible place. This treatment is particularly susceptible to mistreatment.   But only a dedicated designer would attempt its use. Paragraphs may be indicated in

This treatment is based on the idea that each paragraph must be fully filled. Each column's width is adjusted to achieve a perfectly filled rectangle shape. Initial caps must base align with, say, the fourth line of text. Paragraphs may extend as long as necessary, but they must be at least four lines deep, like the initial. Length of each paragraph matters: it wouldn't do to have two paragraphs in a row be the same width. The initial would seem to be floating unattached to the beginning of its paragraph. Such typographic craftsmanship takes time but it elevates the work to a higher level of competence and quality.

Treat paragraphs like individual captions. Each is positioned in a column or it can be hung like a flag on a pole.

One graph follows the previous by aligning on the next baseline. The easiest way to do this is to use tabs.

This treatment breaks copy into bite-size chunks, which is one of the kindest tasks a typographer can do for a reader.

TWO-INCH NAIL SHOT INTO CARPENTER'S BRAIN: HARM NOT SERIOUS

TWO-INCH NAIL SHOT INTO CARPENTER'S BRAIN: HARM NOT SERIOUS

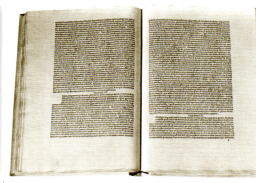

Minus linespacing, taking out linespacing so it is less than the type's point size, is recommended with all-caps settings, where there are no descenders and making type darker is valuable.

A 19th-century parlor game made poems out of texts. By breaking the text into segments and a poem-like position, ordinary prose becomes meaningful and symbolic.

Paragraphs separate ideas by signalling that a new idea is coming. Earliest paragraphing was accomplished with underlines and initial capital letters. Putting space at the beginning of a section is only one way to paragraph. One of the earliest instances of indented paragraphing is found in the *De Antiquitate Judaica* by Joannes Rubeus Vercellensis in 1486.

Line length can be determined individually by "breaking for sense," or breaking copy into natural phrases regardless of line length. Lyrics' sensible breaks are given a breezy, flowing, poetic feeling by their Brazilian artist, Djavan.

Basic ways paragraphing indicates new ideas: no additional space is given so each paragraph simply begins flush left; skipping a line with no indent; indention of the first line with no line space; hanging indent ("outdent"); and hierarchical indention to signal importances.

More imaginative paragraphing: inserting generous space into running text; placing large initials at the starts; and treating each paragraph as a near-separate entity.

only in a large hyphenation zone, has a more uneven right edge because words that exceed the maximum get dragged down to the next line. ⊡ Setting text centered or flush *right*/ragged *left* makes reading difficult because it makes the left edge irregular and hard to find. It may be used for short two- or three-line captions.

Linespacing/Optical linespacing Typography is, among other things, the craft of making fine adjustments so type is as appealing and as effortless to read as possible. It is balancing the letters with space. Too little linespacing, like in this paragraph, darkens an area of type and makes

readers feel claustrophobic. Too much linespacing causes

the reader to become aware of individual lines. Adding

space between lines of type is called *leading*, after the early practice of placing bars of metal between lines of type. ⊡ Linespacing should be sufficient to make returns to the left edge of a column easy, but not so much that the column's integrity as a stack of lines is weakened. ⊡ Types with small x-heights need little linespacing while types with large x-heights need additional linespacing.

Paragraphing is the act of visually separating ideas while maintaining overall unity. There are infinite ways of indicating a paragraph. For example, you may skip a line space (or half a line space, which looks better) or you may indent the first line (the distance is in proportion to the linespacing — but do not also skip a line space).

"It is only shallow people who do not judge by appearances. The mystery of the world is the visible, not the invisible."
Oscar Wilde, in a letter

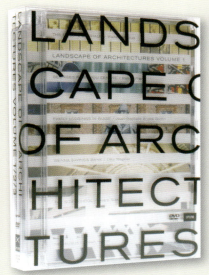

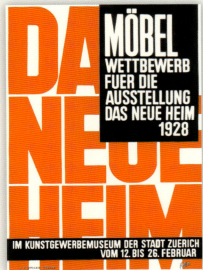

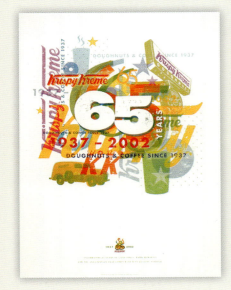

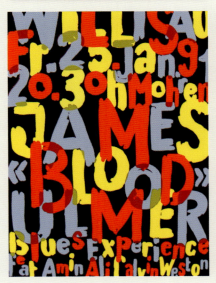

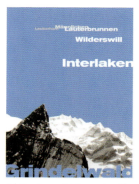

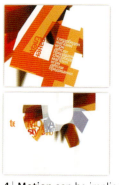

2 | Scale and hierarchy Big objects are perceived as nearer. Use space and size to imply depth. Switch the expected scale of objects for a fresh interpretation.

3 | Perspective Draw three-dimensional letters; distort and skew letterforms; craft three-dimensional letters and photograph.

4 | Motion can be implied by blurring in Photoshop, by slicing an image into pieces, or by repeating an element. Letterforms in motion can also visually interpret stuttering.

5 | Actual dimensionality Use paper's physical thickness; photograph cut letters; relate front and back of sheet; damage the paper and photograph it; cut a hole to see through the paper.

1 | Overlap elements There are three relationships to exploit: **Type in front of image** (*opposite top*): Semi-transparent titling; type on actual lucite box over imagery within; letters cut out of paper appear in front while actually revealing background. **Image in front of type** (*opposite middle*): Scaled type is placed across the tops of five layered newspapers in a 1928 poster; opaque rectangles obscure *non-essential* parts of letterforms beneath; holey art obscures parts of titling. **Type in front of type** (*opposite bottom*): Use opacity with shadow and transparency; overlap letters and reveal shared parts with transparency; 3D print a slipcase that reveals the same letters beneath.

Type in three-dimensional space

Printed space is represented in two dimensions: height and width. The third dimension, depth, can be used as a tool to explain or as an attention-getting technique, though it must always be *implied* in two-dimensional design.

There are five ways of creating the illusion of three dimensions with type. Each can be broadly interpreted:

1 | Overlap elements Placing an object in front of another effectively suggests reality. Image in front of type is far more convincing than type in front of image, but be careful not to obscure the key parts of letterforms so that it can't be read. Ambiguous space is created when one or more of the elements is transparent.

2 | Scale and hierarchy Big objects are perceived as nearer. Use space and size to imply depth. Switch the expected scale of objects for a fresh interpretation.

3 | Perspective The translation of volumes and spatial relationships to two dimensions was perfected only in the 15th century.

4 | Motion Moving objects are more real than stationary objects, so implying motion adds realism.

5 | Actual dimensionality Crafting a real object and photographing it for two-dimensional reproduction is extremely convincing. The more crafted, the better it will stand out.

Type in three dimensions is definitely applicable to logos. Like any design treatment, it should be used to express something conceptually inherent in the company or entity that the mark is to represent.

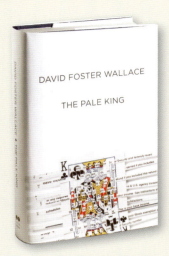

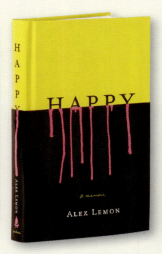

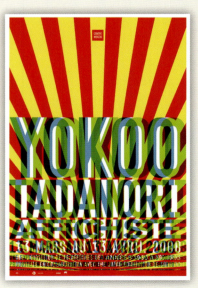

Space curves in this late-1980s Polaroid poster by Mervyn Kurlansky. Shifting baseline angles and Helvetica Bold, about as neutral a type as can be found, are all that are used.

Which is figure and which is ground? Ground usually exists behind but may also be in front of both illustrative or typographic figures. With great

care and intentionality, ground can be ambiguous, existing in both foreground and background simultaneously.

Student understanding includes exploration of pulling background forward and foreground backward. A grid is a useful tool in such studies because it defines space.

Type positioned in the foreground Space or image are in the background and take little or no pain.

Space in front of parts of type while allowing reasonable legibility to remain. Space has become activated and is an equal partner. Type and space *both become figure* with the development of activated ground.

Ambiguous space where space becomes abstract and is not discernible whether it or type is in the background. Either type or space can be perceived as "in front" and frequently can be perceived as both at the same time.

Abstracting type with space

Type exists in space; that is, type is perceived as being in front of its background. Far more dynamic results come from the background being brought to the foreground, so it appears to be in front of type. This works best in display type, where characters and words are large enough to accommodate the insults perpetrated on them. Text type, being small, is more sensitive to being treated with space in the foreground because illegibility is more quickly realized. Besides, once the browser has been hard won into *being* a reader, nothing should dissuade him from *staying* a reader.

The best way to abstract figure and ground is to think of both entities as equally valid shapes. Figures impose themselves on the space in which they exist. Think of it as a black letterform pushing the space beneath it out of its way. You might say the space has "taken all the pain." To abstract type, make the black shapes "take some of the pain," too. Chop off pieces of letters to allow space to come to the front and impose itself on letters.

At left are samples showing the three categories of type and space relationships: space purely in the background; space in front of parts of type (fully integrated and equal partners with the type); and ambiguous space (space itself becomes abstract and it is not discernible whether type or space is in the foreground).

"I wanted to make orderliness invisible. I am an anti-grid man. The best grid is the eye. When you rely on the eye rather than on a grid you're totally free." Leo Lionni (1910–1999)

Cornell's architectural legacy

Cornell University is home to one of the oldest and most respected architecture programs in the United States

The solid foundation in the history, theory, and practice of architecture produces scholars for the next generation of academic leaders. An important feature of the program is its relatively small size, fostering a sense of intellectual community essential to teaching and research. Cornell architecture students and faculty have opportunities to take advantage of the university's world-class library collection, landmark campus in Ithaca, and global footprint and network of alumni and partners. As part of the College of Architecture, Art, and Planning community, they have access to incredible physical resources like Milstein Hall and the Rand Hall Fabrication Shop. Students and faculty are frequently studying and teaching far from Ithaca — in AAP's New York City and Rome, Italy locations or through traveling option studios and other opportu-

nities. The department's core curricula are implemented by faculty from a variety of fields related to the discipline including architectural design, history of architecture and urban development, architectural theory, technology, and representation, and landscape architecture.

For undergraduates, AAP's Department of Architecture offers a five-year professional program leading to a bachelor of architecture (B.Arch.) degree. Consistently ranked one of the top programs in the country, the bachelor of architecture program is accredited by NAAB. The B.Arch. program balances the intensity of a professional education with opportunities to use the resources of a world-class university. The faculty of the department of architecture have developed a highly structured and intensive curriculum, one that em-

Ithaca has dozens of vintage Victorian homes which are ideal subjects for student "character" drawing studies.

Mein Ziel ist es, das vermurkste Gesetz, das ich mitverbrochen habe, wegzubekommen.
Gesundheitsministerin Sabine Oberhauser will ein Rauchverbot in Lokalen

Reichtum ist wie Mist: Auf einem Haufen stinkt er, gut verteilt wird er Österreich zum Blühen bringen.
Caritas-Präsident Michael Landau über die richtige Verteilung von Geld

Willkommenskultur

Wort des Jahres, als Reminiszenz an die Einstellung und die Handlungen der Bevölkerung gegenüber Flüchtlingen

Besondere bauliche Maßnahmen
Unwort des Jahres, „erfunden" von Innenministerin Johanna Mikl-Leitner als Synonym für den Zaun an der slowenischen Grenze

Da können sie so laut schreien, wie sie wollen.
Dagmar Belakowitsch-Jenewein (FPÖ) will Asylwerber im Militärflieger nach Hause schicken

Ein Türl mit Seitenteilen. Es ist kein Zaun.

Bundeskanzler Werner Faymann outet sich in der Frage der von der Innenministerin geplanten Grenzsicherung als semantischer Feinspitz

Ich kämpfe bis zur letzten Patrone gegen so einen Unsinn.
WK-Präsident Christoph Leitl versteht sich im Protest gegen die Registrierkasse als Revolverheld

Wir müssen an einer „Festung Europa" bauen.
Innenministerin Mikl-Leitner beschreibt ihre sicherheitspolitische Vision für den Kontinent

Nur das Amt des Papstes würde mich danach noch interessieren.
Finanzminister Hans Jörg Schelling über seine Pläne nach der Politik

Wenn das achte Weltwunder einträte . . . ja, dann würde ich darüber nachdenken.
Irmgard Griss zu Jahresbeginn über eine mögliche Bundespräsidentschaftskandidatur. Das Wunder trat im Dezember ein

Ich habe es einmal probiert, aber nur gepafft, ohne Lungenzug.
FPÖ-Chef Heinz-Christian Strache über seine einschlägigen Erfahrungen mit dem Konsum von Cannabis

---

Flüchtlinge, die im Freien übernachten müssen in der Republik Österreich – das geht gar nicht.
Bundespräsident Heinz Fischer zur Lage im Aufnahmezentrum Traiskirchen

Wird wohl ka Zwickerbusserl gwesen sein, sondern a solider Zungenpritschler.
Toni Mahdalik (FPÖ) über homosexuelle Liebkosungen im Café Prückel

Das Krokodil tritt ab

Gerald Grosz, erfolgsentwöhnter Obmann der einstigen Regierungspartei BZÖ, gibt sich bei seinem Politikabschied in animalischer Reflexion

Es ist wie ein großes Klassentreffen.
Stefan Petzner überkommen bei seinem Auftritt vor dem Hypo-Untersuchungsausschuss wehmütige Erinnerungen ans Parlament

Wenn wir nicht in nächster Zeit deutlich beweisen, dass wir regieren wollen und können, hat es keinen Sinn, auf Dauer weiterzuwursteln.
Vizekanzler Reinhold Mitterlehner analysiert selbstkritisch die Performance der Regierungskoalition

Die nächsten fünf Jahre werden „oho".

Maria Vassilakou, grüne Wiener Vizebürgermeisterin, verrät dem Koalitionspartner SPÖ ihre Zukunftspläne. Oho? Aha!

Wer nie in der ÖVP war, weiß nicht, was Stillstand ist.
Judith Raab, Oberösterreichs Neos-Chefin

Fast geil finde ich es, dass es uns gelingt, den Kindergarten zu stärken.
Staatssekretär Harald Mahrer freut sich – fast – wie ein Kind über einen Teil der Bildungsreform

Frauen sind Menschen wie wir.
Frank Stronach gibt sich als solider Kenner der Geschlechter

Wer will, der kann. Ich hoffe, sie wollen.
Christian Konrad, Flüchtlingskoordinator der Bundesregierung, über seine Auftraggeber

Ich glaube, es gäbe viele, die das besser machen könnten. Viel schlechter kann man es ja auch gar nicht machen.
Andreas Rabler, SPÖ-Bürgermeister von Traiskirchen, ortet im Flüchtlingskrisen-Management bei seinem Parteichef Werner Faymann Luft nach oben

Wenn ich 22 Stunden in der Woche arbeite, bin ich Dienstagmittag fertig.
Michael Häupl in der Debatte zur Lehrer-Arbeitszeit

Six typographic "flavors" are used in this story-opening spread. The type sizes and placement on the page (higher on the page is more valuable real estate than lower) indicate compara-

tive importances and connections. Note how the headline "bleeds" off the head of the page, which emphasizes the exaggerated space separating the headline/deck from the text.

A grid (helpfully diagrammed in gray) organizes these nine type elements — and perfectly illustrates the distinctive architectural character of the real estate it is selling in the photo.

Each of these four typographic elements has a specific role to aid reading: headline to subhead to text to brand mark. Here the subhead also serves as the ad campaign's tagline.

Display type has a single job: to entice, lure, provoke, and inform browsing readers about the story's value and usefulness *to themselves* so they will engage with the text. Typical display elements are headline, subhead, and caption, as shown in this spread story opener.

Text type contrasts are employed to differentiate items in this "Quotes of the Year" spread. What makes this treatment succeed is the underlying grid — and consistent spacing attributes — that gives structure to such demonstrative typesetting. The two shortest quotes, *Willkommenskultur* and *Das Krokodil tritt ab*, translate as "Welcoming culture" and "The Crocodile surrenders."

 Working type: type with jobs

"*O*ne of the most important differences between being legible and being readable is not only how well you can see what is being said, but whether it is worth seeing.*" Joseph Michael Essex

There are fundamentally two kinds of type: text and display. Text is relatively straightforward: it is the small stuff where the story is, the final destination for browsers who have become readers. But display type — any type meant to attract the reader's attention — can be defined as having nine specific roles. Understanding each of them provides an ability to work with them with intentionality:

- ⊡ Headlines
- ⊡ Captions
- ⊡ Subheads
- ⊡ Breakouts
- ⊡ Coverlines
- ⊡ Contents listings
- ⊡ Department headings
- ⊡ Bylines and bios
- ⊡ Folios and footlines

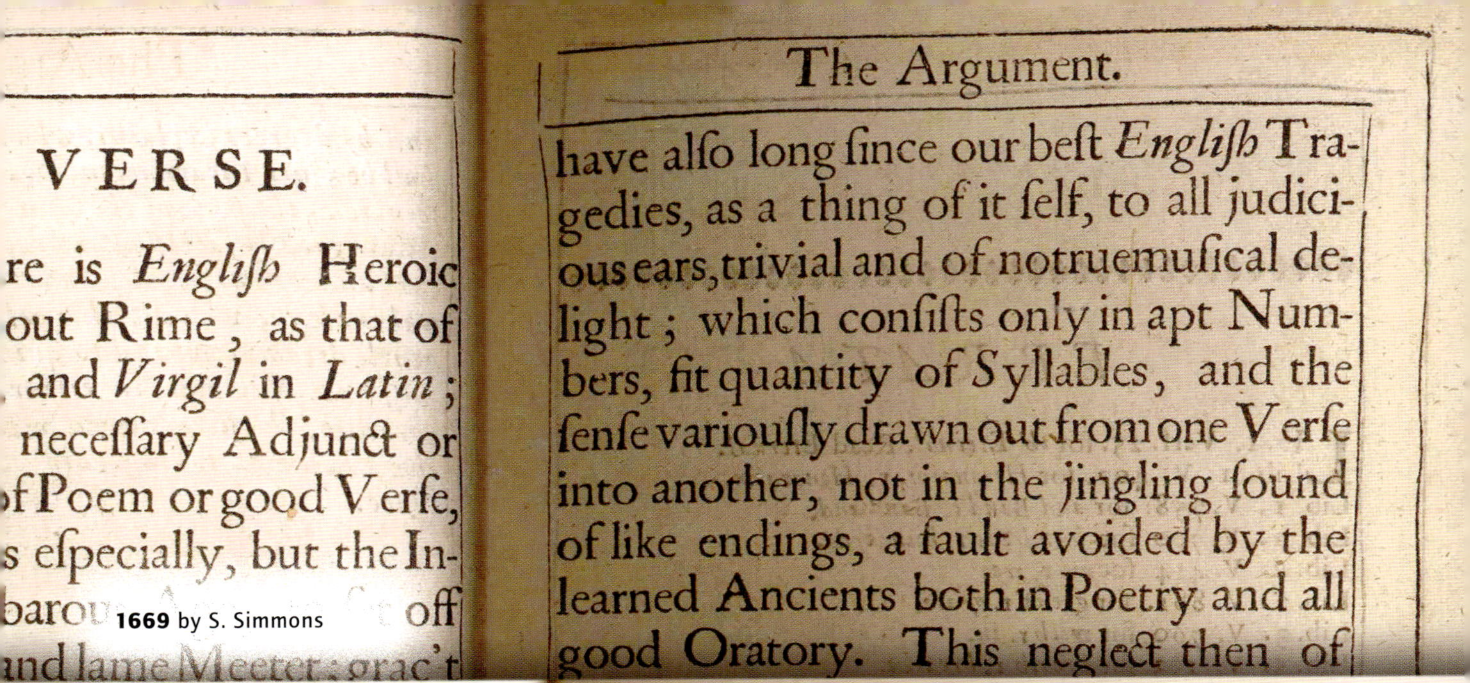

1669 by S. Simmons

VERSE.

...re is *English* Heroic
...out Rime, as that of
... and *Virgil* in *Latin*;
... necessary Adjunct or
...f Poem or good Verse,
...s especially, but the In-
...barou...
...nd lame Meeter: grac't

have also long since our best *English* Tra-
gedies, as a thing of it self, to all judici-
ous ears, trivial and of no true musical de-
light; which consists only in apt Numbers, fit quantity of Syllables, and the
sense variously drawn out from one Verse
into another, not in the jingling sound
of like endings, a fault avoided by the
learned Ancients both in Poetry and all
good Oratory. This neglect then of

1758 by John Baskerville

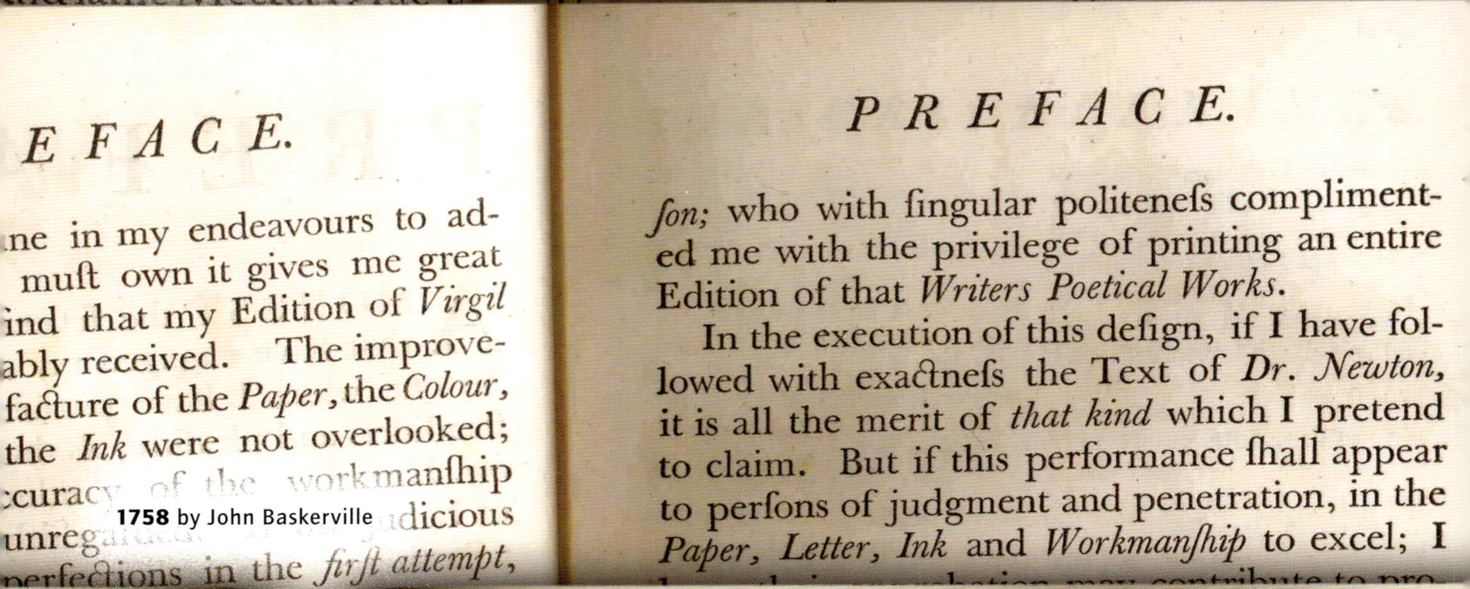

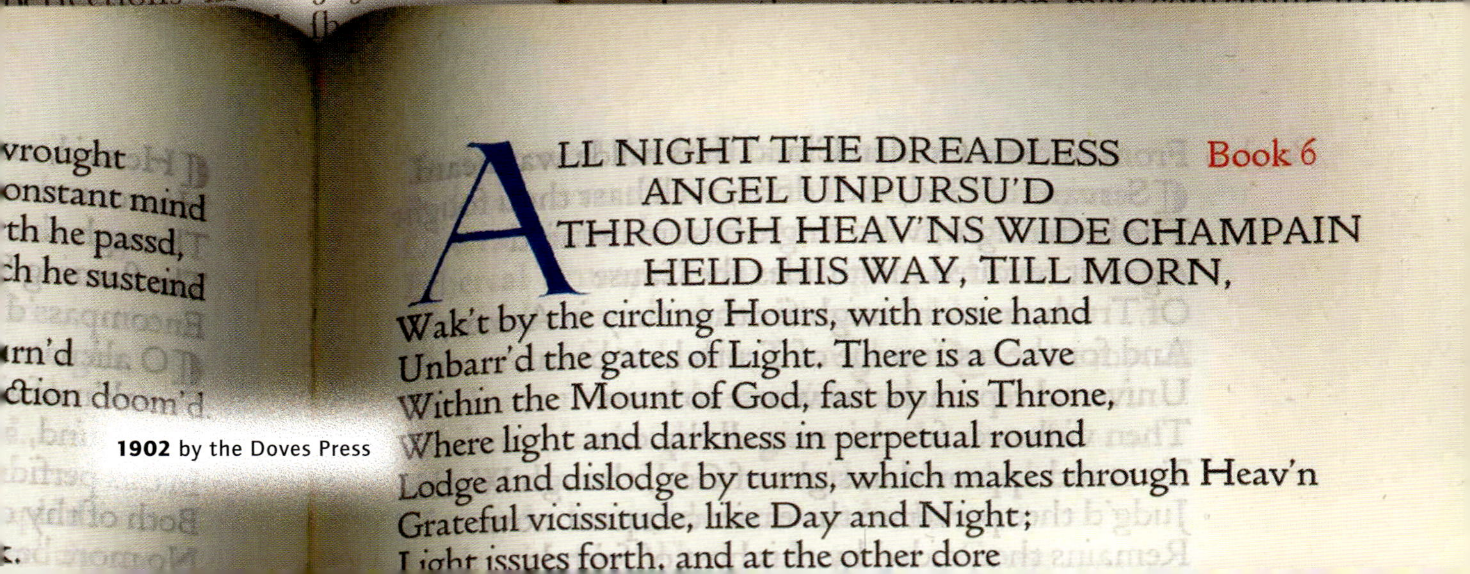

...EFACE.

...ne in my endeavours to ad-
... must own it gives me great
...ind that my Edition of *Virgil*
...ably received. The improve-
...facture of the *Paper*, the *Colour*,
...the *Ink* were not overlooked;
...ccuracy of the workmanship
...unrega... ...dicious
...perfections in the *first attempt*,

PREFACE.

...*son*; who with singular politeness compliment-
ed me with the privilege of printing an entire
Edition of that *Writers Poetical Works*.

In the execution of this design, if I have followed with exactness the Text of *Dr. Newton*,
it is all the merit of *that kind* which I pretend
to claim. But if this performance shall appear
to persons of judgment and penetration, in the
Paper, *Letter*, *Ink* and *Workmanship* to excel; I

1902 by the Doves Press

...vrought
...onstant mind
...th he passd,
...h he susteind
...rn'd
...ction doom'd

ALL NIGHT THE DREADLESS
ANGEL UNPURSU'D
THROUGH HEAV'NS WIDE CHAMPAIN
HELD HIS WAY, TILL MORN,
Wak't by the circling Hours, with rosie hand
Unbarr'd the gates of Light. There is a Cave
Within the Mount of God, fast by his Throne,
Where light and darkness in perpetual round
Lodge and dislodge by turns, which makes through Heav'n
Grateful vicissitude, like Day and Night;
Light issues forth, and at the other dore

Book 6

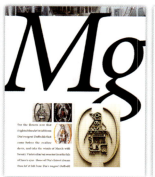

Three settings (*left*) of John Milton's *Paradise Lost* show the evolution of English text, all set in London. Note the improvements in letterspacing and the type's delicacy.

A variety of tones on the page (*above*) tells the reader straight away what is most important and what is less so. Along with positioning on the page, darkness denotes the hierarchy of the elements: our eyes naturally focus on the area of greatest tonal concentration. This is why headlines are bolder type. Using three typographic tones gives the page depth and creates the most satisfying visual mix. Three sequential left-hand department pages use size and tone to differentiate calendar events in a regional magazine.

Text type

There are over thirty thousand typefaces available, some several hundred years old and still used because their proportions are so magnificent, most more recently designed. Selecting the right typeface for your needs is one of the most important decisions you will make. Remember, however, that how you *use* a typeface is more important than what typeface is being used. You must consider both *legibility* and *personality* when selecting a typeface.

You have used all the tricks at your disposal to entice the reader into the text: provocatively written, dynamic display typography, intriguing imagery, visible captions, and well-used white space. Once there, the reader too often finds the text handled as blocks of grayness, as though a 50 percent screen tint is equivalent to words and sentences that actually contain *thoughts*.

Text is the most important part of your message because it contains the greatest amount of information per square pica on the page. It is the ultimate destination for your readers so every design decision should guide readers to it.

The rules for creating excellent text type differ from display type. The fact of text's small size means that spacing between character pairs is nearly insignificant. What is very significant is text's letterspacing and word spacing. The mark of a quality text setting is the evenness of its "color," its lightness or darkness. Even letterspacing and word spacing is a balance between having enough to separate words from each other without so much that it damages the horizontality of the line.

Letterspacing is the space between letters in a word. By completely surrounding individual characters, it defines their shapes. ⊡ Letterspacing and word spacing are controlled on typesetting equipment by setting the tracking. Ordinarily, letter and word spacing are directly related, but it is possible to set them independently, for example to increase letterspacing and decrease word spacing. ⊡ Irregular, arbitrary letterspacing decreases the reader's ability to perceive familiar word shapes and significantly slows reading speed and comprehension. *Kerning*, adjusting the space between specific pairs of characters, smooths out letterspacing by increasing optical consistency.

Word spacing is the space that separates words on a line. Word space should only be *sufficient to separate* one word from the next. Too much word space slows the reader down. ⊡ A flush-left/ragged-right setting is the best way to achieve even word spacing because the spaces stay exactly the same while the ends of the lines flex — some lines are a little shorter than others. Allowing hyphenation creates a "soft rag," or gently curving right

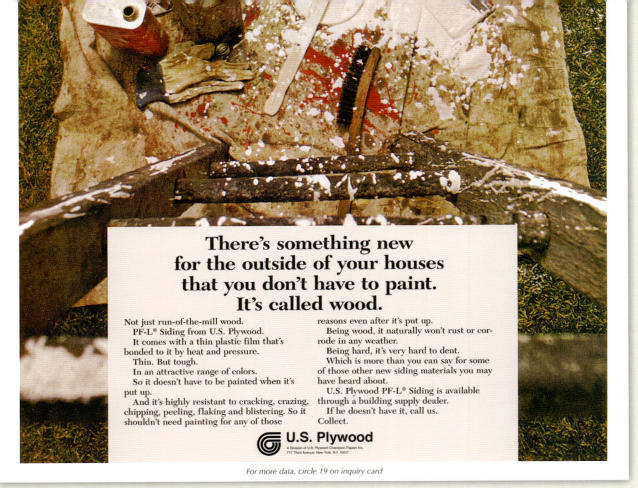

There's something new for the outside of your houses that you don't have to paint. It's called wood.

Not just run-of-the-mill wood.

PF-L® Siding from U.S. Plywood.

It comes with a thin plastic film that's bonded to it by heat and pressure.

Thin. But tough.

In an attractive range of colors.

So it doesn't have to be painted when it's put up.

And it's highly resistant to cracking, crazing, chipping, peeling, flaking and blistering. So it shouldn't need painting for any of those reasons even after it's put up.

Being wood, it naturally won't rust or corrode in any weather.

Being hard, it's very hard to dent.

Which is more than you can say for some of those other new siding materials you may have heard about.

U.S. Plywood PF-L® Siding is available through a building supply dealer.

If he doesn't have it, call us. Collect.

U.S. Plywood
A Division of U.S. Plywood-Champion Papers Inc.
777 Third Avenue, New York, N.Y. 10017

For more data, circle 19 on inquiry card

BIRD to PARADISE.

Just tell us where to and we'll whisk you away to your favorite exotic hiding place. No hoop-jumping, no hidden fees, no hassles. It's turnkey travel—a new, modern way to fly private. Call 877.599.6538 to book your next trip.

XOJET

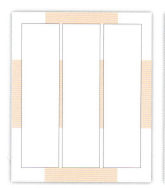

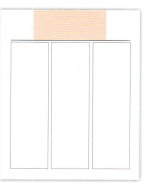

Margins are the four areas surrounding the live area of a page (head, foot, and two sides) and the vertical spaces between columns of type. Generous margins make a

document more appealing by reducing the daunting quantity of text on a page. A deep and consistently applied head margin is called *sinkage*.

Unequal columns may be used when their peculiarity doesn't interfere with reading and when it is plain why the columns are uneven, here agreeing with the image size.

Setting text across the page's width is generally poor design because text becomes overly demanding when there are too many characters per line. Wiggly baselines don't help either.

edge. Prohibiting hyphenation causes a "hard rag," or notably uneven right edge, because entire words that do not fit on a line are dragged down to the next line, leaving a big gap on the right side of the column. The ideal rag is called a "sawtooth" because it has alternating long and short lines. A hard rag is considered poor typography because the zigzag of the right edge is distracting.

Justification is setting lines of type to the same width. This is done by altering word spaces so each line achieves full length, or *measure*. Justified type looks good as long as there are sufficient word spaces to absorb the spacing fluctuations. An average of 8 words per line is a minimum essential for reasonably even justified word spacing. Justified type without hyphenation produces very poor word spacing: the extra white space is inserted throughout the line to make up for the drastic shortage of letters.

Paragraph indents are set in relationship to word spacing (*opposite, above*). A too-shallow indent, the width of a word space, is not adequately visible. These indents are an exaggeration: of the 22 lines of text, half are indented. This makes the left edge of the column extremely uneven and the text look very sloppy.

Line spacing (also known as *leading*, though the days of lead "slugs" separating lines of type are long gone) is the space that appears between the descend-

ers and ascenders of lines of type. Line spacing is added to separate lines of type from one another, making the reading process easier. Proper line spacing prevents skipping or rereading lines of type. Additional line spacing is recommended for long line widths (over about 70 characters), type styles with large x-heights, and for readers with reading deficiencies (the very young, the very old, and poor readers). Additional line spacing improves legibility (*opposite, below*). ⊡ Line spacing is often added when a story is short and must be stretched to fill the space. While a logical method for filling space, it usually draws undue attention to itself. Better ways to fill the space are to enlarge an image or run a breakout. ⊡ Text and the page's underlying grid fundamentally affect the look of visual communication. Josef Müller-Brockmann, the noted Swiss designer, wrote: "Each problem calls for a grid suited especially to itself. It must enable the designer to arrange the [text], captions, and [imagery] so that they are as visually effective as their importance warrants and yet form an ordered whole."

In short, consistent spacing is crucial to making typography attractive and readable. The ultimate goal of letter, word, and line spacing is to make it *invisible*, to avoid self-consciousness, allowing the reader to absorb the meaning and content of the type with as little effort as possible.

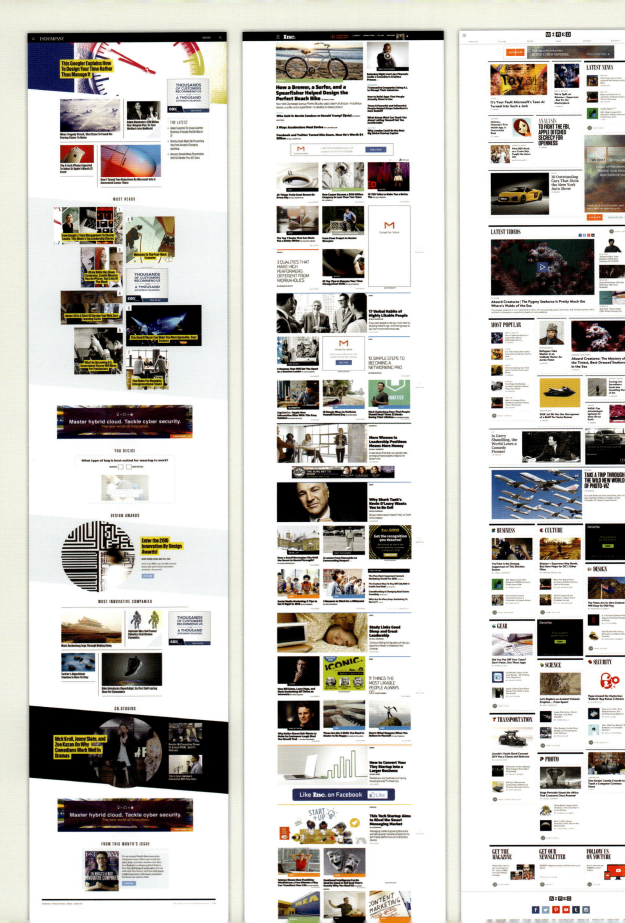

On-screen and print design share the same mission: clear, persuasive communication (*opposite*). All three of these Web sites have corresponding screen and print presence and both platforms are used fully to indicate the richness of their content. Like a magazine, a website's visual identity should remain constant even as its content changes. However, electronic documents aren't constrained to linear structuring the way multipage printed documents are. Unlike a magazine, page numbers are meaningless in a nonlinear environment. Other navigational tools are used in their place.

Web typography

Web sites are magazines. They are brochures. They are both entertainment and informational. Most importantly, they are interactive. But as in any area — and any era — of design, understanding present technological limitations leads to creative solutions.

There are three kinds of Web type: pictures of type, Web-safe system fonts, and @font-face fonts.

Pictures of type offer the greatest creative control, but they can't be indexed by search engines, which is the critical way for Web content to be found. Use pictures of type only to match branding requirements.

Web-safe fonts reside on all computers and are designed specifically for on-screen legibility with larger x-heights and more open counter spaces. They are an easy way to prepare Web type but they severely limit the distinctiveness of your typography because there are a fixed number of such typefaces.

The @font-face choice allows for an nearly infinite variety of typefaces to be used on a Web site. They are protected from being downloaded by the user of the Web page via such font-delivery systems as Fontdeck, Google Fonts, and Adobe Typekit. The fonts reside on a server and cause a slight delay in page loading time, so they are wisely used for display where they are most visible, while Web-safe fonts are used for text.

A "font stack" is a list of types that cascades in descending order of the designer's designated preference: preferred, alternate, common, and generic. The font that appears is the highest one in the stack that is recognized by the CSS instructions. This causes unpredictable visual results for the user.

Type on screen Type on screen is perceived differently than type on paper: we are used to reading printed type that is rendered at 600 to 1,200 dots per inch. Web type must be only 72 dpi. Small type in particular looks dreadful at 72 dpi. The counters, or interior spaces, of low-resolution type appear to fill in, so choose fonts with open counters and large x-heights, and open the letter and line spacing to make individual characters more legible.

▣ **Edit text shorter** Getting ninety percent readership on shorter copy is far better than ten percent readership on longer text.

▣ **Use classic design rules of composition** and type's optimal line length.

▣ **Limit your typeface use** to two fonts: traditionally, display is a heavy sans serif and text is a lighter serif.

▣ **Make your site legible above all else** Select background colors and textures that do not obstructs legibility. Maximize contrast between type and background.

Notebook

HOTELS

Starck's New Reality

When Philippe Starck designed the Royalton Hotel, there were lamps that resembled animal horns and a champagne bar shaped like the inside of a bottle. "In the '80s, the boutique hotel was about design," says Starck. "Today we want something completely different. We don't speak about design." Starck's latest endeavor is SLS Hotels, a new brand meant to "re-explode" the luxury-hotel experience. The first property, SLS Hotel at Beverly Hills, opens next month. Rather than the flashy design motifs of the past, the emphasis is on quieter indulgences. Design retailer Murray Moss will select objects to display for sale in vitrines throughout the lobby. Visitors will be able to sample odd delicacies like caviar cones from food carts. —By Kate Novack

Starck, far left, with SLS Hotels VIPs

AUTOMOBILES

Van with a Plan

THE HIPPIES OF THE '60s imagined a brighter future as they careened around in their Westfalia VW vans. Now Alexander Verdier has made that hopeful future a reality, reimagining the iconic VW cruiser with his new chic and environmentally friendly rendition, the Verdier Solar Power. Awarded the prize for Innovation in New Mobility at the Caravan Salon Düsseldorf—Europe's largest caravanning exhibition—the Verdier Solar Power is a hybrid vehicle outfitted with a system of solar panels, called sun trackers, that provide electricity to the van's many accessories, including an onboard multimedia computer, a wireless Internet connection and a GPS that can calculate, among other things, the vehicle's ideal position in the sun. Although the Verdier won't be available until 2009, reservations can be made now for the $129,000 camper—and it's selling fast. "We think it's possible to connect with nature through technology," Verdier says. "It's for people who care about the environment and prefer to go with a smaller and smarter design." For those seeking a more grounded way to travel, the retro style and modern amenities of the Verdier just might be the way to roll (www.verdier.ca). —By Paige Reddinger

TREND

Giorgio Armani knows a thing or two about the jet-set lifestyle, so it makes perfect sense that his latest accessory venture is the Luxury Traveller Collection, with chic matching luggage sets reminiscent of a bygone era of travel. —P.R.

---

photographs by Adam Ferguson

The Sand and the Fury

Computer chips. Glass. Concrete. The world is built on sand. Mess with the mafias that control it and you could pay with your life.

by Vince Beiser

"If it gets much lower, we'll be out of a job."

Thane Creek's sand will soon be mined out.

> quorundam philofophorum fentétias dige
> ait.Hoc loco dicit aliquis.Credat ergo cęlum
> alios:infta alios.Ego feram aut Platonem:a
> e tutto fuori.Non parla fenon dopo lanno:N
> di fei mefi:elquale prodigio fignifico laruina
> minciono a parlare prefto penono piu a and
> quos ferebat illa aetas nó tam maturos , q̃
> uberes,femper tibi aliquos promeremus:
> nam fiue dolebas aliquid, fiue gaudebas;

Text Convention 7: Type is meant to be read Use your own common sense and clear thinking to make your text type as readable and legible as possible. The first years of type crafting were all about improving the reading experience. These samples, all actual size, are (*top to bottom*) da Spira brothers 1469; Jenson 1470; and Manutius 1495.

Text Convention 8: Typographic *variation* is another way of saying typographic *hierarchy* Differentiating elements on the page is essential, but too many variations confuse the reader. Develop a system of defining *kinds* of information and stick to it. Here are three sizes and two weights. Consistency is perceived as quality.

Eight text conventions Creative text samples generally break typographic conventions such as "use 60 characters per line" or "always add two points of line spacing," but they do so *intentionally*, without compromising legibility. Those of us who work with type must understand text setting "laws" to know when they are being broken and know what to do to compensate for our purposeful violations.

If you follow these eight type conventions and make a few well-placed and highly visible adjustments, you will have clear type that has its own distinctive personality.

Text Convention 1: Text type is sized in relation to the width of the column The wider the column, the larger the type must be because text works best in lines of about 60 characters (*opposite, above*). The bigger red type is set across a wider measure, maintaining approximately the same characters per line as the smaller type above it. We can scan 60-character lines quickly and return to the leading edge of the next line effortlessly. Setting text with more than 60 characters asks for an increase in line spacing. Setting text across a narrower measure causes overhyphenation and, if the setting is justified, will cause very uneven, ugly word spacing.

Text Convention 2: Sans serif type can be just as readable as serif type if you make two adjustments Sans serif typefaces lack the strong horizontal flow of a serif face, so shorten the line length and add line spacing to reduce eye fatigue.

Text Convention 3: Word spacing is determined in proportion to letterspacing If letters are set tighter than normal, word spacing should be set tighter than normal as well.

Text Convention 4: Use space consistently Headlines, subheads, and text need standardized spacing from each other, which shows logic and order.

Text Convention 5: Solutions to typographic problems are built in if you pay attention to communicating clearly. Typography becomes confusing and actually interferes with the message when it is manipulated for its own sake as a self-conscious art form (*opposite, below*). Though beautiful, is its verticality descriptive of this particular message?

Text Convention 6: Consider the audience Selecting a typeface is much like selecting clothing: you neither want to look too peculiar nor exactly like everyone else. Who is the intended reader? Under what conditions will the publication be read? From how far away will it be read? Is it to be scanned for tidbits, or is it to be read from start to finish, like a novel? These factors will help determine the typeface, type size, column width, and line space configurations. Author and design consultant Jan V. White calls this "considerate typography."

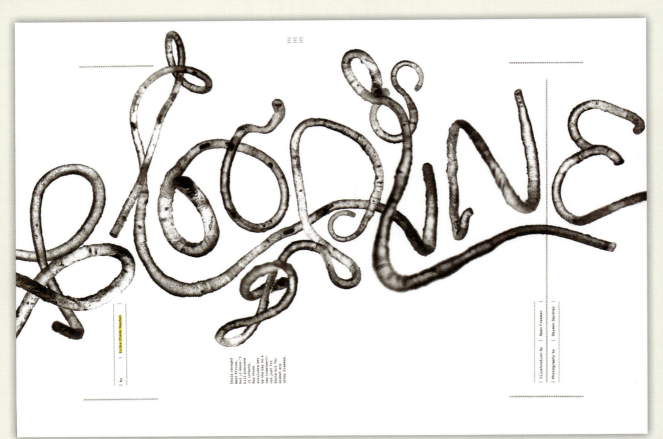

by | Erika Chuck Hayden

Ebola ravaged West Africa, but it doesn't kill everyone it infects. Now those survivors may be the key to a new treatment— not just for Ebola but for almost any other disease.

Illustration by | Sean Freeman

Photography by | Deyson Gaucher

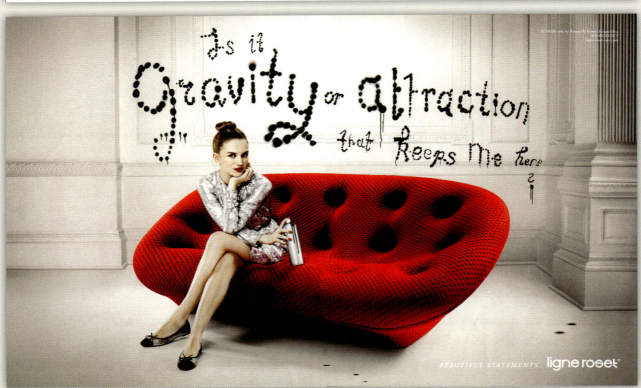

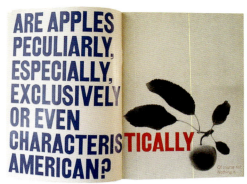

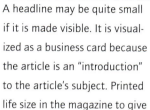

Primary type can be an illustration that happens to be perceived as readable (*left, above*), as in this story opening spread on the Ebola virus. Or it can be rendered in a way that solidly relates it to the image (*left, below*), even crafting it directly in the image.

Anything that interprets the meaning of primary type is a good treatment (*above*).

A headline may be quite small if it is made visible. It is visualized as a business card because the article is an "introduction" to the article's subject. Printed life size in the magazine to give the card maximum believability, the headline, deck, byline, and art credit are all treated as a straightforward but by no means "designed" formal letterpress-printed business card.

Primary display type

Headlines Headlines create the *apparent* personality of printed material (the underlying structure, or grid, actually does most of the work). As primary typography, headlines are intended to stop the reader and persuade him or her to look at the secondary (subheads, breakouts, and captions) and tertiary (text) levels of typography.

Display type is used to draw attention to itself and to lead the reader to the next level of typographic importance, usually the subhead or deck. Most text typefaces make excellent headline faces when set in larger, bolder form. Legible text faces run from a minimum of 8 points to a maximum of 12 points; display type ranges from a minimum of 14 points to an infinitely large size. Indeed, enormous letterforms cropped by the edge of a page can serve as a very effective visual attractant.

Consider the impression you want to create. A typeface's character will be helpful, harmful, or neutral to your message. Match the typeface to the message.

As a general rule, do not use more than two typefaces on one project, and do not use more than two weights of each typeface. If you add italic versions of each weight, you have eight typographic "voices," which should be enough to convey any message. If you need more than eight voices, you are definitely overdefining the differences in the information.

Using visual signals through *relationships of contrast* indicates what is more important and what is less important. Arbitrary emphasis and signal selection, though it may look attractive, will seriously interfere with the readership. Display type sends visual signals that should *demand* attention. It must have sufficient contrast to stand out from the surrounding material. It is impossible to make a headline *too* much larger than text or *too* much bolder than the subhead. But messages can suffer from too much contrast when there are too many typefaces or too many slight variations that the reader perceives as confusing.

Demand attention by increasing typographic contrast using these visual signals:

- **Size** Small/large; big = important; small = less important; big = read first; small = read second.
- **Weight** Thick/thin; the eye naturally goes to the darkest area first, so the most important type is made bolder.
- **Color** Dark/light or black/contrasting color.
- **Stress** Vertical/angled; the letterform's stress determines whether it is roman or angled. Angled type is used for emphasis within an area of roman type.
- **Format** CAPS/lower-case; CAPS/SMALL CAPS.
- **Character shape** Hard/soft; serif/sans serif;

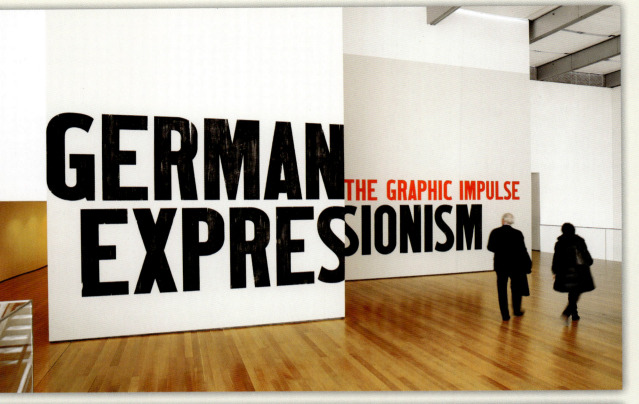

My only love sprung from my only hate! Too early seen unknown, and known too late!

My only love sprung from my only hate! Too early seen unknown, and known too late!

Typographic dimensionality is shown in a real environment — signage at the Museum of Modern Art in New York City — and on the cover of an art school's magazine. The cover letters

were not faked in Photoshop: they were 3D printed and photographed off computer, giving them a far richer, authentic sense of space.

Headlines don't need to be set in type to be effective. Hand lettering — if not necessarily calligraphy ("beautiful writing") — can be the right choice when it is *the right voice*.

Type well used should reflect different tones of voice. These same words presented in six lines "sound" different than when they are presented in three lines.

shape of letterforms; position on the page.

- ⊡ **Character width** Narrow/wide; expanded/condensed.
- ⊡ **Density** Solid/outline; positive/negative; tight/loose.
- ⊡ **Position on the page** vertical/horizontal; top/bottom.

No matter which typographic contrast variation you use, it is necessary to maintain a condition of clear "normalcy" so that the unusual element really stands out. If, for example, about half a page is set in regular and half in italic type, which of the two is asking to be recognized first? Neither is in the majority, and so neither is special, and the reader is simply confused. Follow the 75 Percent Rule: make one element about three times bigger than any other element. It is a good way to remember to have one dominant element.

The effectiveness of display typography is not dependent on the black letterforms, but on the management of the white space between and around the letterforms. Because display type is always brief (to grab the reader's fickle attention), letterspacing, word spacing, and line breaks become very important.

The speed at which words are comprehended is dictated by their typographic presentation. Except in gross instances, the space between individual letters is only noticed when the type is larger than about 18 points. So letterspacing becomes very important in display typography and is somewhat less so in text typography. The optimum letterspacing is invisible. The reader is not even aware that letterspacing exists when it is done well.

Words are strung together to form lines of type. Word spacing is the glue that holds lines of type together. The secret to good word spacing is invisibility. The reader should not be aware of the type they are reading: they should be concentrating only on its meaning. Display word spacing is often too large, the eye plodding across too-great spaces to get to the next word. This significantly slows the eye and makes the reader aware of the process of reading, at which time he stops reading and finds something less effortful to do.

How a line is broken is very important in display type. The aim is to break for sense. A phrase attributed to entertainer Danny Kaye illustrates this point:

I'm so tired I could sleep for a week who would care to join me in saluting the glorious members of our crew.

Words have a rhythm, and the rhythm must be followed for maximum comprehension. Read the words in a headline out loud to find the natural breaks. Don't break a headline to follow a design; rather break a

MONTAUKSOFA®

take a seat, take a stand

Every Montauk Sofa contributes to a Carbon Neutral environment, alternative therapy for a green house gas free planet. montauksofa.com

5.8285 toronto 220 king st. e. 416.361.0331 vancouver 1062 homer st 604.331.2363
6777 new york 51 mercer st. 212.274.1552 chicago 401 north wells st. 312.951.5688

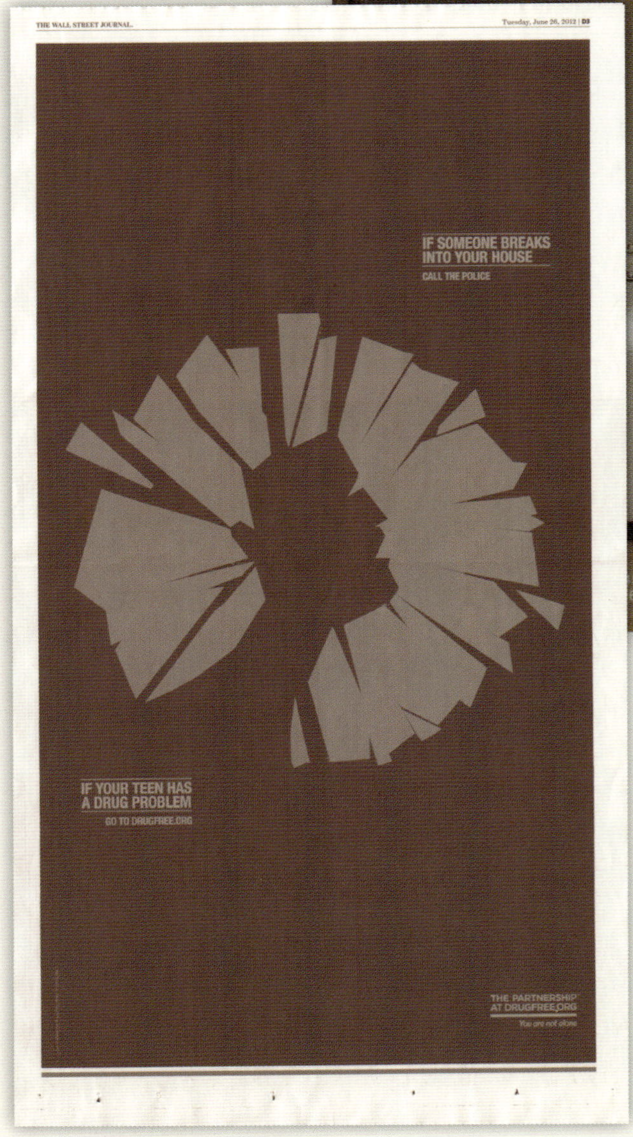

THE WALL STREET JOURNAL.   Tuesday, June 26, 2012 | D9

IF SOMEONE BREAKS
INTO YOUR HOUSE
CALL THE POLICE

IF YOUR TEEN HAS
A DRUG PROBLEM
GO TO DRUGFREE.ORG

THE PARTNERSHIP
AT DRUGFREE.ORG
You are not alone

Word space in headlines can be ignored if another word-separating signal is given, as in this two-word headline for a furniture manufacturer (*left above*). Headlines can be

disguised as captions, demonstrating that primary type transcends categorization, as in this full-page newspaper ad (*left below*).

Dramatic type size changes animate these headlines (*above, left*) in distinctive asymmetric word clouds.

Unexpected contrast of meaning between image and headline

might lead a browser to read the first few lines of the text (*above, center*).

The headline and subhead are defined by changing type color alone (*above, right*).

headline so that it makes the most sense to the reader. Communicate by enhancing the content and exposing the author's thought.

In a complex document, display type (headlines and department headings) should relate in some way to the flag (logo). For a publication to achieve visual unity, the editorial – or non-advertising – pages must be consistent. It is easy to develop a typographic system that uses a few variations of a single typeface. Display type is the most visible type and therefore makes the biggest impact, so typographic consistency is particularly necessary among the logo, department headings, and headlines. This consistency gives a feeling of cohesiveness and unity to the product and reinforces the singular personality of the publication, traits that endear a magazine to its loyal readers and make it more popular with advertisers.

It can be a good idea to change typefaces for a specific feature story, to give it more emphasis in the magazine, which is a correct treatment for a true "feature," or special event. But the headline typography should then remain consistent throughout that one story.

Make headlines smaller and blacker than you might at first think they should be. If the story requires a short headline, add a lengthy blurb describing the article to supply darkness and attract the reader's eye. Reduce the line spacing in headlines to make them darker. Ordinarily,

the rule for line spacing in display type is: "Descenders and ascenders should never touch" — unless it looks better when they do. When ascenders and descenders touch, they create a visual spot on the page that cannot be avoided. All-cap headlines in particular should have no extra line spacing because there are no descenders to fill in the space between lines. Minus leading, or removing line space, makes a headline darker and more visible.

Headlines can be structured to contrast with the text, to stand out on the page. For example, a headline can be stacked in several short lines. Type should reflect different tones of voice. The same words presented in three lines "sound" different than when they are presented in six lines.

In two-line headlines, the second line should be shorter than the first. The short second line encourages the reader to continue on to the text because the end of one element is closer to the beginning of the next.

Headline treatments fall into three broad categories: alignment and position, contrasting type styles, and the integration of type and imagery. These three areas are illustrated by the examples in this chapter. But whatever the treatment, the best headlines are provocatively written and have a point to make. A good headline must be more than just visually attractive; it must be written to say something. It must be *meaningful* to the reader.

HOW LONG WAS THE HUNDRED YEARS' WAR?

One hundred seventeen years, to be precise. And you thought the current conflicts in Iraq and Afghanistan were never-ending—although at this rate, they might be. Iraq has now outlasted World War II, while in March Afghanistan will edge out Vietnam as the longest American war ever.

GULF WAR
1 MONTH, 13 DAYS
JAN. 16, 1991[1]–FEB. 28, 1991

SIX-DAY WAR
6 DAYS
JUNE 5–10, 1967

CIVIL WAR
3 YEARS, 11 MONTHS, 29 DAYS
APRIL 12, 1861–APRIL 9, 1865[2]

WORLD WAR I
4 YEARS, 3 MONTHS, 15 DAYS
JULY 28, 1914–NOV. 11, 1918

WORLD WAR II
6 YEARS, 2 DAYS
SEPT. 1, 1939–SEPT. 2, 1945

IRAQ WAR
6 YEARS, 6 MONTHS, 9 DAYS
MARCH 20, 2003–SEPT. 28, 2009 (AND COUNTING)

WAR IN AFGHANISTAN
7 YEARS, 11 MONTHS, 22 DAYS
OCT. 7, 2001–SEPT. 28, 2009 (AND COUNTING)

AMERICAN REVOLUTION
8 YEARS, 4 MONTHS, 16 DAYS
APRIL 19, 1775–SEPT. 3, 1783

VIETNAM WAR
8 YEARS, 5 MONTHS, 21 DAYS
AUG. 7, 1964[3]–JAN. 27, 1973

[1] WHEN THE U.S.-LED AIR OFFENSIVE BEGAN. [2] WHEN LEE SURRENDERED. [3] WHEN GULF OF TONKIN RESOLUTION PASSED.

RESEARCH BY IAN YARETT

In addition to describing what is important about an entire image, captions may describe parts of an image (*left*) or serve as a translation for abstracted letterforms (*above*).

Pictures and their captions are — or should be — seen as a single unit. Readers expect to be told what they are looking at and a caption is a crucial potential story entry point.

Make captions bolder *or* lighter with extra white space to make them stand apart from the text. This makes them easy

to see and easy to scan quickly, both actions you want your readers to do without effort.

Captions We like explanations. As children, we ask for explanations of the things we see around us. Captions are a printed response to that curiosity. Captions help readers understand what they are seeing and, when the image is complex or puzzling, help them to reach the correct editorial conclusion. Captions serve three functions: they explain the photos; they encourage the reader to want to read the text by summarizing the article they accompany; and they provide another opportunity to give your publication a unique typographic personality.

Captions explain photos Pictures are always the first things scanned on a page. Reading is work; looking at pictures is fun. Humans simply respond faster to imagery than type. Unfortunately, pictures can be misinterpreted and misunderstood, so captions are added — usually beneath, by tradition — to guide the reader to the intended conclusion. ⊡ Captions may explain why the picture is there, they may focus on only a part of the image, or they may put the photo into a different context. Captions should add something to the picture, not merely describe the obvious.

Captions lure readers Captions can be exploited to entice a reader into a story. Attracted by a picture∕caption combination because it breaks the pattern of textual grayness, the reader may then read the headline∕

deck and breakouts and then the text. Captions are often the entry points for readers because they are so strongly joined with photos — which are great interest-creators — and they are short. ⊡ The length of a caption should be neither too long nor too short. Provide enough information to push the reader to the next level of involvement. But a caption contains too much content if paragraphing is necessary. The first few words should be as carefully chosen as a headline's are. Lure readers into completing the caption.

Captions add personality Every typographic element provides an opportunity to contribute to a publication's distinctive look. And every publication deserves a degree of individuality that sets it apart from its competition, in part because it makes advertisers very happy to be seen in quality surroundings. Captions are among the most exploited elements for distinctive treatment, at the forefront of typographic creativity, along with headlines and breakouts. ⊡ Captions have a built-in contrast because of their attendant pictures. But more must be done to make them appeal to the casual reader. Contrast with the text can be increased by setting captions bold sans serif or in a smaller, italicized version of the text face (*see above*). ⊡ Given standard text columns and relatively ordinary display typography, captions can become the most prominent type on the page. This path

A

music be the food of love, play on. Give me excess of it that, surfeiting, the appetite may sicken and so die. That strain again! It had a dying fall. O, it came o'er my ear like the sweet sound that breathes upon a bank of violets, stealing and giving odour. Enough, no more! 'Tis not so sweet now as iot was before. O spirit of love! How quick and fresh art thou, that notwithstanding thy capacity

Love sought is good, but giv'n unsought is better. What a deal o'scorn looks so beautiful in the contempt of his curl'd lip.

receiveth as the sea, nought enters there. Of what validity and pitch soe'er, but falls into abatement and low price, even in a minute.

So full of shapes is fancy that it alone is high fantastical.If music be the food of love, play on. Give me excess of it that,

surfeiting, the appetite may sicken and so die. That strain again! It had a dying at brea upon a bank of violets. Enc no more! 'Tis not so sweet n as it was before. O spirit of love! How quick and fresh ar thou, that notwithstanding capacity receiveth as the sea

B

≥2≤

Love sought is good, but giv'n unsought is better. What a deal o' scorn looks so beautiful in the contempt of his curl'd lip.

C

LOVE SOUGHT *is good, but giv'n unsought is better. What a deal o' scorn looks so beautiful in the contempt of his curl'd lip.*

D

Love sought is good, but giv'n unsought is better.

looks so beautiful in the contempt of his curl'd lip.

What a deal o' scorn

E

ity and pitch soe'er, but falls into abatement and low price, even in a minute. So full of shapes O spirit of love! How quick and fresh art thou, that notwithstanding thy capacity receiveth as the sea, nought enters there. Of what validity and pitch soe'er, but falls into abatement and low price, even in a minute.

Give me excess of it that, surfeiting, the appetite may sicken and so die. That strain again! It had a dying at breathes upon a bank of violets.

How quick and fresh art thou, that notwithstanding thy capacity receiveth as the sea, nought enters there.

Love sought is good, but giv'n unsought is better

music be the food of love, play on. Give me excess of it that, surfeiting, the appetite may sicken and so die. That strain again! It had a dying fall. O, it came o'er my ear like the sweet sound that bre-athes upon a bank of violets, stealing and giving odour.

Enough, no more! 'Tis not so sweet now as iot was before. O spirit of love! How quick and fresh art thou, that notwithstanding thy capacity receiveth as the sea, nought enters there. Of what validity and pitch soe'er, but falls into abatement and low price, even in a minute. Full of shapes is fancy that it alone is high fantastical. If music be the food of love, play on. Give me excess of it that, surfeiting, the appetite may sicken and so die.

That strain again! It had a dying fall. O, it came o'er my ear like the sweet sound that breathes upon a bank of violets, stealing and giving odour. Enough, no more!

dying at breathes a bank of violets. before. O spirit of love! How quick and fresh art thou, that notwithstanding thy capacity receiveth as the sea, nought enters there. Of what validity and pitch soe'er, but falls into abatement and low price, even in minute. Full of shapes is fancy that it alone is high fantastical. If music be the food of love, play on. Give me excess of it that, surfeiting, the appetite may sicken and so die.

'Tis not so sweet now as it was before. O spirit of love! How quick and fresh art thou, that notwithstanding thy capacity receiveth as the sea, nought enters there. Of what validity and pitch but falls into abatement and low price, of shapes is fancy that it alone is fantastical the food of

24

F

capacity rece as the sea, no enters there. what validity pitch soe'er, b falls into aba and low price in a minute. of shapes is fa that it on a b of violets, and giving o Enough, no m 'Tis not so sw as iot was befo O spirit of lo How reathes a bank of vio stealing and p a quick and i art thou, tha

Love sought is good, but giv'n unsought is better.

music be the food of love, play on. Give me excess of it that, surfeiting, the appetite may sicken and so die. That strain again!

It had a dying fall. O, it came o'er my ear like the sweet sod that breathes upon a bank of violets, stealing and giving odor.

No more 'tis not so sweet now as it was before. O spirit of love! How quick and fresh art thou, that notwithstanding thy

G

capacity rece as the sea, no enters there. what validity pitch soe'er, b falls into aba and low price in a minute.. of shapes is fa that it on a b of violets, ste and giving o Enough, no m 'Tis not so sw as iot was bef O spirit of lov How reathes a bank of vio stealing and r a quick and i art thou, tha

Love sought is good, but giv'n unsought is better.

music be the food of love, play on. Give me excess of it that, surfeiting, the appetite may sicken and so die. That strain again!

It had a dying fall. O, it came o'er my ear like the sweet sod that breathes upon a bank of violets, stealing and giving odor.

No more 'tis not so sweet now as it was before. O spirit of love! How quick and fresh art thou, that notwithstanding thy

H

capacity rece as the sea, n enters there. what validity pitch soe'er, b falls into aba and low pric in a minute.. of shapes is fr that it on a b of violets, ste and giving o Enough, no m 'Tis not so sw as iot was bef O spirit of lov How reathes a bank of vio stealing and r a quick and t art thou, tha

L

ove sought is good, but giv'n unsought is better.

music be the food of love, play on. Give me excess of it that, surfeiting, the appetite may sicken and so die. That strain again!

It had a dying fall. O, it came o'er my ear like the sweet sod that breathes upon a bank of violets, stealing and giving odor.

No more 'tis not so sweet now as it was before. O spirit of love! How quick and fresh art thou, that notwithstanding thy

1 This meat hook, which was embedded in the body at its discovery, is now in the Museo della Passo Pordoi 2 The massive valley is already at elevation and accessible to hikers by cable car 3 The remains were found in the cave at the foot of this cliff 4 This walking stick was placed beside the body 5 Saint Bernard of Montjoux points to the cave

The Paleoglaciologist
2nd Quarter

Love sought is good, but giv'n unsought is better

THE EYE

Crocker Motorcycle

A group caption describing several images forces the reader to match the words with the right picture. They perceive this as work. So be nice to the reader and make the numbers or other visual connecting cues visible and very easy to follow.

Reinvent every category of type you use. Captions can be much more than light smudges beneath pictures. They can be the primary type. For example, the "Ayers No.1" layout treats the headline as a caption, explaining the image. The order of information is a natural digression from most to least important.

is not unwise to follow, but it does have one requirement: you must have a supply of good images.

Relating pictures and captions Pictures and captions are inherently joined by meaning. We consider them a single entity. It is important to design a typographic system, to write a typographic recipe, that makes their connection immediately apparent. These are some ideas on caption/picture relationships:

⊡ A coherent typographic system includes positioning captions in regular places. Do not move them for arbitrary or capricious reasons.

⊡ Captions must be physically near the picture. If they do not actually touch — by overprinting or dropping out or mortising — they should not be more than half a pica to a full pica from the art.

⊡ Captions are ordinarily placed beneath a picture. Forcing readers to look elsewhere is fine if the caption can be found easily by, for example, increasing the contrast, or if the alternate position is necessary because the picture bleeds off the bottom of the page.

⊡ Leave at least one line space between a caption and its nearby text to avoid confusion between the two (*opposite,* **A**).

⊡ Connect the picture and caption by joining them on a central axis (*opposite,* **B**). If the caption is set justified, set the last line centered.

⊡ Set the caption to a comfortable-to-read, character-enhancing width (*opposite,* **C**). Match the full width of the picture only if the caption will not be too wide to be easily read. In any case, do not weaken the caption's alignment with the picture by indenting its first line.

⊡ Align a flush edge of the caption with one of the vertical edges of the picture (*opposite,* **D**).

⊡ Contrast rigid, highly structured pages with less formal caption settings (*opposite,* **E**). For example, set captions with one ragged edge with text that is justified. Do not hyphenate captions set in a ragged style. Leave space between the caption and text to increase visibility.

⊡ The caption can be dropped out of a box, which fully or partially overlaps the photo (*opposite,* **F**). This is called a *mortise.*

⊡ A photo can be cropped to make room for its caption (*opposite,* **G**). Cut away the part of the image that is *least* important or, if you are very daring, the *most* important part of the picture.

⊡ The caption's initial or first word can overlap the image (*opposite,* **H**). This is similar to a bold lead in: it highlights the first word as an especially visible element and acts as an umbilical cord between the picture and the rest of the caption.

⊡ Captions can be much more than light smudges beneath pictures. They can be the text or the primary

IN-STORE

Star Power

THE GLOBAL GOURMET ALAIN DUCASSE CHECKS OFF HIS SHOPPING LIST. SANDRA BALLENTINE REPORTS.

1. Alain Ducasse may be celebrated for his multi-starred cuisine, but his latest venture is all about wine. Not only is the dining room of Adour (scheduled to open in January) in New York's St. Regis Hotel surrounded by an open wine cellar, but there's also a state-of-the-art interactive tasting room that enables diners to project the details of a vintage onto their table. "New Yorkers have become much more interested in pairing food and wine, and this is a totally unique approach," the chef says.

2. Two of his pet picks are the 2004 Fombrauge, "an elegant and powerful wine from St. Emilion, a terroir known mainly for its reds," and the 2003 Pape Clément, "an absolute coup de coeur of mine." He would pair them both with his shellfish velouté, a mixture of clams, cuttlefish, squid and bread. "This is a dish that completely sums up Adour," he notes. "It can go with both a white and—unexpectedly—a red."

3. The chef has never met a vegetable he didn't like. In the fall, he combines porcini mushrooms with olive oil, a shallot and fleur de sel and roasts them in chestnut leaves for 20 minutes. "The smokiness of the leaves perfumes the whole." He sources his mushrooms from SOS Chefs of New York (www.sos-chefs.com), Mikuni Wild Harvest (www.mikuni wildharvest.com) and Mushrooms and More (914-692-7288).

4. His custom-made Goyard trunk took a year and a half to make and contains 50 of his favorite kitchen utensils, "everything from dish towels to a marble mortar and pestle." Go to www.goyard.com.

5. Ducasse collects limited-edition hats (about $200) by the Monte Carlo, Monaco-based designer and bespoke tailor Georges Feghaly. Call 011-377-97-97-87-40.

6. He just finished reading "La Trace" by Richard Collasse, the head of Chanel Japan. "I've been fascinated with Japanese culture for years, and the book really captures its nuances."

7. Adour features an enormous mural by the artist Nancy Lorenz. "It's stunning, with gold and lavender tones and real mother-of-pearl." For more information on Lorenz's work, go to www.james grahamandsons.com.

8. A longtime advocate of cooking with local ingredients, the chef also sources the handiwork of nearby artisans for his hotels and restaurants. This plate by Florine Asch, similar to ones used at La Bastide de Moustiers, his country inn in Provence (www. bastide-moustiers.com), is about $205 at Atelier Soleil in Moustiers Sainte Marie.

9. Ducasse cooks his carbs in this snazzy Patrick Jouin for Alain Ducasse pasta pot ($738 at www.alessi.com). (The pasta is cooked slowly with vegetables and stock, almost like risotto.) "At home, I use it to make oblatini with spinach and a four-cheese sauce."

10. On a rare weekend off, he unwinds with a hot stone massage at L'Andana, his hotel in Italy's Maremma region. "They have a thin lavender tart on the spa cuisine menu that pairs nicely with the treatment." Délicieux. Go to www.andana.it.

Houdini wine rack by Metrokane. $13. At Target. Go to www.target.com.

Infinity modular bottle rack by Ron Arad for Kartell. $73 for set of 16 modules. At Kartell, 39 Greene Street.

Setup wine rack by theseventhints for Koziol. $30. At the Conran Shop. Go to www.conranusa.com.

10 Cheap and Cheerful Bottle Picks from Jamie Wolff of Chambers Street Wines.

Hiedler, Kamptal Grüner Veltliner Loss 2006, $15.
Stadlmann, Thermenregion Rotgipfler 2006, $15.
Luneau-Papin, Sèvre et Maine Muscadet sur Lie Le L d'Or 2004, $16.
Cazin, François, Cour Cheverny Cuvée Renaissance 2004, $19.
Bart, Marsannay Grandes Vignes 2005, $20.
Monperthuis, Vin de Pays du Gard la Ramière Counoise 2005, $11.
Baudry, Chinon Les Granges 2006, $16.
Biondi, Guma Etna Bianco 2004, $20.
Zucchi, Lambrusco di Sorbara Rosato 2006, $14.
Montoni, Sicilia Nero d'Avola 2002, $13.

Go to www.chambersstwines.com.

Pile wine rack by Harry Allen for Areaware. $82. Go to www.areaware.com.

Black by Mikael Nilsson for Innermost Furniture. $45. At Clio wine bar and shop. Go to www.cliowines.com.

Bottle stackable wine rack by Jasper Morrison for Magis. $37. At Unica Home. Go to www.unicahome.com.

Cava wine rack by Lawrence Chu for the U+ Collection. $145. Go to www.umbra.com.

Oia wine rack by Hiroshi Tsunoda. $450. At Clio wine bar and shop. Go to www.cliowines.com.

The New Collectibles

SQUIRREL THESE AWAY. BY ANDREAS KOKKINO

BUBBLE ECONOMY
Put this sterling-silver Champagne saver from Mary's Garden into the neck of an open bottle of bubbly to prolong the fizz. $300. At Bergdorf Goodman.

UPMARKET
Be the coolest girl at the farmers' market with Fendi's Giant Chef Knitted Bag in "dreaded" wool. $5,040. At Fendi boutiques nationwide. Call (800) 336-3469.

GOLD IN BOWL
The Winterberry Bowl, from Kiln Enamel, is adorned with a removable branch of gold-plated brass with Pyrex glass berries. $565. At Bergdorf Goodman.

MOISTURIZER
With this plastic Humidifier V.3 from Plus Minus Zero, Naoto Fukasawa has turned a mundane appliance into a whimsical work of art. $279. At Compact Impact. Go to www.compact-impact.com.

RED DELICIOUS
This 10-inch chef's knife from the Italian company Coltellerie Berti is artisan-made and has a red Lucite handle, so even the most inexperienced sous-chef can chop with flair. $226. At Unica Home. Go to www.unicahome.com.

CATCHY
The carved metal Lace-Drain, by Joana Meroz for the Ornamented Life, adds a sink strainer that adds flower power to any kitchen or bathroom. $83. At Rose and Radish. Go to www.roseandradish.com.

LITTLE GULP
The stemmed Sommelier glass by Maxim Velcovsky for the Qubus design studio is a delicate take on the ubiquitous disposable plastic cup. $100 a pair. At MoMA Design Store SoHo, 81 Spring Street.

The New Collectibles

CALLING AHEAD
High tech meets retro styling in the limited-edition wireless Sophie phone from Hulger. $210. Go to www.hulger.com.

TALL ORDER
The hand-painted porcelain Sgraffito vase, by Anna Sykora for Calvin Klein Home, has a lean, Brancusi-like silhouette. $300. To order at Calvin Klein, 654 Madison Avenue.

MIXED MESSAGE
This doormat from the British company Suck UK says, "Come in"—or, when you turn it upside down, "Go away." $25. At Unica Home. Go to www.unicahome.com.

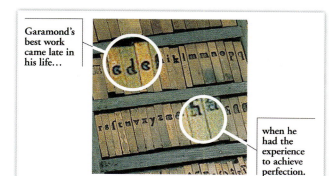

Garamond's best work came late in his life…

when he had the experience to achieve perfection.

Mr Guy wasn't sure he wanted the Doggles on *at first*, but he came to *insist* on them

Complex, compound captions can sometimes be broken into segments and distributed around a photo. Much like the labeling of exploded views, this treatment breaks long copy into bite-size pieces and encourages reading.

Regular-weight type is designed to be read on a white background, not on an image. When placing type in an image area, make the type sufficiently large and bold so that it stands out from the background, whether it is surprinted over in black or dropped out in white from the picture. You may also lighten the photo in a rectangle behind the caption.

typography. By far the most frequently used page layout in advertising is called the "Ayers No.1", after the N. W. Ayers advertising agency in New York, which developed it in the early 1900s. It features a picture on the top two-thirds of the page, a headline immediately beneath the picture, and text and logo at the bottom of the page. This layout has become ubiquitous because it is virtually invisible. It presents information in the most logical order and leaves the design vessel completely unnoticed, throwing all attention to the content itself. What is intriguing about the headline on an Ayers No.1 layout is that, though it is obviously the primary display typography, it acts as a caption, explaining the photo.

▣ Surround the picture and caption with a box. One of the elements may break out of the picture for a more dynamic effect; this is called a partial silhouette.

▣ Captions are usually set in a smaller or lighter version of the text type to help make them recede. Sometimes this smaller type is set across the full width of even the widest illustrations with no additional line spacing. Such lengthy lines are very difficult to read if the caption is longer than a single line. In such cases, open the line spacing or shorten the line length. Readers will bear up for two or three lines, but they will rebel and simply not read longer poorly set captions. Fifty characters per line is an oft-quoted standard, but captions allow greater flexibility than text, so the maximum characters per line can be increased to 60.

▣ Because captions attract interest, it may be desirable to make a whole story look like a caption or series of captions (*opposite*). To do this, you will need a series of photos, fairly short copy, and the willingness to leave some space empty to enhance the picture/caption "easy-read" approach. Here are three variations from a single issue: a four-column grid with the captions in the outer columns; a three-column grid divided into vertical thirds with all images sized to be about the same dimension; and the most free-form format that emphasizes the images on a central axis and irregular space on the perimeter.

▣ Superimposing a caption over a picture presents its own set of problems. It neither enhances the reality of the two-dimensional photo nor improves the type's readability because of the reduced contrast with the background. When superimposing a caption on a photo, place the type in an area of visual plainness. Putting type over a busy background makes it difficult to read.

The combined impact of well-chosen and well-cropped photos and creatively designed captions can coax the browser into becoming a reader. Together, they offer the browser the most compelling reason to become a reader.

SOURCE IT! | HOME FURNISHINGS

TRADE TIPS

New York's most renowned interior designers discuss how Tribeca delivers the goods on nearly every corner. BY AUDRA SHANLEY

Knowing that some of the most creative living spaces in New York are located steps above their sidewalks, Tribeca's shopkeepers marry business with nesting. Here, the storefront community counts more than 50 home design and antiques destinations, one of the largest concentrations locally.

"The key to Tribeca now is seeing it as vital beyond a moment in time," says Jeffrey Billhuber, one of the city's most respected designers. "Just as the Tribeca Film Festival started as a draw for the neighborhood and is now transformed into one of the most successful film festivals in the world, that is happening with the design community in the neighborhood."

While designers and home mavens alike can't go wrong discovering Tribeca's treasure troves, we've asked Billhuber and several of his well known colleagues to name the chart toppers that should start your trip. Tip: See www.tribeca.org for a printable map that pinpoints many stores.

✦ As principal of the 30 year old design firm that bears his name, **T. Keller Donovan** has a few old favorites in Tribeca, but "my new favorite store is **Just Scandinavian**, because they have a bright fresh mix of furniture, fabrics, and accessories." The designer just purchased a 1940s Bullseye mirror, designed by Josef Frank in blue matte lacquer—"which is totally classic and timeless but with a mid-century edge to it." The loftlike store is categorized by room settings so you can target what you need, although the gorgeous kitchen and dining wares may prove distracting. New York- and Miami-based T. Keller Donovan has participated in the Kips Bay Decorator Show House three times. *House Beautiful* has twice awarded him for best show house room; he has made the magazine's top designers list for 10 years. P.O. Box 598, New York, NY 10016; 212 760-0537. Just Scandinavian: 161 Hudson Street, New York, NY 10013; 212 334 2556; www.justscandinavian.com.

SCENES FROM A TRAWL Pass through Just Scandinavian (far left) and you may leave the proud owner of a High Corona chair (left). Other stops on a Tribeca shopping spree include R 20th Century (this page right and middle) and Burden & Izett (bottom).

SUMMER BEER

As the craft brewing industry continues to grow, it continues to get weirder, but in the best way possible. Beer is better than it's ever been, thanks to experimental hops, funky yeast strains, and a spirit of hackerlife ingenuity. It's not just craft, it's science. By Amy McKnight

SAISON ALES Saisons are sturdy farmhouse ales that were traditionally brewed in the winter, to be consumed throughout the summer months. Not so long ago it was close to being an endangered style, but over recent years there's been a massive revival. This is a very complex style; many are very fruity in aroma and flavor. Look for earthy yeast tones, mild to moderate tartness. Lots of spice and with a medium bitterness. They tend to be semi-dry with many only having a touch of sweetness.

INDIA PALE ALES The British Indian army was parched. Soaking through their khakis in the equatorial heat, they pined for real refreshment. These weren't the jolly days of ice-filled gin-and-tonics, lawn chairs and cricket. The first Brits to arrive were stuck with lukewarm beer—specifically dark, heavy, porter, the most popular brew of the day in chilly Londontown, but unfit for the tropics. One supply ship bound for Bombay was saved from wrecking in the shallows when its crew lightened it by dumping some of its cargo — no great loss, a newspaper reported, "as the goods consisted principally of some heavy lumbersome casks of Government porter."

SOUR BEERS Sour beer is beer which has an intentionally acidic, tart or sour taste. The most common sour beer styles are Belgian: lambics, gueuze and Flanders red ale. At one time, all beers were sour to some degree. As pure yeast cultures were not available, the starter used from one batch to another usually contained some wild yeast and bacteria. Unlike modern brewing, which is done in a sterile environment to guard against the intrusion of wild yeast, sour beers are made by intentionally allowing

wild yeast strains or bacteria into the brew. Traditionally, Belgian brewers allowed wild yeast to enter the brew naturally through the barrels or during the cooling of the wort in a coolship open to the outside air - an unpredictable process that many modern brewers avoid.

WHEAT BEERS Wheat beer is beer that is brewed with a large proportion of wheat relative to the amount of malted barley; it is usually top-fermented. Two common varieties of wheat beer are Weißbier (German - "white beer") based on the German tradition of mixing at least 50% wheat to barley malt to make a light colored top-fermenting beer, and witbier (Dutch - "white beer") based on the Belgian tradition of using flavorings such as coriander and orange peel. Belgian white beers are often made with raw unmalted wheat, as opposed to the malted wheat used in other varieties. Other minor wheat beer styles are Berliner Weiße, Gose, and lambic are made with a significant proportion of wheat.

LIGHTER ALES Ales are a type of beer that is light in color and does not contain as much alcohol as other, typically darker, beers. Bitter is an English term for pale ale. Bitters vary in color from gold to dark amber and in strength from 3% to 7% alcohol by volume. Bitter belongs to the pale ale style and can have a great variety of strength, flavor and appearance from dark amber to a golden summer ale. It can go under 3% ABV - known as Boys Bitter - and as high as 7% with premium or strong bitters. The color may be controlled by the addition of caramel coloring. Light ale is a low ABV bitter, often bottled

Headlines are primary typography

Subheads are secondary typographic elements

Speak the speech, I pray you, as I pronounced it to you, trippingly on the tongue. But if you mout mouth it, many of your players, I had as the town crier speak my lines. No do not saw the air awfully much your hand, thus. But use all gentl in the very torrent, tempest, and I may say, whirlwind of passion, must acquire and beget a tempera

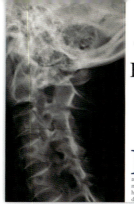

The Elliptical Bone Staircase

Sweeping in one continuous flight from floor to floor found favor, especially in the most spatially-restricted areas

In the beginning of the nineteenth century, the end of the Roman influence and its inspiring force of Renaissance architecture was observed. It is a credit to the English qualities of good sense and self respect that the tendency to extremes which marks the later phases on the Continent gained no hold. in that country. The last phase of the classic tradition, known as the Regency style, remarkable for

your hand, so thus. But use all gently for in the very torrent, tempest, and as I may say, whirlwind of passion, you must acquire and beget a temperate tongue. But if you mouth it, as many of your players do, I had as lief the town crier speak my lines.

Breaker heads are inserted into running text

Do not saw the air awfully much with your hand, thus. But use all gently for in the very torrent, tempest, and as I may say, whirlwind of passion, you must acquire and beget a temperance But if you mouth it, as many of your players do, I had as lief the town crier speak my lines. Put gently your players

---

External subheads are primarily *decks*, which appear immediately below the headline and further explain both the headline and the content of the story.

Another external subhead is the *floating subhead*, so named because it is placed in the margin. The placement of a floating subhead is extremely flexible, with the important

requirement that the subhead be perceived as second in the three-level readership hierarchy of headline/captions to subhead to text.

A third kind of subhead is the *breaker head*, which breaks text into appealing chunks. Position the breaker closer to the text beneath it, to which it naturally belongs.

Secondary display type

Subheads Subheads convinces the reader to continue by explaining the headline. Headlines should convey enough to stop a reader but they often do not contain enough information to give the reader a reason to start directly into the text. A well-written subhead explains its headline and intrigues the reader into continuing on to the next level of information. Headlines that lead to subheads that then lead to text are more effective than headlines that lead directly to text; the reader wants information before committing himself to beginning the text, which takes time to read and is work.

Subheads are considered *secondary* typographic elements (*opposite, top*). They are read *after* the headline and captions but *before* the text. Copy should be broken into three levels: primary information should be in the headlines and captions, secondary clarifying and illuminating information should be in subheads or decks, and tertiary (third-level) information should be in the text.

This basic structure can be varied somewhat. For example, subheads can be replaced by pull quotes or breakouts, or captions can be intended as the primary typography since they are often read immediately. Generally, however, the headline/subhead/text hierarchy is the norm because it serves the reader well with its familiarity based on sound logic.

The unending visual variety of subheads can be classified into two basic forms: "external" subheads that appear outside the text area and "internal" subheads that appear within it.

External subheads that are near the headline are called "*decks*" (*opposite, bottom*). External subheads that are away from the headline and outside the text column are called "*floating subheads*."

Internal subheads are placed within the text column to break up the text. These so-called *breaker heads* are brief synopses of the following paragraphs of text and, as such, should be provocatively written to catch the eye of the casual browser who perhaps managed to avoid being drawn in by the lead headline.

⊡ Using punctuation at the ends of breaker heads creates a tiny pause in the reader's mind, giving a reason not to continue into the text. Do not punctuate there!

⊡ Lead-ins are breaker heads in that they interrupt the text and give the casual browser an entrance into the article (*opposite, bottom*). Choose provocative wording for a lead-in, or the result will be the same as an inherently meaningless initial cap: a mere focal point on which the eye may land (which is still better than endless uninterrupted grayness confronting the reader).

⊡ Breaker heads should generally have a half a line space added above it, not a full line space. A full line

verily I smile and say, with great cunning, "This is no flattery."

Flush left, no indent
Hath not old custom made this life more sweet than that of painted pomp? Are not these woods more free from peril than

Bold lead in
Bold lead in Hath not old custom made this life more sweet than that of painted pomp? Are not these woods more free from peril than the envious court? He

Deep indent with text
Hath not old custom made this life more sweet than that of painted pomp? Are not these woods more free from peril than

Hanging indent
Hath not old custom made this life more sweet than that of painted pomp? Are not these woods more free from peril than

Hanging indent lead in
Hanging indent lead in Hath not old custom made this life more sweet than that of painted pomp? Are not these woods more free from peril than the en-

Breaker with a rule
Hath not old custom made this life more sweet than that of painted pomp? Are not these woods more free from peril than

BREAKER HEAD IN A BOX
Hath not old custom made this life more sweet than that of painted pomp? Are not these woods more free from peril than

This flush left breaker head pokes into the text Hath not old custom made this life more sweet than that of painted pomp? Are not these woods more free from peril than the envious court? Here feel we safe from

THIS CENTERED SUBHEAD POKES HALF IN AND HANGS HALF OUT
Hath not old custom made this life more sweet than that of painted pomp? Are not these woods more free from peril than the en-vious court? Here feel we safe from peril than the

have ventur'd like little wanting child thick upon him. The third day here comes a frost, a killing frost.

Breaker heads that run longer than one or two lines interrupt the text's flow
When he thinks, good easy man, full surely his greatness is aripening, nips his root, and then he falls, as I do. I have ventur'd like little wanting child

his root, and then he falls, as I do. I have ventur'd like little wanting child thick upon him. The third day here comes a frost, a killing frost.

USE 2nd COLOR IN BREAKER HEADS
When he thinks, good easy man, full surely his greatness is aripening, nips his root, and then he falls, as I do. I have ventur'd like little wanting child

his root, and then he falls, as I do. I have ventur'd like little wanting child thick upon him. The third day here comes a frost, a killing frost.

Lead ins
Lead ins are entrances into the text. When he thinks, good easy man, full surely his greatness is aripening, nips his root, and then he falls, as I do. I have ventur'd like little wanting child thick

his root, and then he falls, as I do. I have ventur'd like little wanting child thick upon him. The third day here comes a frost, a killing frost. *[12pts / 18pts]*

Add half a linespace
When he thinks, good easy man, full surely his greatness is aripening, nips his root, and then he falls, as I do. I have ventur'd like little wanting child

his root, and then he falls, as I do. I have ventur'd like little wanting child thick upon him. The third day here comes a frost, a killing frost.

Position a breaker head closer to the copy that follows than to the preceding text
When he thinks, good easy man, full surely his greatness is aripening, nips his root, and then he falls, as I do. I have ventur'd like little wanting child thick upon him. The third day here

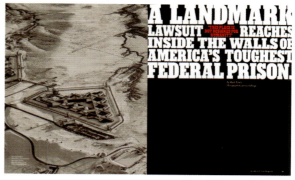

Subheads can take any shape as long as it is recognized as secondary to the primary type, or headline. The form of the subhead in this example is repeated in the byline, creating a rhythm — with enormous help from the two generous word spaces between the three words in the primary type — and design unity.

Carefully written primary and secondary type can be read in either order. A subhead doesn't have to be smaller than the headline — the primary type — if the reading order is clear. Here the dramatic use of color contrast and centered placement makes the red primary type most visible.

space looks too big, chopping the column into segments.

☐ Breaker heads describe the copy they precede. They should therefore be positioned closer to the text they describe — the text that follows — than to the text before them. That proximity signals to the reader that the breaker head describes the following text.

Like headlines, subheads have great potential for effective communication: they help convert a browser into a reader.

Breakouts Breakouts are brief extracts of particularly provocative text. They should be thought of as verbal illustrations that draw the reader into a story. Graphically, they should be highly visible — in strong contrast with their surroundings — and able to easily attract the reader's attention. A potent breakout will give the reader who is casually wandering around a reason to stop and become involved with a story. A subgroup of breakouts are pull quotes, which are brief direct quotes.

Breakouts were invented to solve a particular problem: how to slow or stop a casual reader who is not yet actively reading an article. The solution: enlarge a brief portion that is most likely to make the reader stop and reconsider the article in its entirety.

Breakouts do more than trumpet the most arresting segment of an article. Because they are meant to be read before the text, breakouts also provide an opportunity for typographic preening and experimentation. Their use leads to an over-all elevation of a publication's visual and typographic presentation.

To catch the reader's attention, the breakout must contrast strongly with the surrounding text.

☐ Increase the type size. Use the same font and weight as the text type but enlarge it at least 33% to stand out sufficiently. Surround this size-only contrast with a moat of white space.

☐ Increase the type weight. Make the breakout bolder than the text, or really pump it up by making it bigger and bolder. Experiment by making the text bold and the breakout lighter. Either will work, so long as sufficient contrast exists between areas of type.

☐ Change the color. Run the breakout in a second color or drop it out of a panel of color.

☐ Create an unusual column structure. Eccentric, or uneven, columns are a provocative means of separating kinds of information. If your publication can accommodate eccentric columns — on an opener or because it does not run ads — consider using the narrower column or columns for breakouts. Clear rules for their use must be developed and followed. For example, text may be put in wider columns while breakouts, headlines, and captions go in narrower columns. When using narrow columns, allow the leftover white space to surround the breakout. It

Dangerous Ideas on Design Education

A Manifesto by James Victore

I learned to design the same way I learned to swear: I had to pick it up in the street. I failed out of a university and was asked to leave a design school. But as destiny would have it, I've spent the last 20 years teaching in the class-room, running my own work-shops and lecturing around the world, and I've developed my own ideas about how to teach design, encourage creativity and even inspire creative courage.

...tion's merits or ... an "I" if I were king of ... scathing account ... all wrong; there are ... hothouses of ex-... on the whole has ... s of schooling and ..." as Bob Dylan said), ... different. My own pur-... always been to help ... d creative individuals ... My job is to make it ... high bar. I ask them ... mselves, then make ... ve in those answers. ... ly that they will not ... tition, their gut in ... xciting work. My ... d I don't care.

... d and an idealist. ... s us because good ... e freedom in some-... en we see intelligent ... as smarter; and ... when we see vulnerability in the work we feel closer, more human.

Many of my peers see this as dangerous—I am the fox in Pinocchio, leading the good little boys and girls off to a life in the circus. "But however will they find a JOB?!" they ask. When pushed to invite danger into their work, my students find something much better than a job—they learn to create their own place in this world. I want them to learn to embrace danger. Danger requires bravery. It requires us to risk everything, to do our best work, embrace failure and leave it all on the track.

Herein are a few dangerous ideas about design education.

Weird is good.

Students are attracted to design in the first place because they see the world in a different way, slightly askew. They are weird. Most of them have heard this many times in their lives—and it was not intended as a compliment. But Weird is good; it's an anomaly and it's unique. I teach on the simple premise that the things that made you weird as a

kid make you great as an adult—but only if you pay attention to them. If you look at any "suc-cessful" person, they are probably being paid to play out the goofiness or athleticism or nerdiness or curiosity they already possessed as a child. Unfortunately for most people, somewhere along the road their weirdness was taught out of them or, worse, shamed out of them. Crushed by the need to "fit in," they left their quirks and spe-cial powers behind. But it is our flaws that make us interesting. We need to not only hang on to them, but hone them. I don't try to make my students "Designers." I want to make them "free-er." It's my job to teach them to look inside, to covet their weirdness, to help them direct it and take the rough edges off—or even add a few new ones. It's my job to help students understand and cultivate their individuality and innate weird-ness and turn them into a powerful tool. Weird is good, but only if we put it in your work.

Design is not math. This is what makes the work hard. There are no right answers and very few wrong answers. I've always thought of design more as an innate skill set that we are born with—a small ember waiting to be coaxed into a larger flame. What I see as problematic is when we teach design as if it is something outside of us. As if the students are in an assembly line holding empty shoe boxes, waiting for them to be filled with rules and theories and Photoshop. These tools are important, but they will only get you so far. I don't believe design can be "taught," but rather that it can be "reminded." We need to remind students to use what they already have inside: their history, their loves, their fears. We have to teach students how to use their brains, to make their senses of association and imag-ery sharp and flexible and urge them to seek their own way and express their individuality. We have to push them to think for themselves, form an opinion—and know that their opinions matter. Essentially, we have to "teach" them to be themselves and put it in their work.

In my classroom, the first crit question is always, "What do YOU think?" A student's explanation of her work may start, "When I was a kid, my dad took me to the beach, where we collected stones. . ." "Brilliant! This is relat-able. When you do a good job of telling your

story, your fears, your loves, I see my story, my fears, my loves. Your particular story has meaning to a wider audience. So I spur my students to look inside for answers, not to constantly look outside and drown in a sea of reference materials or look for regurgitated, ready-made answers. They never have to make up a story. They have the story and need only look inside. This frees them from being in the people-pleasing business—looking over their

shoulders for a "popular" answer. Thus, they avoid the world's worst question—"What do THEY want?"—and they understand that the far better question is, "What do I have to say?"

Through this process they learn what others respond to in their work. This trains them to learn who their audience is. They learn that their audience is not me, nor the other students nor other designers, and certainly not onanist

(look it up) design competitions. They answer that their job is not to try to appeal to everyone (a patently impossible task) but to tell THEIR story and find THEIR audience. Ultimately, they'll get paid for it. The more we love what we do, the better off the field will be.

Weird is good; it's an anomaly and it's unique. I teach on the simple premise that the things that made you weird as a kid make you great as an adult—but pay attention to them.

Humans Come Before Design.

After I was asked to leave design school, I began interning for one of my professors, a prolific book-jacket designer named Paul Bacon. Paul worked on his art in a little apartment and paint like a genius. But what he taught me about was wine and auto racing and well-told jokes, and he inspired in me a love of jazz. With these passions and a few of my own, I realized that I had every-thing I needed to be a successful designer.

Most of my college students jumped straight out of high school into a design degree. Personally, I think this is crazy because people. You don't know shit. As a teacher, I am searching for interesting, qualified people. In order to teach you to be a designer, I have to first ensure that

---

My best students have always been the ones who failed some other course of study or life choice—because they carry with them the fire of that experience.

you're a compassionate, curious, intelligent being. I hope that one of you has done some time, or you have traveled, struggled or had children. Once you've suffered, strug-gled or experienced the responsibility of access to the public. My best stu-dents have always been the ones who failed some other course of study or life choice—because they carry with them the fire of that experience. Their peripheral vision is stronger; they can pull from their outside sources, interests and experiences beyond graphic design. I believe in taking a wider view. I think we should encourage everything else, and then design.

... Fuck specialization in branding or advertis-ing. Most branding is cookie-cutter boring, made by specialists. The obsessive concern with the intricacies of any tiny branch of design proves a myopic point of view. You know a lot about a little. I understand the importance of learning the complex rules of typography, but it's like hygiene—know about it, but don't obsess over it. Specializing is something a student should learn or be drawn to on their own. What makes a good designer is how they think. My students' inter-ests in cartography or magic tricks or motorcycle repair makes them better, more interesting and stronger. The best designers are interesting peo-ple first. Smart, funny and curious. Learn every-thing. Then forget it. THEN design.

Creativity Can Be Killed.

Creativity and business do not always make the best fit. Creativity seeks the "New"—new tools, new ways of doing and seeing things. But new is not always welcome. In fact, "new" is generally accepted only after it's been accepted. In any form, whether it's fashion, music, culture, even product—"new" is seen as a threat to the status quo. Design is no different.

Business is the opposite of creativity. Business wants tried-and-true. Business wants safety. Business would like to be creative, but only after the value of that creativity has been proven. Business likes to be in second place because first place is dangerous.

As educators we want to do our students a ser-vice, understanding that they'll accrue debt and need to make a living. In order to make their parents happy and shield our young charges from financial failure, we teach to-the-business. We teach cowardice. In order to get a "job," students are taught that No. 1 is "Please the Client." Newly weighed down by the practical-ities of making other people happy in order to get paid, students lose sight of themselves and the reason they started out on this path. We all

Joseph Campbell put it, "I think the person who takes a job in order to live—that is to say, for the money—has turned himself into a slave." I want students who have a vision and keep their eyes fixed on that goal to avoid getting waylaid along their path.

The problems start down the road. On my You-Tube channel "Burning Questions," we often find ourselves answering queries from mid-career designers who have lost their way, unsatisfied by the doldrums of creating color-corrected, accept-able work. They were conditioned to leave the "creative" part of the business out, and replace it with the merely "clever"—well-behaved little ideas that match the carpet and are so bland that they can pass through a focus group's anus un-scathed. Boring work that succeeds for the mere fact that it offends the fewest number of people.

My first and main concern is to foster confident, creative individuals that the world cannot ignore. It's my job to urge their spark into a flame—to make their worlds larger, not smaller. Design means to see the potential of human-to-human communication, the power of images and the strength in their opinion and personal-ity. It car-ries—the freedom from "making shit up." Smaller means catering to the whims of a client, giving what other people want.

Of course I want my students to be extremely well-paid for their work, but what my students do with their flame, the commercial application of their own damn business. Whether their highest esteem is to pay rent or to shoot for greatness is up to them. It is not the teacher's role to preen students for cubicles and fluorescent lighting, but to prepare them for the longer road. Over prepare them for careers 10 and 15 years down the road. In a field populated more and more by MBAs with color swatches, I push my students for creativity. I want to fill them up with a myriad of creative possibilities—not the correct, logical and marketable answers. As educators, we need to push for experimentation, risk and failure, not supply a safety net and easy access to a 401(k).

their path.

Know that not all clients deserve your attention. Designers are not one-size-fits-all.

Ask the questions. Why are we doing this? What are we contributing to the world?

Have boundaries. Be able to say NO and to never learn the taste of shit.

Ask for More—more time, creativity and always more money.

Learn about money management.

Enjoy your work and the process.

If you don't enjoy it, how can you expect anyone else to?

It is not the teacher's role to preen students for cubicles and fluorescent lighting, but to prepare them for the longer road, to prepare them for careers 10 and 15 years down the road.

Your Work Is a Gift.

The biggest ideal I can try to get my students to understand is that their work is a Gift. This is a fairly abstract idea. When your work is a Gift, it changes how you think about it. It changes why you make what you make and even who you work for. When your work is a Gift, your goal is no lon-ger to please a boss or client—or even to gain a following. You now work to make yourself happy, and you speak directly to your audience be-cause you give them something of value: a piece of you. Designers should understand that this is how they'll be paid best: to be themselves.

What motivates and excites the world is to witness one person, engaged, energized and empowered. This is the path to creativity. This is the way to great work. And ultimately, this is what makes us attractive to clients.

What I propose is a difficult and dangerous path, but then again, my ideas are not for everyone. Just the sexy people. ●

James Victore is a graphic artist, author... Described as "part Darth Vader, part..." Victore is known for his timely wisdom and... and views about design and its place in... He teaches thousands with his weekly... awesome video series, delivers life cha... around the world, and leads Avant-Garde ch... help creative types of all spheres live and... At the helm of his independently run... Victore continually strives to reinforce that... is sexy, strong and memorable, work that... between the sacred and the profane... at the School of Visual Arts in New... 20 years.

A breakout is a short segment of the text that is repeated as display type. It's purpose is to cause a reader to pause and consider engaging with the text, where the full story is.

Pull quotes are a subcategory of breakouts: they are both concise extracts from the text. Making them extremely visible (*here and on opposite page*) is necessary.

Pull quotes are breakouts that trumpet provocative statements made by others. The more provocative the quote, the better: the purpose of pull quotes is to catch passing readers. They are typically signalled with pronounced quote marks, giving the ideas attribution to someone other than the article's author.

is not an extravagant use of paper, but an excellent way of creating a coherent hierarchy on the page.

⊡ Use a display initial. The greater the contrast with the surrounding type, the better. It is almost impossible to overdo it. Found letterforms or objects (reproduced on a copier) make especially unusual, eye-catching initials and can be chosen for their relationship to the subject of the story, thereby enhancing the communicative quality of the breakout.

⊡ Add rules. Rules are visible because they are inherently directional and because they are usually darker than other elements on the page. If heavy enough, the rule creates a useful and unavoidable focal point. Add a rule when a light breakout does not pop off the page.

⊡ Use box rules. These can be embellished to impart a unique character. Be careful not to overuse boxes: they tend to deaden a page and repel readers.

⊡ Surround the breakout with white space. Leave sufficient white space on all four sides, or you may camouflage it amid the textual underbrush. Leave from a half to a full line space above and below and a couple of characters of width on each side but, as always, *optical spacing* is the ultimate determinant.

⊡ Put the breakout inside a shape. Choose a shape that relates to the story's subject, or use a shape that echoes an element in one of the story's pictures.

Using any one of these techniques alone can deliver great results. Adroitly combining two or more of these techniques will create highly visible, unique display type, bound to catch a browser's fickle attention.

⊡ Do not position a breakout too close to its appearance in the text. Readers are looking for the context of the extract. If they find it too easily, they may not read the rest of the piece.

⊡ Insert a breakout in the middle — never at the end —– of a paragraph. This helps the reader read past the breakout by indicating that the text continues.

⊡ A breakout can be one of the most important typographic elements on a page. Do not bury it on the less visible bottom third of the page.

⊡ Combining a distinctive breakout and headline treatment for each feature story clearly tells the reader which pages belong together. It gives a consistency that should be instantly recognizable, especially if the story must be interrupted by advertising pages.

⊡ Finally, it is very important to write breakouts to be as short as possible — two brief sentences or less. Breakouts must be scannable without effort. Long breakouts of three or more sentences dissuade the reader from nibbling. It's simply too big a taste test. The point is to interest, not necessarily to inform. The text carries the information, but the reader must be lured to it.

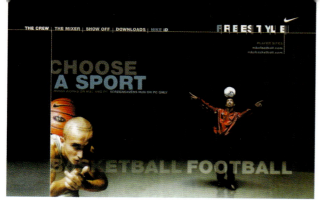

(*Opposite*) If a store window doesn't show products people want in a way they will notice, *they won't come inside where the goods* are to make a purchase. So it is with covers: if the cover does not appeal to the reader's self-interest or arouse their sense of immediacy, they will not make it inside. These three covers are successful at providing reasons to enter the issue.

Web (*above left*) and magazine design both use the same tools to achieve a balance between design contrast and similarity: contrast of typography, position, spatial separation, and color.

Two cover alternatives are a "gatefold" for exceptional horizontal images and a "short sheet," which is used for coverlines while retaining the cover art's unblemished righteousness.

Wayfinding display type

Covers and home pages Covers and home pages have a great deal in common: both are uniquely important real estate. A cover and a home page immediately identify the publication or site. Both deserve a distinctive look and both must promise worthwhile well-organized information within. A home page is a bit more complex than a magazine cover: it must also serve as a linked table of contents.

A typical magazine cover's shape is vertical. Using the top for the most important information and working downward is a convention that is used to define hierarchy. A newspaper's most valuable space is on the front page "above the fold," where the paper is most readily seen. Web pages need to be horizontal to fit computer monitors. On web pages, hierarchy is expressed through presence on the first part of the screen that loads, the part that does not require scrolling to be seen. Scrolling reduces readership by about half. Some web designers refuse to use scrolling and prefer to put such additional information on a subsequent linked page.

Until the late 16th century when printed material remained very rare, alluring covers were unnecessary. The very *existence* of a document was reason enough to take time to read and absorb it. Communication today is so plentiful that we must control how much of it will get our attention. It is therefore vital to be able to indicate immediately the value, or at least the *kind* of information, contained in a design. Announcing information with style and immediacy are what cover design is all about.

Covers create expectation in the reader. They lure the reader into browsing through the inside pages. They supply a sample of what is to come that engenders a sense of needing to *know now*.

A cover establishes identity from issue to issue (while simultaneously signaling a new issue) and claims mental territory distinct from its competition. Both a home page and cover must communicate a sense of urgency and worth. They must fascinate, tease, and involve, and they must relate visually to the pages within.

When designing a cover or home page, four elements — all equally important — must be kept in balance: format, logo, visual, and cover lines.

▣ **Format** Shape and size, use of a frame, texture, weight, thickness — all these establish recognition and continuity. A standardized cover format creates history, value, confidence, trust, and loyalty. ▣ Advertising sizes dictate inside page size, which in turn dictates the size and shape of the cover. But some publications have moved away from tradition and produce square or tall or wide formats. ▣ A gatefold cover can be a powerful attractant if used correctly. Be sure the gatefold's story un-

LOGO

11/18

Primary
cover line
relates to
the image

Cover line
stacked
here

Flush left
cover line

Third cover
line

LOGO

NOV
18

■ Primary cover line relates
to the image and appears
most important on page

■ Flush
left
cover line

■ Cover line
stacked
here

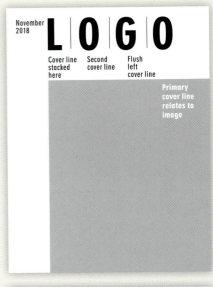

November
2018

L|O|G|O

Cover line
stacked
here

Second
cover line

Flush
left
cover line

Primary
cover line
relates to
image

LOGO

Nov
2018

Primary
cover line
relates to
the image

Cover line
stacked
here

Third
cover line

Flush
left
cover line

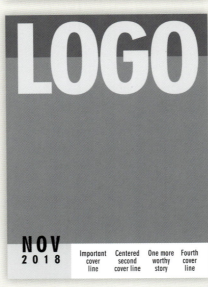

LOGO

NOV
2018

Important
cover
line

Centered
second
cover line

One more
worthy
story

Fourth
cover
line

Cover line
stacked here

Important
second story

LOGO

2018

NOV

LO GO

Nov
06

Cover line
stacked
here

Flush
left
cover line

Primary
cover line
relates to
the image

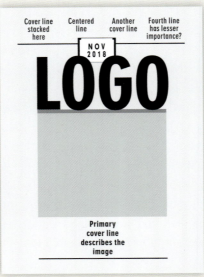

Cover line
stacked
here

Centered
line

Another
cover line

Fourth line
has lesser
importance?

NOV
2018

LOGO

Primary
cover line
describes the
image

Cover line
stacked
here

Flush
left
cover line

Primary
cover line
relates to
the image

LOGO

Nov
18

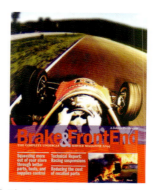

The logo says who you are. The symbol must have character, be applied consistently on all printed and online materials, and it should be closely related to the department headings.

The logo doesn't need to be at the head of the cover if it isn't going to be on a newsstand. Reduce clutter by integrating the issue date and secondary information with the logo.

A special issue calls for a special treatment: the logo and cover lines are drawn in barbecue sauce and photographed on site at the restaurant for this annual issue.

All-type — and in this case die cut — covers are recognized as being special because they are so rare. Using letterforms as imagery sends a compelling, attention-demanding signal.

folds as the cover is opened. Intrigue readers by showing half the image, with the visual "punchline" on the second, inside, panel. ⊡ A frame around the page can become a recognizable and memorable design device. *Time*'s red border is so recognizable it can be purchased printed on mirrors. Similarly, *National Geographic* is known for its yellow border, which is used on nearly all marketing pieces and correspondence as well as on the cover of the magazine. ⊡ To avoid a me-too look, consider an eccentric, off-center border or a partial border. Be sure to leave sufficient border to disguise crooked trimming; ¼ inch is usually the minimum. ⊡ The heft of a publication is usually indicative of its success. It signals the amount of advertising the publication can attract — many magazines gain weight in the two months before Christmas and go on a crash diet in January for lack of advertising pages. *Sports Illustrated*'s swimsuit issue is one of their fattest because advertisers know that particular issue will attract many readers. ⊡ Many publications' covers are printed with an ultra violet (UV) coating to make them shiny and more tactile. UV coating is a protective, ultra-shiny coating that hardens under UV light. It imparts a sense of quality and substance to a publication, to which readers seem to respond. ⊡ Some magazine covers are enclosed by a second, uncoated sheet that is sometimes cut narrower than the cover. On it are printed

cover lines or special messages (for example, "This is your last issue!"). ⊡ Some publications are printed on unusually textured stock or use colored paper or paper with visible additions (little hairs, for example). All these add to the immediate recognizability of the publication.

⊡ **Logo** The publication's title defines who you are. The symbol must have character and be applied consistently everywhere. ⊡ To enable readers to find a publication on a crowded newsstand, the logo must be the dominant element. It should also be dominant if good visual material is not always available. ⊡ If a publication is not sold at a newsstand, the logo doesn't need to be run at the top of the cover. Indeed, the logo does not even need to be horizontal. Marvelous personality and easy-to-execute flexibility can be created by developing a system in which the logo can be placed in any of half a dozen positions, depending on the shape, quality, and internal composition of the visual elements.

⊡ **Visual** or **imagery** The twin purposes of a cover illustration (a term that includes both drawings and photos) are to be noticed and to pull the reader inside. Drawings allow a wider range of graphic techniques than photos and lend themselves to showing concepts, ideas, and humor. Photos, on the other hand, are more believable because they are more realistic. Beauty for its own sake — using either artform — may be admirable, but it

The New York Times Magazine

(VS. ROMNEY + STALLED ECONOMY = 17% CHANCE OF AN OBAMA VICTORY

So, Is Obama Toast?
THE 2012 FORECAST BY NATE SILVER

1. HIS ...
2. THE G.D.P.
3. HOW EXTREME THE REPUBLICAN NOMINEE IS

WHAT HE FEARS:
A STALLED ...MY

WHAT HE NEEDS
4% ECONOMIC

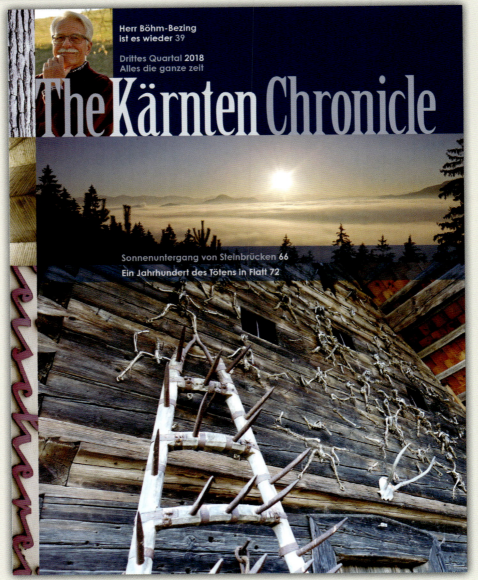

Herr Böhm-Bezing
ist es wieder 39

Drittes Quartal **2018**
Alles die ganze zeit

The Kärnten Chronicle

Sonnenuntergang von Steinbrücken **66**

Ein Jahrhundert des Tötens in Flatt **72**

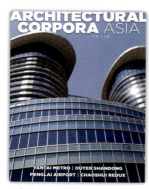

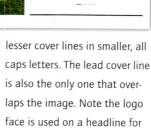

A full-bleed image implies a window to another plane. Particularly on a cover, that is a compelling suggestion of excitement within.

Cover lines use contrasting treatments to indicate the primary story: this cover story is set in larger, upper and lower case, high stroke contrast letterforms to differentiate it from the

lesser cover lines in smaller, all caps letters. The lead cover line is also the only one that overlaps the image. Note the logo face is used on a headline for the publication's *design unity*.

The cover lines, run on a grid at the bottom of the cover, on this daily Austrian newspaper, which is designed like a magazine throughout.

will not necessarily increase reader interest (*opposite, above*). ⊡ Bleeding an image makes it more dynamic by implying continuation. Bleeding on all four sides of the page makes an image look much larger — so large, in fact, that it appears *uncontainable on the page*. But full-bleed photos require an area of relative blandness in color and texture to provide space for cover lines. If no such background field exists, the cover lines should be "mortised" in an area of screen tint color. ⊡ Although reader interest is highest when a cover contains a single focal point, it is sometimes worthwhile to have two pictures on a cover (*opposite, below*). One should be considerably larger, telling the reader that it is more important. A partially silhouetted primary image with the secondary image placed beneath the logo provides a flexible system. ⊡ Readers respond particularly well to pictures of other people. Because portraits look alike, covers with them should be distinguished by printing an area in a distinctive color, including a secondary, non-person image, or changing the color of the logo. ⊡ Many feature stories concern trends or ideas, which must be conveyed by the cover. Use a visual symbol that is not a cliché yet is understandable. A concept cover must be more than a visual pun; it must address and illuminate the meaning of the lead article.

⊡ **Cover lines** These provocations provide other

reasons to pick up an issue. While imagery initially attracts readers, well-written cover lines catch more readers. ⊡ Cover lines persuade readers to pick up a publication by providing several "appeals." A magazine cover that has just one image and one headline will not attract all readers: no matter how important the subject being shown, some readers will fail to respond. Instead of gambling on one idea to bring in the crowds, give the reader a selection of great reasons to pick up the issue and open it. ⊡ Loyal readers, those who already find value in a publication or website and make time to read it thoroughly, will read anyway. It is the *casual reader* for whom cover lines are a necessity. ⊡ The primary cover line describes the main visual, so it must at once be similar to other typography on the cover and act as a caption to the picture. ⊡ If cover lines are to be superimposed on imagery, sans serif type is easier to read and has greater weight when reversing out of an image. Sufficient contrast between type and background must exist or cover lines will be illegible. ⊡ The more sophisticated and upscale the publication, the more restrained the typography should be. ⊡ Repeat the wording of the cover lines precisely on the contents page and on the opening page of each story. It's a reward readers expect for having found the referenced page.

Contents

Contents

---

dl | Big Screen

The Questions

We take a look at the coming month's movies and make it easy for you. By Zac Crain

Shrek the Third
Who: Mike Myers, Cameron Diaz, Eddie Murphy
Even Money
Who: Kelly Scofield, Nick Cannon, Kelsey Grammer
Mr. Brooks
Who: Kevin Costner, Demi Moore, Dane Cook
Pirates of the Caribbean: At World's End
Who: Keira Knightley, Orlando Bloom, Johnny Depp

Hot Rod
Who: Andy Samberg, Ian McShane, Sissy Spacek
Knocked Up
Who: Katherine Heigl, Seth Rogen, Leslie Mann, Paul Rudd
Fay Grim
Who: Parker Posey, Jeff Goldblum, Saffron Burrows

SEPTEMBER
Contents

SEPTEMBER
Contents

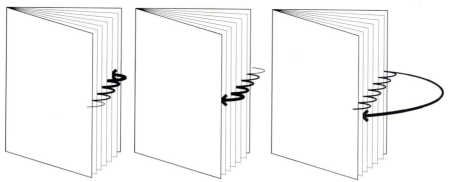

(*Opposite*) Contents pages can be type dominant, as at the top, or image dominant, as at the bottom. If images are used, show same-size details of images as teasers. Photos may be

neatly organized vertically up the side or horizontally across the page's top or bottom, or placed in a seemingly random pattern to contrast with structured type. It is essential that

the headlines and images on the contents page be exactly the same as on story openers so readers know when they have found the article they are turning to.

Contents listings can be put on the cover by simply adding page numbers to the cover lines. This is the fastest way to expedite readers directly inside the issue.

Contents pages There are three ways to read a publication, front to back, back to front, and browse quickly through the issue before returning to the contents page (*see above*). There are two ways to enter and navigate a website, from the home page in and from the page you landed on back to the home page for, among other things, the contents listing. When readers work back to front of a magazine because they enjoy checking regular sections before the feature stories, they are satisfied to discover stories as they progress toward the front of the publication. Readers who work from front to back, on the other hand, are more apt to pause at the contents page for an overview of what the issue contains before leafing through it. They prefer to discover the issue in the order the editors have presented it.

Navigational graphics are wayfinding tools that are equivalent to a magazine's folios, footlines, and department headings. As such, they are a significant part of the site's identity. Like folios, footlines, and department headings, navigational tools must be useful and should be given consistent treatment. Providing constant accessibility to the home page from any other page at the site is essential.

Because the contents page is often read after a preliminary scan of the issue, it provides the reader with a second chance to discover an article. The contents page should therefore present the same article titles, summaries, and images as appealingly and intriguingly as possible. This is very important: if a reader decides an item on the contents page is worthwhile, they have been seduced by the pictures and words on the contents page and will be looking for them. When they get to the story opener, there is no reason for having a different primary image or headline wording. That is solving one problem twice and absolutely does not serve the reader's needs.

A contents page is essentially redundant information. All its information is contained elsewhere, in greater detail and with more hooks to catch the reader. So why would a reader spend any time referring to the contents page? A good contents page must, at the very least, be a clear, simple guide to the issue. But it can be more than that, hooking the reader with its own abbreviated persuasive appeals to turn to a story opener *right now*. It should communicate the issue's worth, value, and fullness as well as its articles' locations. Ideally, it should whet the reader's appetite for the issue. *Fullness*, by the way, is not the same as *busyness*. Fullness suggests depth and quantity, whereas busyness is a symptom of not having chosen a clear hierarchy of information. A busy layout has too many elements jumping out at the reader. It repels readers. White space is as important on

Esquire CONTENTS

June 2008 / vol. 149 / no. 6

CRACKER

[continued on page 14]

ON THE COVER: PHOTOGRAPH BY PLATON/ART DEPT./CPI-SYNDICATION.

Esquire CONTENTS

June 2008 / vol. 149 / no. 6

[continued from page 11]

Esquire CONTENTS

APRIL 2011

VOL. 155

[continued on page 28]

ON THE COVER: MATTHEW MCCONAUGHEY PHOTOGRAPHED EXCLUSIVELY FOR ESQUIRE BY PEROU. SUIT, SHIRT, AND TIE BY DOLCE & GABBANA. POCKET SQUARE BY ROBERT TALBOTT. PRODUCED BY LILIAS HAHN FOR LAH PRODUCES. STYLING BY ARIANNE TUNNEY FOR TRACEY MATTINGLY. GROOMING BY KRISTEN SERAFINO. PROP STYLING BY DIN MORRIS FOR ARTWORKS HOLLYWOOD.

Esquire CONTENTS

APRIL 2011

VOL. 155   NO. 4

[continued from page 27]

Esquire = At the app store now.

This contents listing is made to look like an expanding pull-down computer menu. The articles are organized in page order, which is not helpful: giving reasons to read them is.

This contents listing appeared in a special edition of *Wired* magazine on "The Underworld Exposed." Far from their usual treatment, this dramatically sets a distinct tone for the issue.

The contents page must be easy to use. Clear typographic organization is the most important aspect in attracting readers. Article titles should jump out and page numbers should be placed near the headlines to avoid confusing gaps of space. Avoid *leaders*, or rows of dots used to guide the eye across expanses of emptiness.

this page as on any other. Design some emptiness into your contents page.

The first step in creating a good contents page is to decide what the page should accomplish. What should it show off? Which elements will be emphasized? How wide is the range of subjects covered? Will there be brief descriptions of the articles, or will headlines stand alone? Will there be visuals? Are the authors' names more important than the titles of their articles? Is more than one page desirable or possible?

Esquire magazine used composite images from its various stories for a while (*opposite, above*). This is an ingenious way to relate an entire issue into two entertaining contents pages, one for feature stories and the second for departments. Over time, the composite images evolved into increasingly interpretive, abstract compositions (*opposite, below*). It is evident that the magazine's staff recognized the potential for contents listings extended well beyond merely repeating headlines from story openers and they used it as an opportunity for adding significant value to the reader's experience.

Emphasizing some elements, and necessarily de-emphasizing others, creates contrast, which attracts readers. If all elements are treated equally, the page is gray all over and is more likely to be skipped. Having clearly organized elements makes skimming the page easy. Contents typography must exhibit obvious hierarchy. Titles must be worded exactly as they appear on story openers. A change in the headline wording from the contents to the opener causes confusion once the interested reader turns to the correct page.

The contents may be on the cover. The difference between cover lines and a valid cover contents listing is the addition of page numbers. Cover contents listings are nearly always supported by a complete contents listing inside the publication, because an issue usually contains more elements than space can accommodate on the cover.

The contents should appear on the same page or in the same place in every issue to make it findable. Some readers will turn immediately to, say, page 5 for the contents if they are conditioned to do so. Shorter publications do not need a contents listing because the document is so minimal that readers find scanning the actual pages is easier. In addition to considering what *kind of tool* to provide, consider whether a tool is needed at all.

Information on a contents page can be organized in many ways. Whatever system you adopt, it must provide an immediate inherent visual indication announcing what this page is: a well-designed contents page does not need to be labeled "Contents."

Man at His Best

1. THE CULTURE ›› Mickey Rourke's return, an animated documentary.
2. THE INSTRUCTIONS ›› Three big-batch drinks for a party.
3. STYLE ›› The Esquire Guide to Quality (or: how to shop for yourself).

THE VOCABULARY
(Terms and ideas you will encounter in the pages that follow. Great for conversation.)

- **CRITICAL COCKTAIL** *n:* That drink in a series of drinks that can be the difference between facilitating social interaction and inhibiting it, often the fine line between first-rate sexual performance and inadequate sexual performance. (SEE PAGE 40.)

- **pour management** *n:* THE DISPENSATION OF ALCOHOL INTO THE GLASSES OF PARTY GUESTS, INFORMED BY A DESIRE TO KEEP THEM DRUNK BUT NOT TOO DRUNK. (SEE PAGE 37.)

- **FDR** *v:* To quickly organize, implement, and manage a massive overhaul as soon as you are empowered to do so. Used in a sentence: "Barack Obama is gonna have to FDR the hell out of everything." (SEE PAGE 25.)

- **COCKTAIL GLASS** *n:* A popular yet impractical cone-shaped drinking glass. Also known as a martini glass. (SEE PAGE 38.)

- **the great domestic confusion** *n:* A HISTORICAL ERA (1970s TO THE PRESENT) IN WHICH THE HAPPIEST FAMILIES SEEM TO BE THE LEAST TRADITIONAL FAMILIES. AT LEAST ON TV. (SEE PAGE 28.)

- **REVERSAL ROLE** *n:* 1. A vaguely biographical role landed by an actor in the midst

- **TUGGING THE BUTTONS** *n:* 1. Determining the quality of a shirt by pulling on its buttons to test for sol-

Pants / Trousers

- **TROUSERS** *n:* What the stylish

Man at His Best

1. THE CULTURE ›› Sean Penn as Harvey Milk, the songs of the year.
2. THE INSTRUCTIONS ›› The Great Esquire Chili Cook-Off. And Sex.
3. STYLE ›› How to stay warm and dry and not look ridiculous.

THE VOCABULARY
(Terms and ideas you will encounter in the pages that follow. Great for conversation.)

- **the great bedraggling** *n:* A PERIOD THAT BEGAN IN THE MID-2000s WITH THE PROLIFERATION OF EASILY UPLOADED WEB VIDEOS, WHICH HAVE MADE FAMOUS PEOPLE SEEM UNATTRACTIVE AND NONFAMOUS PEOPLE REALLY UNATTRACTIVE. (SEE PAGE 50.)

- **UNREAL DEATH** *n:* A manner of death so unlikely, shocking, and brutal that it overshadows the life of the deceased. (SEE PAGE 42.)

- **MOLIAN SNUB** *n:* The puzzling phenomenon whereby beautiful, talented, charming actresses (e.g., Keri Russell, Leelee Sobieski, Gretchen Mol) are not in more things. (SEE PAGE 48.)

- **CHILI** *n:* Fundamentally, a stew comprising bits of spiced meat and sometimes beans. Easily corrupted. (SEE PAGE 59.)

- **DUMP** *n:* A blend of chili spices added at precise moments in the chili-cooking process. Done either two or three times, depending on the chef.

- **engineered helplessness** *n:* SURREPTITIOUSLY PLACED INFORMATION IN A CONVERSATION THAT SUGGESTS A FLAW AND BAITS A WOMAN INTO SYMPATHETICALLY ATTEMPTING TO FIX A MAN. (SEE PAGE 70.)

GOOD IDEAS FEATURED IN THIS SECTION:
- GO SEE MILK. (PG. 42)
- ROAST AND GRIND WHOLE SPICES YOURSELF. (PG. 62)
- SHOW SOME HUMILITY EVERY NOW AND THEN. (PG. 70)
- TRY SIPPING RUM, NEAT. BUT FOR THE LOVE OF GOD, MAKE SURE IT'S THE GOOD

- **BARREL PROBLEM** *n:* The effect that the heat in a

- **HOLD THE MONKEYS** *n:* 1. A request made by a bar patron that specifies his cocktail should come without tiny umbrellas, ornamental fruit, or small plastic

---

This Way In

What Lies Beneath

This Way In

AS IF WE'D GIVE AN UNBEARABLE GUY FIVE COVERS

There was no real consensus on how to react to April's stories about Heath Ledger and Admiral William Fallon, but then we showed George Clooney a world video. Nobody felt good about that one.

WHAT THEY WROTE:

Admiral William Fallon

Chuck Klosterman

The Brain Awards

This Way In

WHAT THEY'RE WEARING IN THE MOVIES

AN UNTIMELY EXIT

The Hall of Cultural Significance
The six most intriguing performances this month

THE ROLES

HELP

Cheaper by the Gallon
Where to find the lowest-price gas for weekend wanderings. BY KAIJA HELMETAG

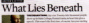

The rapid, frightening rise in gas prices is making cars a prohibitive luxury. Where's the best place to fill up? According to Ralph Bombardiere, director of the state Association of Service Stations and Repair Shops, the answer changes by the day, if not the hour. "The retailer has very little to do with the prices at the pump," he says. "Those are set by suppliers." Via sites like newyorkstategasprices.com, which uses volunteer spotters to post prices daily, we monitored the ever-shifting landscape. Here, eight stations with relatively cheap fuel.

WHERE TO FILL UP WHEN YOU'RE ...

Price for a gallon of regular unleaded gas on May 14.

... COMING HOME FROM NORTHERN NEW JERSEY
Lukoil, 2284 Rte. 4 W., nr. Jones Rd., Fort Lee, N.J.; 201-363-1837.
$3.95

... RUNNING ON EMPTY AND APPROACHING THE LINCOLN TUNNEL
Hess, 833 Tenth Ave., nr. Tenth Ave.; 212-245-8594.
$3.99

... RETURNING FROM IKEA
Amoco, 235 12th St., Jersey City, N.J.; 201-653-3860.
$3.66

... GOING UPSTATE
Shell, 1855 First Ave., nr. 96th St.; 212-426-8351.
$4.07

... DROPPING OFF A RENTAL AT LA GUARDIA
Exxon, 31-02 6th St., at 31st Ave., Jackson Heights; 718-457-1003.
$3.95

... ABOUT TO CROSS THE VERRAZANO-NARROWS BRIDGE
Hess, 204 Fourth Ave., nr. 81st St., Sunset Park; 718-625-7004.
$3.91

... PICKING UP PASSENGERS ON THE WAY TO THE ROCKAWAYS
Exxon, 137-21 Liberty Ave., nr. Van Wyck Expressway, Jamaica; 718-262-0638.

... DROPPING OFF A RENTAL AT JFK
Exxon, 130-11 150th Ave., nr. 130th St., Jamaica; 718-525-5463.
$4.05

By Wendy Goodman

BEST BETS

In the Big-Box Shadows
West 18th Street makes for a very satisfying afternoon of indie-store shopping.

The rare piece of kids' furniture without polka dots or plastic: **children's wooden chair**, $128 at ANC Home, 10 W. 18th St., nr. Fifth Ave.; 212-366-1162.

The paper press in Print Icon's front window actually churns out **custom-engraved invitations** (from $35), 7 W. 18th St., nr. Fifth Ave.; 212-255-4489.

A department store in miniature, Utowa carries accessories like this **straw clutch** along with clothes, cosmetics, and flowers ($65; 17 W. 18th St., nr. Fifth Ave.; 212-929-4800).

For a mid-shopping snack, try the love child of the pretzel and the croissant ($3.50 at City Bakery, 3 W. 18th St., nr. Fifth Ave.; 212-366-1414).

It's cute, sure, but the chile-shape computer mouse also fits the curvature of your palm ($35 at A.I. Friedman, 44 W. 18th St., nr. Sixth Ave.; 212-243-9000).

Wendy Isaacson makes her **heart-shape art pieces** with Durham's water putty, wood pulp, and a secret amount of tap water ("Special Delivery," $448 at Heart Art, 132 W. 18th St., nr. Sixth Ave.; 212-620-3840).

Signed first editions of **Orhan Pamuk's** *Snow* and **Kurt Vonnegut's** *Bagombo Snuff Box* ($300 and $150 at Skyline Books, 13 W. 18th St., nr. Fifth Ave.; 212-759-5463).

Like your mom's oven, but with high-powered burners and delayed-start baking (Northstar, $3,700 at Krup's).

Break out that old crab-salad recipe, best served on a **crustacean-adorned melamine plate** ($83 at West

Department headings bring the primary typographic element, the cover "flag" or logo, inside a magazine (*above*). Recognizable bits of typographic fun, they allow the balance

of a publication to be less remarkable in editorial quietness, which is vital amid noisy advertising. Balancing consistency with necessary novelty to accommodate the variety

of content is the business of the department page designer (*opposite, top*). The structure of a department page is often the best way to impose consistency (*opposite, bottom*).

The cover "flag" is brought inside the magazine by reinterpreting it as department headings. The attributes used here are color contrast, off-center alignment, and all-caps setting.

Department headings Department headings are like road signs that help readers find their destinations. They are vital elements in establishing the cohesiveness and strength of your publication's or website's personality. At best, they work hand in glove with your other display typography to organize and highlight your stories and articles. At worst, they are mismatched smudges in a publication, confusing the reader's need for visual signals.

Departments are topics that appear in every issue. Features, on the other hand, have varying content and a for-this-issue-only specialness. It is unwise to allow departments to outshout features. Departments are toned down by treating their type and imagery in a visually consistent manner. The disciplined quieting of department graphics has a profound effect on the cohesiveness and visual personality of a publication.

The primary display type relationship is between the cover logo, or "flag," and the department headings. This relationship connects the inside and the outside of your publication, making a more powerful impact on the reader and making your publication more attractive to advertisers. Relating prominent display type throughout a publication bestows visual unity. Typographically connecting the cover logo, department headings, headlines, subheads, and breakouts is the most visible way of joining

the editorial matter. This also separates it from the advertising pages. The most direct way to relate all display typography is to use variations of a single typeface.

Department pages are either clustered in the front and back of a publication or scattered throughout its pages. Separated by advertisements, they must immediately be recognized as editorial material. Departments cannot outshout ads (ad agencies are paid great sums to make highly visible pages), so departments must become visible by being related to one another; they make a *cumulative* impact. Giving departments a like treatment is called *formatting*. Formatting department pages achieves two valuable goals: the pages appear to be a large, unified body, and the preparation of each issue becomes easier with more time available for developing exciting feature graphics, where editorial excitement really belongs.

Formatted department pages must follow a style that is consistently applied to enable readers to recognize them. All typographic elements must be handled identically, images must fit into a limited range of sizes, and white space must be treated the same from department page to department page. It takes very little to weaken the format "just this once." With restraint and discipline, departments can be the mortar that holds the diverse elements of a publication together.

A

By OTHELLO the MOOR

I will PLAY THE SWAN *and* DIE IN MUSIC

B

I WILL PLAY by THE SWAN OTHELLO AND *the* MOOR DIE IN MUSIC

C

MISERY ACQUAINTS A MAN WITH STRANGE BEDFELLOWS

A tale that would cure deafness

BY TRINCULO WITLING

D

MISERY ACQUAINTS A MAN *with* STRANGE BEDFELLOWS

A TALE THAT WOULD CURE DEAFNESS

by

TRINCULO WITLING

E

e're you? Over hill, over dale, through bush, through brier, o'er park, o'er pale, through flood, through fire, I can wander anywhere. Swifter than these moon's sphere, and I serve the fairy queen, to dew her orbs upon the green. The cowslips tall her pensioners be, in the gold coats spots you can see. Those be rubies, few fairy favours, in those freckles live their saviours. I go seek some dew drops here and hang a pearl in every cowslip's ear. Over hill, over dale, through bush, through

By STARVELING A. TAILOR

F

e're you? Over hill, over dale, through bush, through brier, o'er park, o'er pale, through flood, through fire, I do wander everywhere. Swifter than the moon's sphere, and I serve thee fairy pro queen to dew's her

orbs upon the green. The cowslips tall her pensioners be, in their gold coats spots you see. Those be rubies, fairy favours, in those freckles live their saviours. I must go to seek some dew-drops here, and hang a pearl in every

STARVELING A. TAILOR

G

e're you? Over hill, over dale, through bush, through brier, o'er park, o'er pale, through flood, through fire, I do wander everywhere. Swifter than the moon's sphere, and who serve thee fairy pro queen to dew's her orbs upon the green. The cowslips tall her pension's be, in their gold coats spots you see those be rubies,

fairy favours, in those freckles live their saviours. I must go to seek some dew-drops here, and hang a pearl in't a cowslips farthin'

By ROBIN GOOD FE*llow*

H

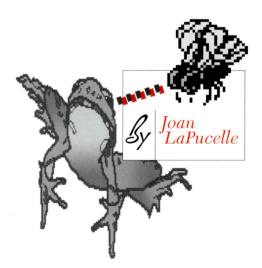

By Joan LaPucelle

they hoist me and show me to shouting varletry censuring Rome? rather a ditch in pt be gentle grave nto me! Rather Nilus' mud lay me ark naked and let ne water flies blow on me. His legs estride the ocean, rear'd arm crested ne world, his voice s propertied adds he atuned spheres,

he meant to quail and shake the orb, he was as to rattling thunder. For his bounty there was no winter in't, an autumn that grew the more by reaping. His delights were dolphin-

Continued on **88**

___ ___ ___

Cleopatra *is a thoughtful and passionate author with a gift for languages. This article, written in collaboration with Plutarch, originally appeared in the Macedonian Herald Sunday Magazine.*

p and show me to shouting varletry censuring Rome? rather a ditch in ypt be gentle grave anto me! Rather Nilus' mud lay me ttark naked and let he water flies blow on me. His legs bestride the ocean, s rear'd arm crested the world, his voice as propertied adds the atuned spheres, and that to friends.

and shake the orb, he was as to rattling thunder. For his bounty there was no winter in't, an autumn that grew the more by reaping he show'd his delights, which were such dolphin-like. 🔘

___ ___ ___

Cleopatra IS A THOUGHTFUL AND PASSIONATE AUTHOR WITH A GIFT FOR LANGUAGES. THIS ARTICLE, WRITTEN IN COLLABORATION WITH PLUTARCH, ORIGINALLY APPEARED IN THE MACEDONIAN HERALD SUNDAY MAGAZINE.

___ ___ ___

CLEOPATRA is a thoughtful and passionate author who has a gift for languages. This article, written in collaboration with Plutarch, originally appeared in the Macedonian Herald Sunday Magazine.

arm crested the world, voice was propertied as the tuned spheres, and that friends. But when he mean to quail and shake the orb, was as rattling thunder. his bounty there was no win in't, an autumn that grew th more by reaping. His deligh were dolphin-like. They show his back above the eleme they liv'd in. In his live walk'd crowns and crowne realms and islands were plates dropp'd from his pock smashed upon the forestage

---

There are eight locations for bylines: near the headline or department heading (**A**), integrated with the headline (**B**), placed near the deck or subhead (**C**), integrated with the deck (**D**), placed near the text (**E**), integrated with the text (**F**), placed in a separate column (**G**), or integrated with an image (**H**).

To avoid cluttering the opening page, distinguish the bio from the text. Make it recognizable by contrasting its type size or style with that of the text, with which it is most easily confused. Set the bio in the same typeface as the text but in italics, or in a smaller size, or flush left if your text is justified. It needs its own typographic "flavor."

Bylines and bios A byline is the author's name. A bio (short for *biography*) is a brief profile of the author, giving pertinent details that express his or her credentials to take the reader's time.

The presentation of bylines and bios indicates the importance of the author. Readers are served by being told up front — somewhere on the first page of an article — who is doing the talking. If the author is not on the staff of the publication, a bio is extremely helpful in describing why the writer is qualified to discuss the topic at hand.

A byline format should be developed and used throughout a publication to make finding the names easy and to make visible those infrequent times when the author is extraordinary and truly deserves to have the byline trumpeted by breaking the normal format.

Bios can be placed at the end of the text on the first page of a story, in a separate column on the opening page, or at the conclusion of the story on the jump ("continued on") page. A horizontal rule is often placed above a bio to separate it from the text.

Bios are often run at the end of an article because it is easy to tack them on there. No preplanning is needed to fit them. But a bio at the end of an article cannot induce a browser to read unless, of course, the article is only one page, making the bio immediately visible. With multiple-page articles, readers have long since made their decision to read by the time they come across the bio. It is more helpful to the reader to place the bio on the opening page.

Bottoms of pages are far less valuable than tops: readers always start at the upper, outer corners when flipping through an issue, then scanning individual pages from upper left to lower right. Put a bio at the bottom of the opening page of an article where it is easily found yet will not interfere with headlines or primary visuals.

Sometimes bios are separated from the stories by being grouped on a single page near the front of the publication. This makes them appear even more important and can serve as an alternate contents page: the reader may peruse the contributors' page to learn who sounds interesting and, by extension, what they want to read first.

A bio is enhanced by including an image of the author. It is always interesting to see something about the subject. Another bland mugshot (head-and-shoulder formal portrait) does not tell much. Select authors' photos by their descriptive quality — their content — rather than their ordinariness. Ask authors to supply their own photos: you never know what you will get. The pictures may be quite descriptive because they will show the authors as they view themselves.

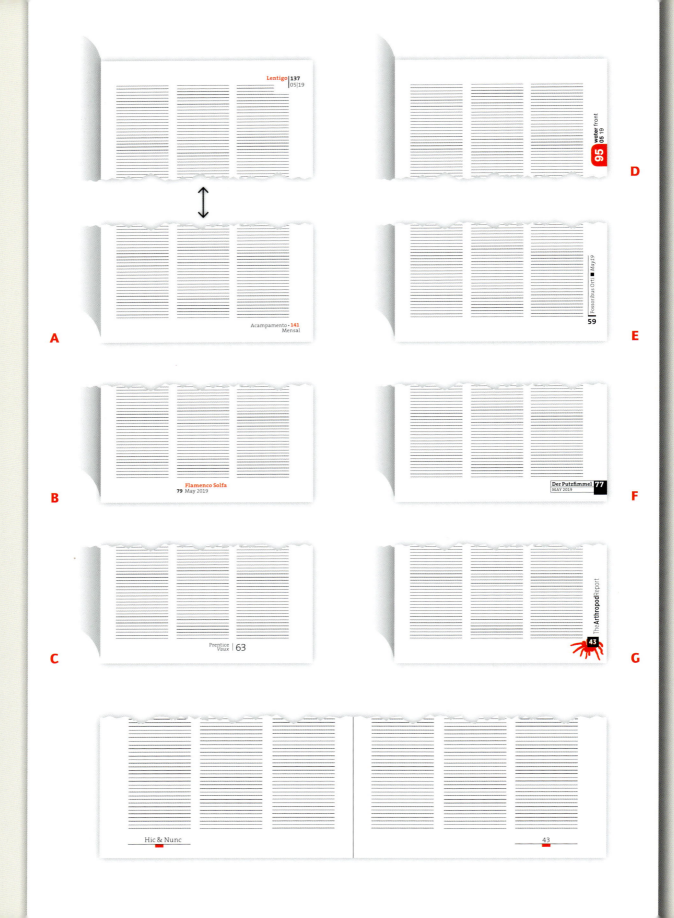

The folio/footline unit can be in the upper outer corner or the lower outer corner (**A**). It can be centered at the foot or at the head of the page (**B**). It can be aligned with the inside edges of text columns, looking eccentrically off-center (**C**). It can be in the outside margin, where the page-turning thumb goes (**D**). The folio/footline can be embellished with rules or bullets (**E**). It can be placed in a shape and connected to the edge of the page (**F**). Or it can be integrated with imagery, particularly useful in feature stories when the art conveys some significant aspect of the story (**G**). *None of these studies are drawn to scale.*

Folios and footlines *Folios* are page numbers. They are a tool to help readers find beginnings. They are not an automatic necessity for some publications.

What publications need folios? Only ones that are long enough to make finding the beginnings — and continuations — of articles cumbersome. And only ones that have a usefully designed contents page that shows off content in a way that persuades browsers to proceed directly to an article.

Who uses page numbers? Only readers who have already visited the contents page and are flipping rapidly through a publication to find a particular article.

Folios are always odd on right-hand pages and always even on left-hand pages (*see above left*). A right-hand page is called a *recto*, which is Latin for "right," while a left-hand page is called a *verso*, which is Latin for "reverse."

Folios must be positioned in the outside margin or in the outer half of the head or foot margin (*see above center*). These are obvious locations as the most visible parts of pages. It is not *required* to put a folio in the lower outside corner, where it traditionally has been stuck and is now placed merely as a default non-decision.

A *footline*, so named because it typically appears at the bottom of the page, contains the name of the publication and the publication date. The footline is also called a *running foot* or a *footer*. When it is placed at the head of the page, it is called a *running head* or *header*. The footline is useful for readers who tear stories out for future reference or for passing on to others because the content is particularly well written and valuable. With a footline, the source of the story is automatically recorded.

Combine folios and footlines into a single perceived element on the page, to reduce the bits and pieces that make a page look sloppy. Their combination is a design opportunity that can dramatically enhance the overall appearance of a publication with little effort. Emphasizing the folio over the footline in this relationship makes it more findable and a more useful tool.

It is not necessary to have a folio/footline on every page, for example, if every story opens on a recto. Place the folios only on rectos, and footlines only on versos (*opposite, bottom*). A variation of the recto-only folio is including both folios on only one page (*see above right*). Or put folios on every page, and split the footline so the publication title appears only on versos and the publication date only on rectos.

Creating unexpected folios and footlines contributes to your publication's personality. Make them echo your magazine logo. Use them as an opportunity to achieve design unity with your other display typography.

"Today's amassment of information [makes it] harder, not easier, to extract essential knowledge. The problem is no longer one of making information available, but of facilitating understanding. That is exactly the role of today's typography: maximizing comprehension." Zuzana Licko

Section Two
What Readers Want

LOSTWITHOUT HIS**PENCIL**
Self-taught,
his paintings
were never
good enough
to frame.

his brother Ernst
n of their father's
mil must have had
d in Olomouc.

never complained
ember his love for
ulius, of whom he
oke glowingly and
He and his brother
ated from the high
ands. He inherited
nt from his father
o profession." So in-
to paint he studied
a.

Hochschule which
ng next door to the
Karlskirche, across
ncert hall: the cen-
na. The doorkeeper
e said there was no
and it was precise-
d been in the teens
as an architectural
pposed to be. Some
He was very happy
oved every memory
ry waltz tune, each

Two friends are walking crosstown discussing the stock market. "How does it work?" "Simple: you buy a dozen chicks, feed them, watch them grow up. Then you buy a rooster. Soon you have more chicks and a whole yardful of chickens. A terrible storm comes and your chickens drown. *Ducklings* you should have bought! That's the stock market." **This is a favorite story told**

by Karl
as she
immig
Olmütz
two-st
window
a marke
interest

Inherently interesting content Four guys saying "BULL" and the headline is "Less talk". The hierarchy leads from one level to the next, to the next, to the *text*.

Arresting pictures Combining parts of connectable images making something new gets attention. Once stopped by the visual, give a provocative first typographic hit, then a secondary hit and maybe, *maybe*, the browser will progress to the text.

Well-built text A variety of typographic weights and limited colors within a structured environment makes text both interesting and legible. Spacing attributes are as important here as they are in display type. Indeed, designers look at the handling of text by their colleagues as a measure of their talent and skill.

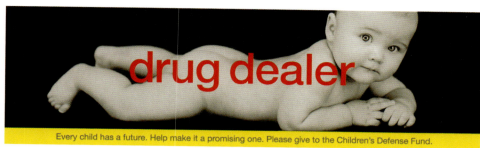

Every child has a future. Help make it a promising one. Please give to the Children's Defense Fund.

Arresting pictures stop me. This picture of an innocent baby is *not* arresting, but its juxtaposed caption — really only a label — forces me to rethink what I imagine I see. In that split of a moment, I continue on to the next level of readership to find out why everything I thought about the picture is wrong.

What makes readers respond

"To catch a mouse, make noise like a cheese." Herb Lubalin

What makes you respond as a reader? If you can codify the visual prompts that catch and keep you interested, you can distill them into good design for others. Here is what works for me:

⊡ **Inherently interesting content** This is a rare commodity. Most content arrives to the designer dull. Good designers and editors expose content by making it *interesting to the reader*.

⊡ **Multilevel readership that encourages scanning** Such hierarchy signals primary, secondary, and tertiary importances in both words and pictures.

⊡ **Headlines that make me want to know more** Primary type's job is to lead the reader to secondary type. The best way to do that is to tell only *the most intriguing part* of the story.

⊡ **Subheads that complete the story** Secondary type's job is to lead me to additional information, whether pictures and their captions or breakouts, pull

LETTERFORM

ABSTRACTION	LEGIBILITY
BEN SHAHN	IGNATIUS
CHAOTIC	ORDERLY
Menhart D	Preissig Ant.
ORGANIC	GEOMETRIC
Benda Romana	Bodoni Light
CASUAL	FORMAL
	SYNCHRO
SPORADIC	SYSTEMATIC
	EMPEROR EIGHT
SPATIAL	FLAT
PENN STATION	EPHESVS
STRONG	WEAK
Mrs Eaves D	Mrs Eaves
ACTIVE	PASSIVE
	News Gothic
EXCITING	DRY

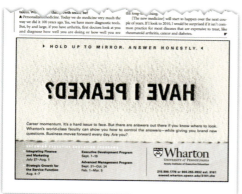

Headlines that make you want to know more can make their points through provocation or abstraction. In this case, the headline is set backward with instructions to hold it up to a mirror. The craft involved in this artwork is exemplary: letterpress printing beautifully photographed to show the paper's grain. This implies a crafted education from Wharton.

Arresting pictures Scale is startling when an object appears to be too close, as if they are just outside a window. A good starting point is life size, which is rarely expected.

Arresting pictures Readers respond to real dimensionality. This book cover for an autobiography uses elements that become representational of a zoological specimen.

Typefaces exist on a spectrum of abstraction and legibility. In other words, they have built-in interest. Most text faces fit within a fairly narrow range of peculiarity because, above all else, they must be highly legible. Display faces, on the other hand, can embody all sorts of quirkiness because their function is to attract fleeting readers (or merely browsers). Nearly every adjective can be used to describe a typeface – so its antonym can be equally applied, as shown in this chart. Awareness of type character and marrying it to specific messages is among a designer's responsibilities. Be careful not to make obvious choices: subtlety in typography is richly regarded.

quotes, or other display material. In few situations is a headline/subhead combination sufficient for me to know subconsciously whether I want to commit to the text.

☐ **Arresting pictures** They help tell the story without my commitment of time or attention. They are cropped and sized to reveal importance. They are not the same as pretty pictures, which may stop me, but, unless they are about beauty itself, do not lead me into the story.

☐ **Intriguing captions** Captions should do a lot more than describe what I can already see for myself. They should help me see the importance of the image and build a bridge to the text.

☐ **Well-built text** That's right, text is *built*, one attribute at a time. Weight, size, column width, letter, word spacing, linespacing, and paragraphing make text either inviting or repelling. Once you've lured and caught me as a reader, don't make me work to read the story. I won't make that effort.

Who's your audience?

Designers stand between the message's sender, the client, and the receiver, the audience. It is our job to interpret content on behalf of the audience so they glean the most meaning and value with the least effort. If you take the designer out of the equation, you have

"To read means to obtain meaning from words. And legibility is that quality which enables words to be read easily, quickly, and accurately."
John Charles Tarr

a. Identify the work and artist

b. Describe the work for the layperson

c. Detail for experts and the especially curious. This third level is present, but it's easily skipped by the average guest.

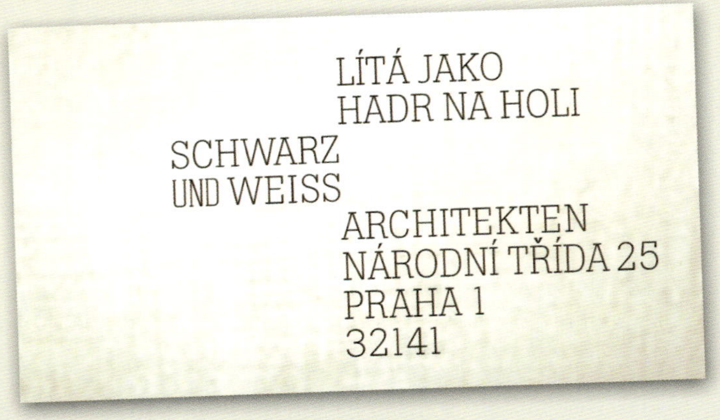

LÍTÁ JAKO
HADR NA HOLI

SCHWARZ
UND WEISS

ARCHITEKTEN
NÁRODNÍ TŘÍDA 25
PRAHA 1
32141

Kaufmännische Ausbildung
Private kaufmännische Kurse

Dr. Sabel
Inh. Therese Sabel
München, Kaufingerstr. 14/2
Telefon 91064

Jahreskurse für schulentlassene Knaben u. Mädchen. Beginn: 16. April

Halbjahreskurse: Beginn: 1. Mai

Unterricht in Einzelfächern. Anmeld. täglich. Angenehme Zahlungsbedingung. *[18767]2-2

Kaufmännische Ausbildung
Private kaufmännische Kurse

Dr. Sabel Inh. Therese Sabel
München, Kaufingerstraße 14,2   Tel. 91064

Jahreskurse für schulentlassene Knaben und Mädchen   Beginn **16. April**

Halbjahreskurse   Beginn **1. Mai**

Unterricht in Einzelfächern. Anmeld. täglich. Angenehme Zahlungsbedingung. *[18767]2-2

Three-level type hierarchy is clear in this magnificent 1906 poster: the primary type is at the top; the secondary type is near the bottom; and the tertiary type — the artist's name, aligned at the cap height and carefully centered — is tiny and way over to the right. It was designed by Julius Klinger (1876–1942), a Viennese magazine and poster designer.

Logos showing a progressive range (*clockwise*) from low abstraction (CLEAN CUT) to high abstraction (BT). Abstraction, like any other design attribute, should be intentionally explored in a full range of studies, pushing toward illegibility, so an *informed choice* can be made for the final mark.

Museum signage (*top left*) typically has three levels so readers can choose how much information they want.

A business card uses flush left alignment of the secondary and tertiary type. Aligning the right edge of the primary type establishes unity.

Jan Tschichold illustrates The New Typography with this before and after example of a 1928 small-space newspaper ad. The before (*far left*), representing traditional typography, has four typefaces and seven type sizes, is centered, and is overly ornamented. The after, which Tschichold designed, has improved legibility through disciplined type contrasts. Though tame by today's standards, such clarified thinking was radical in the 1920s.

raw messages with a lot of visual static that is probably going unreceived because they are sent by people who a) wrongly believe people care about their messages and b) think everyone thinks as they do, so they will respond as they themselves would.

There are many audiences, and each is made of individuals. Individuals are, in turn, members of more than one audience community: a 75-year-old might be a member of a "grandparent" audience, a "frequent traveler" audience, and a "yoga practitioner" audience. How do these audiences differ and what do they have in common? Understanding the *individual* and the *communities* to which each individual identifies helps shape a message so it appeals accurately.

Abstraction and clarity

Abstraction wins eyeballs while clarity keeps them. Abstraction and clarity are the two ends of a spectrum. Neither is "better" than the other, but each has a time and a place for its use.

Abstraction belongs in display type: headlines, subheads, captions, and breakouts/pull quotes. Display type that is merely typeset misses the crucial need to lure and reveal content to the reader. Text, on the other hand, is *not* a place for abstraction. Anything that repels, confuses, or reduces legibility in text hurts the message.

"Maximum meaning, minimum means."
Abram Games

Question type	Response	Visual interpretation			
Yes/No Be alert to local traditions: Xs in Sweden, for example, mean "yes."	Checking a box	☑ *YES*	☐ *NO*		
	Writing YES or NO	__**YES**__	*YES or NO*		
	Circling a choice	(*YES*)	*NO*		
	Deleting a choice	*YES*	*N̶O̶*		
Multiple choice	Checking a box	☐ *Dibble*	☐ *Edger*	☑ *Flail*	☐ *Tongs*
	Writing a choice	__**C**__	*A. Dibble* *B. Edger*	*C. Flail* *D. Tongs*	
	Circling a choice	*Dibble*	*Edger*	(*Flail*)	*Tongs*
	Deleting choices	*Di̶b̶ble*	*Ed̶ger*	*Flail*	*To̶ngs*
Free response Provide enough space for full answers. Character spaces need to be wide enough to accommodate handwriting.	Writing in empty space	CAMSHAFT, CYLINDER & PISTON			
	Writing on horizontal lines	FLYWHEEL TO GEARBOX BEARINGS TO CRANKCASE			
	Writing in defined character spaces	C Y L I N D E R H E A D │ │ │ │ │ │ │ │ │ │ │ │			
Instructions	Instructions at each box	*Bistoury* ☒ *Single* ☐ *Double*	*Colter* ☐ *Single* ☒ *Twin*	*Slotter* ☐ *Double* ☒ *Quad*	
	Instructions grouped near questions	*Indicate small or large size for each* S *Bistoury* L *Colter* S *Slotter*			
Position of answers to questions	Flush right	*Air or bar:* **BAR** *Ditch or drain:* **DITCH**	*Fire or loy:* **FIRE** *Peat or salt:* **PEAT**		
	Following questions	*Ball peen, beetle, or claw?* **BEETLE** *Drop, end, or Stillson?* **STILLSON**			
	Flush left	**AUG** *Auger or bench?* **DIS** *Chamfer or disk?*	**GIM** *Gimlet or keyway?* **STR** *Rotary or strap?*		
	Below questions	*Three favorite mills:* CIDER, PEPPER & TREAD			
	Above questions	CIDER, PEPPER & TREAD *Three favorite mills*			

An all-type hierarchy on a right-hand opener shows three flavors of information, which is good design thinking. But each is set "full measure," or across the entire width of the page,

which makes it look intimidating. Fewer words on each line set larger would make it more appealing: the edited version on the right shows bigger type and fewer characters per line —

reduced from 65 to 70 per line in the original to 50 per line. The "turnover" page changes to the publication's regular text setting. Such subtle changes make type more *engageable*.

A simple type hierarchy uses size in *three equivalent steps*, as shown in the diagram. (The fourth step, for MARKET, is bigger because it had to be sized to match the width of ART + DESIGN.)

Forms have been thoroughly studied for decades. The results for optimizing their usefulness are shown here. The recommended design response is shown first in each category. Forms should be simple to follow and use. Type should be simple and straightforward, without decoration or unnecessary contrasts. Hierarchy can be shown by changing type weight alone. Be sure each question *needs* to be asked: wasting time is something every respondent is aware of. Make it simple to extract and evaluate information. Forms are the most intimate interaction a respondent has with the asker, so they should be considerate and particularly well thought out. The trick to good forms is to make the variety of responses look systematized.

Hierarchy

Hierarchy means "order, ranking, or sequence." If all the elements in a design were presented as being equally important, it would be the visual equivalent of oatmeal: consistently semi-smooth and gray. That's not an effective way to lure and keep readers. So we order type and imagery by importance. In general, bigger and darker means more important; smaller and lighter means less important. In practice any element that agrees with a prevailing visual system indicates "less important" and any element that breaks the system, and thus becomes more visible, indicates "more important."

Use type contrasts to show hierarchy. Edit copy shorter to make type larger. Make the type's entrances findable. Lure readers in and let the content — if it's good — keep them in. While it's possible to subdivide elements into unlimited strata of importances, readers simply do not need more than *exactly* three levels: most important, least important, and all the rest presented as equivalently middling in importance. There will always be a *most* and *least*, so additional subdivisions happen in the middle stuff. These distinctions become meaningless and you're back to semi-lumpy oatmeal.

Design is an "information delivery system." The smoother the delivery — or transfer — of information, the better the design.

"When it comes to handling text, I like to challenge the audience a bit, but I know enough to back off when you really want people to read it."
Michael Mabry

6:62   ∎∎ **Less precision acceptable** Certain instructions may be omitted, however, without endangering the integrity of the proceedings. This is because grand jury instructions need not have the same precision as instructions at trial. [*People v Calbud, Inc.*, 49 NY2d 389, 426 NYS2d 232 (1980)]

> **Example** The failure to instruct on the voluntariness of a defendant's statement is not grounds for dismissal of an indictment. [*People v Davis*, 190 AD2d 987, 593 NYS2d 713 (4th Dept), *leave denied*, 81 NY2d 1071, 601 NYS2d 591 (1993)]

6:63   ∎∎∎ **Evidence constituting a defense** For purposes of determining whether the grand jury must receive instructions on a defense, case law distinguishes between defenses that are exculpatory and those that are mitigating. [*People v Valles*, 62 NY2d 36, 476 NYS2d 50 (1984)]

6:64   ∎∎ **Exculpatory defense** This type of defense would, if believed, result in a finding of no criminal liability. The grand jury must be instructed as to any such defense. Examples include entrapment [*People v Speros*, 186 AD2d 434, 588 NYS2d 562 (1st Dept 1992)], self-defense and agency.

6:65   ∎ **Instructions on alibi evidence** Alibi evidence is in fact exculpatory, but it has sometimes been treated differently from other exculpatory defenses.

Cases are divided on whether, if this type of evidence comes out before the grand jury, the prosecutor must give an instruction on the People's burden of proof on the alibi issue. [*Compare People v Hughes*, 159 Misc 2d 663, 606 NYS2d 499 (Sup Ct 1992) *with People v Crump*, 157 Misc 2d 566, 597 NYS2d 1010 (County Ct 1992)]

6:66   ∎∎ **Mitigating defense** This type of defense is offered to reduce the gravity of the offense committed, rather than to avoid liability. An example is extreme emotional disturbance. The prosecutor need not instruct the grand jury on mitigating defenses. [*People v Valles*, 62 NY2d 36, 476 NYS2d 50 (1984)]

6:67   ∎∎∎ **Limiting instructions** In some situations the prosecutor should give a limiting instruction. Failure to give the instruction may result in dismissal of a subsequent indictment.

6:68   ∎∎ **Impeachment by prior convictions** When a defendant testifies before the grand jury, the prosecution may use prior convictions to impeach credibility on cross-examination. [*People v Gonzalez*, 201 AD2d 414, 607 NYS2d 670 (1st Dept), *leave denied*, 83 NY2d 871, 613 NYS2d 132 (1994)].

Westham
Innisland
Forano

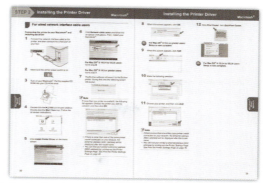

Highway signage must be simple and highly legible from long distances. Type size and spacing have been carefully analyzed and color is used systematically for familiarity and visibility. James Montalbano's *ClearviewHwy* is a type designed for roadside legibility. Tests show it is 25% more legible than *Highway Gothic*, the face widely used on road signs.

Boring but important: this *reference material* is ugly but it is primarily a functional tool. Like a hammer, *how well it does its job* is far more important than how it looks. Reference material's *findability* is essential. Adhering to branding guide lines — even decorating to uphold a minimum designers' sensibility — is semi-okay if it doesn't interfere with finding stuff.

Multilevel typography organizes thoughts into clear levels of importance and usefulness for readers by using a sequence of indentions, as shown by this page from a legal practice guide. This example shows a sequence from general to specific: general information is level one; an explanation of the general statements is level two; and fine points and reference information is in lesser levels. Multilevel type ensures that some percentage of the message is absorbed by nearly all readers, all of whom will recognize the predigested nature of the text. That goodwill envelops a publication or Web site and make it a valued resource.

Information mapping

There are two kinds of information: reading matter and reference material. Reading matter is continuous text like an article or other prose. Reference material is documentation, like an owner's manual or a dictionary, and requires the user's ability to find specific information quickly. Readers judge reference material by its utility more than by its aesthetic attributes.

Both reading matter and documentation can be improved by *information mapping*, a technique that uses segmentation and hierarchical styling — using type weight, size, style, indention, and position — to make the material relatively effortless to read. Reading matter can be mapped by using space, breaker heads, type variations, and ornaments to break text into bite-size pieces.

Reference material is information that readers dip into for specific content. It is typically not the kind of reading in which people want to be engrossed: they rarely use it unless a crisis exists, so *it is not reading by choice*. They just want the facts they're looking for. There are a few design considerations that make documentation more user friendly: ⊡ Display type must be as effective as highway signage. ⊡ Nothing may be done that hurts clarity and usefulness. ⊡ Documentation is often judged on the quality and clarity of its display type. ⊡ Hierarchy of decreasingly useful information is critical.

"Documentation is not reading matter but reference matter. It is a source of segmented information. It is destructive to force documentation to conform to a system developed for traditional printed matter, promotion, and advertising." Jan V. White

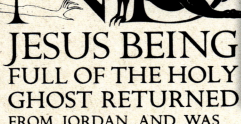

AND JESUS BEING
FULL OF THE HOLY
GHOST RETURNED
FROM JORDAN, AND WAS
LED BY THE SPIRIT INTO THE
WILDERNESS, BEING FORTY
DAYS TEMPTED OF THE DEVIL. AND IN THOSE
days he did eat nothing: & when they were ended, he afterward hungered. And the devil said unto him, If thou be the Son of God, command this stone that it be made bread. And Jesus answered him, saying, It is written, That man shall not live by bread alone, but by every word of God. And the devil, taking him up into an high mountain, shewed unto him all the kingdoms of the world in a moment of time. And the devil said unto him, All this power will I give thee, and the glory of them: for that is delivered unto me; and to whomsoever I will I give it. If thou therefore wilt worship me, all shall be thine. And Jesus answered and said unto him, Get thee behind me, Satan: for it is written, Thou shalt worship the Lord thy God, and him only shalt thou serve. And he brought him to Jerusalem, and set him on a pinnacle of the temple, and said unto him, If thou be the Son of God, cast thyself down from hence: For it is written,

145

Cheddar Cheese

THE main characteristics of Cheddar cheese are its clean, mellow flavour and good keeping qualities. The body is firm and smooth, free from gas holes, and the texture close. The colour is uniform and the rind clean and unbroken.

Cheddar cheese is made from evening's and morning's mixed milk ripened with starter. No cream should be removed from the evening's milk, since this results in a lower yield and the production of a "chalky" cheese.

Treatment of Evening's Milk

The milk is strained into the cheese vat or tub, and in warm weather is at once cooled (preferably by running over a cooler) to a temperature of 65–70° F. The use of a cooler ensures that the milk is evenly cooled and aerated, and the action of the acid-forming organisms is not unduly checked. When cooled in a jacketed vat or tub, the milk must be constantly stirred whilst a steady stream of cold water is circulated through the jacket.

During the evening the milk is stirred occasionally. This prevents a too rapid rising of the cream and results in a thinner layer on the milk the following morning. In cold weather it is not necessary to cool the milk, the vat being covered to maintain the temperature, so that by the following morning it will be about 60–62° F.

After the evening's milk has been treated as outlined above, the acidity is tested. At this stage it is generally 0·17–0·19 per cent and determines the subsequent details of manufacture.

Ripening with Starter

Next morning, the evening's milk is carefully skimmed; the cream is raised to a temperature of 90° F., and then strained back into the milk, the temperature of which has been raised to 70° F. Starter is now added, the amount required varying from 1–2 pints per 25 gal. of milk, according to the acidity of the milk and the time of year. Sufficient should be used, however, to give a correct degree of acidity for renneting in from 1½ to 2 hours after adding.

When the starter has been well mixed in, the morning's milk is added, either in bulk or as it is brought into the dairy.

Acidity Test. The whole is then heated to renneting temperature, i.e., 84–86° F., and the acidity tested. The acidity at this stage (usually 0·19–0·23 per cent) controls the texture, flavour and keeping quality of the cheese and also determines the time taken to complete the making process, which should be 5½–6 hours after renneting. The acidity at renneting should be at least 0·02 per cent above that taken about 30 min. after the evening's milk was received in the dairy. Generally, the acidity of the evening's milk next morning will be from 0·18–0·22 per cent.

BAD Low readability
High legibility

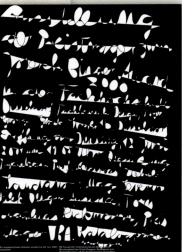

WORSE High readability
Low legibility

IDEAL High readability
High legibility

Readability | Legibility

Readability	Legibility
Unconventional	Functional
Unpredictable	Legible
Disorderly	Orderly
Complex	Simple
Original	Banal
Dynamic	Static

Readability is a built-in certainty with fortune cookies. Our curiosity and self-interest overcomes typographic failings like small size, low color contrast, and poor printing.

Readability, the capacity to attract and hold a reader, and legibility, the capacity to be read, coexist in every instance of typography.

A fascinating combination of braille and type raises two questions: *Does braille provide any degree of readability* and *is legibility defined by the size and height of the dots*?

Readability and legibility tend to be flip sides of one coin: they are not mutually exclusive. Indeed, readers rely on them to work in tandem

to make type speak with the greatest eloquence. This chart shows contrasts that may be exploited to enhance type's readability or its legibility.

Readability 133
Type's capacity to attract and hold a reader's interest.

Legibility 135
Type's capacity to be read under normal conditions.

6 Readability, then legibility

Readability is likely to be a result of good design, not of type but of text. Not 'Times New Roman is readable or unreadable,' but 'a newspaper or a book is reaable or unreadable.'" Gerrit Noordzij

Typography is an information-delivery system like a cigarette is a tar and nicotine delivery system and a mint is a fresh-breath delivery system. Legibility and readability are critical to the efficacy of typography and are among the most misunderstood areas of type. Indeed, many designers use the terms interchangeably, which reduces their usefulness and perpetuates confusion. Let's define terms:

Readability Type's capacity to attract and hold a reader's interest. Readability is macro-typography: it applies to the overall reading experience.

Legibility Type's capacity to be read under normal conditions, that is, the ease with which it can be read. Legibility is micro-typography: it applies to component parts like letters, words, and lines of type.

Like these signs on a door near Prague, every message competes for attention. Increasing type's readability attracts readers' attention.

Space is used as a visual timing device in *Silence*, a collaboration by composer John Cage and designer Raymond Grimaila.

This newspaper's front page is a model of readability. The overall impression is one of clarity and organization with numerous attention-catching entry points.

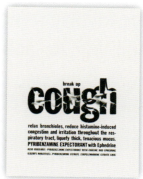

Readability can be created by doing something startling like photographing actual damaged type, which makes the point in this late-1950s pharmaceutical ad by Herb Lubalin.

Type is *readable* in this ad because the hierarchy is clear and it is brief. Note that the display type and logo have a shared variegated treatment.

This page from an early 15th-century Parisian *Book of Hours*, shown actual size, is tiny so it could be handy for reference throughout the day. Its small lettering strains legibility but fine detailing enhances readability. The craftsmanship in its making indicates that it was very expensive to have had made.

First, you have to get browsers to be interested in the type enough to want to read it. You have to increase type's readability to make it subconsciously appealing so browsers become readers. Then you have to make it legible. Readable/illegible type is bad design: you've earned the browsers' attention and desire to read, yet the type can't be deciphered. Unreadable/legible type will simply be ignored.

Readability

Lester Beall said in 1962, "Readability connotes an aethestic pleasantness that makes the type inviting to read. Legibility, on the other hand, does not mean letter-to-letter identification, but the degree of word recognition. Words are, in effect, type-shape associations."

High readability, making something noticeable and interesting, often produces low legibility; that is, making something noticeable also makes it hard to read. Pick your moments to develop readability. Catching readers is the job of display type, not text. Display type is both primary and secondary type elements, those bits that are intended to be read first, describe the story contained in the text, and lure the reader into the text. Display type typically includes headlines, subheads, decks, captions, breakouts, and pull quotes. Holding readers is the job of text. It is the destination to which readers have been

"Type, the voice of the printed page, can be legible and dull, or legible and fascinating, according to the design and treatment. In other words, what the book-lover calls readability is not a synonym for what the optician calls legibility." Beatrice Warde

The following are considerations that affect both type's readability and legibility. An accumulation of carelessness in handling these attributes creates a sense of unreadability. Overlooking just one of these will not necessarily deter a browser, but neglecting as few as two or three may deter even a committed reader.

❶ **Type size** Optimal type size is 10 to 11 point for text. Type that is too small repels readers who can't be bothered. Type that is too big makes skimming difficult and looks inept.

❷ **Type weight** Medium weight produces maximum legibility: the relationship of letterform and counter spaces is balanced.

❸ **Type posture** Paragraphs of italic text are harder to read than roman. Use italics only in short sections for emphasis.

❹ **Line length** Optimal line length is two alphabets (±52 characters). Fewer than 30 characters interrupts reading and causes too many hyphens and, in a justified column, uneven word spacing. More than 65 characters becomes tedious after three lines.

❺ **Letterspacing** Optimal letterspacing is invisible. Experiment with tracking and spacing attributes to eliminate anomalies.

❻ **Wordspacing** Wordspacing should be sufficient to separate words but not so much that it weakens lines of type.

❼ **Linespacing** Linespacing should increase with line length to maintain reading neutrality.

❽ **Justified vs. flush left** Consistent word spacing makes flush left easier to read than justified type. A soft right rag is best: set the hyphenation zone to 0p3. Justified type can make rivers of white when large word spaces stack. Have at least 6 words per line in justified type to absorb uneven wordspaces.

❾ **All caps vs. lower case** All caps are harder to read because word shapes are more similarly shaped. All caps also takes up about a third more space. Use all caps for brief display type.

❿ **Type and background** Black on white is about twice as fast to read as white on black. Reducing contrast between type and background causes loss in legibility and readership.

⓫ **Serif vs. sans serif** Readers prefer serif faces for text reading, so it makes sense to give it to them. Sans serif text

⓬ **Paper finish** High-gloss paper makes images look great but makes type hard to read. Print on uncoated stock and use spot UV coating on images.

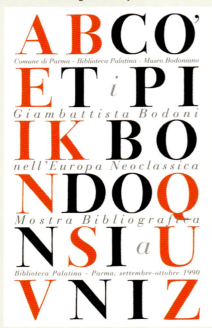

3+4+9 = A decoding game

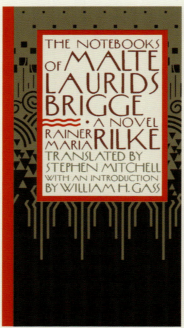

1+4+7+8 = Asymmetrical hierarchy

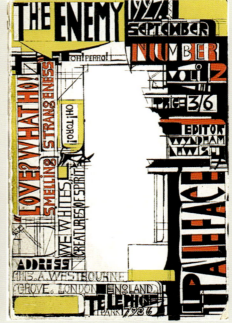

1+2+4+5+7+8+10 = An artistic riff on the numeral 1 announcing the first copy of a magazine

Type size (points)	Min. length (words)	Optimum length (words)	Max. length (words)
6	8	10	12
7	8	11	14
8	9	13	16
9	10	14	18
10	13	16	20
11	13	18	22
12	14	21	24
14	18	24	28

A guide for optimum words per line. In this system, and in English, a "word" is considered to be about four characters, including its following word space.

Max Ernst's 1924 cover for *The Little Review* uses a collection of contrasting letterforms and is unified by the optically equal spacing between them. In comparison, Massimo Vignelli's

1964 cut paper poster for the *32nd Venice Art Biennale* (detail) is unified by its letter-form unity. Contrast is provided only through color.

This billboard is perfectly easy to read – the type is eminently *legible* – but the intentionally changed word order enhances its *readability*.

Combining readability attributes listed at the top of the page can decrease legibility but will increase readability and create character.

lured, so once they are there, don't let anything interfere with their reading experience. Increase *readability* in display type; increase *legibility* in text.

☐ Understand the reader's self-interest. Edit the primary and secondary type so value of the content to the reader is obvious.

☐ Make the design look purposeful. Give display type a distinct treatment that adds to or reveals its meaning.

☐ Readability of small point size display type, for example as captions, is a function of brevity. The human mind perceives groups of two or three as "few." More than three is perceived as "many," so keep small display type short or risk having it skipped.

Increase text type's readability and legibility.

☐ Choose a medium weight of a quality face.

☐ Give it a comfortable size and column width.

☐ Give it invisible, *unselfconscious* spacing.

Legibility

Type is used in the furtherance of communication. Type's legibility, therefore, largely determines the success or failure of communication. If type is more legible, the communication succeeds. If type is less legible, it is a barrier to communication.

☐ Text type has a greater need for legibility than

"Do you think an ad can sell if nobody can read it? You cannot save souls in an empty church." David Ogilvy

"All the News That's Fit to Print"

The New York Times

Late Edition
New York: Today, sunny, a few afternoon clouds. High 77. Tonight, slightly more humid. Low 65. Tomorrow, sun then clouds. High 81. Yesterday, high 81, low 63. Weather map, Page C19.

VOL. CL . . No. 51,874   Copyright © 2001 The New York Times   NEW YORK, WEDNESDAY, SEPTEMBER 12, 2001   El beyond the greater New York metropolitan area.   75 CENTS

U.S. ATTACKED

HIJACKED JETS DESTROY TWIN TOWERS AND HIT PENTAGON IN DAY OF TERROR

A CREEPING HORROR

Buildings Burn and Fall as Onlookers Search for Elusive Safety

By N. R. KLEINFIELD

It kept getting worse.

The horror arrived in episodic bursts of chilling disbelief, signified first by trembling floors, sharp eruptions, cracked windows. There was the actual unfathomable realization of a gaping, flaming hole in first one of the tall towers, and then the same thing all over again in its twin. There was the merciless sight of bodies helplessly tumbling out, some of them in flames.

Finally, the mighty towers themselves were reduced to nothing. Dense plumes of smoke raced through the downtown avenues, coursing between the buildings, shaped like tornadoes on their sides.

Every sound was cause for alarm. A plane appeared overhead. Was another one coming? No, it was a fighter jet. But was it friend or enemy? People scrambled for their lives, but they didn't know where to go. Should they go north, south, east, west? Stay outside, go indoors? People hid beneath cars and each other. Some contemplated jumping into the river.

For those trying to flee the very epicenter of the collapsing World Trade Center towers, the most horrid thought of all finally dawned on them: nowhere was safe.

For several panic-stricken hours yesterday morning, people in Lower Manhattan witnessed the inexpressible, the incomprehensible, the unthinkable. "I don't know what the gates of hell look like, but it's got to be like this," said John Maloney, a security director for an Internet firm in the trade center. "I'm a combat veteran, Vietnam, and I never saw anything like this."

The first warnings were small ones. Blocks away, Jim Farmer, a film composer, was having breakfast at a small restaurant on West Broadway. He heard the sound of a jet. An odd sound — too loud, it seemed, to be

Continued on Page A7

A Somber Bush Says Terrorism Cannot Prevail

By ELISABETH BUMILLER with DAVID E. SANGER

WASHINGTON, Sept. 11 — President Bush vowed tonight to retaliate against those responsible for today's attacks on New York and Washington, declaring that he would "make no distinction between the terrorists who committed these acts and those who harbor them."

"These acts of mass murder were intended to frighten our nation into chaos and retreat, but they have failed," the president said in his first speech to the nation from the Oval Office. "Our country is strong. Terrorist acts can shake the foundation of our biggest buildings, but they cannot touch the foundation of America."

His speech came after a day of trauma that seems destined to define his presidency. Seeking to at once calm the nation and declare his determination to exact retribution, he told a country numbed by repeated scenes of carnage that "these acts shattered steel, but they cannot dent the steel of American resolve."

Mr. Bush spoke only hours after returning from a zigzag course across the country, as his Secret Service and military security teams moved him from Florida, where he woke up this morning expecting to press for his education bill, to command posts in Louisiana and Nebraska before it was determined the attacks had probably ended and he could safely return to the capital.

It was a sign of the catastrophic

Continued on Page A4

AMERICAN TARGETS A ball of fire exploded outward after the second of two jetliners slammed into the World Trade Center; less than two hours later, both of the 110-story towers were gone. Hijackers crashed a third airliner into the Pentagon, setting off a huge explosion and fire.

National

Rolan Hoskin was crushed in an accident at Tyler Pipe in Tyler, Tex., in 2000. Ira Cofer, left, lost an arm in 1997.

James B. Sandler for The New York Times

Agony and Loss at a Texas Foundry

By DAVID BARSTOW and LOWELL BERGMAN

TYLER, Tex. — It is said that only the desperate seek work at Tyler Pipe, a sprawling, rusting pipe foundry out on Route 69, just past the flea market. Behind a high metal fence lies a workplace that is part Dickens and part Darwin, a dim, dirty, hellishly hot place where men are regularly disfigured by amputations and burns, where turnover is so high that convicts are recruited from local prisons, where some workers urinate in their pants because their bosses refuse to let them step away from the manufacturing line for even a few moments.

Rolan Hoskin was from the ranks of the desperate. His life was a tailspin of unemployment, debt and divorce. A master electrician, 48 years old, he had retreated to a low-rent apartment on the outskirts of town and taken an entry-level maintenance job on the graveyard shift at Tyler Pipe.

He would come home covered in fine black soot, utterly drained and dreading the next shift. "I don't know if I'm going to last another week," his twin brother recalls him saying. But

the pay was dece...
his electricity wa...
was just trying to...

On June 29, 20...
job, Mr. Hoskin d...
a huge molding m...
aging, balky con...
Federal regulatio...
conveyor belts to...
caught and crus...
belts be shut dow...
on them.

But this belt...
records show. No...
safety guards. Th...
been trained to a...
running. Less dow...
Now it was about...
alone in the cram...
ening, the footing...
his knees. His le...
head had been pu...

Mr. Hoskin fe...
business that has...
the plant's owne...
court, deliberate...
workers at Tyler...

Mr. Hoskin we...
vately held com...
Ala., that owns T...
world's largest m...
er and water pipe...
gerous employer...
nine-month exam...
Times, the PBS te...
and the Canadian...

Since 1995, t...
recorded in Mc...
dreds of them a...
uments show. Nir...
skin, have been k...
employ about 5,0...
for more than 400...

Awaiting the Aftershocks

Washington and Nation Plunge Into Fight With Enemy Hard to Identify and Punish

By R. W. APPLE Jr.

WASHINGTON, Sept. 11 — Today's devastating and astonishingly well-coordinated attacks on the World Trade Center towers in New York and on the Pentagon outside of Washington plunged the nation into a warlike struggle against an enemy that will be hard to identify with certainty and hard to punish with precision.

The whole nation — to a degree the whole world — shook as hijacked airliners plunged into buildings that symbolize the financial and military might of the United States. The sense of security and self-confidence that Americans take as their birthright suffered a grievous blow, from which recovery will be slow. The aftershocks will be nearly as bad, as hundreds and possibly thousands of people discover that friends or relatives died awful, fiery deaths.

Scenes of chaos and destruction evocative of the nightmare world of Hieronymus Bosch, with smoke and debris blotting out the sun, were carried by television into homes and workplaces across the nation. Echoing Franklin D. Roosevelt's description of the attack on Pearl Harbor as an event "which will live in infamy," Gov. George E. Pataki of New York, a Republican, spoke of "an incredible outrage" and Senator Charles E. Schumer of New York, a Democrat, spoke of "a dastardly attack."

But mere words were inadequate vessels to contain the sense of shock and horror that people felt.

As Washington struggled to regain

a sense of equilibrium, with warplanes and heavily armed helicopters crossing overhead, past and present national security officials earnestly debated the possibility of a Congressional declaration of war — but against precisely whom, and in what exact circumstances? Warships were maneuvering to protect New York and Washington. The North American Air Defense Command, which had seemed to many a relic of the cold war, adopted a pos-

News Analysis

Continued on Page A24

MORE ON THE ATTACKS

RESCUERS BECOME VICTIMS Firefighters who rushed to the trade center were killed. **PAGE A7**

SEARCH FOR SURVIVORS Some people trapped in the rubble for hours were rescued. **PAGE A3**

OFFICIALS SUSPECT BIN LADEN Eavesdropping intercepts after the attacks were cited. **PAGE A2**

TERRORISTS EXPLOIT WEAKNESS Investigators had criticized precautions against hijacking. **PAGE A17**

CASUALTIES IN WASHINGTON An unknown number of people were killed at the Pentagon. **PAGE A8**

FOR HOME DELIVERY CALL 1-800-NYTIMES

Baskerville	Rockwell	Times	Univers
along	along	along	along
along	along	along	along
along	along	along	along
2964	2964	2964	2964
2964	2964	2964	2964
2964	2964	2964	2964

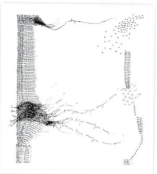

Type degradation and the effects of visual noise on legibility were explored by Linda Reynolds for the British Library.

Ana Hatherly's mid-1970s concrete poetry, or *image-texts* as she called them, are "studies in the illegibility or ambiguity of writing and the disintegration of language." Do you imagine readers care to distinguish between *decipherable* and *illegible* type in anything *except* artwork?

Large-print versions of newspapers and books make reading a pleasure for many and a possibility for some. These examples are shown at a proportionally equivalent size: on the left is a normal front page of the New York *Times* and on the right is a large-print version, both at reduced *but proportionally correct* sizes.

does display type because text type is smaller, so character and word recognition is made more difficult. Anything that gives hard-won readers the slightest awareness of reading text type is bad design.

⊡ Type size is the most abused legibility attribute. Make type too small and you instantly lose all readers for whom small type is hard to see, let alone read. The *New York Times*, among a few other newspapers, has a large print edition that comes out weekly. Stories are edited about in half to make room for the 18-point text, which gives the paper a digest feel. (Their famous "All the News That's Fit to Print" is notably missing from the cover.) Similarly, popular books are available in large-print editions. They, too, look a bit like books for kids, in which text is set large so individual letters and word shapes can be easily discerned.

⊡ Type's legibility is determined in part by the spaces within and immediately surrounding each character. As type's size gets smaller, the spaces must be increased.

⊡ It is thought that serif is easier to read than sans serif in part because it has a built-in horizontal emphasis. Compensate for this by opening the letter and wordspacing just a bit to make sans serif equally legible.

⊡ The alphabet has three letter shapes: vertical, round, and angular. Letters within a single group can be more mistaken for each another: choose a typeface where distinctions are clear.

⊡ As Adrian Frutiger said, "Smooth roads, soft beds, large windows, and sound-proof walls spell comfort to the average human being. The same feelings may be applied to optimum reading comfort of the printed word: suitable paper, sharp printing, well-justfied composition, and clean, open, universally recognized letterforms guarantee optimum legibility."

"The most popular typefaces are the easiest to read; their popularity has made them disappear from conscious cognition. It becomes impossible to tell if they are easy to read because they are commonly used, or if they are commonly used because they are easy to read." Zuzana Licko

You will ask me, Gratius, why this man so delights me. It is because he helps me by refreshing my spirit after the confusion of the law-courts and by resting my senses, wearied by invective. Do you suppose I could find something to say every day on such a variety of subjects, did I not enrich my mind in study? Do you suppose my mind could endure such strains, did I not ease it in these same studies? Indeed, I admit that I am much given to literature. Let others be ashamed—those who have buried themselves in books to the point where they cannot make use of the fruits of their learning for the common good or bring them to light for the consideration of others. But why should I feel shame, gentlemen, I who for many years have so lived that when it was a matter of the time and convenience of others amusement has not distracted me, pleasure has not called me away, not even sleep has stayed me. How then can anyone blame me or be justly angry if I have allowed for the pursuit of my own studies as much time as others give to the management of their affairs, to attendance at holiday performances, to other pleasures, and to rest for body and soul; or as much time as still others devote to luxurious banqueting or even to gaming and ball-playing? In fact, you should grant me this all the more because my studies increase these oratorical abilities and achievements, which, whatever their merits, have never been withheld from my friends in times of danger. However trifling these attainments may seem, I fully acknowledge the source from which I draw all that is most inspired in them. For if I had not from my youth been persuaded by the admonitions of many men and the contents of many books that nothing in life is more to be sought than glory and good repute, in the pursuit of which every bodily torment, every danger of death and exile must be held insignificant, I should never have exposed myself in your defence to so many furious encounters, and to the unremitting attacks of corrupted men. All books, all sayings of the wise, all histories of times past abound in examples, which would be lost in darkness if

Quaeres a nobis, Grati, cur tanto opere hoc homine delectemur. Quia suppeditat nobis ubi et animus ex hoc forensi strepitu reficiatur et aures convicio defessae conquiescant. An tu existimas aut suppetere nobis posse quod cotidie dicamus in tanta varietate rerum, nisi animos nostros doctrina excolamus, aut ferre animos tantam posse contentionem, nisi eos doctrina eadem relaxemus? Ego vero fateor me his studiis esse deditum: ceteros pudeat, si qui se ita litteris abdiderunt, ut nihil possint ex his neque ad communem adferre fructum neque in aspectum lucemque proferre: me autem quid pudeat, qui tot annos ita vivo, iudices, ut a nullius umquam me tempore aut commodo aut otium meum abstraxerit aut voluptas avocarit aut denique somnus retardarit? Qua re quis tandem me reprehendat aut quis mihi iure suscenseat, si, quantum ceteris ad suas res obeundas, quantum ad festos dies ludorum celebrandos, quantum ad alias voluptates et ad ipsam requiem animi et corporis conceditur temporum, quantum alii tribuunt tempestivis conviviis, quantum denique alveolo, quantum pilae, tantum mihi egomet ad haec studia recolenda sumpsero? Atque hoc adeo mihi concedendum est magis, quod ex his studiis haec quoque crescit oratio et facultas, quae quantacumque in me est, numquam amicorum periculis defuit. Quae si cui levior videtur, illa quidem certe, quae summa sunt, ex quo fonte hauriam sentio. Nam nisi multorum praeceptis multisque litteris mihi ab adolescentia suasissem nihil esse in vita magno opere expetendum nisi laudem atque honestatem, in ea autem persequenda omnes cruciatus corporis, omnia pericula mortis atque exsilii parvi esse ducenda, numquam me pro salute vestra in tot ac tantas dimicationes atque in hos profligatorum hominum cotidianos impetus obiecissem. Sed pleni sunt omnes libri, plenae sapientium voces, plena exemplorum vetustas: quae iacerent in tenebris omnia, nisi litterarum lumen accederet. Quam multas

nobis imagines non solum ad intuendum, verum etiam ad imitandum fortissimorum virorum expressas scriptores et Graeci et Latini reliquerunt, quas ego mihi semper in administranda re publica proponens animum et mentem meam ipsa cogitatione hominum excellentium conformabam.

VII. Quaeret quispiam: quid? illi ipsi summi viri, quorum virtutes litteris proditae sunt, istane doctrina, quam tu effers laudibus, eruditi fuerunt? Difficile est hoc de omnibus confirmare, sed tamen est certum quod respondeam. Ego multos homines excellenti animo ac virtute fuisse et sine doctrina naturae ipsius habitu prope divino per se ipsos et moderatos et graves exstitisse fateor: etiam illud adiungo, saepius ad laudem atque virtutem naturam sine doctrina quam sine natura valuisse doctrinam. Atque idem ego hoc contendo, cum ad naturam eximiam et illustrem accesserit ratio quaedam conformatioque doctrinae, tum illud nescio quid praeclarum ac singulare solere exsistere. Ex hoc esse hunc numero, quem patres nostri viderunt, divinum hominem Africanum, ex hoc C. Laelium, L. Furium, moderatissimos homines et continentissimos, ex hoc fortissimum virum et illis temporibus doctissimum, M. Catonem illum senem: qui profecto si nihil ad percipiendam colendamque virtutem litteris adiuvarentur, numquam se ad earum studium contulissent. Quod si non hic tantus fructus ostenderetur et si ex his studiis delectatio sola peteretur, tamen, ut opinor, hanc animi adversionem humanissimam ac liberalissimam iudicaretis. Nam ceterae neque temporum sunt neque aetatum omnium neque locorum: at haec studia adolescentiam alunt, senectutem oblectant, secundas res ornant, adversis perfugium ac solacium praebent, delectant domi, non impediunt foris, pernoctant nobiscum, peregrinantur, rusticantur.

the light of literature did not reach them. How many finely drawn portraits of heroic men have Greek and Latin authors left for us not only to admire but also to emulate! By keeping these models constantly before me during my administration of the republic, I have, through thinking on their greatness, been moulding my own spirit and mind.

VII. But someone will ask, 'What then? Were those great men, whose virtues have been made known through literature, themselves learned in these studies you keep praising so extravagantly?' It is difficult to affirm this about all of them, but I am sure of my answer. Many men of outstanding intelligence and character have led disciplined and sober lives without benefit of learning, simply because their dispositions were naturally akin to the divine. I will even add that character without learning more often attains to praise and honor than learning without character. But I also hold that when the influence of reason and study is added to a natively superior and noble character, we find something uniquely excellent. Such a man was that godlike Africanus, whom our fathers knew; such were Caius Laelius and Lucius Furius, men of the greatest self-control and temperance; of that number was Marcus Cato, that noble old man, who was most brave and, for his time, most learned. These men would certainly never have turned to such studies if their reading had not helped them to understand and cultivate virtue. But if the good results of study were not obvious, and its only goal were pleasure, you would still, in my opinion, consider it the most humane and honorable form of relaxation for the spirit. For other occupations are not suited to all times, all stages of life, all places; but this pursuit inspires the young, delights the old, graces good fortune, offers refuge and solace in bad, charms us at home, never hinders us abroad, watches with us by night, and accompanies us when we journey into foreign lands or retreat to the peace of country life.

SIZE

Large::Small
Tall::Short
Wide::Narrow
Expanded::Condensed

Larger type must be *visibly* larger. A point or two larger at text sizes is not enough – and is useless at display sizes.

Expanded and condensed types are elaborations of the normal members of type families and are thus more difficult to read. Keep such type brief.

FORM

Roman::Italic
Majuscule::Minuscule
Geometric::Organic
Representational::Abstract
Distinct::Ambiguous
2D::3D

Set a phrase in all caps to make it stand out in a lowercase paragraph.

DENSITY

Bold::Light
Thick::Thin
Opaque::Transparent
Stable::Unstable
Filled::Empty
Deep::Shallow

Depending on family, skip *two weights* to make the bolder face look purposeful.

STRUCTURE

Serif::Sans serif
Organized::Chaotic
Aligned::Free placement

A common contrast is sans serif for display (because it fits tighter and becomes darker) and serif for the text (because it is thought to be easier to read at longer lengths).

POSITION

Symmetrical::Asymmetrical
Left::Right
Above::Below
Grouped::Isolated
In front::Behind
Rhythmic::Random

Leaving all other attributes the same, changing position alone is an elegant way to create a focal point.

COLOR

Black::Color
Grayscale::RGB
Dark::Light
Bright::Muted
Warm::Cool
Saturated::Neutral

Though it is tempting to use color as a decorative tool, color contrast must be used as an editorial tool to reveal real differences.

DIRECTION

Vertical::Horizontal
Perpendicular::Diagonal
Forward::Backward
Clockwise::Counterclockwise
Converging::Diverging

Contrast of direction is related to contrast of position and the two can be effectively combined.

TEXTURE

Coarse::Fine
Rough::Smooth
Shiny::Matte

A texture is a surface that can be felt and touched. A pattern is a recurring decorative design or theme. True textures are converted into two-dimensional patterns to be reproduced.

Typographic similarity unites the three elements in Jan Tschichold's 1927 poster. Adherence to an emerging design philosophy resulted in revolutionary creativity.

Typographic contrast separates the Latin, printed in $^{14}/_{16}$ black, from the English translation, printed in $^{10}/_{12}$ italic red, in this excerpt from *Pro Archia Poeta*, an oration by Cicero in 62BC. Yet there is obvious similarity: the column depths are perfectly even, spacing is classically proportional, and the contrasting types are both members of the Bembo type family. Designed by Bert Clarke and letterpress printed in 1967.

There are eight typographic contrasts. Use them when one particular contrast helps convey the meaning of the type. Combining type contrasts strengthens the effect and provides a near-infinite palette of possibilities.

The opposite design philosophy is shown in a patent medicine ad from 1938. An abundance of contrasts overwhelms design unity: there are five separate pieces in this "one" ad.

Strict alignment joins three types into a single unit in Hans Hillman's 1967 German movie poster for the classic 1925 Russian silent film *Battleship Potemkin*.

Connecting unrelated parts into a single thing is work for a designer. Charles Mingus said, "Anyone can make the simple complicated. Creativity is making the complicated simple."

 # Typographic unity

A (publication) consists of five elements: the (content), type, ink, paper and binding. To create a unity from these five elements so the result is not a passing product of fashion, but assumes the validity of permanent value – that should be our desire." Giovanni Mardersteig, *The Apologia of the Officina Bodoni*, 1929

Design is a search for unity. It is a continuous balancing act between sameness and emphasis. Parts must look different to express their content, or else a page will suffer from oatmeal-itis in which everything looks like a unified but unappealing bowl of grayness. At the same time, the parts of a design must be unified so they make a single, powerful impression. Contrasting type styles *that share characteristics* achieves both goals.

Gui Bonsiepe wrote: "Design means, among many other things, arranging elements into a whole that makes sense... In typography, order is mainly a question of relationships within groups of elements and the distribution of these elements on a page." Bonsiepe defines

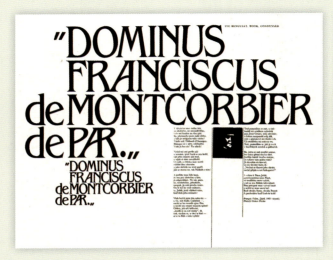

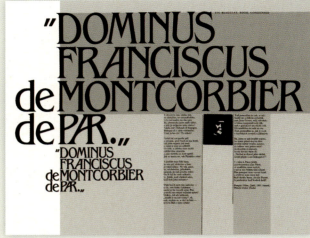

Californian
ABCDEFGHIJKLMNO
abcdefghijklmnopqrstu
1234567890

Franklin Gothic Condens
ABCDEFGHIJKLMNOPQ
abcdefghijklmnopqrstuv
1234567890

Clarendon
ABCDEFGHIJKLM
abcdefghijklmnopq
1234567890

ITC Quay
ABCDEFGHIJKLMNOPQR
abcdefghijklmnopqrstuvw
1234567890

Loire
ABCDEFGHIJKLMNO
abcdefghijklmnopqrstuv
1234567890

Monotype Grotesque
ABCDEFGHIJKLMNOP
abcdefghijklmnopqrstu
1234567890

Menhart Manuscript
ABCDEFGHIJKLMNC
abcdefghijklmnopqrstu
1234567890

News Gothic
ABCDEFGHIJKLMNOP
abcdefghijklmnopqrstu
1234567890

Nicolas Jenson
ABCDEFGHIJKLMNO
abcdefghijklmnopqrstuvwxy:
1234567890

Meta Roman
ABCDEFGHIJKLMNOPQ
abcdefghijklmnopqrstu
1234567890

Other recommended serif types:

Baskerville	Berling	Cæcilia	Caslon	Centaur	Garamond
Geneo	Joanna	Kinesis	Modern 20	Quiosco	Rekja

Other recommended sans serif types:

Akzidenz Grotesk	Frutiger	Futura	Gill Sans	Haptic
Officina	The Sans	Supria Sans	Trade Gothic	Univers

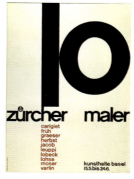

NemBeszélekMAGYARUL

Type that is unified shares design attributes. The counter spaces of *BDV* have been condensed and equally spaced

apart. The height of the all caps *MAGYARUL* agrees with the x-height of *NEM BESZÉLEK*.

Consistent type weight and geometric shapes unite these three letters for a seating company logo by F.H.K. Henrion in 1963. It's a pity the mark isn't for fish.

A single type weight but contrasts of size and position and clear use of space, with color contrast in a lesser role, creates order in Emil Ruder's 1960 typographic poster.

The reasons this design *(far left)* works are:

1| **One type family** in which capitalization is used to differentiate;

2| **Alignment** in which, for example, the repeated *de*'s are hung flush right and the text columns tops align with PAR;

3| **Subtle adjustments** like lowering opening quotes and base-aligning close quotes.

These "showings" are all set $^{25}/_{16.5}$, that is, with minus linespacing. This reveals the relative size of the *x-height*, which is the distance from the baseline to the median of the lowercase letters. Each showing ends on the right side at a different place in the alphabet. This illustrates the type's *comparative width*, which must be considered when choosing a face — and when combining faces.

two kinds of order: 1| **The order of the system** in which each typographic element (headlines, text, and captions) is part of a system. Fewer elements naturally leads to greater order. 2| **The order of arrangement** in which elements clearly relate to each other and the frequency with which elements optically align.

What is *right* with your type?

Because of the constant rain of information on our heads, it is important that we design messages with something noticeably *right* about them. Messages must first be seen, so the focal point must startle. Then they must be legible, so information is gotten across painlessly. If something is *legible*, it *might* be read. If it might be read, it might be *remembered*.

Chefs who use fresh ingredients are a step ahead of chefs who use wilted or frozen ingredients. So, too, designers who use good type have an advantage over those who use whatever is handy. Shown at left are some particularly good types.

Type is the one area in design education in which learning "right" thinking is critical because typography is essentially a logical process. Sensitizing the eye and mind to perceive inherent meaning and real — rather than automatically assumed — differences takes practice and discipline.

"Learn the difference between attention-getting type and information-conveying type. Design accordingly."
Anonymous

The Sauna family is first shown in the book — Regular Italics with two ligatures

'**Read naked**'. — Black

THIS PINK BOOK DOESN'T — Regular

 only contain  — Bold with dingbats

sauna stories, — Bold Italics with one ligature

but it can also be read inside the sauna… — Bold

And it survives! — Swash Italics

Even better, some stories are getting **visible** in a sauna only, — Regular with Bold

at 80 degrees Celsius — Bold Italics

 OR HIGHER. — Regular

---

SNEAUX PRESS

prOGRess

jeFE PRESS

- ■ Size
- ☐ Serif/sans
- ☐ Form
- ☐ Weight
- ☐ Case
- ■ Width

- ■ Size
- ■ Serif/sans
- ■ Form
- ☐ Weight
- ☐ Case
- ■ Width

- ■ Size
- ☐ Serif/sans
- ☐ Form
- ☐ Weight
- ■ Case
- ☐ Width

Sneaux PRESS

PrOGRess

PRESS Jefe

- ■ Size
- ☐ Serif/sans
- ■ Form
- ■ Weight
- ■ Case
- ☐ Width

- ☐ Size
- ☐ Serif/sans
- ■ Form
- ■ Weight
- ■ Case
- ☐ Width

- ☐ Size
- ☐ Serif/sans
- ☐ Form
- ■ Weight
- ■ Case
- ■ Width

LINGUA
TRIUM SÆCULORUM,
QUA
INNOVATUS EST LITERATUS ORBIS
TERRARUM,
ET
*SCIENTIA DIVINARUM RERUMQUE HUMA-
NARUM, AD SUMMUM EVECTA EST*
Fastigium
ARS ARTIUM
TYPOGRAPHIA

[first example — mixed decorative typefaces]

[second example — Czech/Latin text in mixed types]

[third example — Prague text c1740]

Empresa de Transportes
Fluviais de Tavira
Nᵒ 05134
Contribuinte N.ᵒ 501 614 605
QUATRO AGUAS · ILHA · QUATRO AGUAS
Transporte - ADULTO . 200$00
Todas as taxas incluídas
Conservar este bilhete até final da viagem

Mixing types was a necessity when there were simply no letters available. The first two examples show a mixture of typefaces — a truly hideous cacophony, while the third

example merely mixes cases of one size in the headline. Such emergency substitutions had to be made typically at the largest type sizes, where

individual letters were costlier and therefore fewer. One could argue that this third treatment has a bit more unity than the other two. These examples are all from Prague, c1740.

A modern equivalent is a letterpress-printed ticket from a small ferry service in Portugal. The random colection of types gives a rustic, amateurish charm.

This combination of types is both stimulating and unified because it uses members of a single type family. Begun as a black display face, *Sauna*, designed by Piet Schreuder of Underware, includes three weights, each with two versions of italics, 26 ligatures, and 26 dingbats.

Six type contrasts are used in different combinations to produce six very different results. It is perfectly reasonable to consciously craft designs from the list of possible contrasts. Intentional contrast combinations as a *design process* develop alternatives quickly and easily and do not depend on "artistic inspiration."

Combining typefaces

Typographic difference is a tool for developing hierarchy and distinctions between kinds of information. Visually presorting content serves the reader by showing length and complexity. It is easy to make typographic changes that are random or amusing, but it is hard to make thoughtful, purposeful changes that help the message and retain design unity. Too many fonts distract the reader from the work of reading. Mixing types well *to clarify content* is dependent on using adedquate contrasts, but not so much contrast as to break the design's unity.

Daniel Berkeley Updike wrote in the 1937 second edition of his *Printing Types: Their History, Form and Use*, "The problem of choosing types wisely remains precisely what it was (when the first edition of this book was published). Indeed, the necessity for the cultivation of taste and judgment in selection is greater today than it was fifteen years ago, because of the mass of material from which to choose and the delicate differentiations of design in the types themselves. Background, tradition, research, taste, a sense of suitability and practicality must, as in the past, aid one's choice, and then each person must work out the further problem of selection for himself." With the modern proliferation of types, it has gotten considerably more difficult in all these regards since 1937.

"Discipline in typography is a prime virtue. Individuality must be secured by means that are rational. Distinction needs to be won by simplicity and restraint. It is equally true that these qualities need to be infused with a certain spirit and vitality, or they degenerate into dullness and mediocrity." Stanley Morison

Combine Frutiger, a humanist sans serif, with an old style serif. This is 13-point Italian Old Style, a point larger than the Frutiger for x-height equivalency. *Find and make similarities be-*

Combine Syntax, a humanist sans serif, with an old style serif. This is 14-point Nicolas Jenson, three points larger than the Syntax for x-height equivalency. *Find and make similarities between dissimilar types vis-*

Combine Gill Sans, a humanist sans serif, with an old style serif. This is 13-point Adobe Garamond, a point larger than the Gill Sans for x-height equivalency. *Find and make similarities between dissimilar*

Humanists with Old Styles

Combine Avenir, a geometric sans serif, with a transitional serif. This is 12-point Baskerville, the same point size as the Avenir, matched for x-height equivalency. *Find and make similari-*

Combine Neuzit Grotesk, a geometric sans serif, with a transitional serif. This is 13-point Bell, two points larger than the Neuzit Grotesk for x-height equivalency. *Find and make similari-*

Combine Triplex, a geometric sans serif, with a transitional serif. This is 11½-point New Caledonia, a half point size smaller than the Triplex for x-height equivalency. *Find and make similarities between dissimilar*

Geometric Sans with Transitionals

Combine Griffith Gothic, a grotesque sans serif, with a modern serif. This is 13-point Bodoni, one point larger than the Griffith Gothic for x-height equivalency. *Find and make simi-*

Combine Trade Gothic, a grotesque sans serif, with a modern serif. This is 11½-point Veljovic, a point smaller than the Trade Gothic for x-height equivalency. *Find and make similarities between dis-*

Combine Univers, a grotesque sans serif, with a modern serif. This is 11-point Centennial, a point smaller than the Univers for x-height equivalency. *Find and make similarities between dis-*

Grotesks with Moderns

Combine Boton, a slab serif, with a lighter weight of itself. This is 12-point Boton, the same size as the bolder Boton for x-height equivalency. *Find and make similarities between dissimilar*

Combine Cæcilia, a slab serif, with a lighter weight of itself. This is 11-point Cæcilia, the same size as the bolder Cæcilia for x-height equivalency. *Find and make similarities between dis-*

Combine Officina Serif, a slab serif, with a lighter weight of its sans serif counterpart. This is 12-point Officina Sans, the same size as the bolder Officina Serif for x-height equivalency. *Find and make similari-*

Slab serifs with Slab serifs

vibe

COEXISTENCE

These logos use type contrast for expressive interest, but they achieve design unity, which is an essential attribute of high-quality typography.

xfxf

Create type unity between un-related typefaces by matching x-heights. Change the point size of one type in quarter-point increments until visual equivalency is achieved.

bcomw

Match roundness between un-related types by comparing the *b, c, d, e, o, p,* and *q.*

Look for equivalent widths by comparing wider letters, like the *m* and *w,* which show the greatest difference.

Mixing types, by definition, means a condition of dis-agreement. But design calls for agreement, or unity, even among dissimilar parts. Cre-ate unity by choosing types with similar shape, proportion, weight, x-height, typographic color, or even the time period of the typefaces' designs. Keeping half a mind on what is *right* about a given pairing will ensure design unity, what the reader initially sees.

How to combine similar types is daunting. If contrast is needed within an area of serif type, it is better made within a single family, say, with roman and italics, than by using two serif families, where the difference may not be as visible. And even if it is, it will appear jarring and self-conscious rather than smooth and natural.

Choose a family that has a regular and a bold weight; regular italics; regular and bold small caps; and lining and old style figures. In addition to these contrast-ing letterforms, you will have size, case, spacing, and position with which to make meaningful distinctions.

Start by selecting the text face, since this is where the reader will spend the most time. When matching serif and sans serif types, look for inherent similarities: a slightly condensed serif, for example, will look better with a slightly condensed sans serif. Consider a type family that has both serif and sans serif versions because the design unity is built in.

Mixing typefaces is a bit like mixing seasonings when cooking. There may be general agreement among chefs that some flavors go very well with other flavors. But the creative cook is willing to experiment and try new combinations to give diners new eating experiences. The dictum that a designer can get away with anything *so long as it looks like it was on purpose* applies to type com-binations just as it does to every other design decision.

"My primary goal is to inject decisiveness, to show that these words know what they are saying." Susan Casey

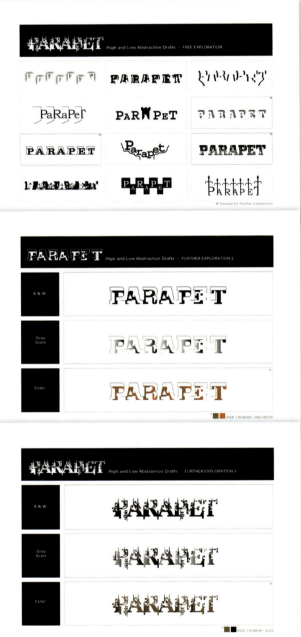

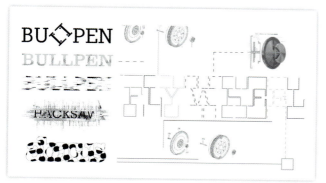

Each student is required to use a slab serif typeface of their choice, thereby causing understanding of type categories. This exercise provides an excellent opportunity to discuss the balance of type and image, an important topic in a designer's education. The "right" balance in this exercise is to emphasize letterform and subjugate imagery.

The exercise also allows a conversation about levels of abstraction in imagery, as shown in this chart. Visual equivalencies of abstraction are shown on the right. The most legible marks (the least abstract) are at the top. Developing similar charts from found samples is a useful freshman exercise.

This is an exceptional record of a student's trail through the design process. Meng Leong Chong generated simple, relatively uninteresting ideas first, but he didn't stop there. He gradually built upon and replaced them for superb, unexpected final results.

Introductory typography exercise

This is an exercise for sophomores. It is not intended as a first experience with type, which must be work with the form of letters and the importance of negative space immediately surrounding letters in a somewhat less illustrative process. The key is to achieve a balance between obviousness and abstraction — mere hinting — at the meaning of the word. This exercise evolves through four critiques — each an opportunity to consider larger ways of perceiving the assignment — before the final is due.

"Creativity is allowing yourself to make mistakes. Art is knowing which ones to keep."
Scott Adams

Purpose To explore typographic abstraction, legibility, and letter-to-letter relationships by designing one source word in three different ways.

The goal is to balance legibility (a quality of efficient, clear, simple reading) and readability (a quality that promotes interest, expression of meaning, and visual pleasure). Is it possible to make a typographic solution both functional (legible) and unconventional (readable)? Ideally, you will cross the line between legibility and readability, or *creative expression*. What choices do you make when abstracting type and inhibiting legibility?

Process, Part 1 Managing abstraction is essential to graphic designers. Like value (lightness and darkness), abstraction is a relative term: by comparison, one thing is more or less abstract than another. You have selected a source word from a list. It is a noun: a person, place, or thing. It can therefore be readily illustrated.

Look up the definition of your word. Use a thesaurus to find equivalent words. Become an expert on your word: when and why was it coined and how has it changed over time? Compile a visual clip file of your word including images, textures, and other extreme closeups that might imply your word without showing it in its entirety.

Process, Part 2 Select a slab serif typeface that is unique in class. Begin sketching ways to integrate your word with samples from your visual clip file. Some sketches will produce more abstract ideas than others: become aware of this comparison. Categorize your sketches in order of abstraction. Select and interpret one idea as a literal (less abstract) study. Interpret another as moderately abstract. Select a third as most abstract. This last will be considered too abstract if your word and its meaning can't be recognized. It may help to think of your word as a restaurant name or book title that illustrates itself.

You must Work exclusively in Illustrator. Use the same slab serif face in each study. Set and convert to outline paths. One study must be RGB and use two colors: 110r 88g 69b plus any other color *except black*. One study must be grayscale and not merely *have* value, but *use* value. And one study must be bitmap (solid black and white only). All studies are to be exactly 54p0 wide and centered on horizontal 51p0x66p0 heavyweight bright white sheets. Export final studies into Photoshop and save as 600dpi RGB/grayscale/bitmap tiffs. Provide digital files with a folder of all preliminary studies; a folder of the final three studies; and a folder of the three final tiff files.

A3 B1 C3 D1 E1 F1

The Masks of GOD

Joseph Campbell

A2 B2 C1 D2 E1 F1

A3 B3 C2 D2 E3 F1

A2 B3 C1 D2 E1 F2

A2 B2 C3 D1 E1 F2

THE CUSTOM OF THE COUNTRY Edith Wharton

A3 B1 C1 D3 E2 F2

A1 B2 C2 D1 E1 F3

A2 B1 C1 D3 E3 F3

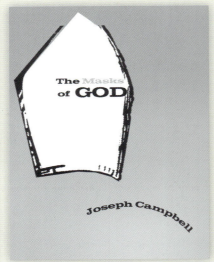

A2 B3 C2 D1 E2 F3

The Masks of God
Joseph Campbell

**The Custom
of the Country**
Edith Wharton

Exile's Return
Malcolm Cowley

Limitations *cause* creativity. Art for this exercise was selected from Dover's collection of steel engravings. They are not chosen for any intrinsic re-latedness to book titles: lack of belonging *requires abstraction* to convey meaning. Book titles for this exercise were selected for their *interpretability*. Novels, because of their broad content on various subjects and their emphasis on the human condition, work well. The extremely wide typeface selected is Clarendon Bold Expanded Round-ed. This peculiar face imposed itself in ways that required creative flexibility. The limitation itself causes unexpected and interesting design solutions.

Each book cover combines assigned variables in different combinations, which are listed beneath each study. The freshness of the designs is a result of the design process used.

Advanced typography exercise

This is a more advanced exercise for juniors and seniors. It has three preliminary critiques before the final is due. Elements, which vary every semester, are assigned so students don't waste time deciding what to use: the exercise isn't about choosing material, it is about choosing what to do with it to convey a message.

Purpose To explore manners of organizing typographic elements, space, and imagery into coherent groups that express hierarchy and show clear relationship finding.

Process, Part 1 Use the 600dpi tiff image provided. Place your image in a Illustrator document so the longest dimension is 3p0 in from trim on a 66p0 x 51p0 page. Print on a bright white, heavy-weight sheet.

Process, Part 2 Design three book covers. The single most important aspect of this exercise is to abstract the type and imagery. Using the chart below, choose one attribute from each of the six columns and combine in a single study. Make a second study using another unused attribute from each column. Combine the remaining unused attributes from each column and combine in a third study. No other elements may be used and no elements, including type, may be repeated. Compositions are to be 42p0 x 55p6 vertical. Execute all preliminary studies full-size. All studies must use the single version of the assigned font. Though using a single typeface keeps you from using *font* contrast, there are five typographic contrasts that remain available: Position (Col A); Value (relative darkness) (Col B); Size (Col C); Base alignment; and type treatments you may add to the font in Illustrator.

You must Explore abstraction and legibility. Show how well you can see and be prepared to defend the logic of precise design relationships.

	A Alignment	**B** Color	**C** Type size	**D** Visual emphasis	**E** System anomaly*	**F** Book title
1	Flush left	Black and white	Maximum of 18pt	Type dominant	Unification/Isolation	*Masks*
2	Centered	B, W, and Grays	Minimum of 200pt	Image dominant	Direction	*Custom*
3	Flush right	PMS 325,328,368	300pt difference	Emptiness dominant	Rhythm	*Exile's*
	These systems create an anomaly based on relative position.	Negative space, whether white or black, must appear in both fore- and back-ground of each study.	One study must use very small type, one must use very large type, and one must use extreme size contrast.	Dominance does not mean exclusivity. Each study must contain all the elements used in the other studies, but they must be differently weighted.	Explore relative position, relative direction, and a break in rhythmic positioning to create an anomaly, or focal point.	

Format Three final prints on high-resolution, bright white heavy-weight paper. Lightly pencil the study's "recipe" on the back of each study. Prepare three 300dpi repro-size files of your final designs. Crop to exactly 42p0 x 55p6 vertical. Name files and your CD intelligently for the user.

* *An anomaly is an element that breaks a visual system and becomes the focal point. For an anomaly to be visible, the system must be consistent and recognizable. Therefore creating an anomaly is really a result of your ability to create a coherent system.*

"Design is about being cheeky enough to question everything. The eyes of a child coupled to the instincts of a bloodhound." Richard Seymour

**Section Three
Creativity**

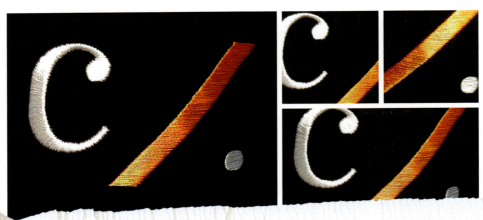

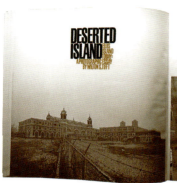

Problem: a story about Ellis Island, the site of entry for hundreds of thousands of immigrants in the early 20th century. Solution: a typographic

cluster of headline, subhead, and byline that illustrates "islandness" positioned in a vast area of empty image.

These two poster diagrams by Yukichi Takada use relative type size to indicate quantity and location of the population's average lifetime (*left*) and energy consumption. What

makes these works fresh is the way type color and type size abstracts familiar shapes of landmasses to describe their messages.

A logo unexpectedly made from stock glyphs is a fresh solution for Caramoor, a classical music venue.

A book thanking donors for a town library expansion reinvents what a "page" is.

QUINTET

Replacing letters with numerals is fairly common, but this example shows particularly sensitive insight into form. A *5* replaces a *UI* in a word meaning a "group of five"; the weight of the much larger *5* is carefully adjusted to its surrounding letters, and the letterspacing throughout matches the space within the *5*.

Fresh vs. familiar

*T*he world is full of inadequate design solutions which merely build on conventional wisdom. *If you don't constantly turn over rocks, you will never notice if something has changed."*
Richard Seymour

The essence of design freshness is recognizing when your work is too comfortable or too familiar.

The definition of *familiar* is safe, automatic, and likely to be accepted. While a familiar presentation may adequately display its message, it does not add value to the message. Some designers are willing to settle, or are perhaps unaware of settling, for ordinary, familiar design solutions. Often, design looks familiar simply because the designer accepted standard treatments without thinking about them (*see next spread*).

The definition of *fresh* is thoughtful, solves the problem in a unique way, and is risky. A fresh presentation adds value to the message. There is, in fact, a correlation between value added and freshness: the more value added to the message through its design, the fresher the

Neon lights were new when this travel poster was designed in 1938, so this was quite an edgy treatment at the time. Freshness is tied to timeliness.

Color consistency and contrast creates order in this near life-size reproduction of a designer's personal statement.

The logo for City Ball, a party in São Paulo, uses contrast of letterform repetition and alignment with looser spiral forms in this design by Guto Lacaz.

Hand lettering and positive/negative contrast of value and baselines reveals editorial meaning on this book jacket.

Hand lettering, or in this case *handcrafting* letters, is Stefan Sagmeister's solution for an Austrian magazine sequence. While highly abstract (they read: *Everything I do always comes back to me*), these six designs are astonishingly original.

solution. It takes informed and interested minds — both the client's and the designer's — to look for fresh solutions. Freshness springs directly from a full diagnosis of the problem. One needs to get inside the problem and turn it over, looking for the unique aspect that will show off its essence. If your design solutions are not unique, if your solutions are applicable to other problems, you haven't dissected the problem fully.

François Colos, a collagist who did a great number of conceptual op-ed illustrations for the *New York Times*, said his biggest problem was coming up with something fresh every year for recurring subjects. "You have for example now the 98th Congress of the United States. It comes every year. What are you going to do for the 98th which is a new statement? And a hundred, a thousand on the economy: it's always the same story. Unemployment, inflation: you made one inflation, two inflation, a hundred inflation drawings, what are you doing for the *hundred and first*? That's the big problem."

As Walter Gropius said, "Design *may* be art." To which I would add, "but only if a design is *fresh*." Design is never art if it is familiar. After all, art is defined as making the familiar look new. And remember timeliness: what was once fresh becomes trite and what is fresh today will probably show its age in the future. The more cutting edge, the more likely a design will come to look dated.

"There is wisdom in turning as often as possible from the familiar to the unfamiliar. It keeps the mind nimble, it kills prejudice, and it fosters humor." George Santayana

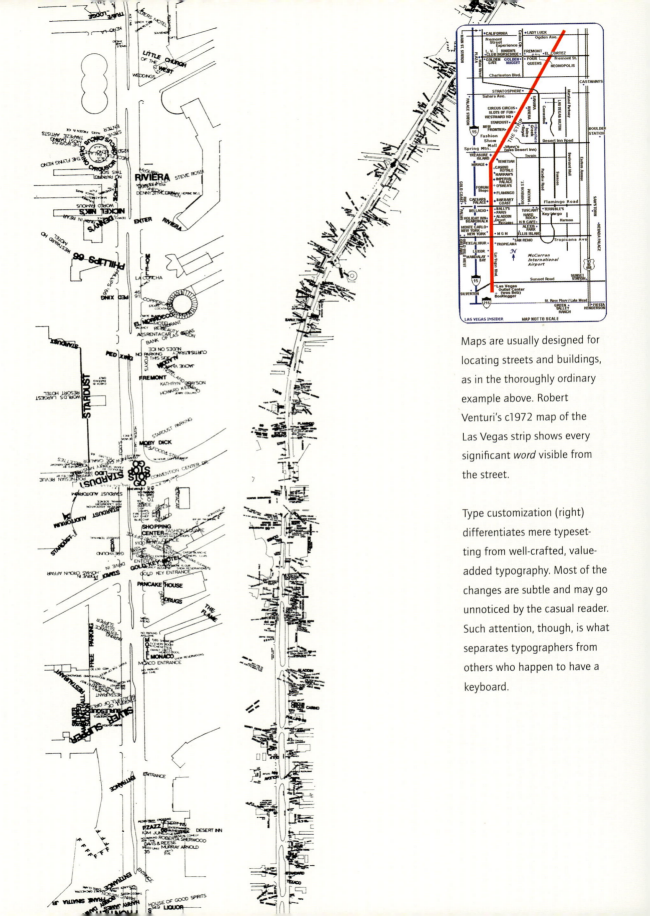

Maps are usually designed for locating streets and buildings, as in the thoroughly ordinary example above. Robert Venturi's c1972 map of the Las Vegas strip shows every significant *word* visible from the street.

Type customization (right) differentiates mere typesetting from well-crafted, value-added typography. Most of the changes are subtle and may go unnoticed by the casual reader. Such attention, though, is what separates typographers from others who happen to have a keyboard.

Art Nouveau was responsible for much of the explosion of expressive lettering that took place around the turn of the previous century, from about 1890 into the 1930s. The at-titude of overthrowing prevailing stodgy attitudes produces a succession of art movements, each quickly replacing its predecessor as artists ("designers" had not yet been invented as a specialty) explored theories, philosophies, and fashions. Comparable exploration continues today, despite the superabundance of information we have become used to.

The unusual dates on Bedřich Smetana's gravestone in Vyšehrad Cemetery in Prague indicate he was born on 2 March, 1824, and died on 12 May, 1884.

Mr. Bedrich Smetana
258 Fulton St.
New York, N.Y. 10038
(212) 555-1645

❶ Ordinary typesetting following styling inherited from mono-spaced typewriters and default computer settings.

Mr. Bedrich Smetana
258 Fulton Street
New York, N.Y. 10038
212-555-1645

❷ Set in a higher-quality font; spell out abbreviation; replace parentheses with hyphen.

Mr Bedřich Smetana
258 Fulton Street
New York, NY 10038
212 / 555 1645

❸ Remove periods and hyphen; replace hyphen with slash; add háček.

Mr Bedřich Smetana
258 Fulton Street
New York, NY 10038
212 555 1645

❹ Add 3 pts optical linespacing above lining numerals; remove slash.

Mr Bedřich Smetana
258 Fulton Street
New York NY 10038
212 555 1645

❺ Replace lining figures with old style figures; remove comma.

Mr Bedřich Smetana
258 Fulton Street
New York NY 10038
212 555 1645

❻ Add 3 pts (*New York*) and remove 3 pts (*212 555*) optical linespacing; italicize telephone; reverse zip code in box.

First draft	Second draft	Third draft	Final design

Hand lettering contrasts with typesetting in this spread from a British design association's annual report.

Robert Massin's 1954 interpretation of Eugene Ionesco's *The Bald Soprano* is an unusual visualization of a play. Each character's dialogue is set in a different font, with typographic size and position used to indicate its delivery. This is a literal translation from spoken sounds to visual signals, which is a common sense approach and eminently defendable. It remains a worthwhile area for continued present-day exploration.

Design is a *process*, not a *result*. These studies show the evolution of five design ideas. Cia Delas uses negative space and the shared shape of the lowercase L and I to connect the two words.

GE Halogen lightbulb package studies show the *benefit* of the bulb without showing the bulb itself.

Lyrica's job brief emphasized the need to express *thirds*. The final uses negative space to enhance distinctive character.

The owner of Prescott Funding simply wanted the symbolism of the bald eagle, so the job was to make an eagle "theirs."

Virclude's marks explore visual representations of "protection" and "aggression."

Five case studies

Designers usually have to get the familiar out of their systems before the fresh ideas begin to flow. The five designs shown on the opposite page all began with perfectly acceptable studies (*far left column*), each selected from a dozen or more initial draft sketches. Second and third passes (*center columns*) show increased individuality and abstraction. Final sketches (*right column*) push abstraction further and add illustrative elements.

Cia Delas, which means *Their Company* in Portuguese, is a Brazilian theater troupe who wanted a mark that would define their group as daring, yet serious and respectful of the nation's performing arts history.

Subtle type changes adjust the importance of secondary type on the GE Halogen Floodlight Bulbs package studies. The GE logo is integrated with the illustration and *HALOGEN* is given a custom letterform treatment.

Identity sketches for *Lyrica*, a pharmaceutical product for neuropathic pain shows the literal illustration of "leaning cards" being replaced by an abstract iteration.

Identity sketches for *Prescott Funding* started with a clean, "trust-worthy" typeface in two weights and sizes, an unexpected word break, and visual alignment. The client asked for an eagle to represent "honor and integrity."

Virclude is a pharma product for hepatitis B. It has a propulsive, battle-ready look.

"There should be a kind of impersonal ease about type — which is, after all, only a medium between writing and reading." Rudolph Růžička (1883–1978)

Lᴇ cruel Neron fit mourir ſa mere, Antonie ſa tante, Britannicus,
Senecque, Corbulon un de ſes Capitaines, & pluſieurs autres de ſes
proches ; & tua lui-même d'un coup
de pied Poppée ſa ſeconde femme.

Fournier

Lᴇ cruel Neron fit mourir fa
mere, Antonie fa tante, Britannicus, Senecque, Corbulon un de
fes Capitaines, & pluſieurs autres
de fes proches ; & tua lui-même
d'un coup de pied Poppée fa fe-

Caslon

Lᴇ cruel Neron fit mourir
fa mere, Antonie fa tante, Britannicus, Senecque, Corbulon
un de fes Capitaines, & pluſieurs
autres de fes proches ; & tua lui-
même d'un coup de pied Poppée

Plantin

BERN HARD

Die Schmal Schrift

ist stets dort, wo es gilt, durch
Raum Geld zu gewinnen, von
unbegrenzter Bedeutung; da-
durch ist sie zu einem unent-
behrlichen Hilfsmittel aller
großen Zeitungs-, Akzidenz-
und Werkdruckereien gewor-
den. Die Favoritin unter allen
guten Schmalschriften ist die

Schmalfette Bernhard-Antiqua

Die Groß-Industrie

verwendet mit Vor-
liebe die Bernhard-
Antiqua. Sie ist das
Rüstzeug moderner
Industrie - Reklame.
Keine Druckerei im
Industriegebiet ohne
Bernhard - Schriften

Bernhard-Antiqua / fett und extrafett

EIN SPIEGEL DER KULTUR

war von jeher die Typographie.
Sie hat fast in jedem Zeitalter die
Wege der anderen gestaltenden
Künste, der Baukunst vor allem, ein-
geschlagen. Wie den Domen der
Gotik die gotische Schrift zeitver-
bunden war, so entspricht auch der
neuen, modernen Architektur die

F U T U R A

Sie ist deshalb und ganz mit Recht

D I E S C H R I F T
U N S E R E R Z E I T

CLAUDE GARAMOND

der bekannte französische Stempel-
schneider, schuf eine grosse Zahl
sehr schöner Schriften, die vielen
Nachschnitten als Vorbild dienten.
Schon vor Jahrzehnten haben wir
durch die in 12 Graden ausgebaute

FLINSCH-MEDIAEVAL

mit der dazu gehörigen Kursiv die
hohe Tradition dieses hervorragenden
Meisters wieder zu Ehren gebracht

Das Hauptgebäude

Z U F R A N K F U R T A M M A I N

das Mutterhaus aller Niederlassungen und Verkaufsstellen, das Zentrum einer weit-
greifenden Verkaufsorganisation. Von hier aus spinnen sich unzählige Fäden rings um
die ganze Welt, nach all den vielen Absatzgebieten und ständigen Kunden des Hauses

DIE BRAUCHBARSTE
GROTESKSCHRIFT

VENUS

14

GARNITUREN

BAUERSCHE GIESSEREI

mager
halbfett
dreiviertelfett
fett
schmal mager
schmal halbfett
schmal dreiviertelfett
breit mager
breit halbfett
breit dreiviertelfett
breit fett
kursiv mager
kursiv halbfett
kursiv fett

Stelle unſeres früheren Verlags-
ſignets treten laſſen. Wir bitten
unſeren verehrten Kundenkreis.
hiervon Kenntnis zu neh-
Leipzig-Reudnitz, am I. Januar

Fiſcher & Wittig

Kunſtverlag und
Buchdruckerei

philobiblon eine zeitſchrift fü

herbert reichner verlag, wien VI (vienna), strohmayergasse 6

Blackletter was widely used in Germany through the first half of the 20th century. Jan Tsch-ichold, the author of *Die neue Typographie*, used it in a student lettering exercise in 1920 (*above left*), a corporate announcement in 1923 (*middle*), and on a Viennese magazine's letterhead in 1940.

This document* ended the use of Fraktur as the official Nazi typeface in 1941, wrongly claiming blackletter was "Schwabacher-Jewish letters." Schwabach is a town in south-central Germany.

Three settings illustrate Beatrice Warde's opening quote at right.

A variety of styles illustrate type in a 1928 German type catalog. Each type was given a treatment thought to show off its inherent quality. Originals are grayscale, too.

* Translation of the Nazi order reads in part: "*3 January 1941... (B)y order of the Führer... It is false to regard ... the so-called Gothic typeface as a German typeface. In reality the so-called Gothic typeface consists of Schwabacher-Jewish letters... the Jews living in Germany also owned the printing presses when ... printing books was introduced and thus came about the strong influx into Germany of Schwabacher-Jewish letters... The use of Schwabacher-Jewish letters by authorities will in future cease...*"

Type and identity

"**S**et a page in Fournier against another in Caslon and another in Plantin and it is as if you heard three different people delivering the same discourse — each with impeccable pronunciation and clarity, yet each through the medium of a different personality.*"
Beatrice Warde, 1933

With repetition, type can come to represent its source and it can come to be identified with a single organization or entity. An extreme example is provided by the Nazis. Blackletter is a writing style that developed in northern Europe beginning about 1200AD. In 1450, when Gutenberg invented movable type in Mainz, he modeled his letters on the prevailing lettering style in the area. Because other parts of Europe adopted types based on the much lighter Italian script writing, blackletter was recognized as Germanic, not least by Germans themselves. Indeed, German typefounders released 218 versions of blackletter typefaces between 1900 and 1940, indicating keen continuing interest in their use. Though difficult to read

Incipit epiſtola ſancti i
paulinum preſbiterum
diuine hiſtorie libris·c

Quem ad finem sese effr
Nihilne te *nocturnum prae*
is vigiliae, nihil *timor pop*
um omnium, nihil hic *mun*

'Monotype' TIMES
New Roman Series
327, available from ⬚ to

Perched atop stair t
fan rooms accent o
of energy-conservir

buzzsaw blades
275 Avocados and 10 Rubber Tires
gold filaments

1450
Gutenberg's
34-line Bible and
Prague Castle

1724
Caslon and the
Spanish Steps,
Rome

1931
Times New Roman
and the
Empire State
Building, NYC

1959
Optima and the
Sydney Opera
House

1998
Tear Drop and
the Guggenheim
Museum, Bilbao

2014
Alda and the
Heydar Aliyev
Center, Baku

Bodoni
Caslon
Clarendon
Fette Fraktur
Franklin Gothic
Frutiger
FUTURA
𝕿𝖎𝖒𝖊𝖘 𝕽𝖔𝖒𝖆𝖓
Trajan

Type has its own identity. These nine typefaces have been "mis-set" in one of the *other* types listed. See if you can determine their right order.

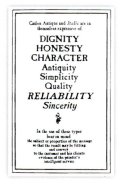

A detail from a 1925 showings book lists nine adjectives for *Caslon Antique*, all of which make the printer — the buyer of typefaces and thus the target of this message — look intelligent.

Sans serif types were avant garde as Tschichold wrote *Die neue Typographie*. This contemporary postcard is by Joost Schmidt.

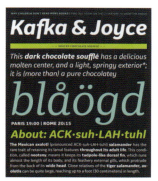

Proprietary typefaces designed specifically for clients (this is for General Electric) saves the need to pay for the use of existing typefaces and supports corporate branding.

Typefaces inevitably represent the culture and time of their design (*opposite*). Clayton Whitehill, in his 1947 *Moods of Type,* shows it thus:

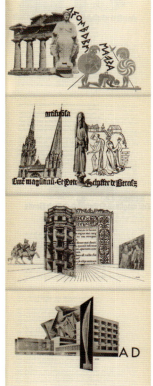

by those not born to their use, blackletter is a highly legible style that creates more unique word-shapes than roman types.

The Nazi's official adoption of Fraktur in the 1930s was a way to state unequivocally that their political party "stood for Germany." As Germany attacked its neighbors and expanded beyond its own borders, the Nazis recognized that Fraktur's Germanness would not help as much and they stopped using it in 1941. The reason the Nazis gave, however, was that it was a "Jewish invention." This was a total fabrication. Blackletter types have not yet recovered from the Nazi's terrible manipulation of national identity and type style.

"Typefaces are (like) ruins. And like so much in art, the history of type design is a continual working over of old forms." Clayton Whitehill, *The Moods of Type*

What typefaces represent

Do typefaces represent anything beyond their own æsthetic quality? Some designers feel all types have a soul and discuss them as an œnophile describes wines: can a typeface really be *pious*, or *materialistic*, or *gluttonous*? On the other hand, is a typeface merely a tool? The answer, not unexpectedly, lies somewhere in the middle. Some types have a soul because one has been bestowed on it. Some types are just shapes — and there is certainly nothing wrong with that. It is a question of perception.

Sans serifs represented modern typography in the early 20th century, particularly after Jan Tschichold's

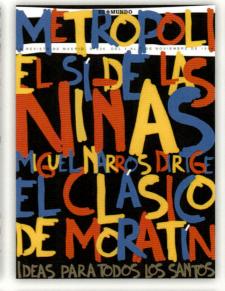
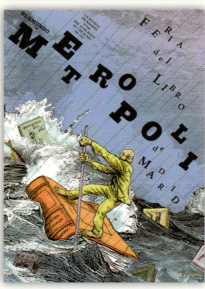

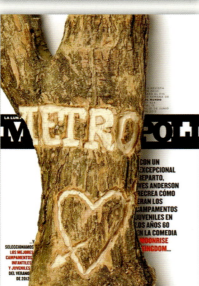

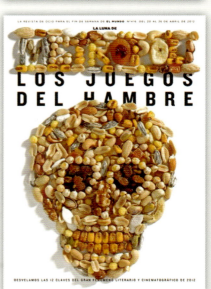

Swedish stamps commemorate the 500-year anniversary of the nation's printing with type, beginning with their first book in 1483. The *Dialogus Creatur-*

arum is a book of Latin fables told by anthropomorphized animals. Printed in Stockholm, five copies survive today.

Studies for a client always include a variety of typographic directions, as for these lawn signs. The particularities of each job define the creativity

called for. The "best" study is the one that most distinguishes the client from his competitors while meeting the assignment's deliverables.

Metropoli magazine is a weekly magazine supplement in a Madrid newspaper. The creative director, Rodrigo Sanchez, has created a recognizable design system in which both the primary imagery *and* the logo of each cover share a unique design treatment. The covers' *alterability* is this magazine's distinctive design attribute.

1928 *Die neue Typographie* defined the movement. Tschichold wrote, "The so-called Grotesque (sans serif) is the only one in spiritual accordance with our time. To proclaim sans serif as the typeface of our time is not a question of being fashionable. It expresses the same tendencies to be seen in our architecture..."

Helvetica represented current sensibility for hundreds of European companies in the latter 20th century. Its appeal comes from two sources: the shapes are highly legible, based as they are on earlier sans serif designs (to some extent, it fulfills Tschichold's call for a type without a personality), but another factor in Helvetica's adoption may be political: the famed neutrality of Switzerland, for which the type was named. This may have played a part during Helvetica's rise to ubiquity during the Cold War decades. It is easy to imagine that the same types would have been far less well received if they had been named "*Soviet State*" or "*Stalinist.*" Antonio Boggeri has called the neutrality of Swiss graphic design "...as perfect as any spider's web, but often of a useless perfection (because it isn't) broken by an entangled fly."

The chart on the next page shows seven categories of symbolism, each represented by six typefaces. You may wonder at or disagree with many of my type designations. That is expected: it is the nature of subjective design. It is this subjectivity, this "because I like it" —

"There are many artists who ... see their value and justification in novelty; but they are wrong. Novelty is hardly ever important. What matters is always this one thing: to penetrate to the very heart of a thing, and create it better." Henri de Toulouse Lautrec (1864–1901)

Symbolism	Typeface samples	
Power Seriousness Sophistication Industry	Caslon Canon Charter CONDENSED SANS	**Frutiger Bold** Linoletter Miller Display Roman
Purity Truth Cleanliness Spirituality	BODONI *Electra Cursive* **Futura No.2 Bold**	Joanna Regular *Lucida Handwriti* Post Antiqua
Neutrality Tranquility Indifference Normalcy	Bell Regular **B O V I N E** Eureka Roman	Garamond Officina Serif Book Poppl-Pontifex
Energy Excitement Danger Vigor	ALPHABLOCK champollion Déformé	Forte Guilty Korakuen
Creativity Passion Dignity Intelligence	**Anatole France** **Armada** ARTS & CRAFTS	MAGMA *Rusch's R-Type* SCHWITTERS ARCHITYPE
Conservatism Security Caution Reliability	**Bureau Grotesque** CASLON *Charpentier Classicistique*	COPPERPLATE FLORIDE Meta Plus Medium
Optimism Kindness Vitality Enlightenment	**Asphalt** BERNHARD GOTHIC **CORVINUS BOLD**	ECKMANN KLEX MOTOR

Franklin Gothic Heavy
Bell Centennial
The Bodonis
Centaur
Helvetica Light
Futura No.2

"Because it is just bold enough." Roger Black ⊡ *"For clarity in the worst circumstances, nothing can touch it... Matthew Carter created a bulletproof rhinoceros that could dance Swan Lake."* Gunnlauger S.E. Briem ⊡ *"...are a must for all cultural documents."* Michael Mabry ⊡ *"It was used with success in two of the most magificent books printed in my lifetime:* the Lectern Bible *and Morison's* Fra Luca de Pacioli." Ronald Mansbridge ⊡ *"In my opinion, it's probably the most readable sans serif face ever designed; it's beautiful and has even typographic color."* Sam Smidt ⊡ *"Futura is one of those faces that looks even better when reversed out, which is a credit to its carefully balanced counterforms."* Erik Spiekermann

Typefaces, like color, can represent more than one idea at a time. These adjective groups are adapted from Jill Morton's very useful *Color Voodoo.* Many of the less familiar types are selections from *Indie Fonts 1* and *2.* Please note that subjective associations are always to be viewed with skepticism: we perceive through the filters of our own experiences. Using subjective feelings is a risky way to explain or defend design decisions: you will lose more contests than you win. If you look at the opposite page and think, "This is ridiculous. How could the author have made such groupings?" remember that is *precisely* what others will think if you use adjectives alone to defend a typeface choice.

whether the "I" is the designer or the client, the author or the reader — that causes discord. After all, everyone has an opinion. If a type choice is refused by a client or colleague after explaining its symbolism, the designer must make another selection, and another, and frequently, another, until all parties are reasonably happy. Some types are very hard to read, so concentrate on symbolism but keep some attention on the type's legibility.

There are five considerations when choosing a typeface:

⊡ **Readers' needs** What are they used to seeing? Should you consciously stretch their comfort zone? Unless your message needs to say "cutting edge," use a time-tested typeface. It may lack novelty, but it will be familiar to your readers and therefore trusted and readable. A type's ability to attract is important in display faces; its ability to be read is essential in text faces.

⊡ **Symbolism** Many types represent the time of their design, or have other meanings.

⊡ **Knowing your client** If your client needs to project "reliability" with "trustworthiness," select a face that conveys those qualities. Also vital is design continuity with the client's previous pieces so the client projects a consistent image.

⊡ **Passing fashion** The more popular the type you are considering, the faster and further out of fashion

"I have always railed against ideological purity. I've found corruption is more interesting than purity." Milton Glaser

M&OTHER
CHILD

ske?tic
THE FORUM FOR CONTEMPORARY HISTORY

That's not a paper cut. It's a finger cut.
I'm going to dream about you my whole life. Or maybe

Frutiger 75 w/Californian Roman

That's not a paper cut. It's a finger cut.
I'm going to dream about you my whole life. Or may-

Meta Plus Black w/ITC Baskerville

That's not a paper cut. It's a finger cut.
I'm going to dream about you my whole life. Or maybe I'll

Geometric 706 Black w/Eureka Roman

That's not a paper cut. It's a finger cut.
I'm going to dream about you my whole life.

Champion Midweight w/Journal Text

That's not a paper cut. It's a finger cut.
I'm going to dream about you my whole life. Or may-

Colossalis w/Comenius Antiqua

That's not a paper cut. It's a finger cut.
I'm going to dream about you my whole life. Or maybe I'll help

Flare Gothic w/Gill Sans Light

That's not a paper cut. It's a finger cut.
I'm going to dream about you my whole life. Or may-

Ignatius w/Linotype Didot

That's not a paper cut. It's a finger cut.
I'm going to dream about you my whole life. Or maybe I'll

Griffith Gothic w/Concorde Nova

THAT'S NOT A PAPER CUT. IT'S A FINGER CUT.
I'm going to dream about you my whole life. Or maybe I'll help you wash your car sometime.

Posada w/Oz Handicraft

A type treatment should be recognizeable so others can't copy it. Swirly letters are recognized as Coca-Cola's. Swirly letters inside an oval are recognized as Ford's.

Hand lettering is used in advertising to evoke a "personal voice," as in this detail of a full-page ad for a car maker. Reading this copy out loud requires an *enthusiastic* voice. Try it.

This full-page-wide newspaper ad is a photograph of a Tiffany light blue box. The ribbon obscures about 90 percent of the the logo, which suggests the concept of a surprise, thus a gift.

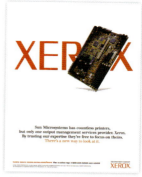

This Xerox ad runs the logo across the page. Its size is large enough that the *O* can be replaced by an image, which is then described in the ad's text.

Two magazine logos by Herb Lubalin use carefully chosen typefaces: *Mother & Child* uses *Goudy Oldstyle*, which has organic strokes and an ampersand borrowed from the italic font; *Skeptic* uses *Clearface*, which has ball terminals that relate to the dot under the question mark.

Optimize job and meaning by experimenting with several type combinations, then decide which solution is satisfactory. In early typesetting, it was impossible to do this: the only fonts available were the ones cut by the printer for his own use. Later, it became possible — but expensive — to use this technique. Today, it is easy.

it will soon be. The opposite of fashion in choosing a typeface is convenience: the font happens to be on your computer, which serves no one's needs but your own.

　▣ **Reproduction variables** Fine serifs and extreme stroke contrasts don't hold up on screen or with poor printing.

Matching type to job and meaning

Type selection is usually the *second* step in a designer's process:

1 Develop the strategy or concept.

2 Choose typefaces that suit the concept: one family for the text (because that is where the reader will spend the most time) and then a display face to complement it. Enormous breadth is achieved if one family is serif and the other is sans serif. This gives inter-family contrasts of style, weight, posture, in addition to intra-font contrasts of size, color, and position.

Mortimer Leach, author, educator, and designer, said in 1963, "Alphabets can portray a variety of feelings or moods, such as stability, strength, an avant-garde quality or that of a past era... At all times, the designer should seriously consider the use of type styles other than those which are currently in vogue. This is not a project for a lazy mind. There are hundreds of alphabets available and waiting to be gainfully re-employed."

"Sometimes there is no need to be either clever or original."
Ivan Chermayeff

Transmitter Brewing was "formed to bring a unique perspective on traditional beer styles to the local NYC beer scene." The labels, which have a recognizeable consistency,

were inspired by the number-ing system from ham radio cards from the 1920s–1950s. Logos have "brand equity," or the recognition earned through repeat exposure. These six

variations prove the efficacy of money spent on advertising. They are customized marks of J. Walter Thompson ad agency's clients to help it celebrate its 150th birthday.

Abstracting letterforms is not only allowed, it is *encouraged* in order to create a definitive personality. Some letter parts are trimmed off to emulate clipped spoken sounds.

A series of opera posters for the Bayerische Staatsoper (Bavarian State Opera) in Munich gives a sense of visual branding through its consis-tent typographic structure. The typographic unity of these posters, designed over years by German designer Pierre Mendell, allows great artistic playful variety in the artwork. This typographic system is defined by the largest type reading vertically in upper and lowercase seriffed letters; the name of the production in smaller horizontal upper and lowercase san serif letters; and all ancillary information in a single much smaller horizontal upper and lowercase sans serif letters with separating rules and consistent spacing between parts across the same column in the same position on the posters.

A type treatment you and your client can own

By *own*, I mean developing a type treatment you are recognized for having and is sufficiently recognizable that others can't copy it. Typographic "ownings" on a global level take years and hundreds of millions of dollars to construct. Fortunately, typographic ownership can be developed at a more local level for a lot less money. All it takes is the willingness to look, to create with distinction, and to stick with the design.

Every client deserves a design treatment for which they can be recognized. Few will admit it, but they want to be clapped on the back by their colleagues and con-gratulated for their company's well-made materials. So a magazine should have a look that is theirs alone and an ad campaign should sell product while reinforcing the sponsor as a unique entity.

Part of owning a typographic treatment is knowing what the direct competition is doing. Another part is knowing what the broader marketplace is doing. For example, the redesign of a magazine must be noticeable against its direct magazine competitors as well as both other magazines with which its readers may be familiar and the visual noise we get from all other sources.

Develop a type treatment that is recognizable, whose characteristics are yours alone. Repeat them so to sustain your ownership of them.

"What's the difference between a logo and a brand? About $500,000."
Louise Fili

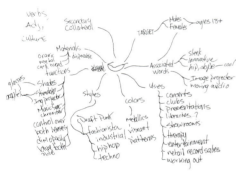

implse

implse

implse

Sensation of *sight*

MEDIAVIEWERS

WWW.IMPLSE.COM

implse MEDIAVIEWERS
WWW.IMPLSE.COM

T 212.217.8868
F 212.217.2764
E OTER@IMPLSE.COM

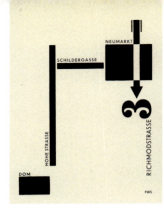

Hot metal type and the dire circumstances in Europe after WWI set severe limitations on designers in the 1920s, which provided extraordinary creative opportunities. These examples,

a diagrammatic map to a Cologne gallery by Franz W. Seiwert (c1926) and a brochure for a photography show by Walter Dexel (1929), use type and printing bars – *plus a*

dynamic use of space – in a revolutionary design process. Dexel, a Constructivist designer, organized the world's first advertising design exhibition in 1927.

This original and enduring mark is a hand-drawn MG ligature. The updated, evolved version ruthlessly abstracts the letters into a severely minimalist form.

Mondrian's *Broadway Boogie-Woogie* (1942–43) served as inspiration for Paula Scher's identity for Manhattan Records. In response to what Scher thought was a depressing sameness of corporate logos "shoved in the upper right corner," she adapted Mondrian's abstract street map of New York City, which was itself inspired by contemporary music. Sometimes boldly interpreting your sources is the right decision and sometimes a more subtle hint is the right decision. Probably recommending the latter, Albert Einstein said, "The secret to creativity is knowing how to hide your sources."

Design is a *process*, not a result. Evolving a solution is a necessary part of the process, as in this logo development.

 **How to evolve type treatments**

"*D*esign requires esthetics, inspiration, and guts. To me nothing is more vibrant than having the power to do something but not having the experience of knowing what's right and what's wrong.*" Tibor Kalman

Every design evolves from an existing model, which may be a current or previous incarnation of the object. For a new business or product, the model may be the competitors' design materials. A design is compared to a client's previous design, the client's competitors' designs, and the broader prevailing design sensibilities of the time.

Most clients want a design to be reminiscent of their existing materials. They aren't looking for a design as much as an *extension* or a *reworking*. This is a good approach as it retains a visual link for their customers.

The development of five projects are shown on the following pages as case studies. They show, among other things, that design is a *process* in which the final result *evolves* and it usually proceeds from complex to simple. But let's be clear: design is work. Really fun work.

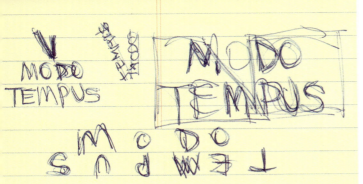

Logo evolution Logo development for a ten-person group that meets once a year for a mystery global adventure. *Fun* and *quality experiences* are to be promoted.

The name of the group, Modo Tempus, is Latin meaning *Now is the time*. The project begins with a few dozen sketches to explore the way the letters and words fit together. This is the crucial step: ideas percolate quickly and it is easy to keep up with them when one leads to another. The notions of *time* and *order* are explored.

The typeface chosen is URW Grotesk for its handsome characters. With four weights, each with italics, it offers plenty of variation for experimentation. The basic typesetting is done in Illustrator that provides editable outlines. The first study uses letters printed individually then cut out and photographed. The photo is contrasted in Photoshop to remove all cut lines and the perimeter is cropped on all four sides to relate the outside to the inside.

Some of the sketches are converted into type, starting with the ones most easily interpreted. Each iteration causes a cascade of alternatives, producing half a dozen or more subtle variations, primarily in spacing. A five-minutes-til-midnight clock is interpreted with a simple gray triangle. Experimental alternating letterform weights livens the otherwise ordinary typesetting. Reordering the letters suggests global hopping — a key feature of the group. Additional exploratory letterform studies.

✋ Combining top and bottom halves of the words leads to the other halves being joined, which are more legible, and in turn introduces the idea of reversing the order of the words to *Tempus Modo*. ✋ A "time shift" is applied to sliced-in-half letterforms. Legibility is affected, but in a logo, this is absolutely permitted if it enhances the unique character of the mark. ✋ This is a combination of the two previous studies. Recognizing such opportunities makes logo design both rewarding and surprising.

✋ Applying an Interrupted Sinusoidal map projection in the background creates a rhythmic composition with a variation of the previous type. ✋ Photographing letters used in office signage — and happily suffering the random angles imposed on their backing tabs — the photo is "posterized" into just two shades. The *D* is very hard to read and the idea is quickly put to rest. ✋ The client's reminder that a number must appear with each annual version of the mark, we revisit earlier studies.

✋ Exploring every word-numeral relationship, the bottom version seems a better balance of sizes. ✋ It becomes apparent that "global" could be easily added and would add needed meaning to the mark. Several variations were done to explore the ideal curve and overlap. ✋ Some fifty studies were developed in total. The final choice is this one. Each year, the numeral indicating changes (1.0, 1.1, 1.2, etc.). After one full cycle, which takes a decade, the first numeral becomes a 2.

Aid to Artisans

Logo evolution Logo development for a nonprofit arts organization The project begins with assessing the existing mark. Clarifying the ATA letterforms, "weaving,"

and roundness are chosen as starting points. The base of an Amazonian basket is scanned and silhouetted in its organically round shape. Edges are soft-

ened and transparent letters are added. Final art has the name set in Trade Gothic Extended beneath the mark.

Determining typographic character is an essential early decision. Studies are made using multiple typefaces, always including the typeface the client *already* uses. This

is a necessary extension of the personality the client has already invested in. Completely overhauling a mark by introducing an entirely new kit of parts is generally a

bad idea because it breaks all visual links to the past. A "logo update" requires at least a nod to what has come before.

 The letterforms are worked into a relationship that uses negative space. It is put in a circle, maintaining that one similarity to the original mark.

 News Gothic Bold Condensed Italic is notched in the A's. The T is extended through the bottom of the circle and the entirety is textured in Photoshop.

 A somewhat less obviously manipulated version is matched with all-caps News Gothic Bold Condensed Italic, angle-aligning the three T's.

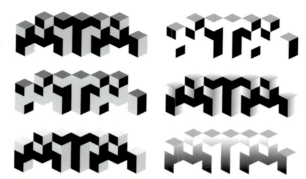

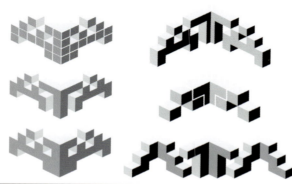

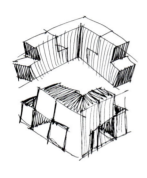

The ideas of weaving and dimensionality lead to another abstraction of the ATA letters. Shown here is the first letter A.

An isometric grid is set up and the shapes are prepared. Studies explore value, complexity, and legibility.

Asymmetrically set News Gothic Expanded complements the rigidity of the mark with organic alignment.

The dimensionality of the previous studies evolves into simpler abstraction.

Using the same isometric grid, the essence of the two letters, A and T, are explored. Every idea can be expressed as either advancing or receding studies.

The final contrasts the abstract letterforms with a curvilinear shape and a simple setting and exact sizing of the name.

Weaving and roundness are characteristics that need development, so several previous studies are revisited.

A new woven pattern is applied. The isometric grid is converted to a beehive-like pattern that fits behind previous marks and suggests a circle.

Note the typeset capitals are stacked beneath the midpoint of the circle, asymmetrically relating to the circle.

Magazine evolution A magazine redesign is a complex challenge. There are hundreds of little pieces, each of which must be made to agree or, with care, disagree with the overall format. *Vistazo* is the newsmagazine of Ecuador. Shown are three covers in its evolution in three steps over eight years. Coverlines are nearly as important as the logo in defining character.

✋ *Vistazo* began as a project to keep the presses busy at a leading printery in Ecuador. The 3D version was to be the last iteration before a redesign. The logo was set in Futura Extra Bold (*bottom left*) and ✋ variations of both figure and ground were thoroughly explored.

✋ The dot over the *i* was too visible, so it was absorbed into the background. The final mark is the last one at bottom right.

✋ The logo is the most important typographic element for a magazine. It is most recognizable — or should be — and it sets the tone for all other display type. Department headings are the second most important type because they connect the inside pages to the cover. These four variations were among twelve sets prepared.

✋ The folio/footline is another recurring element that unifies the editorial pages in a magazine. These are four sets of studies.

Berling Roman
Last night I took a stroll through the center of Guayaquil. The clouds were dark in the east and I expected rain, but it never came. As six turned into seven, more people crowded the sidewalks. Verandas cover virtually all the sidewalks. They must be there because it rains

Adobe Caslon Pro
Last night I took a stroll through the center of Guayaquil. The clouds were dark in the east and I expected rain, but it never came. As six turned into seven, more people crowded the side-walks. Verandas cover virtually all the sidewalks. They must be there because it rains frequently.

Giovanni Book
Last night I took a stroll through the center of Guayaquil. The clouds were dark in the east and I expected rain, but it never came. As six turned into seven, more people crowded the sidewalks. Verandas cover virtually all the sidewalks. They must be there because it rains frequently.

Charter Roman
Last night I took a stroll through the center of Guayaquil. The clouds were dark in the east and I expect-ed rain, but it never came. As six turned into seven, more people crowded the sidewalks. Verandas cover virtually all the sidewalks. They must be there because it rains

El éxito genera más éxito

Este Gobierno ha sido el más represivo de todos

ANTONIO VARGAS

Last night I took a stroll through the center of Guayaquil. The clouds were dark in the east and I expected rain, but it never came. As six turned into seven, more people crowded the side-walks. Verandas cover virtually all

El éxito genera más éxito

Este Gobierno ha sido el más represivo de todos ANTONIO VARGAS

Last night I took a stroll through the center of Guayaquil. The clouds were dark in the east and I expected rain, but it never came. As six turned into sev-en, more people crowded the side-walks. Verandas cover virtually all

✠ Text studies at reproduction size must be carefully evaluated: this is where read-ers spend the most time. Legibility matters the most in these studies. ✠ Charter was chosen for text and many studies are done to develop the secondary type charac- teristics. Though workaday, the simpler is preferable to the more complex because its delivery is more legible.

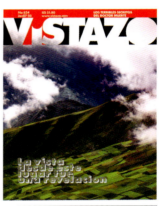

✠ The cover format calls for imagery to run up into the logo, though it doesn't have to, and coverlines to align in one of three columns at the page's head. Cover composition is relatively easy: select a great photo, write a catchy headline, and use any version of Futura, including what the client calls "the crazy ones," to make a special piece of typographic art. ✠ The finished cover is immediate, distinctive, and attention-getting. It's underlying structure is nearly infinitely interpretable.

✠ The makeup of the magazine includes departments, which are recurring topics of interest in every issue, and feature stories, which are, by definition, special to that one issue. Departments use a three-column grid to accommodate partial-page ads. Features use any grid, so long as they don't look like departments. ✠ This feature story looks different from the rest of the editorial matter, standing out with inherent specialness, exactly as it should.

Business card (top left)

RISK CAPITAL MANAGEMENT PARTNERS
1750 Broadway, Suite 1900
New York, NY 10019

David C. Shim

Voice: (212) 998-1817
Fax: (212) 998-1818
Cell: (917) 998-1819
shim@rcm-rcm.com

◢RCM◢

Business card (top right)

Hang RISK CAPITAL
Skip one line
Risk Capital Management Partners
David C. Shim
1750 Broadway
Suite 1900
NYC NY 10019
212 998 1817
Skip one line
917 998 1818 cell
212 998 1819 fx
shim@rcm-rcm.com
Equalize optical space on top, bottom, and right

Business card evolution ✋ Typical of startups, this business got card is from a print shop. The result is unexceptional design, including the logo.

✋ Once the business got on its feet, it needed to be presented more appropriately. This is one of about two dozen preliminary type studies completed for internal evaluation.

AG OLD FACE

✋ The original logo (top), designed by the founder, needed reinterpretation. The RCM/triangles relationship was the natural starting point.

✋ Cropping in on the edges of RCM makes a neat alignment. Four examples from a series of about twenty variations explored stacking, repetition, and order.

✋ The final logo. It retains all the elements of the original with the addition of a quirky point of view.

Business card (bottom left)

David C. Shim
Risk Capital Management Partners
1750 Broadway
Suite 1900
NYC NY 10019
212 998 1817

917 998 1818 cell
212 998 1819 fx
shim@rcm-rcm.com

Business card (bottom right)

David C. Shim
Risk Capital Management Partners
1750 Broadway
Suite 1900
NYC NY 10019
212 998 1817

917 998 1818 cell
212 998 1819 fx
shim@rcm-rcm.com

✋ Corporate design is comparable to a business suit: simplicity and dignity is imperative. Using order and alignments describes status, business practice, and philosophy.

AG OLD FACE

✋ Once the direction is determined, a variety of executions are run to compare subtle differences. There are a limited number of possible relationships: explore and exhaust all of them.

GRIFFITH GOTHIC

RCM

David C. Shim
9179981818 cell

Risk Capital Management Partners
1750 Broadway   2129981817
Suite 1900   2129981819 fx
NYC NY 10019   shim@rcm-rcm.com

✋ One purpose of studies is to identify *TRADE GOTHIC*
types that create a unified design that
projects *timeliness* but not *faddishness*.

RCM

Risk Capital Management Partners

David C. Shim

1750 Broadway
Suite 1900
NYC NY 10019

212 998 1817 office
917 998 1818 cell
212 998 1819 fax
shim@rcm-rcm.com

✋ More than individual lines, information *URW GROTESK*
groupings are manipulated. Space is carefully attended to.

David C. Shim

Risk Capital Management Partners   **RCM**

1750 Broadway
Suite 1900
NYC NY 10019

212 998 1817
917 998 1818 cel
212 998 1819 fax
shim@rcm-rcm.com

✋ It is decided that the company name *BARMENO*
will be larger and darker. The alignment of
PARTNERS unifies the design.

David C. Shim
917 998 18 18 cel

1750 Broadway
Suite 1900
NYC NY 10019

212 998 1817
212 998 1819 fax
shim@rcm-rcm.com

RCM **Risk Capital Management** Partners

✋ Putting the company name at the bot- *ELLINGTON*
tom of the card is counterintuitive, but
suggests the company thinks in fresh,
dynamic ways.

RCM

Risk Capital Management Partners

David C. Shim

1750 Broadway
Suite 1900
NYC NY 10019

212 998 1817
917 998 1818 cel
212 998 1819 fax
shim@rcm-rcm.com

✋ Approaching completion, compare this *ROTIS SEMI SANS*
design to the original print shop card.
Notice how differently the same company
presents itself.

RCM

Risk Capital Management Partners

David C. Shim

1750 Broadway
Suite 1900
NYC NY 10019

212 998 1817
917 998 1818 cel
212 998 1819 fax
shim@rcm-rcm.com

✋ Centering the mark over the left edge *ROTIS SEMI SANS*
of RISK on the final card concentrates the
empty space. This format is adapted to
website, letterhead, envelope, and forms.

Logo evolution Logo development for a reformulated pharmaceutical product that is long acting (*LA*). ✋ The first step is trying various typographic directions to get familiar with the problem.

✋ The second pass tries simpler faces that can be used in a supporting role with imagery.

✋ The third pass adds illustrative ideas to type treatments. Some studies include the drug's generic name, an eventual requirement.

✋ A highly abstracted *L* and *A* that suggest building blocks, strength, and dynamism. Multiple studies explore relative emphases.

✋ Federal requirements require the drug's generic name at half the logo's point size. Note the alignment of elements and consistency of sizes.

✋ Horizontality is chosen over the squarer format. Branding colors are blue and gold. The type is *Interstate*.

✋ The idea, "What if the *I*'s talk to each other?," came up in an agency meeting. Increased human interaction is a benefit of this drug.

✋ Bending the *I*'s makes them look more human with the dots becoming heads. The cost of this adjustment is a slight decrease in legibility.

✋ The final mark uses the NEW ONCE DAILY "eyebrow" as a conversation between the two *I*'s. This type is *News Gothic*.

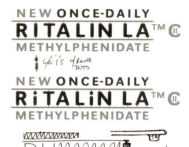

✋ This started as an example using a typeface called *Plastic Man*. Studies were made using alternate types in a similar format to suggest playfulness.

✋ The two legally required ancillary "bugs" are incorporated into the primary type.

✋ *NEW ONCE DAILY* is reduced to the width of *RITALIN*. This type is *News Gothic Rounded*.

✋ The mark suggests cooperation, playfulness, and process. You may see an abstract face, though this was not promoted as an attribute.

✋ The cyclic motion of the mark is reiterated in the horizontal bars. These studies tended toward busyness more than the others.

✋ The final logo centers the mark over *RITALIN* and sizes *NEW LONG ACTING* with *RITA*. This type is *Trade Gothic*.

✋ One of the basic typeset studies evolved to highlight the long-acting properties of the drug via a rising sun. The first studies were too abstract.

✋ These are six of the dozens of studies produced in Illustrator. They are better at suggesting "daytime" and "improvement."

✋ *NEW ONCE DAILY* has been de-emphasized and the dots over the *i*'s imitate the sun's shape. This type is *URW Grotesk*.

Design is interesting when developed in the areas *between* the three elements designers use: type, image, and space.

Egyptian hieroglyphics c2500BC places large illustrations directly beneath the text so their nearness connects them. This treatment is just as effective today.

An elaborately drawn initial is an illustration and focal point in this detail of a page from Francesco Petrarch's *Trionfi*, illuminated by Ricciardo di Nanni in Firenze c1450.

Captions are embedded directly into each frame of this 1470 German woodblock so illiterate readers could more easily understand the text's meaning.

Monks were revered as copyists for their manuscript writing. Adding illustrative elements was done by other specialists. As the demand for books grew through the 14th century, copying them became a commercial activity in bigger cities. Step-by-step instructions on how to illuminate a manuscript were prepared in the 15th century for the new practitioners

Name the animal outlined. If you took a moment to reconcile the image with its label, you succumbed to the *Stroop Effect*, which is the momentary delay when the brain processes conflicting messages. This describes the fundamental relationship of pictures and their descriptive words: do they reinforce each other or do they only happen to be near each other?

Type and imagery

I n special cases the particular way type is used makes the difference in the communication. But unless typography is being used as central to the communication — as the pivotal illustration — what makes the communication work is always the content."
Saul Bass

Type and image. Image and type. These are the two visible elements of design. Though inherently different, they are almost always seen together. They come with plenty of contrast. What takes thought, though, is how to make them harmonize by sharing attributes.

Scott McCloud, author of *Understanding Comics, The Invisible Art*, offers the following evolution of type and imagery. Egyptians placed their hieroglyphics near images, like extensive captions, so the words and pictures would work together for clear communication. Early European woodblock printing matched pictures with textual captions. As images increased in representational quality, type increased its power to express abstract thoughts using its abstract characters. Finally, with both

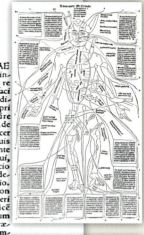

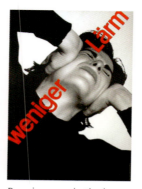

Following the upheaval of the First World War, Kurt Schwitters works with fragmented collage. "The Scarecrow" is a 1925 children's issue is of his *Merz* magazine. He asked,

"Couldn't we make a picture book using nothing but typographical elements?" His invention helped propel type's use as a malleable, expressive medium.

By using axes in the image, Josef Müller-Brockmann (1914–1996) creates an "x" by crossing the figure's arms and type in this 1960 poster for the Swiss Committee to Combat Noise.

"Splitting in half" is interpreted in both the image and the word in this 2004 poster by Pierre Mendell.

Relate by position The caption surrounds the image in a 1519 book; captions are directly linked to parts of a 1491 "exploded view" diagram; and individual lines of type in a caption are integrated directly into the image.

Relate by layering Image dominates over type on a book cover where odor wafts in the foreground and a brand mark is overlaid on a logo. Type dominates over image on a repurposed map and on a book cover with a backward title.

representational and abstract issues achieved, there was nowhere left but for words and images to begin their inevitable journey back to a central, shared language. Imagery would become more abstract as type became more representational. This happened in the early 20th century, first by the Expressionists, then by the other avant garde movements. Art became abstract and expressed ideas. Writing became specific and vernacular.

Relating type to image

The first step in consciously developing a type and image relationship is recognizing that type and image are fundamentally *different* and our job is to develop *similarities* to achieve design unity. The second step is choosing whether the type or the image will be dominant. The image, as the default "non-decision," is typically dominant. Dominance ordinarily refers to quantity: an image is said to dominate when it is the largest element on a page. But dominance can also be applied when one element imposes itself on another element, which is to say, it *gives* the pain. A subordinate element is one that is imposed on by another: it *takes* the pain.

The third step is to recognize that the subordinate element must be made to agree with the dominant element. There are four basic relationships, with an infinite number of ways to execute them.

"Formerly pictures were used to supplement or amplify words. Now words supplement and amplify pictures."
Clayton Whitehill,
The Moods of Type, 1947

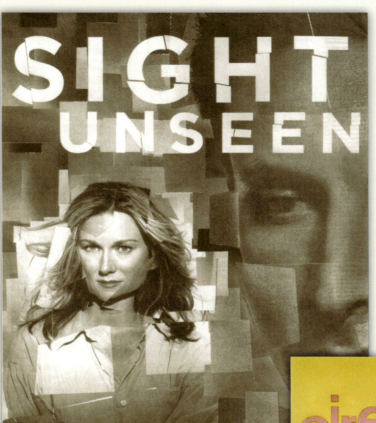

SIGHT UNSEEN

SIGHT UNSEEN BY DONALD MARGULIES WITH BYRON JENNINGS
ANA REEDER BEN SHENKMAN SET DESIGN DOUGLAS W. SCHMID
JESS GOLDSTEIN LIGHTING DESIGN PAT COLLINS ORIGINAL MUSIC
JOHN GROMADA PRODUCTION STAGE MANAGER ROY HARRIS DIRECTED BY DA

MTC
MANHATTAN
THEATRE CLUB
AT THE BILTMORE
261 WEST 47TH ST

PREVIEWS BEGIN MAY 6
TELECHARGE.COM NOW OR 212-239-6200/800-432
MANHATTANTHEATRECLUB.COM. GROUPS 212-398-838

SHARP AND ABSOLUT VODKA
PROUDLY SUPPORT MTC

PHOTOS BY MIRANDA PENN TURIN

sirenella

palais de cristal

largo cairoli de via pozzone in via rovello 16

sirenella

palais des danses

sirenella

Relate by layering The sponsor's name is ghosted into the background behind the figure's head, making it more than a subliminal message but less than a neon sign. Such intentional, delicate relationships suggest self-assured sophistication and quiet elegance, two attributes of Omega watches and their carefully chosen spokesman, Mr. Clooney.

Structural simplicity is an effective way to make type and image look "in agreement." The grid in the composite image sets up a comparison with the new car that embodies a ninety-year history of automotive improvements in this spread ad.

Relate by shared characteristic TREATMENT Type and image are both cut and refit in an ad for a Broadway show. ANGLE The baseline of the enormously fat *B* is angled to match the car's front wheels. DIRECTION Secondary type explodes from a drummer.

▣ **Relate by position** TYPE NEAR IMAGE Type near an image is perceived as a captions. Whether as little clots of type beneath pictures or as headlines splashed across the page, captions are read before the text. Captions are therefore display type: type that is meant to entice and lure. Captions satisfy readers' curiosity and help them understand what they are seeing and how they are to interpret the picture. As tools for enticement, captions should be carefully worded and not very long.

▣ **Relate by layering** The ultimate position of nearness is *on top of*, so this might be considered a subset of the preceding relationship. IMAGE OVER TYPE makes image look more real by making it look dimensional. If too much type is covered, it makes type hard to read. TYPE OVER IMAGE is much less persuasive. It negates the reality of the image and invariably makes the type hard — or impossible — to read.

▣ **Relate by space and alignment** POSITION, SIZE When type and image are both affected by space, they are unified. When the height or width of an image is equal to type, they are unified.

▣ **Relate by shared characteristic** TREATMENT, SHAPE, DIRECTION, ANGLE, COLOR, AND TEXTURE This is a huge category. One example may suffice: if the headline that goes with a picture of, say, a beach scene is given a sand treatment, the two elements will be unified.

"Design should be used to communicate ideas with wit, simplicity, and intelligence."
Marcello Minale

WIRED

SPECIAL REPORT

HOW THE U.S. ALMOST KILLED THE INTERNET— AND WHY IT STILL COULD P. 62

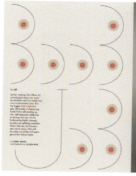

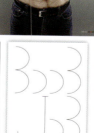

Letterforms and images joined into characters A self-descriptive illustrative element is joined to a letterform to explore the figure-ground relationship and legibility.

Letterforms and images joined into characters This category differs from **Image in the shape of letterforms** because here removing the illustration leaves legible letter-

forms. This is the above artwork without the illustration.

Picture fonts Any character or glyph that is *keystroke accessible* is embedded in a font. The sample on the left is from 1760, the one on the right is 243 years younger.

Letterforms and images joined into characters Combining a drawing of a skull with the *at* character is the product of the ideas of "death" plus "internet." This is a pretty simple thinking process, but the result benefits from its execution: the scale of the primary element, the solid black background that sets off the fade from white to red, and the symmetrical arrangement.

Type as image

Sometimes the best way to tell a story is with type alone. The meaning and power of written language can be most persuasive. In these circumstances, simple letters simply arranged are enough.

Other times a story is best told by developing type into an enhanced focal point. There are seven ways to do this and, be warned, each one of them takes a toll on legibility. Consequently, apply these ideas to display type only. Text is too fine, and readers too harried, to tolerate much fooling around with small type sizes. As in all things creative, examples are interpretable and can overlap categories.

▣ **Letterforms and images joined into characters** These are *augmented letterforms*. Letterforms and imagery are given about equal emphasis, but removing the imagery allows the letterforms to remain legible.

▣ **Picture fonts** These are collections of keystroke-accessible images. They can be used as spot illustrations, as bullets for emphasis, or, when repeated, as borders and separators. The first picture font was a set of movable type *fleurons* ("flowers"), made by Giovanni and Alberto Alvise in 1478. After about 28 years of movable type, this was a radical recognition that bits of reusable metal could print images instead of letters. Picture fonts are also called *symbol fonts*, *ornament fonts*, or *dingbats*.

"People who love ideas must have a love of words, and that means they will take a vivid interest in the clothes that words wear." Beatrice Warde

MARRIAGE

ꟼꟼꟼꟗꟼꟼꟼꟗꟼꟼꟼꟼꟗꟼꟗL

ꟼꟼꟗꟼꟼꟗꟼꟼL = minimal

MADISON SQUARE GARDEN

GUGGENHEIM MUSEUM OPEN FREE TUESDAY EVENINGS

89th St & 5th Ave
5 to 8 pm
Made possible
by a grant from Mobil

Vɪrclude®
Entecavir

wordplay

Wolfgang
Amadeus
MOZART
Symphony
No.

America's answer!
PRODUCTION

BIANCO

Letterforms arranged to illustrate the message's meaning Parentheses and brackets are combined: using familiar characters in such original ways takes the ability to see freshly.

Letterforms chopped and arranged as image Hand lettering allows maximum flexibility when making letterforms fit into an illustrative shape.

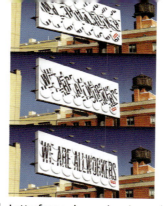

Letterforms chopped and arranged as image A moving billboard rotates parts of letters on subtle white-on-white gears so the message makes sense only intermittently.

Letterforms overwhelmed by image so they nearly disappear The overall impact of such treatments takes priority over understandability — this is poetic typography.

Letterforms arranged to illustrate the message's meaning Purposeful illustrations using only letterforms to both state and show their meaning.

Image in the shape of letterforms Images and letterforms that cannot be separated.

Letterforms chopped and arranged as image A building's form is revealed; *v* becomes activated as a virus; the *LWA* becomes a digital man; a human face is "drawn"; flip *WORDPLAY* upsidedown; *MOZART* and *40* are reduced to the least letter parts necessary to read; the composer, performers, and recording label are woven into a composition.

Letterforms as part of the image Letterforms integrated with illustrative elements.

▣ **Letterforms arranged to illustrate the message's meaning** Keen observation, free imagination, plus strong intention can turn many words inside out so they *show* what they mean. This is harder than it looks, but is a praiseworthy mental exercise. This is different than **Letterform and images joined into characters** because removing the illustration here necessarily destroys the letterforms.

▣ **Image in the shape of letterforms** Non-letterforms are arranged into legible letters and words but the emphasis is on imagery. If letterforms are too subordinate, legibility suffers. Be sure that the illustrative subject is appropriate to your message.

▣ **Letterforms chopped and arranged as image** The image is entirely made of parts of letterforms. Type that becomes image through abstraction typically trades *legibility* for *readability*; that is, it adds to the type's strength to attract attention.

▣ **Letterforms as part of the image** Type inserted into or substituted for a part of an image. This is a relatively easy and a particularly convincing way to unify execution with meaning.

▣ **Letterforms overwhelmed by image so they nearly disappear** By definition, type plays a very subordinate role in this category. Clear communication is not key in this category!

"There aren't many raw parts in typography. I like the idea of using type as though it were paint. That way I can get back the rawness."
Ivan Chermayeff

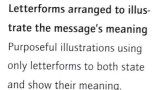

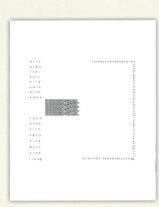

LA PELLE D'OCA = *goose bumps*   DARSI ALLA MACCHIA = *go into hiding*   FAR ALA = *to make way*

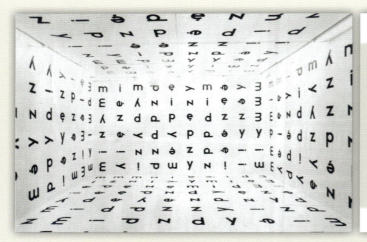
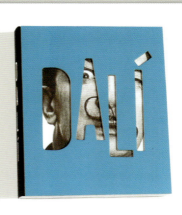

All lettering and type, shown here from various periods in history, has color and texture. *About 800 years ago in what is now Germany, handwriting evolved from Carolingian — an open and light style — into a very dark and condensed style. This was in part to make most efficient use of precious vellum. It became known as *textura* because, with little with which to compare it, Europeans thought it looked like the texture of rough fabric (*far right*). This bit of history illustrates that type has *inherent texture*. We are so familiar with type today that its textural quality has become all but invisible. But texture is still there for useful exploitation.

Texture can be exploited as a way of indicating areas of text type, as shown in these student exercises; texture added to words may be decorative, but is best used when it conveys *meaning*.

Four logo studies that use drawn dimensionality.

"*Between*," a 1977 artwork by S. Drozdz, puts flat type in a dimensional space. A diecut *Dalí* book cover reveals the artist within (and beneath) his own name.

Takenobu Igarashi crafted a series of alphabet sculptures in the 1980s. This is his letter *F*. Actual letters can be photographed, as in this detail from an editorial page from *Esquire* and signage in Portugal.

Texture and dimensionality

Text type is said to have "color" and texture,* which are closely related. *Texture* can differentiate areas of text type, as shown by the student studies at the top of the opposite page. Texture can also be used as a fill on display letterforms.

In this age of increased visual competition, display type has to be provocative. One technique that makes type literally stand out is *dimensionality*, which can be digitally made or can be crafted and photographed. With few exceptions, the handcrafted is always preferable to the all-but-perfect digitally crafted because handcrafted human imperfections make it more visible.

With the proliferation of three-dimensional (height+ width+depth) rendering software, dimensional display type has become almost ordinary. As with all type treatments, the purposefulness of a particular technique defines its success or failure as mere noisiness. In other words, does the dimensionality express appropriate *meaning*, or is it only a trick?

Texture and dimensionality are illustrative approaches, subsets of the categories of *letterform and image joined into a single entity* and *type overwhelmed by image so it nearly disappears*. These treatment can be used to relate headlines to images and thereby achieve design unity, the Holy Grail for visual communicators.

"*Typography of swirling patterns, shapes trapped in texture are sophisticated examples of expressionism.*"
Tom Carnase

CAVALLERIA RUSTICANA

PAGLIACCI

Pietro MASCAGNI + CAVALLERIA RUSTICANA + ピエトロ・マスカーニ

カヴァレリア・ルスティカーナ

Ruggero LEONCAVALLO + PAGLIACCI + ルッジェーロ・レオンカヴァッロ

パリアッチ（道化師）

東京二期会オペラ劇場
Tokyo Nikikai Opera Theatre

公益財団法人 東京二期会 60th Anniversary
2012年二期会は創立60周年を迎えます

Textile Textile
Rental Rental

Developing perfect display type, in this case a magazine flag, begins with a sketch. After setting the type in Illustrator, convert to paths and finesse the *shapes*. Note the spacing improvements made between every character pair (hairlines show the "after" spacing), the joining of the XT and the EN into ligatures, and the shortening of ascenders to get tighter line spacing. Preparing an outline file will force you to attend to every letter-to-letter, word-to-word, and line-to-line relationship, ensuring that nothing is overlooked.

This type is ITC Berkeley Old-style, a digital interpretation of Frederic W. Goudy's 1938 typeface for the University of California Press.

Dimensionality and, in this example, thematic argumenta-tiveness in these two operas is implied by slicing letters and using handcrafted shadow smudges. Was this poster craft-ed off computer and carefully photographed for reproduction, or was it crafted on computer in Photoshop? If you can't tell, it is a step in the direction of truly adding value to a design.

Preparing display type

Display type is usually the big stuff, so every mistake or oversight that you might get away with in text is magnified. Display type isn't "big text." Instead of typing in the copy, designating its point size, and allowing defaults, prepare the type as an outline file in Illustrator. An outline file can be scaled without losing resolution. A file made in Photoshop, by comparison, is a bitmap file that will degrade when enlarged.

To achieve the next level of typographic excellence, the letterforms themselves should be changed at display sizes. From 1450 through the 1950s, metal type had to be cut in specific sizes. (This is, by the way, the source of the sizes listed on a computer's pull-down font menu.) The typefounder made subtle differences to type pro-portions and spacing for each size as he cut the fonts. Larger type sizes allowed greater detail while smaller sizes required larger counters and weightier thin strokes. Beginning in the 1950s, the phototype process set type of any size using a single negative, usually optimized for an average setting of 12 points. This forced a significant compromise at the largest and smallest sizes.

For the first two decades of its existence, digital type has continued that palliative model. More types are now being made that have two or three family "lines" to be used at small, text, and display sizes.

"Design which afflicts communication is bad design; it cannot be esthetically satisfying, but to illiterates."

Gerrit Noordzij

*"Of all the achievements of
the human mind, the birth
of the alphabet is the most
momentous."* Frederic W. Goudy

Section Four
Typography Timeline

A 22,000-year-old cave painting of a bison. Cave paintings were messages made for the community to see. Such works are today called *murals*.

A variety of proto-writing styles show drawing preceded writing. The oldest known proto-writing dates from c3000BC.

c1800BC Mesopotamia (present-day Iraq) is home to livestock traders who invent notations for their own use on small clay pads.

c1200BC Sumerian cuneiform (from the Latin *cuneus*, meaning "a wedge," the tool used to make the marks) used stylized pictograms.

Photo by Marvin A. Powell

12 Handwriting and lettering until 1450

"**T**ype evolved as a way of putting the word into non-face-to-face communication. Electronic media have (made) the relation of type to sound more meaningful. There's a kinship between expressiveness in typography and sound through control of such elements as rhythm, volume, montage, pauses, pace, style, accent, clarity, and tone." Tony Schwartz

The development of Egyptian hieroglyphics ("sacred writing") begin as a symbol system that is unrelated to spoken language.

Hieroglyphics and a quicker writing style, hieratic script, develop in parallel, culminating in a cursive abstract system.

The development of Hebrew hieroglyphics shows a transition from representational to abstract. Chart by linguist Zev Bar-Lev.

The edged pen, made from hollow cane, reed, or quill, was the primary writing instrument for centuries.

HIEROGLYPHIC	HIEROGLYPHIC	HIERATIC SCRIPT	HIEROGLYPHIC	HIEROGLYPHIC BOOK SCRIPT	HIERATIC SCRIPT	HIEROGLYPHIC	HIERATIC SCRIPT	DEMOTIC SCRIPT
2900BC	2000BC		1500BC			500BC		300BC

Hieroglyphic	Meaning	Linearized	Written	Modern
	Camel		גמל	גמל
	Righteous		צדיק	צדיק
	King		מלך	מלך
	Not		לא	לא
	Hear		שמע	שמע

c3,000BC Egyptian hieroglyphics

c3,000BC Hitite hieroglyphics

c2,000BC Babylonian cuneiform

c1,600BC Cretan linear script

c1,100BC Phœnician "soundscript"

c1,000BC Cuneiform script

c1,000BC Egyptian hieratic script

c1,000BC Late Phœnician script

c2000BC Sheets of papyrus, a swamp grass, are used as writing material. Layers of the inner fiber are cut into strips, dried, then interwoven and soaked and dried again. Papyrus can't be folded without cracking, so it has to be rolled. Papyrus rolls are called volumes (Latin *volvere*, to roll).

c3000BC–c1000BC The evolution and development of writing encompasses representational symbols that were unrelated to spoken language. These eventually became nonrepresentational symbols *signifying sounds*, joining spoken and written language into a unified learning process.

Stylized drawings of things became symbols, or pictographs (*picto*=image, *graph*=drawing) around 3,000BC. Pictographs show things, so a pictograph of a cow, for example, could mean either an animal used for food or a unit of wealth, since cows were used for trading. Pictographs couldn't represent ideas very well, so ideographs, which show ideas and actions, evolved. Ideographs had to be learned because the marks were symbolic. Society grew into two distinct groups: those who could understand ideographs, and those who couldn't. Eventually, ideographs could no longer describe the increasingly complex societies in which they were used. There was a huge difference between spoken and written languages. Around 1800BC, the Phœnicians, a successful trading society on the eastern shores of the Mediterranean Sea, reasoned that if symbols represented specific sounds, they could be joined as sounds were. Their revolutionary system directly connected spoken sounds to writing. Instead of two distinct languages, only one needed to be learned. They spread their system as they traded with others. The Greeks adopted their system around 800BC and added vowels and named the letters. The Romans adopted the Greek system within two hundred years and added the *G* and *Z*.

Written language started with Egyptian hieroglyphics. Their system stayed local but the idea of writing, at first to keep track of belongings for trade, was an idea whose time had come. It began appearing throughout the region, eventually spreading westward to Greece and Italy.

Alphabetic writing uses symbols that represent sounds. This was a development by the Phœnicians, who assigned their 22 spoken sounds distinct characters. Other languages defined their own sounds and adapted existing marks and introduced new ones.

YEAR		CHARACTERS IN ALPHABET
1,600BC	Phœnicians (Syria and Lebanon) develop alphabet that represents specific sounds.	22
800BC	Greeks adopt Phœnician alphabet, taking 15 characters and adding nine of their own, and add word spaces and punctuation.	24
700bc	Etruscans, then Romans, adopt Greek alphabet, taking 18 characters and adding seven.	25
400BC	Anglo-Saxons (northern Europeans) adopt Roman alphabet, adding one character.	26

474BC Etruscan inscription from Syracuse shows earliest Roman interpretation of Greek letters.

The evolution of Greek to Latin (Roman) letters. Only the first half of the alphabets are shown here to make the characters as large as possible.

Remnants of Greek letters can be seen in this c200BC Roman tomb. These letters are incised in the stone grave marker of L. Cornelius Scipio.

Scrolls were first written across the width of the roll, held vertically. Later, the characters were written parallel to the roll, which was held horizontally.

c1600BC–c499AD

c1600BC First alphabet developed in the Middle East. Though it contains no vowels, its characters represent spoken sounds. **c1500BC** Chinese develop ideographs. **c1400BC** Ten Commandments incised on stone tablets. **c950BC** The Phœnicians, building on alphabets by the Egyptians and Chaldeans, take a very significant step further, directly linking specific sounds to nonrepresentational symbols. Phœnician traders bring their alphabet to the Greeks, who then carry it to the Etruscans. **c850BC** Semites use first punctuation |vertical strokes separating phrases. **c600BC** Earliest dictionary written in central Mesopotamia, indicating need for various peoples to understand growing lexicon. ⊡ Torah, first five books of the Bible, written by exiles in Babylon. ⊡ As societies develop, the only writing is either God's or the King's words, giving all writing great significance. IN THE 6TH CENTURY BC, THE GREEKS, WHO AT THE TIME HAD ONLY CAPITAL LETTERS, USED A METHOD OF WRITING IN WHICH ONE LINE LED IMMEDIATELY TO THE NEXT, WHICH THEN BECAME BACKWARD READING, THEN TO THE NEXT, WHICH BECAME RIGHT READING, THEN FORWARD AND BACKWARD ON DOWN THE COLUMN. THIS WAS KNOWN AS BOUSTROPHEDON, OR "AS THE OX PLOWS." IT HAS BEEN SUGGESTED THAT SUCH WRITING WOULD

c700BC Early Greek looks much like the Phoenician alphabet.

c400BC Greek Lapidary ("carved") type is the Greek's interpretation of the Phoenician alphabet and the forerunner of Latin majuscules.

SENATVS VLVSQVE·ROMAN)·TITO·DIVI·VESPASIA
72AD Roman Monumental Capitals from the *Arch of Titus.*

TRAIANO·AVG·G MAXIMO·TRIBPO
114AD Roman Monumental Capitals from the *Trajan Column,* built to commemorate victory over Decebalus eight years earlier. This is the source of all serif fonts.

LIQVITVREIZEPHYROPVTRI DEPRESSOINCIPIATIAMTVA
c150AD Handwritten *Quadrata,* or "Square Capitals." Vellum's smoother surface was preferred over papyrus at this time.

FELIXOSEMIEROVES M·FOVEEAGNEMESIB
c300AD Rustic Capitals, a condensed square capital, saved valuable vellum and was quicker to write.

uETAS PERPlAC> QUEINGENIATE
c350AD Uncials ("Inch High"), with curves and rudimentary ascenders and descenders.

c450AD Half Uncials, the precursors of today's lowercase letters, resulted from ever-quicker writing.

c500AD Roman Cursives, not intended for permanence, were a faster, more fluid writing style. This shows variations of each character.

130AD Roman Monumental Capitals are inscribed on a gateway honoring Emperor Hadrian in Shropshire, England.

9AD Tomb inscription of a Centurion shows developing Roman monumental capital. A skilled craftsman could carve three characters per hour.

c50ad Roman Cursive from Pompeii shows flamboyant ascenders and descenders.

c100AD Romans write on wax-covered wood with a metal stylus. Speed causes letters to be joined and to become angled. It was difficult to read until two

Oxford scientists in 2002 use computers and complex lighting to reveal what is hidden. Two samples of this temporary, quick writing are shown.

TODAY BE MORE EFFICIENT WITH THE ADDITION OF BRACKETS AS GUIDES. SHORTLY AFTER THE ADVENT OF BOUSTROPHEDON, STOICHEDON, A TERM THAT MEANS "BY ORDERLY RANKS," BEGAN TOBEUSEDINSOMEPARTSOFGREECE. LETTER SWEREWRITTENINONEDIRECTIONANDTHEYWE REEVENLYSPACED. SUCHPRECISIONWASSOONP ROVEDINEFFICIENTANDTHEPRACTICEENDED. **C300BC** Alexandria, the world's cultural center, has two libraries with 500,000 scrolls, which are both burned to the ground by Roman soldiers in 48AD. ⊡ Chinese invent paintbrushes made of hair. **C250BC** An Egyptian papyrus embargo forces the need for an alternative in Greece and Rome. Parchment, made from sheep and

goat skins, is invented in Bergama. Parchment can be written on both sides and folded, so codices and books replace rolls. Requiring the skins of 300 animals for a single Bible, and running out of livestock, scribes use the Chinese technique of breaking down cotton fiber in water and flattening the slurry into sheets. ⊡ The surface of valuable parchment can be scraped and the hide used again. Such manuscripts come to be called palimpsest, or "scraped." Some famous works have been discovered beneath later writings, including Cicero's long-lost 51BC *On the State* under a 7th-century copy of a Saint Augustine work. That a pagan work was erased to make

Early Christian capitals use ligatures and abbreviations to make the it hard to read on purpose: outsiders would be unable to decipher the message.

c230AD The Gospel According to St. John.

A codex, the earliest book-form with folded pages, c250AD. Made from parchment (animal hides glued together into a

long strip and folded), they opened to two facing pages. The modern equivalent is called a French fold.

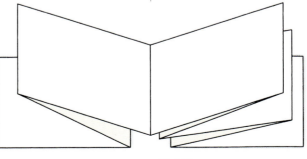

500AD Monks illuminate hand-copied manuscripts as the early Middle Ages begin, developing punctuation as well as dozens of character variations to make each line equal in length. This "justification," or evenness of column edges, is thought to please God with its perfection.

C700AD The Book of Kells (Latin Gospels), Ireland. It is the most highly regarded book of the Dark Ages (500-1450AD) because of its perfected minuscule letters. According to Calligraphia Latina, a 1756 book, Irish law "metes out the same price for the shed blood of a scribe as for a bishop or a king."

room for a Christian one is typical of a palimpsest book. **59BC** Posted in public spaces, first daily news document founded in Rome. **C400AD** Woodblocks used to print textiles in Egypt. ☐ Black ink invented in China. **C476AD** With the fall of the Roman Empire, the skill of writing is practiced almost exclusively in monasteries. With the exception of illuminated manuscripts, not much other writing is produced for nearly 1,000 years, when movable type is invented. ☐ Letters have always been made in the way that is easiest. Angular letters resulted from chisels on stone. Curved letters developed after papyrus and vellum accommodate pen and ink.

500–999AD

C500AD Ornamental initials, from the Latin *initials* meaning "*beginning*," are used by monastic scribes in the 5th and 6th centuries to give their manuscripts an unusual treatment. These enlarged letters evolve into illustrations and, over centuries, become identified with bookmaking of the highest quality. Gutenberg includes such decorative initials in his books, and they have been used by designers ever since. ☐ The dot over the letter '*i*' introduced. It is used at first as an accent to indicate a double '*i*,' which is no longer used. **C700AD** The Chinese develop block printing. **C860AD** Cyrillic alphabet, based

868AD The Diamond Sutra, the earliest dated block-printed book, is on seven sheets of paper glued into a single strip (*bottom*). An exceptional example, it is discovered in 1900 in a secret room with 40,000 other scrolls. The block printing technique is brought to Europe around 1420.

C900AD Roman cursive script has pronounced decorative ascenders and descenders.

931AD Certificate in Scriptura Longior minuscules with all-capitals.

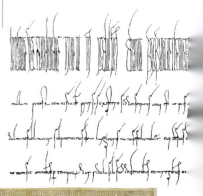

c780AD Merovingian Script, from the Rhone River area of France.

790AD Carolingian Minuscule ("Small Letter") develops at the dictate of King Charlemagne to unify holy texts.

Carolingian Minuscules become more formalized between **c750AD** (*top*) and **c850AD**.

IVLIVS
114AD Trajan Column

IULIUS
900AD

JULIUS
1400AD

900AD Capital *U* introduced for use within words. Five hundred years later, *J* replaces *I*, at first only at the beginnings of words.

on the Greek alphabet, is developed by missionaries to Moravia, now part of the Czech Republic. **C875AD** The Middle Ages bring more rounded letters — a consequence of new writing tools — and a more condensed style, which formalizes in the next 300 years into Textura, the northern European lettering that Gutenberg copied for his type. **C950AD** At about the time of the turn of the first millennium, books and reading were held in such high esteem that, typically in monasteries throughout Europe, an annual book exchange took place. The head librarian would solemnly read the book title that each monk had borrowed the previous year, collect the book,

and assign the next year's book, one per person. It is likely that the monastic residents read more than a single book per year, but this was their minimum, and those who didn't finish their one book "shall confess his fault prostrate and ask for pardon," according to Francis Wormald's *The Year 1200: A Background Survey*.

1000–1399

The letters we use today are derived from two distinct sources: capitals from Roman inscriptions and lowercase letters from Medieval handwriting. ◨ Roman letters are today used by about a third of the world's population.

Numerals develop quickly after the concept of zero is invented in India. Renamed as they are brought west by merchants, "Arabic" numerals are intro-

c250AD India *Nana ghat*

814AD Arabs adopt Indian numerals

c900AD India *Devangari*

950AD Eastern Arabic

duced in Spain in about 950AD and brought to France 40 years later. Arabic are shown in reverse order because it is read right to left.

976AD Spain *Ghobar*

1400 Italy

1545 Paris *Claude Garamont*

1908 New York *M.F. Benton, News Gothic*

c975AD Runic characters are brought from southeast Europe around 250AD. Based on the Latin alphabet, it is simplified from 24 to 16 characters.

f u t h o r k   h n i a s

975AD A psalter from southern England shows more-rounded letters.

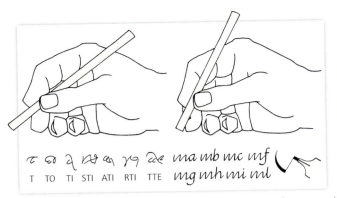

Late Roman cursive shows many variations of a single letter, here the letter *t*. Given the coarse papyrus paper imported from Egypt, writing requires changes

to make the pens work smoothly. Simply changing the way the pen is held increases writing speed and changes the way letters are shaped.

Byzantine letters were considered high art at the time of their writing. Shown here are samples from 1000 to 1425.

c1100 Late Carolingian Minuscules from northern Italy.

The other two-thirds use a variety of languages. ◩ The 1,000 years prior to type's invention, about 500–1450AD, are the Dark Ages, so called because the increase in mankind's knowledge had slowed to nearly nothing. Hand-copied books couldn't keep up with increasing demand. With type's invention in about 1450, knowledge became immediately accessible to many more people. Movable type is among the most important developments in human history. **1000** *Beowulf* manuscript written in Anglo-Saxon, a precursor to English language. **1041** Pi Sheng invents movable type made of baked clay and glue in China. The sculpted glyphs are glued onto a metal sheet, printed, and removed from the sheet for reuse. **1200** Textura, or Gothic, script develops. Legibility is not the chief concern of this heavy, condensed handwriting style: fitting many characters into a small space is. It fits about twice as many characters into the same space as its predecessor, Carolingian. **1221** Goose quill first used for writing. **1253** Arabic numerals introduced in England.

1400–1449

Written materials until now are notably scarce. Reading by the ordinary person is limited to inscriptions on buildings. The invention of movable type printing

1328 The *Book of Hours* of Jeanne d'Évreux, a 3½"x2½" personal prayer book created for the Queen of France, is a strikingly intricate work of art.

c1350 German manuscript writing with flourishes. This is called *textura* or *blackletter* because of its darkness and density. It is used north of the

Alps, throughout Germany and France. By the late 1400s, the letters have evolved to be so condensed and dark that they have become hard to read.

1380 The first translation of the Bible into English is not welcomed: "the pearl of the Gospel is scattered abroad and trodden underfoot by swine."

IOANNES WICLEFVS ANGLVS.

ymæchrmétjcorumæ c350AD Late Roman cursive	*cor, ydem profecto funt fe* c1250AD Early Gothic script
atnon fytcnoícu c450AD Semiuncial	*Magnus dominus et* c1400AD Angled Gothic script
rca confentiant ucn c900AD Carolingian script	*ditte familie mē, Onefimus do* c1450AD Textura type
go Emulare g& penitent c1050AD Carolingian script	*quorum maieftate fug* c1480AD Humanistic script
ad'o cõuuffif, ferału artij aliq, c1200AD Carolingian script	Sic splendente domo, claris c1500AD Humanistic type

c1200 Condensed letters with pronounced vertical strokes become exaggerated into Gothic blackletter in northern Europe. This permits more characters

to fit into less space, making the best use of expensive parchment (limed sheep and calf hides).

c1300 Every monastery had a *scriptorium*. It was sometimes the only heated room. *Scriptores* wrote about four large pages per day. The monastery at

Murano includes the exhortation, *"The pious man should copy books and render them more plentiful ... the spiritual life is nothing without books."*

changed everything. Printing — primarily in the form of books, from its inception in 1450 through the mid-1800s — is the greatest development in history: it makes knowledge available to everyone. It is a revolution that causes regional languages to be standardized, drawing the public away from Latin and the religious structure that has shaped society. By stimulating thinking, it leads directly to the Renaissance. ▣ The demand for books increases: one Florentine bookseller employs up to 50 scribes at one time. *Written* books are about to be supplanted by *printed* books. ▣ Block printed, or *xylographic*, books are the world's first mass-produced objects. Each

page was carved as a complete entity. ▣ Playing cards were among the earliest instances of block printing in both the east (China) and the west (France, Germany, and Italy). ▣ Wood type forms begin to be replaced by metal, which can be cast, engraved, and etched — and used for more impressions without degradation. **1440–1449** Gutenberg takes the existing printing press, a repurposed grape press for wine making (and block printing), oil-based ink, and the eastern invention of movable type, and adds the crucial component: a way to manufacture many copies of letters quickly in metal molds. As a jeweler, he was an expert at casting.

c1420 The initial of every sentence is illuminated in this small, beautifully lettered *Book of Hours* from Flanders (now northern Belgium).

1423 Earliest dated woodblock printing in Europe. Both the type and illustration of St. Christopher are on a single block of wood.

c1440 Gutenberg begins experimenting with movable type in Strassburg, where he lives from 1434 to 1444. He produces the *Sibylline Legend*,

a short booklet. Strassburg has a claim to the earliest movable type printing, but Mainz is where Gutenberg printed the first *book* with movable type.

gebē Die gene mit ſchreckē wohien Die got nye erkante noch forchtē en Riemā mag ſich ōbergē nicht Vor ð gotliche angeſiecht Kriſtus wil do urtel ſprechen· Dñ wil alle boſzheit rechen Die nie ge dacht den willē ſin Den wil er gebē ewige pin Dñ wil den gutē gebē Bi vñ ſreuie

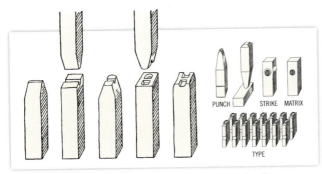

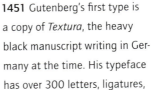

As a goldsmith, Gutenberg's invention of movable type is a natural evolution: he is accustomed to working with molds and duplication. Type founding is the process of striking a carved relief letter into softer metal to make a female, into which molten metal is poured to make multiple copies.

1451 Gutenberg's first type is a copy of *Textura*, the heavy black manuscript writing in Germany at the time. His typeface has over 300 letters, ligatures, and abbreviations, necessary for justification. The type is hand set, locked, inked, and printed. Gutenberg checks a page proof just taken from his press.

13 Type 1450-1913

To be creative means doing the contrary of what every pre-established system wants you to do. To be creative means to try to do something that has never been done before, to build out of nothing something that can have enormous value. Creativity requires a state of non-control, of limitless courage. And that is why conformism is creativity's greatest enemy." Oliviero Toscani

"Under a cloak of classical respectability there is something incongruous about Garamond. As a design, it is somewhat irregular, yet this (doesn't) detract from the harmony of the type." Romek Marber

1451 Bookmaking required four distinct specialists: the typefounder, the papermaker, the printer, and the binder. For the first many decades of printing, the typefounder and the printer were one person, which leads to a multitude of letterform designs. Each printer has his own limited catalog of types to offer. Papermaking requires prodigious amounts of water, so the papermaker has to be near its source: note the waterwheels immediately outside his window. Typesetting takes place in the background as two printers work the press. Binding is done remotely with thread, glue, leather, and pressure.

TYPEFOUNDER

PAPERMAKER

PRINTING OFFICE

BOOKBINDER

grecox: Ariftoricus
neftella. Hi omes pcip
memorãt. Appollodc
ucro enã legatos Eric
mína Romã deporta

1452 Johannes Gutenberg (1394–1468) creates movable, reusable type and prints 160 copies of his *42-line Bible*, a 1,300-page work in two volumes. Marking the birth of typography, such an ambitious and beautiful piece wasn't his first attempt at printing: he prepared himself by printing a brochure and some lesser pieces. A sample of Gutenberg's type and a spread from the *42-line Bible*, the first book printed with movable type.

1465 Sweyenheym and Pannartz's first type, for Cicero's *De Oratore*, in Subiaco, Italy, looks like a cross between *blackletter* and local humanistic lettering.

The 150-year period following Johannes Gutenberg's invention of the printing press and movable type is known as the Renaissance. Gutenberg's invention cannot be separated from this coincidence. It was an era that sought and defined beauty and expressed creativity in many areas. ☐ The greatest type designers are all masters of both printing technique and letterform artistry, and their letters show their understanding of technology. Punches, the original master letters, continue to be handmade until the 1890s, when an American company introduces a punch cutting machine. **1460** Albrecht Pfister of Bamberg produces the first book including both woodcut illustrations and type. **1464** Earliest printed books are reprints of existing works and are made to look as similar to the manuscript works as possible for market acceptance. Printers soon begin making changes in letters and style that make printing its own art. ☐ Conrad Sweynheym and Arnold Pannartz become "journeymen" and move to Subiaco, near Rome, with their press and blackletter types from Mainz. But Italians aren't accustomed to such letters and Sweynheym and Pannartz are forced to craft letters designed after the region's manuscript writing. In due course Blackletter is used for religious material while *Littera Antiqua* is used for secular content. ☐

1467 Sweyenheym and Pannartz's second typeface, *Speculum Humanae Vitae*, shows more Latin characteristics. This trend continues, rapidly diverging from northern European blackletter to more readable Italian letterforms, as shown in these modern interpretations of historical originals.

1470 Nicolas Jenson (1420–1480) was a Frenchman who moved to Venice. This was his first type (shown actual size, about 16pt), and was made for his *Eusebius*. The first true Roman (rather than blackletter), its proportions and elegance remain a standard by which all text types may still be measured.

a bõeftiffime a
Nam & facra f
ndat inquiéf u
pera laudabié.
icef negotiátur.

ACEGMfgomty
Trajanus Semi-Bold

ACEGMfgomty
Goudy Thirty

ACEGMefgomty
Poliphilus
(facsimile of Aldus' 1499 type)

hebræos
tranfitiu
nõ fcript
ad rectan
totius generis origo Habraam n
iuftitiã quã non a mofaica lege(f
Moyfes nafcitur)fed naturali fu
atteftatur. Credidit enim Habra

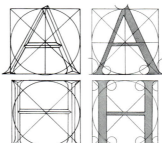

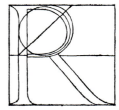

1476 Erhard Ratdolt's ornamented title page is the first time author, title, printer, place, and date are listed. Note the use of fleurons, or *flowers*.

1478 Giovanni and Alberto Alvise produce the earliest fleuron font. Also shown is their little-known typeface from the same year.

1480 The Renaissance brings about studies in letterform perfection based on geometry and numerical proportion. The earliest studies are by Felice

Felicianus, Andrea Mantegna, and Damianus Moyllus. Later studies will be developed by Pacioli, Fanti, Vicentino, Dürer, and Tory.

Movable type printers institute type changes to reduce cost and increase efficiency. Initials become smaller, and ornamentation and illustrations are added and printed in a single pressing with the type. **1470** Johannes de Spira (a transplanted German originally named Johann von Speyer) opens the first printery in Venice, one of the most active trading centers in Europe, and produces the first fully roman typeface, basing it on humanistic handwriting of the area. This marks the shift from Gothic to roman typefaces throughout Europe. ⊡ Nicolas Jenson, a Frenchman, begins printing and making types based on manuscript writing in Venice. Rather than perfecting the beauty of individual characters, Jenson sets out to create an even typographic color in multiple lines of type. His interest is equally in the spaces within and surrounding letters as in the letter shapes themselves. ⊡ For the first 20 years of movable type printing (1450–1470), books have no title pages. They don't *need* them because there are still so few books. **1472** England's first printer, William Caxton, learns the art in Belgium, where he prints the first book in English. He imports *blackletter* fonts to London, then develops his own faces, which become known as *Old English*. **1476** Competition among printers becomes fierce. Partly to stay ahead of

1495–1501 Aldus Manutius (1450–1515) and his typecutter, Francesco Griffo de Bologna (1450–1518), base their roman type on Jenson's. Its modern interpretation is *Bembo,* named for Pietro Bembo, the author of the book of its first use. A shrewd businessman, Manutius next creates a graceful, slanted type after the local Venetian writing style to fit more characters on a page for his new 3½"x 6" "pocketbook" line. Making only lowercase letters, Manutius uses his type with Roman capitals. This slanted style became known as *italic,* though "Roman" types also come from Italy.

1484 William Caxton (1421–1492) is the first printer in England, beginning his work in 1472. He translates many foreign works into English, becomes the first English bookseller, and prints Chaucer's *Canterbury Tales*. The type shown is actual size from his *Prologue to Eneydos*, 1490.

1493 Anton Koberger's sketch and printed page of his *Nuremburg Chronicle* shows the detail to which printers planned the complex craft of making a page. Full pages of text didn't require such preplanning, save for leaving space for the illuminated letter to be added afterward.

the crowd, Venetian printer Erhard Ratdolt produces the first ornamented title page for Johannes Montenegro's *Calendarium*, a treatment that is immediately and widely copied. Ornamented title pages evolve into today's book covers. Two years later, Giovanni and Alberto Alvise design movable type illustrations of flowers and leaves that can be repeated as borders. *Fleurons*, or "flowers," are initially rejected by fellow printers, but shortly become popular because they are fun to make and allow self expression. **1485** As a consequence of William Caxton's efforts in England, Theodore Rood of Oxford writes (in Latin) in the first edition of *Letters of Phalaris*: "The art which the Venetians had to be taught by the Frenchman Jenson, Britain has learned by its native genius. Cease, ye Venetians, sending us any more printed books, for now we sell them to others." **1488** Moritz Brandis of Leipzig invents type families by creating the first semibold version of an existing text face. **1490** Ludolf Borchtorp, a mathematician and engraver, cuts the first Cyrillic types for the printer Szwajpolt Fiol in Kraków. **1500** The first 50 years of movable type printing (1450–1500) are called the *Incunabula* (*swaddling clothes*, or *infancy*). The books printed then were by about 1,000 scholars who became craftsmen so they could print and educate

1500 After the first 20 years of movable type printing (1450–1470), there are more than 100 printers in Europe, primarily in northern Italy and southern Germany (*above*). By 1500, printing expands to 200 cities and is practiced by about 1,000 scholars who have taught themselves the craft.

Handsetting type from a type case. After each page was printed, the letters would be put back into the case for reuse.

c1500 Typecast matrices from Prague show how letters are made in a mold, then separated and finished.

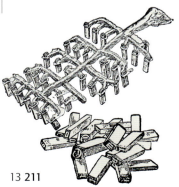

13 211

Johann Trithemius of Sponheim (1462-1516), a lover of knowledge and author of more than 30 books, he was also considered a dangerous occultist.

1517 Old technology — hand copying — vs. new technology: this is a detail of the earliest known drawing of a printing press.

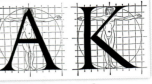

c1525 Geoffroy Tory (1480-1533), a French printer and calligrapher, helps move France from *blackletter* to Roman type. His studies of letterform proportions based on the human body are inspired by da Vinci's sketches. Tory introduces printed decoration and ornament, and teaches Claude Garamont.

others, spread among 200 cities. On the cusp of the Renaissance, they sensed that their communities were ready for learning. In this 50-year period, 35,000 titles are printed, for a total of 10 to 12 million copies. The average "run" of a book's printing is 250 copies.

1500–1599

1500 Page numbers are used for the first time. ⊡ Abbot Johann Trithemius of Sponheim, near Mainz, Germany (1462–1516), writes: "In the city of Mainz, located in Germany on the banks of the Rhine (and thus not in Italy as some have falsely written), was invented and devised by the Mainz citizen Johann Gutenberg that marvelous and previously unheard-of art of printing and the impression of books... O blessed art of printing, long to be remembered as belonging to our age!... Now that this marvelous art has been discovered, it is henceforth permitted to an unlettered person to become as learned as he will." Printed books were nevertheless thought of as second rate well into the 16th century. 1516 As the development of printing types begins to replace monastic scribes, Trithemius builds a library that, at his death, numbered 2,000 volumes, half hand copied and half printed. Trithemius writes that the hand copying of

1523 Ludovico Arrighi's (1475–1527) capital alphabet, considered perfected majuscules, and italic minuscules, both from *Il modo de temperare le penn*.

1525 Albrecht Dürer (1471–1528) focuses some of his extraordinary creativity on perfected — ideal — forms of letters in *"The Art of Measurement."*

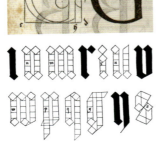

1540 Robert Estienne uses fellow Frenchman Claude Garamont's types at the *Imprimerie Nationale.* He refers to printers as "Children of Gutenberg."

Mayan syllabari, 16th century. Phonetic equivalencies of a Spanish *a* is translated as the Mayan *ak*, meaning *turtle*, and written as a turtle's head.

uilísque prudentiæ, Mediolar
nuerunt.Incidit Galuanius in
lanum à Federico AEnobarbo
rerum geſtarum gloria , & qu
calamitate memorabilis . Cap

ta jaċtabit audacia
urbis vigiliae, nihil
nihil hic *munitissin*
que moverunt? Pat
omnium horum c

1526 Giovanni Baptista Verini draws a complex, interwoven composition using seven letters.

1535 Claude Garamont (1500–1567), whose name was changed to *Garamond* on a 1592 Frankfort specimen sheet, opens a foundry and is first to sell his types to other printers, thus creating type founding as a separate activity. Brings Roman types to France, where they replace *blackletter* in use. His types (*left*) have been called "Universal Romans" because of their proportional perfection. Monotype's 1922 revival is the first of many.

texts is better than printing, but, ironically, he uses a Mainz printer, Peter von Friedberg, to duplicate his *Praise of Scribes*. In it, he writes, "Nobody should say or think: 'What is the sense of bothering with copying by hand when the art of printing has brought to light so many important books; a huge library can be acquired inexpensively.' I tell you, the man who says this only tries to conceal his own laziness." Trithemius offers four reasons that hand copying is better than printing: parchment lasts longer ("Parchment will last a thousand years, the most you can expect a book of paper to survive is two hundred years."); hand copied texts are more aestheti-cally pleasing; they are beautifully illuminated; and they are more accurate in their spelling and syntax. 1550 It takes about six months to produce a complete font. The punches take three months; striking, justifying (cleaning up) the matrices and making the molds takes about four weeks. 1569 Robert Granjon of Lyons crafts gothic, roman, italic, and Civilité fonts, a flamboyant, hard to read lettering used in Paris. 1569 Christophe Plantin of Antwerp begins his *Polyglot Bible*, showing simultaneous translations in Latin, Greek, Hebrew, Aramaic, and Syriac. He publishes it three years later. 1592 The first known typeface "showing," or sampler, is printed in Frankfurt.

Samples of 16th-century italic handwriting (*top to bottom*): 1516 Cardinal Caravaial to Henry VIII; 1517 Archbishop of Sienna to Henry VIII; 1530 For-mal italic book hand; 1570 Italic chancery. Gradual improvements in ink and paper's smoothness allow greater freedom in written self-expression.

1611 The First Edition of the King James Bible. The 7-year completion of this translation represents the most significant step toward standardizing the English language. Two versions were printed, the "He Bible" and the "She Bible," due to a typographic error in Ruth 3:15.

Flamboyant initial caps in a variety of styles: **B** 1485, Paris; **O** 1521, Augsberg; **X** 1580, Italy; and **N** 1611, London.

GARAMOND, JEAN JANNON 1621

GARAMOND 156, MONOTYPE

1621 Jean Jannon's (1580–1658) *Antiqua*, after Claude Garamont (*top*). Jannon's types are mistakenly used in a seminal 1911 revival of *Garamond*.

1632 Richard Shorleyker, London, title page of printer's showings book featuring "Spots, as Flowers, Birds and Fishes &c..."

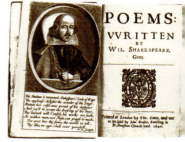

1640 Shakespeare's poems were first printed 25 years after his death in this pocket-sized edition.

1600–1799

Russia and some of its neighbors use Cyrillic, an invented alphabet in the 9th century AD. Based on Greek, it has additional letters to accommodate the sounds of Slavic speech. ⊡ Since 1450, when Gutenberg invented movable type, improvements in typecasting and type use are stylistic, but don't really make the system more efficient. Paper gets smoother, ink becomes more consistent, and type gets finer and more even in color. But type is still set one letter at a time. **1605** First public library is founded in Rome. ⊡ First true newspaper, *Niewe Tijdinghen*, founded in Holland. Contains political and social news, trials, births and deaths, sports, theater reviews, and international news delivered by Dutch seafarers. **1609** First weekly newspaper appears in Strasbourg, the *Avisa Relation Oder Zeitung*. **1620** Gutenberg's press has been in use for almost 200 years without much alteration. But its impressions are uneven, requiring letters that have little contrast, and they fade in spots. The Blaeu press gives even pressure and permits letterform development. **1621** First English newspaper is a translation of the Dutch *News Currents*, which includes "Newes from Italy, Germany, Hungarie, Spaine and France." Newspapers appeared across Europe in this

1682 Peter de Walpergen *Fell Roman* and *Italic*, a Dutch Old Face bought for the Oxford University Press.

1684 Nicholas Kis (1650–1702), a Hungarian in Holland, produces a Bible in Hungarian. His types are temporarily attributed to Anton Janson in 1919.

1693 *King's Roman* (*right*), designed by a committee for use by the Imprimerie Royale, is the first "rational design" based on geometry and grids.

c1700 An anonymous specimen sheet (detail) from England shows fairly rough letters. There are four sizes of roman letters and one size of Old English.

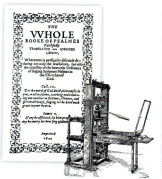

1640 First book is printed in America by Stephen Day in Cambridge, Massachusetts, and his press, the first in America.

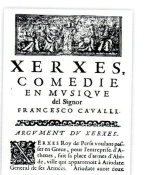

1660 Venetian Francesco Cavalli's play *Xerxes* is performed at Louis XIV's marriage in France. This is the first page of the opera's synopsis.

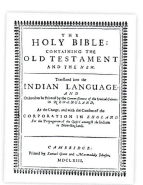

1663 The Bible is translated into Algonquin (an entirely new typeface was needed) and printed in Boston by Green and Johnson.

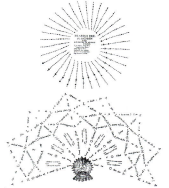

1666 A spiral labyrinth poem and a more complex 1738 version give fresh form to a type-set message. Metal type made these very difficult to make.

period: 1620 in Austria, 1634 in Denmark, 1636 in Italy, 1645 in Sweden, and 1661 in Poland. **1663** London has 60 printers. ☐ First true magazine, containing specific information tailored for a particular audience, is published in Germany. **1690** First American papermill founded in Philadelphia. ☐ Printing is firmly positioned as a business rather than as a personal cause. **1695** After three year's work on the order of Louis XIV for the Royal Printing House, the first typeface that transitions from old face to modern is readied. A conscious effort to build letters using geometry rather than humanistic structure and to relate roman and italic versions, Philippe Grandjean

(1666–1714) used a 48x48 unit grid on his *Romain du Roi*. This is the first important change in printing types in 250 years and precedes Baskerville in England, Firmin Didot in France, and Giambattista Bodoni in Italy by decades. **1702** The *Daily Courant,* England's first daily newspaper, is founded. **1714** Henry Mill receives an English patent on his typewriter. **1719** Wood first proposed as a paper source by a Frenchman, who recognizes the wasp's ability to chew wood and regurgitate it for their nests. Wood is used as paper in 1801 by Mathias Koops in England. Paper is at the time made of cotton and linen rags, but there isn't enough cloth to keep up with the

1710 Russian *poluustav* type of the 16th century is an imitation of medieval script (*left*). But it echoes the old ways and Czar Peter I wants a modern alpha-

bet. After three years of development, he still finds characters he "doesn't like" and crosses them out. He approves this final version of *Civil Type* in 1710.

1718 The first color printing in America, by Andrew Bradford, uses red and black inks in this announcement for a bakery.

1724 William Caslon's (1692–1766) *Old Face*, based on Dutch types of the time. This is the first significant type to be made in England.

RAH SELL
-MAKER, in BROAD-S1
this Method of in
and the Publick in ge
g MUFFINS and CRUM
nbly thanks her Friends
itreats the Continuance c
her conftant Endeavour
er gratefully acknowled;

ABCDEFGH
LMNOPQRS
VWXYZ12
abcdefghijkln

13 215

it froidement
on ne pend pa
spoſer de cer
eſſus ils paſſèrent dans le
Un inſtant après , Monſie

ABCDEFGHIJK
LMNOPQRSTU
VWXYZ&123456
7890abcdefghijkl
mnopqrstuvwxyz?

1742 Forbidden by law to copy the *Romain du Roi* of Grand-jean, Pierre Simon Fournier (1712–1768) develops similar, though more condensed, high-contrast types, which in turn lead to Bodoni's even crisper types. Fournier's types are used by W.A. Dwiggins to create *Electra* (*inset*) in 1949.

Making metal type: a master letter "punch" is crafted out of metal, then hardened (*left*). The punch, held in a vise, is punched into a softer metal "matrix" to make a reverse female mold (*right*), into which molten metal is poured to make multiple copies to be used as printing characters.

ever-increasing needs of printers. The linen wraps from Egyptian mummies, each of which provided about 30 pounds of fabric, are used, and *rag pickers* are paid to find remnants in the garbage, sometimes drying them on clotheslines. Wood becomes economical in 1860, after a German invents a wood grinding machine and a Canadian processes a sheet of paper made from ground wood. **1742** Pierre Simon Fournier produces his first specimen sheet in Paris. His shaded and ornamented letters bring fresh vitality to printing. **1760** Hermann Zapf says "If Bodoni had merely continued to copy Fournier – as he did during his first years – his books would not be out-standing achievements. It was not until he used printing types in the style of his time that his books became truly representative of his age." **1757** John Baskerville (1706–1775) says, "Having been an early admirer of the beauty of letters, I became insensibly desirous of contributing to the perfection of them." Baskerville was a perfectionist. Fellow printers found his types unattractive, though their opinions may have been affected by his disdain for religion, which was then central to English life. Didot and Bodoni found great inspiration in Baskerville's work, which links Caslon's *Old Style* types to their own *Moderns*. **1775** There are about fifty printers in the thirteen colo-

1768 Bodoni designs the first of many versions of what became known as *Modern* faces, with hairline serifs and heavy vertical strokes.

BODONI

re, Catilina, patientiâ
ror iste tuus nos elu-
et? quem ad finem sese
frenata jactabit auda-
a? nihilne te nocturnum

1776 William Caslon's types are adopted by many US colonial printers and are used for the original settings of the Declaration of Independence.

In CONGRESS, JULY 4, 1776.
A DECLARATION
BY THE REPRESENTATIVES OF THE
UNITED STATES OF AMERICA,
IN GENERAL CONGRESS ASSEMBLED

1783 Firmin Didot (1764–1836), a third-generation printer and type founder, begins cutting types based on his father's roman alphabets.

ABCDEFG
LMNOPQ
VWXYZ&
7890abcde
mnopqrstu

1808 Robert Thorne's *French Canon* (*top*), and Thorowgood's 1822 *Canon Modern* show the transition from very bold face to fat face.

ABCDEF
ABCDE
ABCDE
a b c d e f

Tandem aliquan A B C D 1 2 3 4 5 6 7 8 9 0

From an original Baskerville specimen of 1777

Tandem aliquan A B C D

American Type Founders' *Baskerville* made from Baskerville's original matrices

Tandem aliquan A B C

English Monotype *Baskerville* of 1923, recut in 1936

1757 John Baskerville (1706–1775) improves the printing press, ink-making, and paper's smoothness. These complement his type (straight serifs, extreme contrast, and vertical emphasis), which transitions from *Old Style* faces to the *Moderns*. Baskerville's types are used privately until his death, then sold and used only occasionally. Monotype releases a version in 1923 and *Baskerville* has since been one of the most used text faces in the world.

1768 Giambattista (*John the Baptist*) Bodoni (1740–1813) becomes head of the royal printing house in Parma.

nies of the United States. They help foment revolution, which begins the following year with the Declaration of Independence. **1796** Archibald Binney and James Ronaldson start the first permanent type foundry in the United States. Ronaldson writes to Thomas Jefferson on July 3, 1822, "...the genius of Arch Binney simplified the [typefounding] process, and by putting it within the reach of a greater range of talent, there are now in the US six letter foundries." Binney invents a way to eject type from its mold, making it possible to produce 6,000 characters per day, up a full 50 percent. ⊡ Making metal type: The punch-cutter would reproduce letters by making a master, called the *punch*, from steel. The spaces enclosed within the letter were formed with a "counter punch," and then the outer parts of the letter were cut away. The letter was tested as it progressed to ensure an accurate rendition of the original drawn letterform. The finished letter punch was then tempered to harden it. It was then punched into a softer metal, which became the female mold. The mold was worked to accommodate the type's width, then placed in a holder into which molten metal was poured to create multiple male copies that would be used on the printing press. **1798** Aloys Senefelder invents lithographic printing.

1816 Sans serif *hand-drawn* letterforms existed for hundreds of years before William Caslon IV's *Egyptian* type (*top*), which had only capitals.

1817 Vincent Figgins (1766–1844) adds even more darkness to display type be developing the first *slab serif* types, calling them "Antiques."

Giambattista Bodoni creates a succession of high-contrast types, totalling 298 typefaces. Shown are some of his hardened punches and a page from *Divina Comedia*. Bodoni's refinements culminate in what many believe are the most elegant, mechanically perfect letterforms ever designed.

ABCDEFGHIJ
NOPQRSTUV
TO BE SOLD
ANTIQUE LECTURE
CANTER
ROOM

ABCDEF
HIJKLM
speculato
mansions
equipages
and parks

D alla letterata Fire
delle sue Biblioteche
un po' di destrezza e
nell' anno 1789 la divi
niere brutture purgat

einde ad Jus Caesareum ani-
opulit. ... profe-
a celebr ... unus
n maxi ... it au-
nibus ... terea
eo era ... o mi-
as con ... quo-
tinentia, ac morum integri-

Quousq; tandem abutère, Catilina,

1818 Bodoni's *Manuale Tipografico* is published after he dies. It contains 142 of his roman alphabets with many italic and decorative types.

A *rebus*, the combination of pictures and text, is represented in this German work from 1820.

ABCDEF
HIJKLM
OPQRST
VWXYZ

c1825 *Schreeflooze Kapitalen, Series 510* from Enschedé en Zonen, a Dutch type house started in 1703.

ABCDEFG
Roman
KLMN
Antique (Heavy serifs)
STUVWX
Gothic (Sans serif)

1827 Darius Wells invents a way to mass produce wooden display letters, making large-scale printing common. There are three basic style groups.

1800–1913

During the 1800s, readership in the United States explodes from 5.2 million to 75 million. The public school system is introduced, papermaking begins using wood pulp, and steam and electricity replace foot-powered presses. ⊡ The Industrial Revolution brings *hot type*, type made by forcing molten lead into casts of each character, which is melted and reused after each job. Mechanical typesetting technologies evolve throughout the century as competing systems vie for dominance. This speeds the printing process and spurs expanded typestyle offerings for use in the newly formed advertising business. ⊡ The

Arab world uses three writing systems, each of which can be written very quickly: Naskh, the universal language, and two styles used for headings and inscriptions: Solloss and Kufic, used in many of the greatest mosques. **1816** William Caslon IV (the great, great grandson of William Caslon) uses first sans serif *type*, though the Greeks used sans serif *letters* 1,400 years earlier. ⊡ Graphic design evolves markedly during the 19th century, as industrialization sweeps the Western world. **1839** Niepce and Daguerre invent photography in France. ⊡ Large wooden letters used for printing and for sand casting to make metal copies, which lasted far longer. ⊡ Progressively

Setting type by hand requires placing individual characters into a composing stick. The lever on the left is moved to set the measure, or line length.

1850s Machine-carved wooden display faces proliferate in quantity and exuberance through the second half of the 19th century.

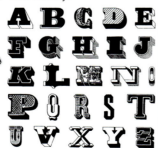

1851 This poster shows the cacophony of types that printers use in the mid- to late 1800s. Anything will be done to increase a message's visibility.

1865 The "writing ball" was invented by the director of a school for the deaf in Copenhagen. Typewriters are sold commercially beginning in 1873.

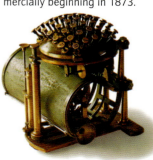

ABCDEFGH
OPQRSTU
abcdefghi
rſstvwxyz

1834 Johann Heinrig's title page showing his sans serif face along with a blackletter and a decorative serif.

1840 The "Pianotype" composing machine, made by Young and Delcambre, had justification and matrix distribution capabilities.

ABCDEFG
HIJKLMN
OPQRST
UVWXYZ
1234567890

1844 Sans serif from Vincent Figgins II, a style that was widely copied. His father is credited with having coined the term "sans serif."

ABCDEFGHIJ
MNOPQRSTU
XYZ&abcdefg
klmnopqrstuv
yz1234567890

1845 *Clarendon*, first slab serif, introduced in England as a display face. It is distinguished by bracketed serifs and greater stroke contrast.

ugly type used because of the Industrial Revolution, in which speed and cost were paramount concerns. ▫ The Industrial Revolution brings major speed improvements in typesetting for the first time since Gutenberg invented movable type. As speed increased, cost decreased and generated even more information to readers worldwide. Knowledge increased at a startling rate. But automated typesetting machines, which still made bits of metal with raised characters on them, could not kern, so what we would consider open letterspacing was normal. **c1860** Printing quality suffered in the throes of the Industrial Revolution. Henry Stevens, a Vermont-born rare-book seller in London and recognized proponent of fine printing, wrote, "The disagreeable fact that our books are deteriorating in quality is assumed for the present and taken for granted. The fault exists and is daily becoming more and more manifest... Our printing presses are teeming and steaming with books of all sorts (with some striking exceptions) not up to the mark of the high calling of book-making. It is no excuse to say that the rapidity of production has been largely increased. That amounts merely to confessing that we are now consuming two bad books in the place of one good one... It is not the amiable public that is so hungry for cheap print-

1866 *Alden Typesetter and Distributor #2*, a steam-driven machine, uses a rotating wheel (*right rear*) to return characters to storage channels.

1867 *Fette Fraktur*, an updated blackletter, is released by Bauer in Frankfurt. *Blackletter* has come to represent Germany.

1885 *Lagerman Composer, Justifier and Distributor* is a two-man machine: one to load font casettes and one to pull a three-ring letter selector.

Upper- and lowercase are blended together in Tuer's type with maximum x-height to save space for uses like "the crowded columns of a newspaper."

lustrates the kind
strings in which loc
palities are kept. Ar
of the local govern
has been holding a
-lic inquest on the
the Brighton corpor
row 55.000l. This e

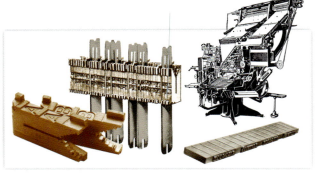

1886 The Blower Linotype machine is the first line-casting machine in the world and replaces letter-by-letter typesetting.

1886 Ottmar Mergenthaler perfects his *Linotype* matrix and type-casting machine. A keyboard operator types, releasing female letter molds

from a rack at the top of the machine. Gravity drops them into position and molten lead is poured in to cast a male, printable line of type.

1890s *Tobaccos of Popov's Tobacco Factory and Trading House, Moscow*, a fine example of merging letters and image into a single statement.

ing and cheap books; but the greedy provider of cheap and cheaper books with which the public is crammed like Strasbourg geese, that are in fault. This downward tendency is not so much the fault of the consumers as the manufacturers. The manufacture of a beautiful and durable book costs little if anything more, it is believed, than it does to manufacture a clumsy and unsightly one. Good taste, skill, and severe training are as requisite and necessary in the proper production of books as in any other of the fine arts." **1886** After several attempts, Ottmar Mergenthaler perfects his *Linotype* matrix and type-casting machine. As the keyboard operator types,

letter molds drop into position and entire lines are cast at once. Because of the key-like matrix on each letter, returning the characters is now automated, too. Until the Linotype machine, all type has been handset one letter at a time, a method essentially unchanged since Gutenberg's invention in 1450. **1890** In a response to sweeping industrialization and mass-market design, William Morris (1834–1896) commits himself to craftsmanship, beauty, and quality. In addition to furniture, fabric, and stained glass design, Morris' Kelmscott Press revives the art of fine printing. Morris designs three typefaces: *Golden Type* in 1890, *Troy Type* in 1892, and *Chaucer*

1892 American Type Founders forms when 23 small foundries merge. This brings the American type foundry business into alignment and profitability.

In 1893, ATF releases *Jenson Oldstyle*, a revival of the 1460 face. Full sets of metal fonts cost from $9.10 for 72 point to $2.00 for 6 point.

1892 Henri de Toulouse-Lautrec uses vernacular letterforms to emphasize the sheer joy of living, as in this small poster for *Les Affiches Illustres*.

1894 *La Revue Blanche*, magazine cover by Pierre Bonnard, Paris, uses wonderfully organic letters with uneven baselines and extended ascenders.

1890 William Morris (1834–1896) *Golden Type* (*above left*): "This type (by Nicolas Jenson) I studied with much care, getting it photographed to a big scale, and drawing it over many times before I began designing my own letter." Morris overwhelms his distinctive type with floral patterning, spends about 20 years designing jewelry, wallpaper, and stained glass windows before turning to type design in 1890. This helps explain Morris' attraction to decorative design. Erhard Ratdolt worked similar territory in 1477 (*above right*) with an ornate woodblock-framed page.

Type in 1893. His politics are as illustrative of the man as his art: Morris declines an Oxford University professorship and naming as poet laureate. **1892** Faced with industry-wide frustration at the lack of manufacturing standards, American type manufacturers agree to adopt a single point system for type measurement. Then more than half merge into a new entity, The American Type Founders, which dominates the type design and manufacturing field for decades to follow. ATF consolidates its many existing types, discarding near-duplicates, and has an initial offering of about 750 faces. ATF expands many existing typefaces into families and begins designing all its new typefaces in families. By 1923, they offer over 8,000 faces. It isn't difficult to imagine the enormity of the task of composing those pages, one line, or one letter, at a time. ATF begins to decline in importance — succumbing to competition though proving that type founding is a profit-making business — in 1935. **1892** William Caslon's types, having been used for the original settings of the US Declaration of Independence (1776) and the US Constitution (1787), are revived by the American Type Founders as *Old Style*, then renamed *Caslon 471*. **1893** Joseph Phinney of The Dickenson Type Foundry in Boston, one of the brand-new members of ATF,

1896 German type foundry Berthold releases *Akzidenz Grotesk*. *Akzidenz* is the source of a revival as *Helvetica* in 1957.

1896 Bertram G. Goodhue *Cheltenham* for the Cheltenham Press in New York City. The redrawn face is adopted by the New York *Times* in 2003.

1897 *The Inland Printer* magazine cover, by J.C. Leyendecker, USA. IP is the first magazine to use a changing cover design with each issue.

1898 Eleisha Pechey *Grotesque 8* for Stephenson Blake Foundry. "*Grot 8*" is available in only one weight and has multiple quirks in its design.

DEFGHIJKL
PQRSTUV:
Z&123456?
abcdefghijk;
pqrstuvwxyz!

ABCDEF
MNOPQ
WXYZ&
hijklmno

ABCDEFG
LMNOPQF
WXYZ&12
90abcdefgh
opqrstuvw:

1900 Morris Fuller Benton *Century Expanded*, based on Linn Boyd Benton's and Theodore Lowe DeVinne's *Century* for *Century Magazine* in 1894.

ABCDE
HIJKLM
PQRST
WXYZ&
456789

1902 Frederic Goudy (1865–1947) *Copperplate*. Goudy began designing types only after he turned 30 and produced about a dozen classics.

Letterforms went through dynamic reinvention in the early 20th century. These are samples from European posters made between 1902 and 1926.

1902 Felix Vallotton's periodical covers relate image and type and help define the Viennese Art Nouveau movement.

begins development of a type family based on Nicolas Jenson's 15th-century types. This revival results in *Jenson Oldstyle*. ⊡ Halftone printing begins to replace line art illustrations. ⊡ Type and design stagnate at the end of the 19th century, with relatively few typefaces available. Bookmakers and artists who care have to make their own types for their private presses. They model them after 15th-century types and contemporary calligraphy. The Germans and French lead the way with the most idiosyncratic type designs, often as direct statements against the machine age that is quickly forming around them. 1900 The Vienna Secession group, also known as the Union of Austrian Artists and led by Gustav Klimt and Koloman Moser, breaks away from the stuffy Viennese Creative Artists' Association. They experiment with new ideas, particularly centered on the active use of space in art and architecture. ⊡ Type is still in the printer's domain. Indeed, the typesetter and the typographer are the same craftsman. Designing as a separate profession has not yet broken away from the printery. 1902 There are about 6,000 Linotype machines in use since their introduction in 1886. ⊡ Otto Eckmann and Peter Behrens design faces for the Klingspor foundry in Germany. Behrens is an early practitioner of what comes to be

1904 Willhelm Woellmer's *Siegfried*. His Berlin foundry specialized in blackletter fonts, but this one is a combination of blackletter and art nouveau.

1905 Will Bradley's (1868–1962) posters change America's design sensibility and he is hailed as "one who has helped develop culture in this country."

1907 Morris Fuller Benton *Clearface*, here shown in ITC's 1979 revival version. Benton headed the ATF type development team for 35 years and

oversaw the design of dozens of typefaces. His 1908 *News Gothic*, the first type designed as a family and redrawn for optical equivalency at each size.

ABCDEFGHIJK
LMNOPQRSTU
VWXYZ.GOBELIN
abcdefghijkl
lmnopqrsstuv
1234567890
TYPE.wxyz.ROSE
MINERVA.SEVILLA

The INTERNATIONAL
STVDIO
An Illustrated Monthly Magazine of FINE & APPLIED ART *Edited by* CHARLES HOLME *Published by* JOHN LANE The Bodley Head at 140 Fifth Ave New York Price 35 cents ❧ Yearly Subscription £3.50 post paid

ABCDEFGI
MNOPQRS
XYZ&1234
90abcdefgh
nopqrstuvw

ABCDEFGHIJKL
NOPQRSTUVW
Z&abcdefghijkln
opqrstuvwxyz12
567890$.,"-:;!?"

ABCDEFGHI
LMNOPQRS'
VWXYZ&ab
efghijklmno
stuvwxyz12
567890$.,-':

1903 Morris Fuller Benton *Franklin Gothic*, initially offered in a single weight. Named for Benjamin Franklin, this is America's first sans serif.

1903 Logo for the letterhead of the Wiener Werkstätte (*Vienna Workshop*), designed by Koloman Moser. Moser cofounded the company with

Josef Hoffmann, both of whom were heavily influenced by the Vienna Secession, a group of painters, sculptors, and architects who sought to synthesize

all the arts. Moser's and Hoffmann's purpose was to push back against "low quality mass production and the unthinking imitation of old styles."

known as corporate identity, developing a logo and its application for Allgemeine Elektrizitäts Gesellschaft, or AEG. ◻ In anticipation of agitation that erupted in the First World War — and in response to it — some artists in Europe conclude that the times need a new way of communicating. Eleven movements overlap and succeed each other in the first half of the 20th century. Steven Heller writes, "There is *always* an artistic avant garde. Once accepted, that avant garde becomes fashionable and, after its turn on the fashion wheel, becomes mainstream." **1909** Filippo Marinetti publishes his Manifesto of Futurism in a Parisian newspaper. ◻ The early 20th

century is a time of a succession of avant garde art movements, almost entirely in Europe. Artists and designers intently follow each others' work and either add to it or refute it in their own works. Each movement is a response to what has come before, and each is intent on overthrowing the prevailing attitudes and values of the Victorian and Arts & Crafts movements that survived until the turn of the century. Between 1905 and 1935, Expressionism is followed by Cubism, Futurism, Dadism, de Stijl, Constructivism, the Bauhaus — which introduces the clean, uncluttered typography that is still a standard — Art Deco, Surrealism, and Modernism.

1911 Frederic Goudy *Kennerly*. Commissioned and first used in a book published by Mitchell Kennerly, a British publisher.

1913 Alphonse Mucha's lettering is indicative of the Art Nouveau movement. This poster is for a friend's daughter who excelled at the cello.

1913 Morris Fuller Benton *Cloister Old Style*. An early interpretation of Nicolas Jenson's 1469 roman. Comparable to *Centaur, Jenson,* and *Legacy*.

1913 Ludwig Hohlwein's *Das Plakat* magazine cover, Germany, shows a new spatial structure and contrast between type and image.

CDEFGHI
MNOPQR
UVWXYZ
defghijklmn

ABCDEFGH
MNOPQRR:
UVWXYZal
ghijklmnopqrst
xyzt Qu &abcde

HE mental pro... ing vary so wi... that, short of w...ght. There is a futile to try to ...d, fast by his of approach to ...ts in perpetual

1914 Bruce Rogers *Centaur*, for a book called *The Centaur*. Rogers was inspired by Nicolas Jenson's 1470 *Eusebius* (*top*), an inspiration for Emery

HIS WAY, ...ours, with rosi...

Walker's own *Doves* (for his Doves Press) in 1900. Walker's business partner tossed the metal letters into the Thames in a fit of pique.

c1915 The Merganthaler Linotype machine is adopted across the Unites States and around the world, replacing slower handset type.

ABCDEFGHI... NOPQRSTUV... &abcdefghijkl... rstuvwxyzfiffff... 4567890$.,"-:;!?

1915 Morris Fuller Benton *Century Schoolbook*, based on 1890s *Century* by Linn Boyd Benton. This design is the result of early legibility studies.

14 Type 1914-1945

I n the sense in which architecture is an art, typography is an art... Every work of architecture and typography depends for its success on the clear conveyance of intentions from one human mind to others." Beatrice Warde

Why 1914–1945? The period from the First World War until the beginning of the Second World War propelled

"In all affairs it is a healthy thing now and then to hang a question mark on the things you have long taken for granted." Bertrand Russell (1872-1970)

1916 *Il Pleut (It's Raining)*, G. Apollinaire's concrete poem shows message and presentation joined into one. It was later typewritten by a friend.

1919 D. Stempel AG in Frankfurt revives Anton Janson's (1620-1687) *Janson Antiqua*, made from Janson's original matrices.

1920 Lazar M. Lisitskii (1890–1941) *Red's Wedge is the White's Death*. This constructivist poster is a powerful revolutionary statement.

1921 Ladislaw Medges' *Broom* magazine cover, USA. *Broom* is a poetry and literary magazine that offers opportunities to many young artists.

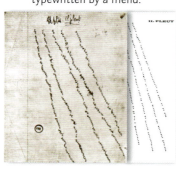

ABCDEFG... IJKLMNOP... RSTUVWX... Zabcdefghijkl... nopqrstuvwxy... 1234567890ß&

Lettre d'une jolie femme
à un monsieur passéiste

ABCDEFGH
OPQRSTUV
abcdefghijkln
uvwxyzæœefit
1234567890.,

*Handlettered effec
seldom attempted i
but the designer c
face was very succ*

Colwell Handletter Italic

Wood types are used by artists in several movements: Cubism, Dadaism, Futurism, and Constructivism. Shown here are

two works by Filippo Tommaso Marinetti from 1915 and 1919. (This is a love poem: *chair* means *flesh* in French.)

1916 Frederic Goudy *Goudy Old Style*. Drawn after the Venetian Old Style model, *G.O.S.* has a slightly enlarged x-height.

1916 ATF releases the first type designed by an American woman, Elizabeth Colwell.

change across the arts. Artists and designers, whose gift it can be said is a greater sensitivity to their environment, reacted to the human cataclysm with a sequence of artistic movements, each necessarily rejecting the others, each exploring the present truth as they saw it. Artists who used the word reflected the new reality in radical new ways: being intelligible in traditional ways was not the point, being expressive in their outrage was. In addition, the war made traditional art materials, including paper, very hard to come by, so their art was partly caused by happenstance of what they could find to use. ▣ The Constructivists had the most

interest in typography of the avant garde artists in the early 20th century. This may be a reflection of their belief that their works are art objects. ▣ Bruce Rogers (1870–1957), one of the most influential typographers in American history, is an artist who designs types for new manufacturing techniques without compromising the highest standards of form and color. Rogers designs *Centaur* and *Metropolitan*, among several others. Raised in Indiana, he moves to Indianapolis, then Boston for his primary client, a quarterly arts magazine. He becomes a trade book designer, then the director of fine editions at Houghton Mifflin. He designs his own versions of *Jenson*

c1920 Dadaism born in Switzerland. *"Dada,"* a term that has no meaning, identifies an anti-art avant garde movement that emphasizes absurdity ("word

salads" and "image salads") by using the printer's random on-hand art and, in the middle sample, spontaneous deconstruction of a clock.

1921 Oswald B. Cooper *Cooper Black*. Designing types was a sideline for Cooper, who thought of himself as a lettering artist. His lettering jobs often grew

into complete typefaces. "No one has done more than Cooper to combat ugliness in American advertising." *Thomas J. Erwin*, J. Walter Thompson, 1923

ABCDEFGHIJKL
MNOPQRSTUVW
XYZ&12345678;:
90abcdefghijklm
nopqrstuvwxyz?!

c1921 Dadaism spreads from Switzerland to Germany, then Holland, where Theo van Doesburg evolves it into de Stijl (*The Style*).

1925 Alexander M. Rodchenko (1891–1956) *Lengiz Publisher: Books on All Sorts of Knowledge*. This is a great example of type as "frozen sound."

1925 Eric Gill's carved alphabets, an unequaled modern standard. Gill applied his knowledge of stone letter carving into his typefaces.

abcdefg jklmnop stuvwx

1925 Herbert Bayer (1900–1985) *Bayer*, a unicameral type (only one case), which is a significant step in the search for maximum simplicity.

and *Caslon* for use in specific books. A few years later he reworks Jenson's *Eusebius* and creates *Centaur* for the Metropolitan Museum Press (although its first use is on Guérin's *The Centaur*) followed by the *Oxford Lectern Bible, Fra Luca de Pacioli*, and a new translation of *The Odyssey*. Rogers has been called a master at achieving Beatrice Warde's acclaimed typographic crystal goblet: "the vessel which contains without distortion the thought of the author." In fact, Rogers is a refined reader and thinker and comes to advise — and even edit — his authors, among them Winston Churchill, Ezra Pound, and Willa Cather. ▣ Walter Gropius, German architect and teacher, helps found the Bauhaus in Weimar after the First World War. Gropius sees a more integrated relationship between the artist and industry. He seeks to reduce the compromises that machines imposed while bringing the artist into the business mode and to "humanize the rigid, almost exclusively material mind of the businessman." This is a conscious effort to attack the artistically vapid terrain of the industrial revolution, in which speed and cost are the primary concerns. The Bauhaus strives to invent new standards for an age that is examining time and space by reexamining the purpose of design in society. ▣ Stanley Morison and Eric Gill are central to

1926 Heinrich Jost (1889–1948) *Bauer Bodoni*. This is probably the best of many early 20th-century *Bodoni* interpretations.

1926 Rudolph Koch *Wilhelm Klingspor*, named after the German Klingspor type foundry. Koch also designed *Kabel* and *Neuland*, among other faces.

1926 The Bauhaus ethic is shown in this magazine cover by Herbert Bayer. The concentric circles represent a roll of printing paper.

1926 A chart shows the relationship of metal type body (*left*) to printed letter and the names of common type sizes.

ABCDEFGHI
NOPQRSTU\
Z&abcdefghij
opqrstuvwxy
1234567890$

ABCDEFE
KLMMOPE
TUVWXYZ
4567890abcd
klmnopqrstuvw

OFFSET
BUCH UND WERBEKUNST
7

Type Body	Size of Face	Size in Points	Name*
Hm		6	Nonpareil
Hm		8	Brevier
Hm		10	Long Primer
Hm		12	Pica
Hm		14	English
Hm		18	Great Primer
Hm		24	Double Pica
Hm		30	Five-Line Nonp.
Hm		36	Three-Line Pica
En		48	Four-Line Pica

1925 Jan Tschichold's *Typographischen Mitteilungen*, in black and red, shows the new dynamic, asymmetrical typography that considers emptiness.

1925 Paul Renner (1878–1956) *Futura* with a page from the original 1928 Bauer Type Foundry catalog and a showing of Renner's original letters and

replacements suggested and adopted by the foundry. Futura popularizes sans serif types with its geometric simplicity and lack of obvious weight change.

c1926 Kurt Schwitters' Pelikan symbol and Piet Zwart's (*zwart* means "black") personal mark use combinations of letters and stock metal printing shapes.

---

the development of typography between the two World Wars, 1917–1940. Morison oversees typeface design for the Monotype Corporation. Gill designs a sans serif that remains one of the most popular faces in use today: *Gill Sans*. ▣ Linotype and Monotype machines compete for business by offering differing technologies. Both machines have limitations: maximum type size is 48 and 60 points respectively; the maximum line length is 36 and 60 picas respectively, and the Linotype requires that bold and italic characters be the same width as roman, forcing some undesirable compromises in counterform shapes and spacing attributes.

1920–1929

The early 1900s are a time of freeing typography from the strictures of the previous century. The Arts and Crafts movement of the late 1800s is an example of the classic refinement that has been achieved. ▣ The world is now changing rapidly at the close of WWI. Cubism, de Stijl, Suprematicism, and Dadaism are flourishing. The Russian Revolution in 1917 propels Russian artists to new ways of seeing. The revolution ruins nearly every physical tool they have to work with, so imaginative use of what is left lying around is essential. Printing sizes, for example, depended entirely on what paper is

---

1926 Emil Rudolph Weiss (1875–1942) *Weiss*. Notable for its top-heavy vertical strokes and the quirky cap *B*, *M*, *S*, and *U*.

c1927 Several initials show great fluidity and imagination and reflect the artistic attitudes and explorations being made in the 1920s.

1927 Moholy-Nagy develops "typophoto," combining type and image into "the new visual literature," as in his 1929 collaged cover for a brochure for

14 Bauhaus Books. Moholy-Nagy helps found the Bauhaus school in 1923, integrating technology and industry into the arts.

ABCDEFGH
MNOPQST
UVWXYZ&
fghijklmnopc
wxyzff12345(

1928 Fantastic letterforms are the style in Europe. These are all drawn for specific use, not made into metal type, which would have been impractical.

1928 Stenbergs' *Berlin, Symphony of a Great City*, a photomontage that depicts man and machine working as one, an important theme of this period.

Calligraphic experience, the ability to render letterforms, is shared by all type designers in the early 20th century. These sketches are by Rudolph Koch.

Dutch Moderne logos from the 1920s and 1930s. The short-lived movement for design elegance existed between the two World Wars.

---

already at a print shop. ☐ Lazar (El) Lissitzky meets and becomes enormously impressed with Malevich, who is pressing Cubism and Futurism to their ultimate ends: abstract art. Lissitzky emphasizes space, simplicity, the tension between objects and typography, and photomontage. He develops a list of requirements of good typography: 1) printed words are seen and not heard; 2) concepts are communicated through words and letters; 3) concepts should be expressed with the greatest optical (not phonetic) economy; 4) the layout must reflect the content's rhythm; 5) sequence of pages are like a cinematographical book; 6) the page and the endless number of books must be overcome. **1923** The Bauhaus School, led by transplanted Hungarian László Moholy-Nagy (pronounced *Mahóy-Náj*), Theo van Doesberg, Walter Gropius, and Herbert Bayer, expand on Lissitzky's ideas and address the problem of mechanization head on, as in this statement: "There is no essential difference between the artist and the craftsman. Proficiency in craft is essential to every artist." From 1919 to 1933, when it is closed by the Nazis, the Bauhaus makes an indispensable contribution to the arts. The Bauhaus marks the birth of graphic design as a separate academic profession and discipline. At its closing, most of its artists move

---

1930 Rudolf Wolf (1895–1942) *Memphis* (*top*), essentially a slab serifed *Futura*, inspires many similar interpretations of sans serif types in the 1930s.

ABCDEFGHI
JKLMNOPQR
abcdefghijklm
Cairo (Intertype)
ABCDEFGHIJK
Karnak (Ludlow)
ABCDEFGHIJ
Beton Light (Bauer)
ABCDEFGHIJKl
Rockwell Medium (Monotype)
ADBCEFGHIJK
Scarab (Stephenson Blake)

1930 R. Hunter Middleton (1898–1985) *Tempo*. Every foundry wants its own Futura. Middleton is the type director of the Ludlow foundry for 50 years.

ABCDEFGHIJ
NOPQRSTUV
YZ&abcdefgh
nopqrstuvwx
34567890$.,

1930 William Addison Dwiggins (1880–1956) *Metro*. Dwiggins designs this, his first typeface, on a dare by Merganthaler Linotype.

ABCDEFGH
NOPQRSTU
YZ&abcdefg
nopqrstuvwx
234567890

1930 Wladyslaw Strzeminski *From Beyond* book cover reduces letters to their stylized shapes — and uses the three primary colors plus black.

1925 Jan Tschichold's *Typographischen Mitteilungen*, in black and red, shows the new dynamic, asymmetrical typography that considers emptiness.

1925 Paul Renner (1878–1956) *Futura* with a page from the original 1928 Bauer Type Foundry catalog and a showing of Renner's original letters and

replacements suggested and adopted by the foundry. Futura popularizes sans serif types with its geometric simplicity and lack of obvious weight change.

c1926 Kurt Schwitters' Pelikan symbol and Piet Zwart's (*zwart* means "black") personal mark use combinations of letters and stock metal printing shapes.

the development of typography between the two World Wars, 1917–1940. Morison oversees typeface design for the Monotype Corporation. Gill designs a sans serif that remains one of the most popular faces in use today: *Gill Sans*. ⊡ Linotype and Monotype machines compete for business by offering differing technologies. Both machines have limitations: maximum type size is 48 and 60 points respectively; the maximum line length is 36 and 60 picas respectively, and the Linotype requires that bold and italic characters be the same width as roman, forcing some undesirable compromises in counterform shapes and spacing attributes.

1920–1929

The early 1900s are a time of freeing typography from the strictures of the previous century. The Arts and Crafts movement of the late 1800s is an example of the classic refinement that has been achieved. ⊡ The world is now changing rapidly at the close of WWI. Cubism, de Stijl, Suprematicism, and Dadaism are flourishing. The Russian Revolution in 1917 propels Russian artists to new ways of seeing. The revolution ruins nearly every physical tool they have to work with, so imaginative use of what is left lying around is essential. Printing sizes, for example, depended entirely on what paper is

1926 Emil Rudolph Weiss (1875–1942) *Weiss*. Notable for its top-heavy vertical strokes and the quirky cap *B, M, S,* and *U.*

c1927 Several initials show great fluidity and imagination and reflect the artistic attitudes and explorations being made in the 1920s.

1927 Moholy-Nagy develops "typophoto," combining type and image into "the new visual literature," as in his 1929 collaged cover for a brochure for

14 Bauhaus Books. Moholy-Nagy helps found the Bauhaus school in 1923, integrating technology and industry into the arts.

1928 Fantastic letterforms are the style in Europe. These are all drawn for specific use, not made into metal type, which would have been impractical.

1928 Stenbergs' Berlin, *Symphony of a Great City*, a photomontage that depicts man and machine working as one, an important theme of this period.

Calligraphic experience, the ability to render letterforms, is shared by all type designers in the early 20th century. These sketches are by Rudolph Koch.

Dutch Moderne logos from the 1920s and 1930s. The short-lived movement for design elegance existed between the two World Wars.

already at a print shop. ▢ Lazar (El) Lissitzky meets and becomes enormously impressed with Malevich, who is pressing Cubism and Futurism to their ultimate ends: abstract art. Lissitzky emphasizes space, simplicity, the tension between objects and typography, and photomontage. He develops a list of requirements of good typography: 1) printed words are seen and not heard; 2) concepts are communicated through words and letters; 3) concepts should be expressed with the greatest optical (not phonetic) economy; 4) the layout must reflect the content's rhythm; 5) sequence of pages are like a cinematographical book; 6) the page and the endless

number of books must be overcome. **1923** The Bauhaus School, led by transplanted Hungarian László Moholy-Nagy (pronounced *Mahóy-Náj*), Theo van Doesberg, Walter Gropius, and Herbert Bayer, expand on Lissitzky's ideas and address the problem of mechanization head on , as in this statement: "There is no essential difference between the artist and the craftsman. Proficiency in craft is essential to every artist." From 1919 to 1933, when it is closed by the Nazis, the Bauhaus makes an indispensable contribution to the arts. The Bauhaus marks the birth of graphic design as a separate academic profession and discipline. At its closing, most of its artists move

1930 Rudolf Wolf (1895–1942) *Memphis* (*top*), essentially a slab serifed *Futura*, inspires many similar interpretations of sans serif types in the 1930s.

ABCDEFGHI
JKLMNOPQR
abcdefghijklm
ABCDEFGHIJK
Cairo (Intertype)
ABCDEFGHIJ
Karnak (Ludlow)
ABCDEFGHIJKI
Beton Light (Bauer)
ABCDEFGHIJK
Rockwell Medium (Monotype)
ADBCEFGHIJK
Scarab (Stephenson Blake)

1930 R. Hunter Middleton (1898-1985) *Tempo*. Every foundry wants its own Futura. Middleton is the type director of the Ludlow foundry for 50 years.

ABCDEFGHIJ
NOPQRSTUV
YZ&abcdefgl
nopqrstuvwx
34567890$.,

1930 William Addison Dwiggins (1880–1956) *Metro*. Dwiggins designs this, his first typeface, on a dare by Merganthaler Linotype.

ABCDEFGH
NOPQRSTL
YZ&abcdefg
nopqrstuvwx
234567890

1930 Wladyslaw Strzeminski *From Beyond* book cover reduces letters to their stylized shapes — and uses the three primary colors plus black.

ODBEEHIJKLMN
VWCG
&
ABCDEFGHIJKL
MNOPQRSTUV
WXYZabcdefgh
ijklmnopqrstuv
wxyz

ABCDEFGH
OPQRSTUV
&abcdefghijk
tuvwxyzæœf
1234567890.,

abcdɛE
fghijk
lmNop
qrstuv
WXYZ

1928 Eric Gill (1882–1940) *Gill Sans*, loosely based on his teacher Edward Johnston's London Underground signage (*rear*). Gill was commissioned by the Monotype Corporation to create a sans serif to compete with *Futura*. He made a humanistic sans that remains one of the most legible sans serifs.

1929 Stanley Morison *Bembo*, a revival of the 1495 original by Griffo. It is named after the author of the manuscript Griffo used, Pietro Bembo.

1929 Jan Tschichold *Tschichold*, a unicameral type. This is the ultimate geometric sans serif: there is nowhere left to go. Note the alternate *E* characters.

to the United States and, in 1937, Moholy-Nagy establishes the new Bauhaus in Chicago. Other US schools begin offering graphic design in the late 1940s. The American Bauhaus evolves into the International Style, which has prevailed since 1950. ⊡ Magazine design is a significant part of the design revolution, particularly the covers, where it is believed readers are most pliable. Art Nouveau with its organic curves evolves into a more geometric style, which becomes known as Art Deco, named after the International Exhibition of Decorative Arts in 1925. ⊡ The poster is a commonplace event in Russia. Posters are used to make political, social, and marketing announcements and color every town, factory, and school. They promote Russia's achievements, wealth, and dreams until the late 1980s, when posters are replaced by television as the primary means of mass communicating in Russian society. **1929** Herbert Matter works with A.M. Cassandre and Le Corbousier in Paris. He moves to Zurich to work with Anton Stankowski and Walter Herdeg before moving to the United States and reinventing *Vogue* and *Harper's Bazaar* magazines. ⊡ Perhaps as a result of the Industrial Revolution, Eric Gill is a critic of commerce and of machines and, most interestingly, of typography. He is quite a curmudgeon:

1931 Herbert Bayer *Bayer-type*, a unicameral, serifed "universal" experiment. Compare to the maximum simplicity of *Tschichold* in 1929.

1931 Lucian Bernhard *Bernhard Gothic*. This is a detail from the original 4-page booklet announcing the release.

1931 Eric Gill *Joanna*. Named for his daughter, Joan, this face is designed for use at his private press. It is first used in his own *An Essay on Typography*.

c1932 Kurt Schwitters, a leading Dadaist, makes the *Systematic Letter*. Consonants are narrow and square and the vowels are fatter and round.

abcde
jklmr
stuvv

BERNHARD GOTHIC MEDIUM CONDENSED
ABCDEFGHIJKLMNOPQRSTUVWXYZ&
abcdefghijklmnopqrstuvwxyz .,-'""::!? $1234567890¢¢
$1234567890   ÆFKMПШ
CHARACTERS FONTED AND SOLD SEPARATELY

HE WHO FIRS
he who first short
HE WHO FIRST!
he who first shorten

ABCDEFGH
NOPQRSTU
YZabcdefgh
opqrstuvwx
123456789

MŪSꞳK ꞳM Lēben dɛ
20 ŪhR dꞳRꞳGꞳeR
WARSꞳhAUS beRũ
POLNꞳSꞳheR MeꞳSꞳ

ABCDEFGH
OPQRSTUV
abcdefghijkl
uvwxyzfifffflf
67890$.,"-:;!

1932 Berthold Wolpe *Albertus*. This glyphic face, based on stone inscriptions rather than handwriting, becomes popular for use in all-capitals settings.

ABCDEFGHIJ
KLMNOPQRS
abcdefghijklmno
rstuvwxy123456

1932 Stanley Morison (1889–1968) *Times New Roman*. Morison serves as the typographic advisor to Monotype Corporation for 25 years and oversees the development of dozens of classic faces. He is hired to improve the typography of *The Times* of London. The set of metal fonts weighs 35 tons.

Italian logos from the 1930s and 1940s. Art deco and Futurism are visible in these works. Harsh political realities are evident in other samples.

"The only way to reform modern lettering is to abolish it." "There are as many different varieties of letters as there are fools." Master printers are "a bunch of morons."

1930–1945

In December 1936 *Time* magazine reports: "In Budapest, surgeons operated on Printer's Apprentice Gyoergyi Szabo, 17, who, brooding over the loss of a sweetheart, had set her name in type and swallowed it." ▣ In the same year, the most popular types in the *British Fifty* books competition are: *Baskerville* (8 winners); *Bembo* (6); *Fournier* (5); *Perpetua, Poliphilus, Walbaum* (4 each); *Centaur, Caslon* (3 each); and *Times New Roman, Lutetia, Imprint, Bell* (2 each). ▣ Tony Stan, a type designer in the 1970s and 1980s, primarily for the International Typeface Corporation, says of his typographic education, "In the late 1930s, three typefaces were used the most: Bodoni, Caslon, and Futura. I soon discovered the balance of each letter and how one form reacted next to another. It became apparent that balance was synonymous with legibility, readability, and beauty." Similarly, Imre Reiner (1900–1987), designer of fifteen faces, says, "A typographer should never limit himself to being modern in the sense of current fashion. He should strive to

1937 Lester Beall (1903–1969) designs a series of posters for the Rural Electrification Administration. Beall is inspired by the Bauhaus.

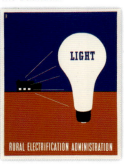

1938 R. Hunter Middleton *Stencil* (*left*) vs. Gerry Powell *Stencil* (*right*). Released within weeks of each other, Powell's version found greater success.

ABC ABCI
IJK IJKI
QRS QRS
YZ& YZ&
7890 7890

1938 Lucian Bernhard (born Emil Kahn, 1883–1972) *Bernhard Modern*. Self-taught type designer and artist, he begins work for the ATF in 1922.

1939 W.A. Dwiggins *Caledonia*. Inspired by *Scotch Roman* (*c1813*) and *Bulmer* (*1790*), this is his third (of twelve) and most successful typeface.

ABCDEFC
JKLMNO
RSTUVWX
abcdefghijk
opqrstuvw

ABCDEFG MNOPQRS XYZ&1234 0abcdefgh opqrstuvw

Preissig Anti
ABCDEFGHIJK
abcdefghijklmno
A&C
afghi

1934 Monotype In-House Design Studio *Rockwell*. Morris Fuller Benton, Frank Hinman Pierpont, and Stanley Morison help in its development.

1934 Nationalist poster, Ladislav Sutnar, Prague. An information graphics specialist, he invents parentheses around telephone area codes.

1936 Heinrich Jost *Beton*, meaning "concrete," becomes a popular advertising typeface. This announcement poster is designed by Alexey Brodovitch.

c1930s Czech typographer Vojtech Preissig designs types and books. These book plates are for himself and an American friend.

produce work which will stay unaffected in its artistic value by the tastes of future generations." **1942** Isidore Isou develops his ideas for Letterist poetry in Romania. "Letterism" is an avant garde movement and its core idea is that language requires the deconstruction of words into letters. Isou moves to Paris in 1945 and affects a wider audience. One Letterist insight is that, given an abstract work, a representational element will become the focal point; given a realistic work of, say, a landscape, a human being will become the focal point; and given a portrait, letters will become the focal point. Letters, they conclude, are therefore the most potent symbols in any art. **c1945** Photographic advances make phototypesetting practical. A film negative of each character is exposed through a lens onto light-sensitive paper. The same negative can make any size letter, ending the need for optical adjustments in letterform design as the size changes, and leading to a slight diminution of type standards. *Phototype*, also called *cold type*, sparks a flood of new typefaces, most for display use. ▣ As post-war society and culture evolve through the 1920s, '30s, and early '40s, artists and designers react to mechanization and mass production. Whether in support or rejection, they view undisguised modernity as threatening.

1941 Bert van der Leck's de Stijl-inspired type used in *Flax* magazine. Perhaps familiar by today's standards, this was then a progressive effort.

1941 Alexey Brodovitch art directs *Harper's Bazaar*, inspriring and expanding the design possibilities of all magazines.

1942 "Lettrism" develops in Romania and Paris in the work of Isidore Isou and Maurice Lamaitre. This 1950 example is by Isou.

1945 Georg Trump *Schadow Antiqua*. This is a slab serif but with a forward-thinking modernist attitude. Note the tail on the Q and the *j*'s angular descender.

ABCDEFGHIJK
PQRSTUVWXY
abcdefghijklmn
yz chckßfl äöü &
1234567890.,-:;!·?

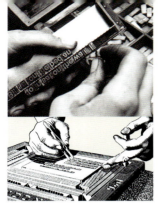

Handset type requires sure fingers and eye-to-hand coordination (*top*). Setting lines and locking them in a chase is essentially the same as in 1450.

Italian logos from the 1940s and 1950s. Futurist simplicity has run its course and increased decoration is emerging, with residual hints of Art Deco.

1946 Czech designer Oldrich Menhart's *Manuscript Antikva* and *Kursiva*, two of his many calligraphic typefaces (*top*). Menhart also drew initial sets.

Three elegant Dutch stamps from the middle of the 20th century: 1947, Eva Besnyö; 1962, Car van Weele; 1962, Otto Treumann.

15 Type 1946-1982

Typography, the perfect fusion of form and meaning in which beauty is born, is raised from mere craft and can claim the title of a philosophy... Thus the printed word is in touch with the spirit." Raul Mario Rosarivo

At the end of the Second World War, the economies of the western world began to grow and people had

"The time to recognize typography on its own has arrived." Founded in 1946 by some of the industry's leading practitioners, the Type Directors Club is formed in New York City.

1950 Bradbury Thompson (1911–1995) *alphabet 26*. A unicameral solution: the black letters use uppercase design; red use lowercase design; blue have

only one design. Thompson says of his *Westvaco Inspirations* series, "I was privileged to produce designs where images and words were synonymous."

1950 Hermann Zapf (1918–2015) *Palatino* (named for a 16th-century scribe). This marked-up proof is a preliminary of Zapf's first typeface design.

1950 *Dom Casual* is the first commercial phototype face. Its use is as a prototype to reduce the financial risk of introducing a new metal typeface.

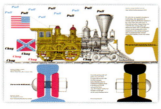

1947 Viktor B. Koretskii (1909–1998) *Let's Reconstruct!* The headline in this Russian poster is drawn to look like shavings, relating lettering to image.

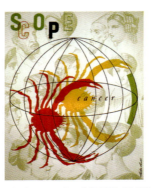

1948 Lester Beall (1903–1969) designs *Scope* magazine for Upjohn. He uses collages of old steel engravings and flat areas of transparent color.

ABCDEFGI
MNOPQRS
XYZ&1234
90abcdefg
nopqrstuvw

1948 Jackson Burke *Trade Gothic*. Because of its elegant simplicity and condensed form, *Trade Gothic* becomes one of the most versatile types ever drawn.

1949 Hand-lettered poster for the International Mediterranean Games in Palermo. Such hand-drawn lettering yields variety and innovation.

more money, more time, and a higher quality of life than ever before in history. Books, advertising, and magazines all become far more plentiful, in part aided by the development of better quality printing and color reproduction. Television is introduced in the 1950s, bringing an entirely new medium that requires lots of visual presentation. Graphic design becomes an increasingly important aspect of differentiating competing goods and services. **1946** Photosetter introduced by Intertype. **1947** "Formerly, pictures were used to supplement or amplify words. Now words supplement and amplify pictures." Clayton Whitehill, *The Moods of Type.* **1950**

The first phototype face is developed as a cost-saving prototype. Ed Rondthaler, President of Photo-Lettering Inc., says, "Cutting a new typeface has always been the typefounder's most hazardous gamble. To convert a new alphabet from drawing to metal type is an expensive undertaking, and no foundry dares embark on such a project until it is absolutely sure that the style will more than pay for itself. Photo typesetting removes the gamble: a test run of the proposed type will determine its popularity and disclose any design flaws. This approach was first used in 1950, with a commercial testing of Dom Casual by Photo-Lettering for a full year

1954 Georg Trump (1896–1985) *Trump Mediæval.* Also called *Imperial* when released by C.E. Weber in Stuttgart. Interpretation of old style models.

1954 Viktor B. Koretskii *Careless Talk — Enemies Help!* uses calligraphic lettering to imply looseness and typeset words to imply organization.

"The realization came to many of us in the early '50s that type was ... a creative and expressive instrument." Herb Lubalin (1918–1981)

1954 Ladislav Sutnar designs brochures for Marquardt Paper. This spread is from an issue on "Controlled Visual Flow."

ABCDEFC
MNOPQF
WXYZ&1
890abcdef
nopqrstuv

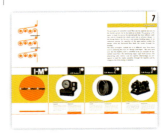

1955 Saul Bass's poster for *The Man with the Golden Arm*. Bass alternated between movie titles and trademark design throughout his career.

1956 Sutnar's poster for Addo-X, a Swedish adding machine manufacturer. Characters are simplified to zeros and symbols in geometric forms.

1956 Emil J. Klumpp (1912–1997) *Murray Hill*. Named for an area of NYC where advertising agencies were then concentrated.

1957 Konrad Bauer & Walter Baum *Folio*. This is remarkably similar to *Helvetica*, which was under development at the same time. Note the alternate cap *R*.

before metal casting was undertaken." ⊡ Regarding type, design, and communication, Walter Zerbe writes in *Typographische Monatsblatter*, "In typographical design the artist's whole personality is revealed … carefulness or superficiality, expert knowledge or ignorance, whether he acts subjectively or objectively. With the objective outlook, he will make typography subordinate to the content: the content decides the form… But with the subjective approach, the content is always subordinated to the form." **1954** First phototypesetting machine sold for commercial use. This begins a revolution in letterspacing and typographic flexibility impossible with metal type.

Compugraphic broadens the market by selling a lower-cost machine beginning in 1968. ⊡ Perhaps the most significant change in the post-war period is the introduction of television. Herb Lubalin, one of America's most notable designers, says "Television has had its effect on the reading habits of the American people. We are becoming more accustomed to looking at pictures and less interested in reading lengthy copy. These influences have created a need for experimentation with new graphic forms. One important result is what I refer to as the 'typographic image.' The use of typography as a word-picture gives designers greater creative scope. In

1957 Charles Loupot (1892–1962) produces a series of posters for St. Raphael restaurant that become increasingly abstract.

1958 Hermann Zapf *Optima*, a semi-sans, wanted to name his "serifless roman" *New Antiqua*, but the marketing director wanted a catchier name. The

forms, nearly none of which have straight lines, are based on inscribed letterforms dating from 1530 in church of Santa Croce in Florence.

1958 Slug casting operators type in characters so their matrixes fall into place and the line of type is then cast from molten metal into a "slug."

ABCDEFGHIJ MNOPQRSTU WXYZabcdef jklmnopqrstu yz12345678

21 variations sur un thème unique

1957 Adrian Frutiger *Univers*. This is the first type family completely planned before fonts are drawn. All 21 weights are introduced at once. "*Univers* (is) the most versatile gothic to be found in metal. It is a costly and heroic achievement." Ed Rondthaler, quoted in 1962.

ABCDEFGH MNOPQRS WXYZabcd jklmnopqrs xyz1234567

Helvetica

1957 Max Miedinger (1900–1980) & Edouard Hoffmann *New Haas Grotesque*, a revival of *Akzidenz Grotesk* (1898). It is rereleased in 1960 as *Hel-vetica*. *Helvetica* becomes ubiquitous — and invisible — when it is adopted as the native sans serif on personal computers in the 1980s.

composing a typographic picture, a tight-knit unity of elements is necessary. We have therefore had to take liberties with many traditional rules which have come to be accepted as criteria for good typography. Sometimes, this 'playing' with type has resulted in the loss of a certain amount of legibility. Some consider this a deplorable state of affairs, but the excitement created by an image sometimes more than compensates for the slight difficulty in readability... Typography is not an end product. But, for the first time, we have emerged with typography that is distinctly American and which is contributing its influence to the rest of the world."

1958 The first international seminar on typography, *The Art and Science of Typography*, is hosted by Aaron Burns (future cofounder of the International Typeface Corporation) and Will Burtin in Connecticut. **1959** Photo-Lettering Inc.in New York publishes *Alphabet Thesaurus No.1*, containing 3,000 faces. It is a revelation and an immediate hit with designers.

1960–1969

1961 Ladislav Sutnar publishes *Visual Design in Action*, an expansion of an exhibit he co-planned. Sutnar describes three attributes of design: **1) Visual interest**

1960 Freeman "Jerry" Craw (1917–) *Craw Clarendon*. Craw says, "If I need a type to achieve a certain style or mood, somebody else needs it (too)."

Craw Clarendon Book
Craw Clarendon
Craw Clarendon Condensed
Craw Modern
Craw Modern Italic
Craw Modern Bold
Ad Lib
CBS SANS
CBS-DIDOT
Craw Canterbury

1960 Gene Federico designs an elegant 16-page booklet in a series on *Experimental Typography by American Designers*. His emphasis is on empty space.

NORTHERN SPY
JONATHAN
GRIMES GOLDEN
WINESAP
BEN DAVIS
RED ASTRACHAN
WEALTHY
HUBBARDSTON
LADY
EARLY JOE
GOLDEN PIPPIN
HOWARD BEST
CRANBERRY PIPPIN
MAIDEN BLUSH
PRIDE OF GENESEE
GLADSTONE
PHILADELPHIA SWEET
CHENANGO

1962 Aldo Novarese *Eurostile*, which starts as an all-caps face called *Microgramma*.

ABCDE KLMNO TUVWX abcdefg opqrstu

A phototypesetting negative contains a single character size and uses a lens to change the typeset size.

FORMATT No.5387 — SPACEAID' ALPHABET — *TRADEMARK
AAAAABBCCCCCDDD
EEEEEEEEEFFF GGH
HHIIIIIJ KKLLLLM
MMNNNNN OOOOP
PPQRRRRRSSSSS

Letraset instant lettering — 72pt CLARENDON BOLD — HAAS — 774 — U.S.A Order No. 11-72-CN
CCDDE;
EFGGH;
KLLLM;
NOOOP
RSSSTT

1962–1963 Formatt and Letraset type sheets introduced. Formatt letters are printed on adhesive-backed clear plastic sheets. Individual letters are cut out and composed on a board, then photographed. The flexibility to determine display type spacing is put directly into the designer's hands.

Letraset dry transfer letters are rubbed down as a headline is composed, leading to a new style of intentionally cracked and torn letterforms.

1964 Corporate identity grows in importance as industry begins to globalize with less specific marks, as in F.H.K. Henrion's and Tom Geismar's logos.

A force of inventive design which will excite and hold attention. **2) Visual simplicity** A simple design through precision and ordering has the power to communicate directly. **3) Visual continuity** A smooth flow with rhythm, direction, and unity for increased comprehension. **1962** Newly emerging phototype, first tried about 1910, can be linespaced in as little as half-point increments, giving designers new-found flexibility. Phototype provides the technology to minus letter and line space, previously impossible because of the physical limitations of working with blocks of metal. As Ed Rondthaler, president of Photo-Lettering, says, "The irregular shapes of many letters do not easily conform to the rectangular blocks of metal type. The letter *H* forms a perfect rectangle and fits naturally on a rectangle, a *V* does not. It should be placed on a triangle, and *O* on an oval. Forcing every letter onto a metal rectangle cramps the type designer's style, and virtually guarantees poor spacing... The typographer of the future will view his work from the 'top side' — the reading side — rather than from the 'bottom side' as now. His concern will be more with art and less with the mechanics of assembly. He will use photography where it offers advantages, and metal where it is better." ▣ Steven Heller says of phototype: "I believe history will

An example of "all-display type advertising." Enlarging the text to unavoidable and maximum ease-of-reading size, the entire ad becomes appealing.

1967 CBS News develops two typefaces: one has light traps to counteract screen fill in. The other is heavier to counteract reversed type's weight gain.

Near illegibility that represents the concert experience is used as an identifying style in the psychedelic poster movement in the mid- to late 1960s.

1968 Figured text, a technique in which the form contrasts with the text, is used in Claus Bremer's *Taube* ("Dove").

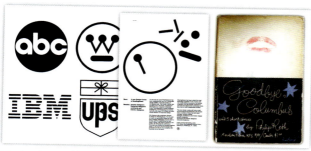

"Design is a problem-solving business. It provides a means of clarifying, synthesizing, and dramatizing a word, a picture, a product, or an event." Paul Rand. Shown is a selection of his work from 1961–1968.

1964 Jan Tschichold *Sabon*, with preliminary sketches. The design of the roman is based on *Garamond* and the italic is based on a Granjon type.

1967 Adrian Frutiger *Serifa*, a slab serif version of his *Univers*. Three weights (45, 55, and 65) are shown here.

record the development of phototypography as merely a bridge between hot metal and digital." ⊡ The 20th century sees the split between type as a structural material and type's visual appearance. Until the development of phototype, setting type is an exercise in manipulating bits of metal, whether as the letters or as the spacing between them. This imposes very limiting constraints on what is possible. But as a consequence of the freeing theories of Constructivism and Dadaism in the 1920s and the Bauhaus in the 1930s, type becomes more plastic — formable — resulting in typographic playfulness and experimentation with the artist's, rather than the reader's, needs chiefly in mind. As early as 1962, critics complain that typographers are showing contempt for readers by developing visual riddles, a compulsion to appear original, and a disconnection between the message and the type that expresses it. **c1964** The mid-1960s sees typography evolve from "the old one-two ad presentation" (getting attention and then presenting the sales pitch) into what came to be known as "all-display type advertising," in which the entire message was immediately presented. All-display typography was defined as dramatic headlines and text exceeding 18 points. Critics asserted that "excessively large" type was

1968 Adrian Frutiger OCR-B (Optical Character Recognition, *top*), a computer-legible font that is more human-legible than OCR-A, a previous all-caps face.

1969 The first digital typesetting machine in the United States is installed in the US Government Printing Office. Developed by Linotype and CBS, the Linotron 1010 can set the Old and New Testaments in 18 minutes: amazing then but very, very slow by today's standards.

1970 International Typeface Corporation (ITC) founded by Aaron Burns, Ed Gotschall, and Herb Lubalin. In 1973 they start publishing U/lc.

High resolution

Low resolution

ABCDEFGH
MNOPQRS
XYZ&12345
abcdefghi
ÆAŒEAFA

1970 Herb Lubalin & Tom Carnase *Avant Garde*, which grew out of the 1962 logo and a series of headline applications for *Avant Garde* magazine.

1971 *Belles-Lettres*, a complete photo alphabet of twelve nude models is a "typeface" made by a group of five Dutch artists.

ABCD 4567 abcde
EFGHI 890!". fghijk
JKLM #$?=: lmnop
NOPQ >□_^ qrstuv

1971 *Vidifont 28-line*, an interpretation of the 1967 *CBS News 36 alphabet*, is the first font developed for immediate CRT on-screen use. *Vidifont* began

solving the problems of on-screen curved and angled letterforms. The 28-line designation is the number of scanning lines rendering characters.

now shouting at readers and that such treatment was a passing fad. ⊡ Phototype makes its impact felt: "In the past five years (since 1959), there has been an increase in asymmetric placement, closer setting of the lower case, and much greater awareness of space as a design element. However, the almost universal use of a sans letter could be nearly — but not quite — as dangerous as the blind acceptance of a debased Trajan Roman, for so long the hallmark of public lettering." John Brinkley, *Lettering Today*. **1965** Dr. Rudolf Hell introduces *Digiset* and merges his new company with Linotype Corporation, making Linotype/Hell. The *Digiset* can process 6,000 characters per second through a cathode ray tube (CRT) onto photo paper. ⊡ Herb Lubalin is a source of amusing and insightful quotes: "Unfortunately, too much is said about good typography and not enough set"; "If what we do with type is effective, we don't care if it is called pretty, ugly, or pretty ugly"; "When a good ad is set right, no one notices the letters — they're too busy reading the words." **1969** International Typeface Corporation is founded. Because ITC types are licensed only to select typesetting manufacturers, their typefaces become known and valued for the ability to be set consistently anywhere, a boon to national and international corpo-

1974 Ikarus is the first program to outline characters to make digital fonts. Ikarus can "interpolate" characteristics to quickly form type families.

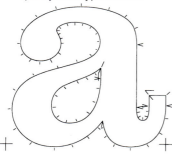

1974 Herb Lubalin *Lubalin Graph* is his own *Avant Garde* with serifs added. Lubalin provides alternate characters and multiple ligatures.

ABCDEFG
JKLMNOF
TUVWXYZ
123456789
ÆAŒEAFA

1974 Adrian Frutiger *Frutiger*. Originally designed as *Roissy* for signage at de Gaulle Airport in Paris and converted to five weights plus italics.

ABCDEFGI
MNOPQRS
XYZ&1234
90abcdefg
nopqrstuv

1978 Hermann Zapf ITC *Zapf Dingbats*. Zapf did 1,200 sketches, of which 360 were chosen in three groups of 120 symbols each.

The Cooper Union New York

c1971 Tom Carnase *New York* magazine logo. Carnase is an expert at hand lettering as well as type design, having created 17 faces.

ABCDEFGI
MNOPQRS
WXYZ&abc
ijklmnopqrst
yz12345678

1971 International Typeface Corporation releases new version of Morris Fuller Benton's 1914 *Souvenir*. It becomes symbolic of 1970s graphic design.

WHI
AB

1974 Technology increases printing speed at high visual cost. Dot matrix printers have pins that push inked ribbon against the paper (*top*). They

HAS FOUR
WHICHEVE
ABCDEF
ABCDEF

can print 165 characters per second but lack resolution. Non-impact printers (*above*), the forebears of today's ink jet printers, have higher resolution.

rations. ITC cultivates revivals and original types from designers worldwide.

1970–1982

Phototype dispenses with the practice of altering versions of a typeface as its size increases in order to maintain optical consistency. Generally, a face would get lighter as it got larger. Instead, phototype uses a single master font, usually 12 point, and uses a lens to enlarge or reduce the type size. **1972** A group at MIT develops a way to render type in grayscale on screen, reducing pixelation and increasing legibility. **1974** Digital type gets a boost with the invention of *Ikarus*, a program that uses vectored outlines to create type. **1975** Steve Jobs' and Steve Wozniak's Apple I developed. **1976** Monotype Lasercomp introduced, the first laser phototypesetter. **1977** Xerox 9700 printer uses digital fonts at 300dpi. **1980** New Wave and Deconstruction grow in popularity. **1981** Matthew Carter and Mike Parker found Bitstream, the first all-digital independent type foundry, in Cambridge, Massachusetts. **1982** Adobe founded. Their first offering is *PostScript*, a language that allows type and images to be combined in a single document, making *desktop publishing* possible.

1978 Matthew Carter *Galliard*, an interpretation of a 16th-century type by Robert Granjon. It is notable for its extraordinarily long serifs.

ABCDEFC
LMNOPQ
VWXYZ&
67890abcc
klmnopqrs

1979 Erik Spiekermann *Berliner Grotesk*. Based on a 1913 face, Spiekermann also designs *Meta* and *Officina* type families in the 1990s.

ABCDEFGH
NOPQRSTL
Z&123456
abcdefghijk
qrstuvwx

1981 Bitstream's *Charter*, designed by Matthew Carter for laser printing and optimized curves and angles for 300dpi low-resolution legibility.

ABCDEFGI
MNOPQR;
WXYZ&ab
hijklmnop
vwxyz123

1982 Massimo Vignelli elected to the NY Art Directors Club Hall of Fame for work including that with Knoll. Receives the AIGA Gold Medal the next year.

ABCDEFGHIJKLMN(
VWXYZ&abcdefghij
stuvwxyz$123456;

ABCDEFGHIJKLMNC
WXYZ&abcdefghijkl
tuvwxyz$1234567

ABCDEFGHIJKLMN(
VWXYZ&abcdefghij
rstuvwxyz$12345€

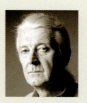

1983 Apple introduces Lisa, the first useful home computer. It flops. The Macintosh is introduced the next year and modern typographic history begins.

1984 Tom Geismar *Public Broadcasting System* logo. By flopping the P, "What had been the initial P became an image of 'everyman.'"

1985 Charles Bigelow and Kris Holmes *Lucida* and *Lucida Sans*, types designed for then-common 72 and 300dpi low-resolution printers.

1985–1989 Four logos using letterforms by Pentagram Design. *F* is for a music publisher; *R* is for a railroad; *S* is for the Scottish Trade Centre; and *T* is for Tactics.

16 1983 onward

In former times producing a typeface was an effort architectural in scale. A typeface was exquisitely expensive to cut. The choice to make one had a you-bet-your-company gravity to it." Mike Parker, Bitstream

"Type is a beautiful group of letters, not a group of beautiful letters."
Matthew Carter

Today's use of type is based on centuries of typographic evolution, on thousands of improvements based on our

1987 Sumner Stone *Stone Sans*, part of a family that includes sans, serif, and semi-serif versions in a full range of weights, all designed for low resolution.

ABCDEFGHIJk
RSTUVWXYZ{
ijklmnop1234
ABCDEFGHI
RSTUVWXY
ijklmnop123

1988 Adrian Frutiger *Avenir*. Two-story lowercase *a* and other features makes this a more legible geometric sans serif face than *Futura* or *Avant Garde*.

ABCDEFG
LMNOPQI
VWXYZ&1
67890abcc
jklmnopqrs

1988 Otl Aicher (1922–1991) *Rotis*, an extensive family similar to *Lucida* and *Stone*. *Rotis* is named for the German town in which Aicher lives.

ABCDEFGHI.
NOPQRSTU\
YZ&abcdefg
mnopqrstuv
z?!1234567

1989 Newspapers worldwide (here from Detroit, Washington, and Norway) use shorter stories, more graphics, and magazine-like typography to lure readers.

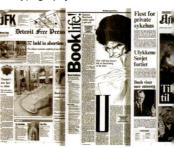

ABCDEFGHIJKL
MNOPQRSTUVW
XYZ&;abcdefghi
jklmnopqrstuvw
1234567890@?!%

1986 Adrian Frutiger *Linotype Centennial*, commissioned to celebrate the 100th anniversary of Linotype, is an update of the Century family. Linotype had a total of 150 hot metal faces, and now adds about 100 new digital faces *per year*. The need for digitized versions of existing typefaces explodes.

DEVICE
DEVOTION
erasure
Garish Mor
OSKAR
Thickhead
violation
Where's Mar
Wooly

1986 Fontographer allows anyone with a Mac to make typefaces. The random and scratchy results become known as *grunge font*s.

...und ich will bei euch wohnen

1987 Blackletter is used for both its religious and German nationalistic meanings by Manfred Butzmann. The image is a handle on a boxcar.

need to record ideas and share knowledge. Each major step forward — from the development of the characters themselves to the technology of presses, paper, and inks — is driven by the opportunity to increase efficiency and lower the cost of production. The digital revolution that begins in the 1980s is the most significant change in written communication since Gutenberg's invention of movable type in 1450.

1983–1989

Adobe introduces Type 1 PostScript for Apple computers. ▣ Apple develops the Lisa, the first computer to have windows, pull-down menus, and a mouse. **1984** Apple introduces the Macintosh computer. **1985** Aldus introduces PageMaker 1.0, a program that combines text and graphics, for the Macintosh. With it, the "desktop publishing" revolution begins. ▣ The Apple LaserWriter is the first printer to use the PostScript language. **1986** Altsys introduces Fontographer, a program that allows typefaces to be made entirely on the computer. Now anyone with a Mac can make typefaces — and they do. Over the next decade, so-called *grunge fonts*, type designs of roughly drawn and butchered characters, become wildly popular. **1987** Post-modernism reacts against the cleanli-

1989 Carol Twombly *Trajan*, an accurate reproduction of the 114AD capitals on the Trajan Column in Rome, which are considered ideal letterforms.

ABCDEFC
IJKLMNC
QRSTUVV
YZ&1234!

1989 Arthur Baker *Amigo, Marigold,* and *Visigoth*, three of his calligraphic faces. These may be popular as counterweight to computer sameness.

ABCDEFGHIJKI
abcdefghijklmnop
ABCDEFGHIJKLM
abcdefghijklmnopqrstu
ABCDEFGHIJK
abcdefghijklmn

1990 Freda Sack and David Quay form The Foundry in London, where they research and develop the *Architype* revival series of 20th-century types.

Architype All
ARCHITYPE AUBE
architype ballr
architype bayer-
Architype Ren
Architype Renner
ARCHITYPE SCHWJ1
ARCHITYPE

1990 Erik von Blokland and Just van Rossum *Beowolf*, in which each character iteration is changed as it is placed. Infinite variability is added to type.

ABCDEF
NOPQRS
Z&123456
fghijklm
wxyzAB

1990 Robert Slimbach *Minion*. First released as a Type 1 font, then reissued in 1992 as a Multiple Master font, allowing multiple-axis adjustment.

ABCDEFGHIJKI
RSTUVWXYZ8
ijklmnop1234!
*ABCDEFGHIJKI
RSTUVWXYZ&
ijklmnop1234!*

1991 Erik Spiekermann *Meta*. A popular example of a humanist sans in extensive families, here shown with the old style figures option.

ABCDEF(
LMNOPQ
WXYZ&ab
jklmnopqr
yz;?!12345

1991 Brian Willson *Attic Antique*. Willson says, "It resembles the broken serif type you might find in a hundred-year-old textbook."

Keedy Sans
Democratica
Elektrix Bold
platelet thin
Dogma Bold
Suburban Bold
Base Twelve

1990–1996 Rudy Vanderlans tests legibility and typographic standards in *Emigré*, his avant garde magazine. The types he commissions become iconic.

ness and precision of the International Style. ▣ Adobe introduces Illustrator, an outline-based drawing program. ▣ QuarkXPress begins competing with PageMaker. **1989** Canon introduces the first color laser printer. Apple begins making color computers and monitors.

1990–1999

Adobe introduces Photoshop for Macintosh, the image manipulation program that becomes the industry standard with the addition of a PC version. **1992** Adobe introduces Multiple Master font technology. The user selects variations between one, two, or three pairs of design characteristics, spectrums whose breadth are created by the type designer. Choices may include weight, width, posture, and serif. **1993** According to the Type Directors Club Call for Entries to their worldwide typography competition, the goal of typographic invisibility is changing. "Typographic standards that have been around for 500 years are now coming under fresh scrutiny from creative, resourceful designers." ▣ TrueType GX font encoding introduced by Apple. Automatically replacing ligatures and alternate characters, TrueType GX provides optical character alignment. TrueType GX becomes AAT, or *Apple Advanced Typography*, a few years

1995 Peter Matthias Noordzij *PMN Caecilia*. It has many weights, all with small caps and old style figures.

1996 Jean Lochu *Loire*, an updated Didone face. Its small x-height makes this a somewhat inefficient face, but it is a distinctive and readable text.

1997 The Font Bureau is a new all-digital type foundry, but their catalog is reminiscent of type showings at the turn of the 20th century.

2000 *ITC Bodoni Seventy-Two*, a revival from the 1818 *Manuale Tipografico*. Three sizes accurately represent Bodoni's original size-sensitive types.

ABCDEFG
NOPQRST
YZabcdefg
nopqrstuv
23456789C

ABCDEFG
MNOPQRS
WXYZ&ab
ijklmnopqrst
1 2 3 4 5 6 7

ABCDEFGHI
LMNOPQRST
VWXYZÆŒ
abcdefghijklm
pqrstuvwxyzfi

1994 Nancy Skolos and Tom Wedell craft actual dimensional typography and photograph it. Mistaken for Photoshop manipulation, it is hailed as fine craft.

1994 Matthew Carter *Mantinia*, featuring an extensive set of ligatures and enlarged capitals. Based on Renaissance artist Andrea Mantegna's letters.

1994 N. Mazzei and B. Kelly *Backspacer*. They say, "*Backspacer* is an homage to the 1930s typewriter…the shadows symbolize the passing of time."

1995 Bob Aufuldish *Whiplash*. Aufuldish quips, "(Whiplash is) baroque modernism for the new millennium."

later. ☐ Designer's exploration of digital possibilities overtakes clarity of communication as the goal. **1994** Luc(as) de Groot completes *FF Thesis*, a type family with 144 fonts, the most comprehensive family ever produced at one time. It contains three groups: sans serif, semi-serif, and serif. Each of these is available in eight weights, from Extra Light to Black, and each weight is available in six variants: Plain, Italic, Small Caps, Small Caps Italic, Expert, and Expert Italic. De Groot includes five styles of numerals: old style figures in the plain font, lining figures in the small caps font, and tabular figures (mono-width lining figures to help set columns) in the expert font, plus superior and inferior numerals for setting fractions. ☐ Rudy Vanderlans says, "There is a new generation of graphic designers who, before ever considering what their favorite typeface is, will design a new one. I rank myself among them." **1997** Adobe and Microsoft merge Type 1 and TrueType font formats. **1998** Adobe introduces InDesign, its page makeup program that offers superior type controls over either QuarkXPress or PageMaker. ☐ The quickly expanding universe of digital resources provides limitless choices. Handcrafting is on the decline as designers sit in front of blank screens waiting for creative inspiration.

2000 *Emoticons*, faces made with key-stroke characters, evolve to add humanity to email, used by early adopters since 1983, but widely since 1994.

2001 The OpenType format allows far more glyphs per font, and thus is more useful. This update of 1992's *Myriad Pro* by Robert Slimbach, Carol Twombly, and Fred Brady includes old-style figures and additional diacritical marks for worldwide Latin-based alphabets, as well as Greek and Cyrillic glyphs.

2001 *Sumeria*, a digital font for a presumably limited readership, becomes available. Based on cuneiform (wedge) writing c1200BC.

16 243

Top row

Hail Mary grace, walking stairs, I can't through with I got to get ou

2001 Frank Heine's *Dalliance* is released by Emigré Fonts. This eccentric typeface is based on writing from a 1799 map.

1234567890
ΛΛБΒΓΔΔΕЖЗ
ЗИКΛМНОНО
ПΡϹΤΥФΧЦЧ
ЧЪШЩЫΙΠЪЬ
ЭЮЯЇΉΙΈΉΘЙ

2002 Innokenty Keleinikov *Letopis* (*"Chronicle"*), a revised 16th-century *poluustav*-style Cyrillic alphabet.

2002 Brad Holland gives his ad for the Newspaper Association of America humanity, personality, and, perhaps most important of all, readability.

OHAAMELAUI
HOOFTFTNNU
OLAEHRFTOO
AAMEUSAE SAC

OHamburge fonstiv nature Hoffnung Oberfoerster Hornisse Otto amuse s tee inserat moostauben monsunrege abteigruft nortvone gabe turnverein

2002 Linotype releases *Optima nova*, a completely redrawn and re-spaced version with true italics of Hermann Zapf's 1958 hot metal type.

2000–Present

OpenType font format develops. Adobe and Microsoft join to extend Apple's TrueType encoding to accommodate larger character sets (from 256 glyphs to 65,000) and increase their fonts' functionality. It is no longer necessary, for example, to change fonts for foreign languages, to access expert sets for special characters or to replace ligatures. They can be substituted automatically and be "read" during spell checks and searches. OpenType is built on Unicode, which allows for cross-platform use. **2001** Adobe discontinues Multiple Master fonts. ⊡ *The New Testament* of the *Bible* — all 180,568 words —

is engraved on the face of a 5mm ($\frac{3}{16}$" or ■) square silicon chip by a team from MIT and a private archiving software firm. **2002** The New York *Times* reports that humans stored five exabytes (5 billion gigabytes) of new information this year. This one year activity is equivalent to *every word ever spoken in the history of mankind*. Telephone use in this one year adds another 17 exabytes. This is proof that we are in information overload and that typographic messages must be compelling and clear. **2003** *Unicode Standard 4.0* released. Begun in 1990, *Unicode* is a *single font* containing every alphabet of every language in the world. A transparent program,

Bottom row

2006 German postage stamp design uses realistic tactility and monochromatic full color to express and celebrate a school for the blind.

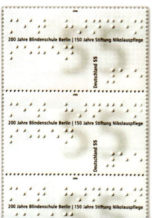

2007 Seven of the 21 winners in the Type Directors Club worldwide typeface competition are non-Latin. Quality type is increasingly global.

2008 This Japanese poster detail shows that letterforms from any language continue to be abstracted — so they themselves become the artwork.

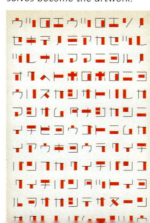

2009 Motion graphics and movie titles become a category in the Type Directors Club type competition. This is a Brazilian winner.

ABCDEFGHIJKLMNOF
ABCDEFGHIJKLMNOPG
2003 DIGITAL MONTICELLO

ABCDEFGHIJKLMNOPQ
ABCDEFGHIJKLMNOPE
1892 OXFORD, 12 PT.

ABCDEFGHIJKLMNOP
ABCDEFGHIJKLMNOP
1949 LINOTYPE MONTICELLO

lls *Creativity* **Drugs**
igles *Waist*
ligned **Muse**
llaz **Trailer**
North
jority **Stanc**
lden's 313 **Dun**

humanists of the
Simplicity and Efficiency
The evolution of handwriting, from the earliest pictograms to our current alphabet

Cancellaresca Formata

The Mystery of the Creative Process & Typographic Protocol

Adobe Systems introduces Brioso Pro, a new font software package in the growing library of Adobe Originals typefaces, designed specifically for today's technology. *The Adobe Originals typefaces have been consistently recognized throughout the world for their quality, originality, and practicality.*

Adobe Systems introduces Brioso Pro, a new font software package in the growing library of Adobe Originals typefaces, designed specifically for today's technology. The Adobe Originals typefaces have been consistently recognized throughout the world for their quality, originality, and practicality.

Twin
Cold
Twin
warm

2003 Linotype's *Monticello* for Thomas Jefferson's papers is latest and most accurate revival of Binney & Ronaldson's 1796 *"Pica Roman No.1."*

2003 Display typefaces from a variety of designers. The web becomes the primary route for researching and buying fonts, which reduces per-font cost.

2003 Robert Slimbach *Brioso Pro*, an extensive family based on Italian Renaissance handwriting. *Brioso* is optimized in four "opticals," or size ranges.

2003 LettError introduces *Twin*, a morphing multiple master typeface. "Formality," "informality," and "weirdness" can be adjusted by the user.

it allows people to use computers to communicate worldwide in any language without actively participating in its translation. Called the most far-reaching and ambitious multilingual project in history, *Unicode 4.0* contains 96,000 characters. It encodes characters for 55 languages, including the Mediterranean Linear B, Cherokee, Cypriot, Limbu, ogham, Osmania, Sinhala, Tai Le, Tagalog, Tibetan, and Ugaritic. The project will be complete when all 148 languages now in use worldwide are included so that anyone, anywhere, can use a computer in their own language. ⊡ All of Adobe's fonts are released only in OpenType format. **2004** Macs and PCs use the exact same font files, a remarkable achievement in coding that cements OpenType's role in the future. ⊡ Saad D. Abulhab develops a simplified Arabic alphabet that is bidirectional, making it easier to read for Westerners — and computers. **2005** Type options on the Web are limited: Web-safe type is necessary — and common. Expressive type must be a picture of letterforms. **2009** Microsoft releases Internet Explorer 8 with improved support for CSS and RSS. **2012** @font-face allows distinctive typefaces to be downloaded for on-screen use only. **2015** Monotype's Typecast becomes a free tool that offers 3,650 "live" fonts and type control for use on any website.

2010 This cover of *New York* magazine contrasts crispy Didot with a hand-cut paper holes environment to imply depth for a special double issue.

2011 Mike Barker makes great use of 3D software to embed type into an aerial photo of Manhattan for this poster.

2012 An alphabet drawn by a variety of artists illustrates key words in technology. Shown are Datamining, Geolocation, jQuery, and Narrative.

2013 ZXX, a font family that can't be read by OCR scanners, preserving user anonymity, becomes a useful and intriguing online asset.

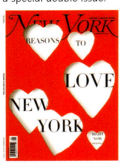

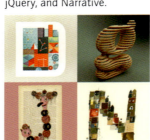

Appendix: Twenty-six letters evolve over three eras*

Pre-Alphabetic Writing

3000BC Egyptian Hieroglyphics	2900BC Babylonian Cuneiform	2500BC Ethiopic	1500BC Samaritan

Alphabetic Writing

1300BC Phoenician	1000BC Early Greek	800BC Classical Greek	700BC Etruscan	300BC Roman Formal	114AD Trajan Column	400 Rustic Capitals	600 Uncials

Not all writing systems used the twenty-six characters we now have. Early systems used many more glyphs and some used fewer as we gradually formalized written language and added visual representations to the sounds we make.

700 Half Uncials	800 Carolingian Minuscules	1300 Blackletter	Typographic Writing

Typographic Writing columns:
- 1450 Gutenberg's Movable Type
- 1465 Sweynheym & Pannartz
- 1470 Jenson's Roman
- 1514 first Italic
- 1525 Albrecht Dürer
- 1695 Grandjean's Romain du Roi
- 1816 Wm Caslon IV Sans Serif
- 1834 J. Heinrig Sans Serif Lowercase

(The chart shows the letters A–Z in each of these historical typefaces and scripts.)

"We use the letters of our alphabet every day with the utmost ease and unconcern, taking them almost as much for granted as the air we breathe. We do not realize that each of these letters is at our service today only as the result of a slow process of evolution in the age-old art of writing." Douglas C. McMurtrie

Glossary

Selected peripheral terms are listed alphabetically at the end of the Glossary. These terms are historically important, but they aren't central to modern typographic usage.

Accented character Added mark ("accent") indicates changed sound. See *Diacritic*.

Aldine Typography that is derived from Venitian printer Aldus Manutius and his type cutter, Francesco Griffo, c1500.

Alignment Edge Run alongside a common edge. Optical alignment is always more important than measurable alignment.

Alphabet A language's characters that represent spoken sounds, arranged in their traditional order.

Alternate character Character differently designed, which may replace the primary version.

Ampersand The sign (&), Latin *et*, meaning *"and."*

Anti-aliasing Smoothing the jagged edges of on-screen type and digital images.

Antiqua or **Antikva** Early Roman type drawn by Niccoli and Poggio based on northern Italian manuscripts of the 11th and 12th centuries.

Antique A display-type style from the late 1800s to the early 1900s.

Aperture The openings in letters like C, S, and a. See *Counter*.

Apex The part of a letterform where two lines meet, as in A, M, V, W.

Apostrophe Mark showing missing letters, possessives, or single close quote.

Arm Stroke unattached on one or both ends, as in the uppercase F, L, T, X.

Ascender Part of lowercase letters that extend above median in b, d, f, h, k, l, t. See *Descender*.

Asterisk The sign (*) used to indicate a footnote.

At @ sign used since 1536 to mean "each one for the price of," has been reborn in email addresses. Known as "cat tail" in Finland, "cinnamon roll" in Norway, "elephant's ear" in Sweden, "little dog" in Russia, "monkey tail" in Holland, "small snail" in France and Italy, "spider monkey" in Germany, and "strudel" in Israel.

Axis The primary angle of stress of a letterform.

Back slant Leftward type posture. Compare to Italic, slanting to right. Hard to read in any but extremely short segments.

Ball terminal Rounded shape at end of an arm like c, y in Bodoni (cy) and Clarendon (cy).

Bar The horizontal stroke of a letterform like F, H, T, Z.

Baseline Implied line on which letterforms sit.

Beardline Invisible line indicating the bottom of descenders.

Bicameral Two alphabets joined together, as upper and lower case as Latin alphabet. *Unicameral* and *Tricameral* typefaces exist.

Bitmap font A font made of pixels for on-screen viewing. Also called *Screen font*.

Blackletter Heavy, angular types based on medieval quill script. Used by Gutenberg as first metal type. Its five categories: *Bastarda, Fraktur, Quadrata, Rotunda*, and *Textura*.

Body copy Primary text of article (as distinguished from headings, display type, captions, etc.). Usually in medium weight and 8 to 12 points in size.

Body size Height of type. Originally the height of metal block on which letters were cast. Digital type's body size is measured slightly beyond highest and lowest points of characters. See *Point size*.

Bold Face heavier and wider than roman style of same face. See *Light face*.

Bowl Round forms of body of uppercase C, G, O, Q, and lowercase b, c, d, q, o. Large bowl indicates a large x-height. Also called *eye* or *counter*.

Brackets Braces: { }. Square brackets: [ ]. Parentheses: ( ).

Calligraphy Hand-drawn letters. From the Greek meaning "beautiful writing."

Cap height Height of capital letters, measured from baseline to top of uppercase. Some lowercase ascenders exceed cap height.

Capitals Uppercase letters, from inscriptional letters at the head, or capital, of Roman columns. Cap line Implied line at top of capital letters.

Caption Explanatory copy referring to image and usually read first. Habitually placed below image.

Caret The symbol (|) used to indicate insertion. First used by 13th-century scribes.

Carolingian script 9th-century script developed for Emperor Charlemagne.

Case In metal type, shallow rectangular box for metal type with compartment holding each character, caps in an "upper" case, others in "lower" case.

Centered Midpoints of each element placed on central axis. The ragged outer edges are mirror images.

Chancery Handwritten typestyle with long, graceful, curved ascenders and descenders.

Character Any letter, numeral, or punctuation mark.

Character map or **Keyboard layout** Table that assigns glyphs to specific keystrokes.

Character set Letters, figures, punctuation marks, symbols in a font.

Character width Horizontal dimension, including neighboring empty space.

Cold type Printing not produced by hot-metal process. May use foundry type, typewriter, phototypesetting, or digital setting. See *Hot metal*.

Colophon Information at end of book or Web site describing its production.

Color, typographic Lightness or darkness of an area of type affected by texture, type size, posture, weight, and letter-, word-, and linespacing.

Column rule Vertical line between columns of type.

Compose In metal type, to set type.

Condensed Narrow version of typeface fitting more characters into a given space.

Contrast, typographic Variation between thick and thin strokes of a letter. Helvetica has little contrast, **Bodoni** has high contrast.

Copy Wording to be set in type.

Counter Space completely or partially closed, in letters like *A, B, C, S, a, e, o, u.*

Cross bar or **Cross stroke** A horizontal stroke connecting two stems, as in A, H.

Cursive Typefaces with fluid strokes that look like handwriting. Similar to Italic, but looking more handwritten.

Dashes Horizontal punctuation marks: long (—) em-dash; medium (–) en-dash; short (-) hyphen.

Descender Part of lowercase letters below baseline in *g, j, p, q, y.* See *Ascender.*

Descender line Implied line marking the lowest point of descenders in a font.

Diacritic Mark added to a character to indicate a changed sound, e.g., acute (*é*), tilde (*ñ*), and umlaut (*ü*). See *Accented character.*

Dingbats Illustrative characters in a typeface. Also called *Picture font* and *Flowers.*

Diphthong A ligature made of two vowels like œ and æ.

Display face Decorative typeface meant for larger sizes, often illegible at text sizes or long passages.

Display type Letterforms whose purpose is to be read first by its large size, bold weight, or prominent position.

Drop cap A large initial set into the top left corner of body copy. A drop cap's baseline must align with a text baseline. See *Stickup initial.*

Ear Small stroke attached to some lowercase letters like the **g** and **r**.

Egyptian A group of display types with slab serifs. Design coincided with mania for ancient Egyptian discoveries in the 1830s.

Ellipsis Single character of three dots (…) indicating an omission. Spacing distinct from three periods in a row (. . .).

Em Unit of measurement based on a square of the size of type being used. An em of 10-point type is 10 points wide by 10 points tall. Often used as spacing definition for paragraph indents.

Em dash The longest dash in a typeface (—) separates thoughts within a sentence. It should not have spaces added on either side (—) to avoid excess width, which draws accidental attention to itself.

En Unit of measurement based on a vertical rectangle of half the size of type being used. An en of 10-point type is 5 points wide by 10 points tall.

En dash Medium-length dash separates numbers. When used in text, usually flanked by a space (–). Also used in place of a hyphen for compound adjectives.

Erratum Latin for an error discovered after a document has been printed. In case of extreme insouciance, its plural is *errata.*

Expanded Wider version of a typeface. Also called *extended.*

Expert set Additional characters enriching as companion to a basic set. May include old style figures, small caps, ornaments, alternate characters, and swashes.

Face Named group or family of type like News Gothic or Perpetua. Also, in metal type, the raised printing surface of a type character.

Family Group of typefaces derived from the same typeface design. Usually includes roman, italic, and bold versions. May include small caps, old style figures, expanded, condensed, and inline versions.

Figures Either Arabic numerals (*1, 2, 3, 4, etc.*) or Roman numerals (*I, II, III, IV, etc.*).

Flush *Aligned* or *even.* Flush left (even on left side and ragged on right); flush right (even on the right side and ragged on the left). Flush on both the left and right is called *justified.*

Flush paragraphs Paragraph in which the first word is not indented.

Folio Page number.

Font A *digital file* that contains a typeface, a set of characters with common characteristics: capitals, lowercase letters, numerals, punctuation etc. In metal, a font is a single typeface in a single size. See *face, typeface.*

Footnote Short explanatory text at foot of a page, typically set smaller than the text it describes.

Foreword Introductory copy not written by the author of a work.

Format General appearance or style of a design or area of type.

Foundry Where metal type is manufactured. Modern type foundries are digital.

Foundry type Type cast in metal for hand composition.

Geometric Class of sans serif developed in the Bauhaus: **Futura** and Avenir.

Gothic Another name for *Grotesque.*

Glyph Character in a font.

Grid Skeletal guide used to ensure design consistency. Should show trim size, image areas, margins, type widths, and blank spaces.

Grotesque or **Grotesk** Class of sans serif considered ugly when introduced in mid-1800s: **URW Grotesque** and Franklin Gothic.

Gutenberg, Johannes Inventor of movable type in 1450. His 42-line *Bible* of 1455 was first book produced with his technology. Looked like the handwritten books of the time, but could be duplicated in quantities and speeds never before achieved.

Gutter Space between columns and on either side of the bound inside margins of multiple-page documents.

Hairline Thinnest strokes of a typeface. Thinnest line output device can make, usually ¼ point.

Hand set Type composed in a stick one metal letter at a time.

Hanging indent Paragraphing where first line stands out at left. Sometimes called an *outdent* or *flush and hung.*

Hanging initial Letter placed in the margin next to body copy.

Hanging punctuation Allowing lines that begin or end with punctuation to extend a bit beyond the column width for optical alignment. An indicator of typographic sensitivity and craftsmanship.

Headline Title or primary type in a composition.

Hot metal Typesetting and printing using type cast of molten lead.

House style Publisher's preferred spelling, punctuation, capitalization, spacing.

Humanist Class of sans serif similar to handwriting, not too mechanical or geometric, with angled emphasis: **Formata** and Syntax.

Incunabula *"Cradle"* Books produced with movable type in the infancy of printing, 1450–1500.

Indentation or **Indention** Any setting that is short of the full column measure, usually from the top left corner of text.

Inferior figures Small letters or numerals printed at the foot of ordinary characters (H_2O). Also known as *subscript.*

Initial A letterform at beginning of a paragraph for visual contrast or to signal beginning of a section of text.

Inline A character in which the interior has been carved out for a highlight effect: Ramona and CASTELLAR.

Italic Types that slant to the right, based on 15th-century Italian Renaissance script. First italic designed by Aldus Manutius, 1501. Italics must have letters that are distinctly different from the roman version

of the typeface, like a and *a*, or it is an *oblique* version, like a and *a*.

Justification Aligning both left and right sides of a column of type by distributing space evenly between words and, if necessary, letters.

Kern (noun) Part of the letter that extends into space of its neighbor. In metal, each individual letter had to be hand filed.

Kern (verb) Removing space between specific letter pairs to achieve optically consistent letterspacing. See *Tracking.*

Layout Rough design of placement of type and images and spaces.

Leaders Pronounced *"leeders."* Line of dots leading eye across wide space, often in listing contents.

Leading Pronounced *"ledding."* Space between lines of type that appears between the descenders of one line and the ascenders of the next. Name comes from metal days when strips of lead were inserted between lines of type. Digital leading is added above a given line of type.

Lead-in Pronounced *"leed-in."* First few words of a paragraph set differently to attract attention.

Legibility The ability to distinguish between letterforms. See *Readability.*

Letterspacing Equivalent to *tracking*, describes spacing between letters: tight, loose. See *Kern.*

Ligated A typeface with connected letters, usually a script face: *Brush Script* and *Zapfino*. Individual pairs of ligated letters are called *ligatures.*

Ligature Letters paired as one, for consistent optical spacing: fi and fl.

Light face Lighter version in the density of a typeface. Opposite of *Boldface.*

Line spacing Preferred term for leading. See *Leading*.

Lining figures Numerals that are equivalent to the cap height of the typeface (ABCDE0123456789). To be used in charts and in all-caps settings. Also called *modern figures* and *ranging figures*. See *Old style figures* and *Modern figures*.

Linotype First hot metal machine that composed type assembled by keyboard matrices of the characters into slugs and automatically redistributed the characters after casting the slugs. Invented in 1886, it dramatically speeded the previous hand-set typesetting process. Similar to *Intertype*.

Logo Greek for "*word*." Abbreviation for *logotype*, a visual identifying mark.

Logotype In metal type, a word or several letters cast as one unit. Also, company's identifying mark read as a word.

Lowercase Non-capital letters like *a, b, c*, etc. Term from location of the drawer (case) beneath its upper drawer (case) containing the capitals (caps): *A, B, C*, etc. Lowercase used to be called *minuscules*.

Majuscules See *Uppercase*.

Manuscript Literally "written by hand," thus prior to typesetting. Also the original prepared by author.

Margin Space at four edges of a page. head-, foot-, outside-, and gutter- (the margin facing the opposite page).

Mark up Specifying every detail necessary prior to type setting.

Measure The width in picas of a line or column of type.

Median Top edge of the x-height, the implied line defining the top of lowercase letters that do not have ascenders. Also

called *mean line* or *waistline*.

Medium Weight of typeface midway between light and bold. Also called *regular* and *normal*.

Metrics Information that manages spacing attributes of a font, including character widths, sidebearings, kerning pairs, and line spacing.

Minuscules See *Lowercase*.

Minus leading Reducing space between lines of type to give it a more unified texture and darker look. Used with all-cap display. With U/lc display, check how ascenders and descenders overlap. See *Leading*.

Modern Typeface with vertical stress, strong stroke contrast and unbracketed serifs: Bodoni and Didot.

Modified sans serif Sans serif faces with partial serifs to increase legibility: Optima and Rotis SemiSerif. Also called *Semiserif*.

Monospaced type Faces where each character occupies same horizontal space. Remnant of typewriter technology. Figures in charts are more legible when monospaced. See *Variable spaced type*.

Monotype Trade name for typesetting machine invented in 1887 by Tolbert Lanston of Ohio.

Multiple master Fonts with user-defined, adjustable characteristics like width and weight, called *instances*.

Neo-grotesque Class of sans serifs designed since 1945: Univers, Helvetica.

Oblique Angled typeface whose roman characters have been mechanically slanted to the right, not redrawn. See *Italic*.

Old Style Types from 15th–16th centuries, characterized by diagonal stress and bracketed serifs: Caslon, Garamond.

Old style figures Numerals whose heights vary so they blend into a paragraph of text (abcd0123456789). Sometimes called "text figures," and mistakenly called "lowercase figures." See *Lining figures*.

OpenType Cross-platform type coding that allows a font to be used on both Macintosh and Window machines. Also allows for almost limitless number of characters in each font.

Optical alignment Adjusting elements or letterforms "by eye" to appear perfectly aligned, often better than being mechanically aligned.

Orphan Last word left at top of column. Ultimate careless practice. See *Widow*.

Ornaments Decorative characters (✿❋✤) used to embellish typography.

Outline font Mathematical representation or vector of characters that can be scaled to any size and resolution. Also called *Printer font*.

Outline type Letterforms whose edges are drawn but whose interiors are left empty. See *Inline*.

Parentheses Rounded characters ( ) used with text. See *Brackets*.

Period A punctuation mark (.) that indicates a full stop.

Phototypesetting Setting type by means of light exposed through a film negative onto light-sensitive paper. Introduced in 1960s, replaced by digital typesetting in mid-1980s.

Pica Space measurement, one-sixth of an inch; 12 points. Because it perfectly accommodates type measurement, it is useful to use the pica as default for planning all design space. Approximately equivalent to European *cicero*. See *Point*.

Pi font Font made of mathematical symbols ($\sqrt{}$ ∞ $\measuredangle$ $\simeq$ $\hbar$ $\rightleftharpoons$ $\succ$ ∂).

Point Type measurement, one-twelfth of a pica; $1/72$ of an inch. Basic unit of vertical measurement of type. Equivalent to European *Didot point*. See *Pica*.

Point size Size of a typeface measured by points from just above the top of the ascenders to just beneath the bottom of the descenders. Invented in 1737 by Pierre Fournier. Also called *Type size*.

Posture Angle of stress of a typeface. There are three postures: roman, *italic* or *oblique*, and backslant.

Proofreading Exacting process of reading set type against the manuscript, checking for accuracy. Until advent of digital typesetting, proofreading was done by specialists. Now done by designer with spell-checking software.

Punchcutting Process of cutting letters into steel, then punching the letters into softer brass matrices, from which lead type is cast.

Punctuation Non-alphanumeric characters used to clarify meaning by breaking text into phrases and sentences. (.,;:–!?).

Ragged Type that set with one edge rough: flush left/ragged right or flush right/ragged left. Rough rag: hyphenation zone is either set to a wide measure or is not used. Smooth rag: hyphenation zone is set to less than a pica. Ragged left type is difficult to read beyond three lines.

Raised cap See *Stickup initial*.

Readability Quality of reading, determined by letterspacing, linespacing, paper-and-ink contrast, among other factors. See *Legibility*.

Recto Any right-hand page in a bound document. Odd numbered. See *Verso*.

Reference mark A symbol in text connecting related information (*, †, ‡, etc.).

Reversed out White or light color "dropped out" of a dark background.

Rivers Accidental vertical strips of white visible when word spacing is greater than line spacing, avoided by careful typography.

Roman An upright, medium-weight typeface style, based on the classical lettering found on the Trajan Column in Rome and the later humanistic writing of Italian Renaissance scribes. Two classes: *Old Style* and *Modern*.

Rough rag Type set without hyphenation, causing a pronounced variation in line length. See *Tight rag*.

Rule A printed line.

Runaround Type set around an irregular shape. The ideal distance is one pica, enough space to separate but not to dissociate the type and image.

Run in Text set without paragraphs.

Running head Line of reference repeating on every page, usually near folio.

Sans serif From French "without serifs." Type without cross strokes at the ends of limbs and usually of consistent weight. Four classes: *Grotesque* or *Gothic*, *Geometric*, *Neo-Grotesque*, and *Humanist*.

Screen font See *Bitmap font*.

Script Type designed to imitate handwriting, typically joined. Four classes: *Blackletter* or *Lombardic*, *Calligraphic*, *Formal*, and *Casual*.

Serif A small terminal at the end of an stroke or arm of a letterform.

Serif, bracketed A serif where the area between the stroke and serif has been filled in with a curved triangle.

Serif type Type whose limbs end in cross strokes and usually have variation in character stroke weight. Four classes: *Old Style*, *Transitional*, *Modern* or *Didone*, and *Slab* or *Egyptian*.

Set width The width of a character and its side spaces.

Side bearing The digital space between the left-most (or right-most) edge of the letterform and the edge of the space in which the character exists. Each character has two side bearings: left and right. Side bearings ensure that letters don't bump into each other, unless on purpose.

Slab serif Type with especially thick serifs, as in all Egyptian typefaces.

Slug In hot metal type, a line of cast type. When stacked with other slugs, it becomes a column. After printing, the slugs are melted for reuse.

Small cap figures Numerals designed to be used with a small caps alphabet.

Small caps Capital letters that are about the size of x-height of their lowercase. Unlike capital letters set a few points smaller, true small caps are proportionally drawn to same weight as their lowercase characters.

Solid Type set without additional linespacing, as 12/12 (12-point type on 12 points of linespacing, measured from baseline to baseline).

Spacing The space and its arrangement between and around letters, words, and lines of type. It is said that spacing is 90 percent of typographic practice.

Stem The main straight stroke of a letter.

Stickup initial A large initial set at the top left corner of body copy. Its baseline must align with the baseline of the first of text. Also called *elevated cap* or *raised cap*. See *Drop cap*.

Stress General direction of a letter, whether vertical for romans, or diagonal for italics.

Style Variations of a typeface, including roman, *italic*, **bold**, light, condensed, and extended.

Subhead Secondary type that explains the headline and leads to the text.

Subtitle Explanatory type that follows the title of a book.

Superior letters The small letters (X^AX-$^BX^C$) or figures ($X^1X^2X^3$) set next to normal characters. Also called *Superscript*.

Swash characters Old Face italic types with calligraphic flourishes: *Nicolas Jenson Italic, Loire Italique*.

Swell The thicker parts of curved strokes.

Tabular figures Numerals designed to occupy the same width, for use in vertically aligning tabular data.

Tail A character's last stroke, usually diagonal and leading from left to right: K, Q, R.

Terminal The hanging stroke of letters like *a, c,* and *f*. There are five styles of terminal: *ball, beak, finial, half-serif,* and *teardrop*.

Text The main portion of a story. See *Copy*.

Text face Types designed for maximum legibility at 9 to 12 points reading size. Also called *Bookface*.

Texture The overall impression of an area of type. Determined by typeface, size, linespacing, color, and column structure.

Tight rag Type set with a small hyphenation zone, causing minimal variation in line length. See *Rough rag*.

Titling Type that is only available as capitals and to be used at large sizes.

Tracking Adjusting overall letter and word space in a line or paragraph. See *Kern*.

Transitional Serif types developed in late 18th century between Old Face and Modern, sharing characteristics of both: Baskerville, Ehrhardt.

Tricameral Three related alphabets that could include, for example, UPPERCASE, lowercase and SMALL CAPS. See *Bicameral*.

TrueType Outline font format that eliminates the need for a separate screen font.

Turnover Type that continues on a subsequent line.

Type Keystroke-accessible, repeatable letterforms for reproduction. In metal type, a rectangular block, having on its surface a relief character to be printed.

Typeface Set of characters of a certain design and bearing its own name, like BEN SHAHN, Eureka, or Linolschnitt. A typeface usually includes alphanumeric figures (letters and numerals), punctuation, accents, and symbols. See *Font*.

Typo A typographical error.

Typographer Historically, one who set type. Current usage, one who practices art and craft of designing with letterforms as well as designing letterforms themselves.

Typographic color See *Color*.

Typography The art and craft of designing with letterforms.

Type size See *Point size*.

U&lc (Upper & lower case) Typesetting using upper and lowercase letters. The normal setting for the bicameral alphabet.

Uncial From the Latin *crooked*. A calligraphic typestyle with rounded letterforms that combines some upper and some low-

ercase letters in a unicameral style.

Unicameral An alphabet with only one case, including Hebrew and Roman titling faces. See *Bicameral*.

Uppercase Capital letters like A, B, C, etc. Term comes from the placement of the drawers containing the cap characters below the lower case (a, b, c, etc.) characters. Used to be called *majuscules*. See *Lowercase*.

Variable spaced type Type in which each character is assigned its own width as determined by the character's inherent width. See *Monospaced type*.

Verso Any left-hand page in a bound document. Even numbered. See *Recto*.

Waistline See *Median*.

Weight The lightness or darkness of a typeface.

Whiteletter Lighter types used in Italy in 15th and 16th centuries, contrasted to *blackletter* in northern Europe.

White space Emptiness that exists behind and around letterforms. Essential to typographic clarity and legibility.

Widow Last word of paragraph carried over to top line of next column. Looks careless and should be corrected. See *Orphan*.

Word space Correct word spacing is not noticeable: just enough to separate words but not enough to break a line of type into chunks. Proportional to letterspacing: if one is open, both must be open. Lowercase *i* can be used as a starting guide.

Wrong font Font that computer could not find, so used substitute.

X-height Distance from the baseline to the median in lowercase letters. It is the height of a lowercase x, which has neither ascender nor descender.

These additional terms are historically important to the understanding of how typography got where it is, but they aren't central to modern typographic usage.

AFM (Adobe Font Metrics) A file in which a font's character widths, kerning pairs, etc., are stored.

Agate Five-point type and "agate line" spacing (5¼ points, or 14 to the inch) used in newspaper advertising.

Aldine Typography that is derived from Venitian printer Aldus Manutius and his type cutter, Francesco Griffo, c1500.

Analphabetic Characters that lack a place in the alphabetical order. Diacritics such as the umlaut, and characters such as the asterisk, are examples.

ATF (American Type Founders) The largest metal type foundry in the United States, founded in 1892, by merging several small foundries.

ATM (Adobe Type Manager) A program that accesses the outline version of a typeface for on-screen display.

Banner A headline that extends across the full width of a page or spread.

Bastard In metal type, a letter foreign to the font in which it is found.

Bastarda A cursive Gothic letter style with pointed descenders and looped ascenders used in Germany in the 15th century. William Caxton, England's first printer, introduced Bastarda to England in 1476. See *Blackletter*.

Batter Metal type that is damaged or worn and gives an imperfect impression.

BCP (Bézier Control Point) A handle that controls the curve described by mathematical equations in PostScript outline fonts. Named for French computer scientist Pierre Bézier.

Bevel In metal type, the sloping surface rising from the shoulder to the face of the letterform.

Bitmap A character image represented as a pattern of dots or pixels on a screen. See *Outline*.

Bolding Using a computer's ability to synthetically create bolded typeforms. These are not the same, nor as good, as authentic bold fonts.

Cap line The implied line at the top of capital letters.

Character count The total number of characters and spaces in a manuscript.

Chase A metal frame into which type and blocks are fitted in preparation to print a page. The type is held in place by furniture and quoins.

Cicero A European unit for measuring the width, or "measure," of a line of type, equal to 12 Didot points. The cicero is slightly larger than the Anglo/American *pica*.

Composing stick In metal type, a portable l-shaped holder for hand setting letters.

Compositor In metal type, the person who prepares type for printing.

Contents In multipage documents longer than eight pages, a listing of its sections, stories, or chapters.

Didot point European unit of type measurement established by Frenchman Firmin Didot in 1775.

dpi (Dots per inch) A measure of screen or printer resolution.

Drop folio A page number placed at the bottom of a page when most page numbers are positioned at the tops of pages, as in the first page of a chapter.

Dry transfer lettering Rub-down characters invented in England in 1961. Their use precipitated a more playful approach to display typesetting.

Enschedé The most famous Dutch printing company, founded in 1703 by Izaac Enschedé.

EPS (Encapsulated PostScript) Computer document file format used to transfer PostScript files between applications.

Estienne A firm of Parisian scholar-printers, founded in 1501 by Henri Estienne.

Ethel A French ligature of the *o* and *e* letters (œ).

Eye See *Bowl*.

Finial A flourish at the end of a main stroke in some typefaces. See *Terminal*.

Fleuron and **Flower** See *Ornaments*.

Forme In metal type, type and blocks locked in a chase for printing.

Fount English term for *Font*. Pronounced "font."

Fraktur A style of German blackletter originating around 1510. See *Blackletter*.

Furniture In metal type, bars of metal or wood below type height placed around a form of type to fill the space in a chase.

Galleys In metal type, printed proofs.

Hair space In metal type, the thinnest space between type.

Hinting Mathematical formulas applied to outline fonts to improve the quality of their screen display and printing on low-resolution printers.

Imprimatur Latin meaning "*Let it be printed.*" In early books, it indicated that permission to print the work had been given by an authority.

Imprint Required by law, the name of the printer and the place of printing.

Intertype Similar to *Linotype*.

Legend Stand-alone descriptive copy that relates to an image. See *Caption*.

Lockup In hot metal type, the preparation of a completed page, or *form*, of type and images by securing it in a *chase* with *furniture* and *quoins*.

Ludlow In hot metal type, a machine composing display-size type in slugs with matrices assembled by keyboard and hand-distributed back into the machine after casting. Precurser to *Linotype* and *Intertype*.

Magazine In hot metal type, container for type matrices on a typesetting machine.

Matrix In metal type, brass or bronze "female" mold used in typesetting machines to cast "male" letters from molten metal. See *Punchcutting*.

Misprint A typographical error. See *Typo*.

Modern figures See *Lining figures*.

Mold In hot metal type, the part of a typesetting machine in which molten lead hardens into printable slugs.

NFNT (New FoNT) Macintosh font numbering system which assigns numbers to screen fonts.

Octothorp The number or pound sign (#). So named because it indicates eight farms surrounding a town square.

Optical character recognition (OCR) Software that converts a scanned page into raw text without keyboard operation.

Pixel (PICture ELement) The basic unit of screen display. More pixels per inch results in improved resolution.

PostScript Adobe Systems' page description software. Using a complex mathematical formula, characters and images are defined as outlines and printed as dots.

Printer font See *Outline font*.

Proportionally spaced type See *Variable spaced type*.

Quad In metal type, pieces of blank metal under type height that are used as spacers.

Quadrata A class of Blackletter type.

Quoins In metal type, wedges used to tighten spacing material around the type form.

Relative unit A fraction of an em space, and therefore proportional to the type size.

Repetition The simple repeating of an element.

Resolution The number of dots per inch (dpi) displayed by a printer or pixels per inch on a screen, which determines how smooth the curves and angles of characters appear. Higher resolution yields smoother characters.

Rhythm A strong, regular, repeated pattern of an element, a movement, or a sound.

Rotunda A class of Blackletter.

Round Hand Types with rounded letters.

Rubrication The insertion of handwritten initial letters in early printed books.

Shoulder In metal type, the non-printing surface of type or a slug.

Spaceband In hot metal type, device with moveable wedges that expand between words to bring the line to full measure in Linotype and Intertype machines.

Teardrop Overhanging part of a swash letter.

Text figures See *Old style figures*.

Textura A class of Blackletter.

Thick space A unit of measurement equal to one-third of an em.

Thin space A unit of measurement equal to one-fifth of an em.

Type case In metal type, a shallow tray of metal or wood divided into compartments to contain the characters of a font of type.

Type family All styles and variations of a single typeface. May include italic, bold, small caps, etc.

Type foundry The place where type is made. In metal type, the place where type was designed, punches cut, matrices punched, and metal type cast. In digital type, as little as a single computer.

Type high In metal type, the height of the type block. In the United States, type high was .918", while in Europe, type high varied from .918" to .979".

Typescript A typed manuscript. Raw copy to be formatted into a design.

Type speccing In all predigital typesetting methods, estimating the space typeset copy will occupy.

Upright A roman typeface or regular sans serif face that stands vertically.

Vertex The point where a character's stems meet at its lowest joint.

Bibliography

I have selected the most important books on design and typography in the last fifty years. Some I have only seen; many I own and love.

The important thing about a bibliography is to have a road sign that points to further knowledge on a subject. Discovering books that help you understand and see a vast subject like design and typography in a new way is worth the effort.

You may note that many of these books are released by the same few publishers. Visiting these publishers' Web sites will lead you to many other worthwhile texts.

Some of these books are out of print. Of these, a few are being made available again every year. Many can be found as out of print selections at online auction sites.

The Type Directors Club Annual. New York: Harper-Collins Publishers, published annually.

Bartram, Alan. Five Hundred Years of Book Design. New Haven: Yale University Press, 2001.

Blackwell, Lewis. 20th Century Type (remix). Corte Madera Calif.: Gingko Press Inc., 1998.

Bringhurst, Robert. The Elements of Typographic Style. Point Roberts, Wash.: Hartley & Marks, 1997. 2nd ed.

Burns, Aaron. Typography. New York: Reinhold Publishing Corp., 1961.

Carter, Sebastian. Twentieth Century Type Designers. New York: W.W. Norton, 1995.

Conseguera, David. American Type Design & Designers. New York: Allworth Press, 2004.

Dair, Carl. Design with Type. 1952. Reprint, Toronto: University of Toronto Press, 1982.

Fertel, Dominique. La Science Practique de l'Im-primerie. 1723. Reprint: Farnborough, England: Gregg International, 1971.

Frutiger, Adrian. Type Sign Symbol. Zurich: ABC Edition, 1980.

Garfield, Simon Just My Type. New York: Gotham Books, 2012.

Gill, Eric. An Essay on Typography. Boston: David R. Godine, 1988.

Ginger, E.M., S. Rögener, A-J. Pool, and U. Pack-häuser. Branding with Type: How Type Sells. Mountain View, Calif.: Adobe Press, 1995.

Hollis, Richard. Graphic Design: A Concise History. New York: Thames and Hudson, 1994.

Hutchinson, James. Letters. New York: Van Nostrand Reinhold Company, 1983.

Jean, Georges. Writing: The Story of Alphabets and Scripts. New York: Harry N. Abrams Inc., 1992.

Kelly, Rob Roy. American Wood Type: 1828–1900, Notes on the Evolution of Decorated and Large Types. New York: Da Capo, 1977.

Lawson, Alexander. Anatomy of a Typeface. Boston: David R. Godine, 1990.

Lupton, Ellen, and J. Abbott Miller. Design Writing Research. New York: Kiosk Books, 1996.

Macmillan, Neil. An A–Z of Type Designers. New Haven: Yale University Press, 2006.

McLean, Rauri. The Thames and Hudson Manual of Typography. London & New York: Thames and Hudson, 1980.

Miller, Brian D. Above the Fold, 2nd ed. Blue Ash, OH: HOW Books, 2014.

Morison, Stanley. A Tally of Types. Jaffrey, N.H.: David R. Godine, 1999.

Norton, Robert. Types Best Remembered, Types Best Forgotten. Kirkland, Wash.: Parsimony Press, 1993.

Peckolick, Alan. Teaching Type to Talk. New York: Pointed Leaf Press, 2013.

Rand, Paul. A Designer's Art. New Haven: Yale University Press, 1985.

Remington, R. Roger, and Barbara J. Hodik. Nine Pioneers in American Graphic Design. Cambridge, Mass.: MIT Press, 1989.

Rogers, Bruce. Paragraphs on Printing. New York: Dover Publications, 1979.

Rondthaler, Edward. Life with Letters... As They Turned Photogenic. New York: Visual Communication Books, Hastings House Publishers, 1981.

Ruder, Emil. Typography: A Manual of Design. Adapted by Charles Bigelow. New York: Hastings House, 1981.

Spencer, Herbert. Pioneers of Modern Typography. Cambridge, Massachusetts: The MIT Press, 1982. 2nd ed.

Spiekermann, Erik. Rhyme & Reason: A Typographic Novel. Berlin: H. Berthold AG, 1987.

Thompson, Bradbury. The Art of Graphic Design. New Haven: Yale University Press, 1988.

Tracy, Walter. Letters of Credit: A View of Type Design. Boston: David R. Godine, 1989.

Tschichold, Jan. Asymmetric Typography. Trans. by Rauri McLean. London: Faber and Faber, 1967.

Index

Colophon

Bamboo Vanishing Point
Gloss white lacquer
Rossa Corsa Taranis
Scuderia Ferrari
Pininfarina Nanotech
Cambiano & Prima

Thinking in Type, Second Edition is set in ITC Quay Sans™, a humanist sans serif typeface designed by David Quay (1948–) at The

Foundry in London and issued by URW in 1990. Designed in three weights, each with corresponding italics, ITC Quay Sans™ has very subtle stroke thickness contrast and tiny flares at stroke ends – not quite a semi-serif and certainly not a serif typeface. Both these attributes make it a particularly readable typeface and useful for both text and display settings.

David Quay, who lectures widely and has taught letterform design and typography at several colleges in England, has designed more than two dozen typefaces with Freda Sack at The Foundry. He now lives and works in Amsterdam.

Thinking in Type, Second Edition was designed and typeset by Alexander W. White. It was printed in China by Asia Pacific Offset.

Credits

All illustrations by the author unless otherwise indicated here. Every effort has been made to identify the designer of the works. Credits will be happily updated in the next edition of this book. My thanks to each and every designer and art director whose work was selected as a superior example of typographic excellence. **1** PORTRAITS EMIL WEISS; SYMBOLS HENRY DREYFUSS; **CHART** VISIBLE LANGUAGE MAGAZINE **5** TAXI DON DYER; OHE STUDY ERIC GILL; TAXONOMY MAXIM ZHUKOV **11** NO SAUL STEINBERG; **8** LOGOS UNKNOWN **13** ABSTRACT BACKGROUND UNKNOWN **15** COMIC WORDS UNKNOWN; FCUK UNKNOWN **19** AN TERENCE MENG-LEONG; CK MARIOS GEORGIOU; YF XIN BAI WU; XF MICHAEL JIN; ZB MICHAEL KWAN; SZ/SZECHUAN JOY SCOTT **21** 0 THROUGH 9 JASPER JOHNS **23** BAZAAR HENRY WOLF; TONNAGE DON EGENSTEINER, AD; FAUSTS UNKNOWN CZECH DESIGNER **25** PEOPLE VS IRS TRACY MA & RICHARD TURLEY, CDs **29** PALATINO STUDY HERMANN ZAPF **31** ALPHABET OF LOGOS A ART LOFGREEN; B JACK & CHRIS HOUGH; C CARL GRAF; D AUTHOR; E JOHN STONEHAM; F KENNETH HOLLICK; G UNKNOWN; H SCOTT RAY & ARTHUR EISENBERG; I ROLF HARDER; J WOLFGANG HEUWINKEL; K CYNTHIA VAUGHAN; L WALTER BERNARDINI; M BILL GARDNER; N TERRY JEAVONS; O JOHN STEGMEIJER; P JOHN MASSEY; Q AUTHOR; R ART LOFGREEN; S STUART ASH; T GARY TEMPLIN; U FÉLIX BELTRÁN; V AUTHOR; W DC STIPP; X AUTHOR; Y STUART ASH; Z MICHAEL SCANLAN & TOM CUTTER; MOUKA CZECH FOR FLOUR **35** ANTIQUERIA UNKNOWN **37** PDDDD FREDERIC GOUDY; DUNHILL UNKNOWN **39** JAPANESE FONTS MERALD E. WROLSTAD; H LOGO WOODY PIRTLE; E LOGO NORMAN IVES **43** BATMAN UNKNOWN; AVANT GARDE HERB LUBALIN & TONY DISPIGNA **45** COMMA PAULA SCHER; VODAPHONE UNKNOWN; JE PARS DEMAIN FRENCH FOR *I'M LEAVING TOMORROW*; DANKE GLEICHFALLS GERMAN FOR *THE SAME TO YOU*; QUERÍA DESAYUNO SPANISH FOR *I'D LIKE BREAKFAST* **47** NATURAL HISTORY UNKNOWN **49** PAINTED SERIFS EDWARD CATICH **53** LICENSE PLATES SCOTT MARZ & CRAIG WELSH **55** PS POSTER BARK DESIGN; NASTY SPACE AD MESS UNKNOWN; **1** ROSANNA GONZALEZ; **7** UNKNOWN; M SCOTT LOPRESTI; M CARLOS OROPEZA **57** NYCSEX PENTAGRAM; PLATAANIT KOSTI ANTIKAINEN; **3** ABSTRACTION STUDIES UNKNOWN; MUSIC X4 UNKNOWN; HEWITT UNKNOWN; MISSING U'S AD UNKNOWN **59** UROPAN ARIANE SPANIER **63** C'EST BON FRENCH FOR *THAT'S GOOD*; TUNCZYK POLISH FOR *TUNA FISH*; AVELÃS PORTUGUESE FOR *HAZELNUTS*; VASÁRNAP HUNGARIAN FOR *SUNDAY*; **3** LOGOS UNKNOWN; FEDEX LOGO LINDON GRAY LEADER; **2** BOOK COVERS GRACE ABBOTT **67** ESV UNKNOWN **69** DJAVAN CD GUALTER PUPO & JOÃO BONELLI **71** NEEDING ALICE GENAUD, JEAN-PAUL LEHFELD, JASON LITTLE & BRAD STEVENS; LANDSCAPE MASAYOSHI KODAIRA; I SUPPORTED ARIANE SPANIER; LE PARISIEN PHILI; MÖBEL ERNST KELLER (1928); WHERE ZSUZSANNA ILIJIN; KRISPY KREME ELLIOT STRUNK & KEVIN POJMAN; JAMES NIKLAUS TROXLER; ON SUCH A HELEN YENTUS; MISALLIANCE MARC COZZA; MOTION x2 MAXIM IVANOV; ROBERT KLAINTEN STEFANIE SCHWARZ; EXPO ENZO FINGER; JEG WICTOR LEONARD FAANES; NIL ITALO MORO; PAPERMANIA BOB GILL; T NORMAN IVES; GRAPHIS ALAN FLETCHER; PLEXIGLAS ANTON STAANKOWSKI (1938) **73** PALE KING MARIO J. PULICE; GERMANS DIVE CHRISTOPHER SERGIO; HAPPY REX BONOMELLI; HELL'S CATHERINE CASALINO; ALLES FONS HICKMANN; MOZART UWE LOESCH; SCHLYSS NIKLAUS TROXLER; **10** 2012 TIZIANA ARTEMISIO & MATTHIAS KANTEREIT; JAZZ PAUL ROGERS; YOKOO ORANGETANGO; POLAROID MERVYN KURLANSKY; IRAQ MICHAEL BEIRUT; VASTAANOTTO FINNISH FOR *RECEPTION*; TEQUILA WUQUAN WU **75** KLEINEZEITUNG UNKNOWN; AMERICAN GAIL BICHLER, DD; SOUTH BEACH UNKNOWN; CANADIAN CLUB UNKNOWN **77** FEASTS UNKNOWN **79** WOOD UNKNOWN; BIRD PARADISE UNKNOWN; CANDY CANE UNKNOWN **81** FAST CO FLORIAN BACHLEDA, TED KELLER & ALICE ALVES; INC. BLAKE TAYLOR, CD; WIRED BILLY SORENTINO, CD **83** NOTEBOOK HENRY CONNELL, DD; THE SAND BILLY SORENTINO, CD; ONE HUNDRED COMPASS **85** BLOODLINE BILLY SORENTINO, CD; GRAVITY UNKNOWN; APPLES GENE FEDERICO; MR CONGENIALITY GAIL BICHLER, CD **87** GERMAN EXPRESSIONISM JESSE REED; DESIGN ED PUSZ & DAVID ROBINSON; MISSING UNKNOWN **89** MONTAUK UNKNOWN; DRUGFREE UNKNOWN; ENGINE PATRICK MITCHELL & KRISTIN FITZPATRICK; CORN UNKNOWN; CONTRACT TO COMPLETION UNKNOWN **91** HOW LONG UNKNOWN; MENACE WING LAU **93** CROCKER SUE LLEWELLYN **95** STAR POWER CALEB BENNETT **97** TRADE TIPS FABRICE G. FRERE & MARIANA OCHS **99** DOUBLE CALEB BENNETT; LANDMARK GAIL BICHLER **101** DANGEROUS IDEAS KYLE J. McDONALD; PATRICK HENRY CONNELL **103** AMERICAN WAY J.R. AREBALO, JR., DD; MENTAL FLOSS WINSLOW TAFT, CD; ELLIMAN KATHLEEN GATES, DD; FREESTYLE BETTINA SHERAIN **105** OPER TIM FINKE, TIMO HUMMEL, SVENJA VON DÖHLEN & STEFFEN WIERER; BEST BBQ T.J. TUCKER; NOVUM MARC CLORMANN & MICHAELA VARGAS CORONADO **107** 17% CALEB BENNETT & GAIL BICHLER; NIDO FRANZISKA KRONAST & AXEL LAUER; UNSER MANN UNKNOWN **109** CONTENTS DESIGN MANAGEMENT INSTITUTE; THE TALK JANET FROELICH, CD; MARKETS OF PARIS EMILY CRAWFORD, AD; THE QUESTIONS J.R. AREBALO, JR., DD; CONTENTS CONTENTS SUE LLEWELLYN, CD **111** ESQUIRE UNKNOWN; NY PUBLIC LIBRARY MARC BLAUSTEIN; WIRED WYATT MITCHELL & MARGARET SWART **113** ESQUIRE UNKNOWN; CHEAPER/BIG-BOX UNKNOWN; 02 FABRICE G. FRERE, CD **121** LOST EMIL WEISS; TWO FRIENDS EMIL WEISS; LESS TALK UNKNOWN; DRUG DEALER E. STEINBERG **123** HAVE I PEAKED? UNKNOWN; SHEEP UNKNOWN; SPEAK MEMORY MICHAEL BIERUT **125** SCHWARZ UND WEISS EMIL WEISS; DIE LUSTIGE JULIUS KLINGER; CLEAN CUT STEINER ODDLØKKEN; GLASS KIT HINRICHS & AMY CHAN; BT UNKNOWN; BRAIN DAMAGE UNKNOWN **127** BACKGROUND CALEB BENNETT & GAIL BICHLER; MARKET UNKNOWN **129** WESTHAM JAMES MONTALBANO; STEP 2 UNKNOWN **129** AND JESUS ERIC GILL; CHEDDAR CHEESE BRITISH GOVERNMENT PRINTING OFFICE, c1946; AUSSTELLUNG ANDREAS UEBELE & EICHER SIEBDRUCK; FORTUNE COOKIE UNKNOWN; BRAILLE UNKNOWN **133** DAGEN (*THE DAY*) PETER LINCK; COUGH HERB LUBALIN **135** ABCO UNKNOWN; MALTE DANIEL PELAVIN; THE ENEMY WYNDHAM LEWIS, 1927; LITTLE REVIEW MAX ERNST; BIENNALE MASSIMO VIGNELLI; FORECLOSURE UNKNOWN **137** NYT UNKNOWN **139** IWAN JAN TSCHICHOLD; VENOS UNKNOWN; POTEMKIN HANS HILLMAN; SEX GOD & GREED UNKNOWN **141** DOMINUS HERB LUBALIN; BDV (BASLER DRUCK UND VERLAG) JOOS HUTTER; NEM BESZÉLEK MAGYARUL HUNGARIAN FOR *I DON'T SPEAK HUNGARIAN*; COX F.H.K. HENRION (1963); ZEURCHER EMIL RUDER **143** READ NAKED PIET SCHREUDER **145** VIBE ANISA SUTHAYALAI & ALLISON WILLIAMS; COEXISTENCE FONS HICKMANN **147** PARAPET STUDIES AND PROCESS PANELS TERRENCE MENG LEONG CHONG; BULLPENS MICHAEL JIN; HACKSAW WASCAR SANTOS; ABACUS MELISSA MEDINA; FLYWHEEL CHRISTOPHER CHAPMAN; LOGO/CHICKEN/AMPERSAND CHART ADAPTED FROM *VISIBLE LANGUAGE* MAGAZINE **149** TOP ROW JOEL MENTOR, COLETTE WAITE, WUQUAN WU; MIDDLE ROW ROSANNA GONZALEZ; JOEL MENTOR; DANIELLE RODDEY; BOTTOM ROW VASHEENA DOUGHTY; JOEL MENTOR; CARLOS OROPEZA **153** CARAMOOR LOGO UNKNOWN; LIBRARY BOOK UNKNOWN; DESERTED ISLAND HERB LUBALIN; MAPS YUNKKI TAKADA; QUINTET PIERRE VERMEIR **155** EVERYTHING I DO STEFAN SAGMEISTER; EGYPT UNKNOWN; IMAGINATION MATTHEW BECKERLE; BALE DE CIDADE GUTO LACAZ; EVERYTHING IS ILLUMINATED JONATHAN GRAY **157** VEGAS MAP LINE ROBERT VENTURI; VEGAS MAP GRAYS UNKNOWN **159** EYE-POPPING VINCE FROST; CROCODILE ROBERT MASSIN **161** SIX TYPE SHOWINGS UNKNOWN **163** DIGNITY HONESTY UNKNOWN; KAFKA & JOYCE MIKE ABBINK, PAUL VAN DER LAAN & PIETER VAN ROSMALEN; FOUR PAGES CLAYTON WHITEHILL **165** METROPOLI COVERS RODRIGO SÁNCHEZ & MARÍA GONZÁLEZ; STAMPS M. FRANZÉN, Z. JAKUS, L. SJÖÖBLOM & Z. JAKUS **169** MOTHER & CHILD HERB LUBALIN; SKEPTIC HERB LUBALIN; COCA-COLA UNKNOWN; FORD LOGO UNKNOWN; FORD AD UNKNOWN; TIFFANY UNKNOWN; XEROX UNKNOWN **171** BAYERISCHE STAATSOPER PIERRE MENDELL; TRANSMITTER JEFF ROGERS; THANKS x6 GRAHAM CLIFFORD; INTERNATIONAL VOICES MATT FERRANTO **173** IMPLSE DAVID TORO **187** ULRICHI JOHANN SCHÖFFER, 1519; BODY MAP JOHANNES DE FORLI, 1491; HOW MUCH EVERYONE BEK; ESPÍRITOS LASHAWN WIGGINS; CARDINAL HEALTH WU QUAN WU; MAP RYMN MASSAND & KAI ZIMMERMAN; SCHLINK MICHAEL GLIDDEN **189** SIGHT UNSEEN UNKNOWN; STABLE TOM BROWN & JOSHUA PAUL; SIRINELLA MAX HUBER, 1946; OMEGA UNKNOWN; LINCOLN UNKNOWN **191** WIRED @ BILLY SORENTINO, CD; TYPE/IMAGE CHARACTERS ALULEMA, BARRIA, BENITEZ, BROWN, DOUGHTY, FORONDA, GODINA, GONZALEZ, LI, LOPRESTI, OROPEZA, PEREZ, RODDEY, TERRANOVA; BOB JOB CHELSEA CARDINAL & FRED WOODWARD; WOMEN'S HEADS JORGE ALDERETE **193** MARRIAGE HERB LUBALIN; MINIMAL IGOR ANDJELIC; NUMERALS UNKNOWN; MADISON SQUARE WU; ABCs x3 UNKNOWN; GUGGENHEIM IVAN CHERMAYEFF; VIRCLUDE AUTHOR; LWA AUTHOR; PEOPLE MERVYN KURLANSKY; WORDPLAY JOHN LANGDON; MOZART 40 UNKNOWN; MAHLER UNKNOWN; ATH ERIC GILL; PRODUCTION JEAN CARLU, 1942; BIANCO SEPO, 1926; BIKINI FONS HICKMAN; PARENTHESES FONS HICKMAN; DOCKERS UNKNOWN; WE ARE ALL JESSICA WALSH & STEFAN SAGMEISTER; ABCD UNKNOWN; DINING FOR FRIENDS HAYES HENDERSON & WILL HACKLEY **195** TEXTURE STUDIES x2 CHIRAG BHAKTA & AMY PUTNICKI; **4** LOGO ALICE TONGE & CHRIS WOOD; "A" LOGO UNKNOWN; TRL LOGO UNKNOWN; SU LOGO AUTHOR; DALÍ ROMAIN HISQUIN; F TAKENOBU IGARASHI; FIRST UNKNOWN; APARTADOS ALGARVE, PORTUGAL **197** CAVALERIA OSAMU MISAWA

Books from Allworth Press

Designers Don't Have Influences by Austin Howe (5 x 7½, 320 pages, paperback, $16.95)

The Education of a Graphic Designer, 3rd ed by Steven Heller (6 x 9, 368 pages, paperback, $19.99)

Classic Typefaces: American Type and Type Designers by David Consuegra (8½ x 11, 320 pages, paperback, $19.95)

Design Firms Open for Business by Steven Heller and Lita Talarico (5½ x 8¼, 224 pages, paperback, $14.95)

POP: How Graphic Design Shapes Popular Culture by Steven Heller (6 x 9, 288 pages, paperback, $24.95)

Design Disasters by Steven Heller (5½ x 8¼, 240 pages, paperback, $14.95)

Graphic Design History by Steven Heller (6 x 9, 352 pages, paperback, $29.99)

Star Brands by Carolina Rogoll (7 x 9, 256 pages, paperback, $24.99)

Brand Thinking and Other Noble Pursuits by Debbie Millman (6 x 9, 320 pages, paperback, $19.95)

Design Literacy by Steven Heller (6 x 9, 304 pages, paperback, $22.50)

Starting Your Career as a Graphic Designer by Michael Fleishman (6 x 9, 384 pages, paperback, $19.95)

Advertising Design and Typography by Alex W. White (8½ x 11, 224 pages, paperback, $22.99)

The Elements of Graphic Design, 2nd ed by Alex W. White (8 x 10, 224 pages, paperback, $29.95)

The Art of Digital Branding by Ian Cocoran (6 x 9, 272 pages, paperback, $19.95)

Design Thinking: Integrating Innovation, Customer Experience, and Brand Value by Thomas Lockwood (6 x 9, 304 pages, paperback, $24.95)

Building Design Strategy: Using Design to Achieve Key Business Objectives by Thomas Lockwood and Thomas Walton (6 x 9, 256 pages, $24.95)

Citizen Brand: 10 Commandments for Transforming Brands by Marc Gobé (5½ x 8½, 256 pages, paperback, $24.95)

To see our complete catalog or to order online, please visit www.allworth.com.

About the Author

Alex W. White is an award-winning design consultant and typographer working in Greenwich, CT. He is the author of several bestselling books

on design and typography, including Allworth's *The Elements of Graphic Design* and

Advertising Design and Typography. He served as the president and

is Chairman Emeritus of the Type Directors Club. A third-generation designer, White is chairman of

the graduate program in design management at SASD/UB and has taught at Parsons, Syracuse, FIT, the Hartford Art School, and CCNY. He holds a terminal degree in advertising design from Syracuse University and a BFA in graphic design from Kent State University. *alexanderwwhite.com*

Leo **Lionni**   El **Lissitzky**   Herb **Lubalin**   Alvin **Lustig**   Laszlo **Maholy-Nagy**

R. Hunter **Middleton**   Stanley **Morison**   Gerrit **Noordzij**   Mike **Parker**   Jim **Parkinson**

Alexander **Rodchenko**   Bruce **Rogers**   Ed **Rondthaler**   Stefan **Sagmeister**   Paula **Scher**

Erik **Spiekermann**   Ladislav **Sutnar**   Bradbury **Thompson**   Kathleen **Tinkel**   Jan **Tschichold**

Massimo **Vignelli**   Mark **van Bronkhorst**   Beatrice **Warde**   Wolfgang **Weingart**   H.N. **Werkman**